MW01644566

Boomtown New York

Bolivar NY 1825-2025

by

George Christman Bradley

Scarlett Windigo Press
Deering, New Hampshire

2025

Published in the United States of America by George C. Bradley, d/b/a Scarlett Windigo Press, 671 E Deering, Road, Deering, NH 03244

First Edition

CATALOGING DATA

Bradley, George Christman

Boomtown, New York: Bolivar, New York 1825-2025

United States-History-New York State

United States-History-Local

United States-History-19th Century

United States-History-20th Century

United States-History-Oil and gas development

Includes a bibliography and index

ISBN:

All illustrations are either in the personal archives of the author, or in the collections of the BRAG Historical Society, the collection of the Pioneer Oil Museum of New York, the collection of the Bolivar Free Library, the Pioneer Oil Museum, or of the Bolivar-Richburg Central School system. Others, except as otherwise credited, are in the public domain.

For

Bob & Jack & Little Beaver
and
Ragnar & Freyja, & Bjorn

Table of Contents

Acknowledgements

Although I have thought about this project for a long time, I have always known that I would never be able to do a creditable job if I attempted to do it alone. Even had I done so, I would have been in the debt of the historians who have taken on this task before me, the most important being John P. Herrick, who produced his book about Bolivar in the 1950s. That book, *Bolivar, New York, Pioneer Oil Town*, and the issues of the *Bolivar Breeze*, which he founded and which are readily available on line, are core sources for anyone interested in the little town so many of us grew up in. Nearly as important is Facebook's *Bolivar New York Fan Page*, with its thousands of photographs of the locale and people who made Bolivar, New York what it was. Among those who created and annotated the albums there, the most important contributor has been Tom Manning, who, like me, moved away from Bolivar decades ago, but whose mind appears to spend a good portion of most days dwelling on its past. He has spent countless hours proofreading and commenting on this text, and has contributed the articles about John P. Herrick and the Fire Department. Steve Yehl and Bob Dunbar have also put many hours into the Fan page. Janice Rhodes has offered me constructive suggestions, and sent a myriad of historical nuggets, and all of that was much appreciated. I often thought that my late father, John D. Bradley, could recall just about every day of his life. He had a large repertory of stories and anecdotes about the people he got know or hear about during the sixty years he lived in the village. I heard a few of them often enough to commit them to memory, and I made notes of many others- but not nearly all of them- and where possible I have shared them here. Many people have been kind enough to record their recollections of the time they spent in Bolivar, and to share those with me. Among them are former police chief Rick Whitney, former school superintendents Tom Boedicker and Bob Mountain, Norene Ferris, Dustin Allen, and Kelly Lounsberry. Others, like Lance Shaner and Scott MacDonell, have helped me flesh out the lives of their ancestors and relatives who were important to Bolivar's story.

Modern times and the wonders of the digital age make it possible to sit at home and read newspapers hundreds of years old, and much of what you read here I have uncovered just by reading the *Bolivar Breeze* or other community newspapers which are available on line. Almost all of those newspapers are no longer issued, so I have no idea how the person who tries to update this for the 250th will go about locating the material. I did much of the work on the Sesquicentennial book, which was written pre-internet and before home computers, and the online sources that helped provide the fodder for the story of Bolivar up to 1970 are of little or no use afterwards, so I wish that person luck! Many of the photographs and illustrations you find here I found via the Bolivar New York Fan Page on Facebook. The thousands of photos and captions there cover most of what people want to remember about our town, although finding particular items can sometimes be a challenge- not the fault of those who regularly contribute, but rather of Facebook algorithms and the like. If you want to browse that collection, first look for "Photos", then "Albums," where the pictures are loosely grouped by topic.

Although the information housed at the Allegany County Clerk's Office is available on line, most of it is only available only for a fee. The current county clerk, my cousin, Rob Christman, has been very helpful to me in locating information which would have taken me much longer to get. The Christmans have ties to the western part of the town since the the 1890s. The records of the Holland Land Company can be checked over at the library of SUNY Fredonia. Despite the help of the professionals there, we were unable to uncover the names of those who accompanied Benjamin Ellicott when he located the southeastern corner of the town, and the notes about what they found when they did their job, thus also being the first people of European heritage to set foot here.

I consider this book a work in progress. Many of you who read this will probably put it down thinking, "how come he didn't mention him or her or this or that." Maybe I knew about who or what and decided it just didn't fit; but more than likely, I simply didn't know, or overlooked notes I had in the rush to get this done in time for the celebration of 2025. Thanks to the wonders of modern computer printing, revising a text and creating a second or third edition is relatively easy. So I invite anyone who thinks anyone or anything was slighted by what is contained here to please let me know. Give me the story, and if it makes sense to revise or expand the contents, it can happen. The same goes for factual mistakes. Speak up- let's get them fixed! As an historian and lawyer by training, I feed on facts, not fantasies. I have already started a file for the second edition.

This book is in part a personal memoir of the forty-five years I spent being a Bolivar boy. Many of my contemporaries describe their childhoods in Bolivar as growing up where Beaver Cleaver lived. I feel the same way. It was just a great place and time to be, and to be from. If I didn't think so, I would not have undertaken the writing of this. But I know such an experience and attitude has not been universal, and if that was the case for you, please forgive me for letting my own experience color my description of those years and this place.

A note on photo credits: Except for those for which credits are given, the photos contained in this volume are in the personal collection of the author. Others are in the collections of the BRAG Historical Society, the collection of the Pioneer Oil Museum of New York, the Bolivar Free Library, the Pioneer Oil Museum, the Bolivar-Richburg School, or of the Bolivar New York Fan Page. Others were provided by Lynne Morrison and Scott MacDonell. All are reproduced here with the permission of those entities or the owners thereof. The photo on the front cover shows R. Allen Glintz and John D. Bradley getting ready to promote the Bolivar Men's Cub minstrel show of 1951 in John's 1914 Saxon automobile. It too is from the author's collection.

The Population of Bolivar, New York

	Town	Village	Total
1830			449
1840			408
1850			708
1860			959
1870			959
1880			1029
1890	2233	???	
1900	2035	1208	3,253
1910	2282	1318	3,600
1920	1979	1146	3,125
1930	2813	1725	4,538
1940	2628	1344	3,972
1950	2680	1490	4,170
1960	2441	1405	3,846
1970	2391	1379	3,770
1980	2496	1345	3,841
1990	2361	1261	3,622
2000	2223	1172	3,395
2010	2189	1047	3,236
2020	2051	1010	3,061

In the Beginning

Four hundred years ago, near the summit of the hill rising to the west of the present-day village of Bolivar, fires burned. Corn roasted, beans boiled. Nuts roasted and cracked, the meats passing into mouths while the shells went back into the flames. Raspberries might have served as dessert. Native Americans parlayed and enjoyed the summer harvest inside a seven acre circular compound of two, perhaps three, longhouses, surrounded by an earthen rampart topped by a wooden wall. They sat about chipping away at pieces of flint carried from afar, making arrow points with which to hunt and defend themselves.

Those natives, forerunners of the Seneca, used that compound for around seventy-five years, from about 1550 until 1625 or so, and then they abandoned it. The forest grew back, shading, then shrouding, the old camping ground. The longhouses collapsed and rotted away. The forest grew ever more dense, concealing the fact that there ever had been anything man-made there at all.

Why the natives stopped using it we do not know, but it could have been something we hear much about today: climate change. The "Little Ice Age" reached its climax just about then, the winter of 1608 being noted as brutally harsh throughout New England and Canada; and we know how blustery winter still can be on the hilltops of Allegany County. Or perhaps it was the coming of the white man. The first French missionaries arrived around Cuba in 1627. Regardless, times changed. The natives left, and the hilltop citadel, the first known settlement in what would become the town of Bolivar, faded out of memories.

None of the valleys that lead through the town of Bolivar were part of native trade routes. Those ran along wider lowlands which connected the Genesee and Allegany rivers. The busiest ran from what we call Belvidere westward along Van Campen Creek and over the gentle divide where the waters run west toward Cuba, into Oil Creek and on into the Allegany. Another route took travelers farther south up the Genesee valley, past the future site of Wellsville and into Pennsylvania and the valley of the Oswayo, which then took them to the Allegany. So, although occasional trappers and traders may have come up over the West Notch and into the valley of the Little Genesee, or may have ventured from the Genesee up Marsh Creek and into the Honeoye Creek valley running westerly just north of the southern border of the future town, they were few in number. The routes those travelers blazed attracted few others. They were only that, paths that never gained enough traffic to become roads.

And so it remained for nearly two hundred years. The path up to the native compound on Bucher Hill, which came up the far, western slope of the hill from the Town of Genesee, had been so well and deeply traveled that it could still be found, even though the compound itself had been swallowed by the forest, but other signs of human habitation, if there were any, wore away. The native Americans may have still camped nearby, for Zephaniah Smith, the first man to build a cabin in the Little Genesee valley, claimed that it had been burned by Indians in 1818- but he still promoted the area to his friends back in the Catskills as a good place to make a fresh start.

From the early 1620s onward, the European exodus to North America continued apace, a steady flow of 4,000 or 5,000 people a year, making a total of 950,000 by 1790. Those immigrants propagated and filled the earth as the Bible told them to, so the population of the original thirteen states then stood at 3,900,000, most crammed east of the Appalachians. The pressure to expand into the west was irrepressible.

Land

Looking southwest about 1890 from the hill overlooking Maple Lawn Cemetery, the LeSuer and Millard farms, some of the earliest land settled in the town outside what became the

The British created a legal quagmire for the land laying between Albany and Lake Erie. The Crown gave it to Massachusetts, then gave it to New York, then decided to reserve it for the Iroquois nations. And finally, they lost the Revolutionary War and left. Negotiations to solve the conflicting claims began in the mid-1780s, shortly after the war ended. A partnership named Phelps & Gorham made a deal to buy Massachusetts's claim, but in short order found they couldn't make the payments. Robert Morris, the entrepreneur who had been a principal financier of the Revolution, stepped in and took over their position, but subsequently he too ran into financial problems. He courted Dutch bankers, and in 1793 Morris sold most of his rights in western New York to a consortium of five banks from the Netherlands, which were collectively referred to as The Holland Land Company.

The Dutch recognized that the first step in opening up western New York to settlement, (and making sales), had to be putting an end to the claims of the Iroquois. This was accomplished at the council of Big Tree, held near Geneseo in

1797. The natives kept 200,000 acres of land and surrendered all of their legal claims to the other 3,000,000 acres. The Holland Land Company could now offer clear title to settlers. First, however, the land had to be surveyed, so plots could be described and deeds written. The company made a plan: divide the tract into townships six miles square, then subdivide each township into sixty-four "great lots" of about 320 acres each. To do this, they needed a first class team of surveyors.

They already had the right man to lead the project on their payroll. Before venturing into New York, the Dutchmen had purchased 1,500,000 acres in northwestern Pennsylvania. The imposing Joseph Ellicott, thirty-four years old, standing six-feet-three, went west to survey those lands in 1794. He was a son and apprentice of Andrew Ellicott, a legendary figure among American surveyors, whose greatest claim to fame was being selected by President Washington, (himself a surveyor), first to establish the southwestern corner of New York State, then, in 1791, to lay out Washington, DC according to the plan prepared by the French architect, Pierre L'Enfant.

Initially, Joseph worked with his father and his brother, Benjamin, finding New York's corner, before laying out the streets of the District of Columbia. But he was pulled away by Secretary of War Henry Knox to establish the boundary between the state of Georgia and the Creek nation. Completing that job, he returned and finished the work at the capital. Since he had experience working with his father on the New York-Pennsylvania border and then with the Dutch lands in Pennsylvania, he was a logical choice to survey the Holland Land Company's purchase in western New York.

Benjamin Ellicott joined older brother Joseph at Canandaigua in the summer of 1798, and he was given the job of establishing the southeastern corner of the company's lands. That corner was described as being twelve miles west of a previously marked point in the 42nd parallel, the southern boundary of New York State. Working his way west along the line, on July 5, 1798, Benjamin Ellicott and his team established the point from which to begin work on the eastern boundary of the Holland Land Company's tract, on the south side of Honeoye Creek, not far from the present-day crossroads of Alma. There they placed a large block of stone inscribed on three sides and on the top, and turned their transit north. The stone they set is still there, marking the southeastern corner of Town One, Range One of the Holland Land Company's survey. It would take twenty-five years for that town to attract enough settlers to justify having a government of its own, and also a name: Bolivar. Benjamin Ellicott and his surveying team thus became the first American citizens we know of to set foot in our Town of Bolivar.

Just eight years later, in 1806, the New York legislature received numerous petitions to form new counties. "Extensively circulated," a grand total of 750 male citizens collectively signed petitions to form three new counties: Niagara, Cattaraugus, and Allegany. The act creating Allegany County passed on April 7. James Stevens, William Ramsey, and Phillip Church received appointments as commissioners to locate the county seat. Church had acquired 100,000 acres at a foreclosure sale in 1801, so it was only fitting that the location fell in his parcel, and he also got to pick the name: Angelica.

The new Allegany County included a large expanse of land east of what the Holland Land Company owned. Initially, all of the company's land in the county, approximately the western half, was organized under one town government, called Caneadea. Joseph Ellicott estimated that 23,000 settlers had moved on to company lands by the end of 1811, and two thousand more over the coming year, most finding good land to work on the flat lands near Lakes Ontario and Erie. Those who drifted up the Genesee Valley and toward the Southern Tier were few and far between. The census of 1810 identified a total of sixty-one households, (337 people), living in "Caneadea," an area that would eventually be divided among twelve town governments. Among those early settlers were family names that sound familiar still: Jennings, Nobles, Hungerford, and Leonard being a sampling. But most of those new arrivals to the Holland Company's lands in Allegany County had settled in the broad and fertile valley, (by Allegany County standards), running westward from Angelica through Friendship and on to Cuba. None had as yet settled on the forested hillsides of Town One, Range One.

The first man who came to the Bolivar area with the intention of staying, if only temporarily, went by the name of Zephaniah Smith. He was near fifty years old, a Revolutionary War veteran, and perhaps a veteran of a second war, probably also serving in a militia regiment raised during the War of 1812. That war had put a huge damper on the settlement of Western New York. The British had seized both Fort Niagara and Buffalo, burned every farmstead they came to, and caused thousands of newcomers to flee to the east, where they stayed until the war ended in 1814.

In 1816, Smith made his way west from Unadilla, a small settlement forty miles northeast of Binghamton, looking for fresh territory where he could set traps and hunt. He made his way to the Genesee Valley, then up along Knight's Creek, over the gentle divide near Allentown and Vosburg, and into the upper reaches of the Allegany River system. There he built a small, log hunting cabin roofed with birch bark, on a spot barely south of Town One, Range One's northern boundary, along the creek just south of the present-day Richburg Cemetery, and there he found enough game to keep him coming back for three seasons, until he discovered his cabin burned, by Indians he thought. Indians or not, he "returned to Otsego County with glowing reports of this region abounding with meadows and forests." There were more than 23,000 acres available in Town One, Range One, on which settlers could try to make a go of it. Thanks to Smith, and to the sales materials put out by the Holland Land Company, those acres started to attract settlers.

It was a good time to think about heading farther west in New York State. The center section of the Erie Canal opened in 1819. By 1823 it was complete all the way from Albany to Rochester, providing efficient transportation for people and their belongings to reach the Genesee River Valley, along which settlers could travel south to the Holland Company's holdings in the hills of the newly created Allegany County.

We don't know exactly what route those first settlers of Bolivar took, whether south from Rochester or along a southern route similar to the one Smith had taken. We do know who the first ones were, and a great many were from one family: the Cowles. Timothy Cowles, age forty-four, a Vermont-born son of a Revolutionary War soldier, arrived on December 18, 1819, with his wife, Anna Wilbur Cowles, and two boys, Alvin T., age 11, and Erastus, a newborn babe who had come into the world in Friendship near the end of their journey.

Having planned a trip to arrive in a wilderness location in mid-December, it is obvious that Timothy Cowles had great faith in the presence of game, and in his ability to hunt. Smith had described a land abundant in both meadows and forest. Timothy built a cabin for his family on Great Lot 61, about three miles south of Smith's camp, where the valley widens thanks to the inflow of streams from Foreman Hollow and Horse Run, and which was almost certainly mostly meadow. The cabin was small, and for that winter at least, its doorway was covered only with a blanket; but they managed. Asa Cowles arrived two months later, along with his wife, a son, and a daughter. Before the census taker came round, Austin Cowles had also taken up residence, with a wife and two girls under sixteen.

The first settler on Phillips Hill was, unsurprisingly, John Phillips. Born in Vermont in 1802, he came to Bolivar in 1822 and began clearing his farm. He also cleared a sled road from his property to Knight's Creek. Only two other families lived along the route into Scio. He was a noted hunter, and once killed a deer with an ax not far from his house, where he would live for sixty years.

Most of the early settlers bought their land on contract, putting down a small part of the purchase price, being obligated to make annual payments for many years to cover the balance owed plus accrued interest. Therefore, very few deeds were recorded in these early years showing who was living in the town. The first settlers to pay for and take title to property in the town were William and Sally Wilbur, who, on December 15, 1827, bought and paid for the southern 100 acres of Great Lot 55 for $290.75. This plot was also undoubtedly mostly meadowland, and included the heart of the valley where what we know as Root Hollow Creek flows into the Little Genesee. Extending north from Root Hollow, it included the lands that would become the heart of the village, from South Street nearly to Plum. There the Wilburs settled with, (by 1830), their six children.

They didn't stay long. In 1829, the Wilburs sold thirty acres "on the east side of the road running from Ceres to Friendship," which we refer to as Main Street. Twenty-six of those acres were picked up by partners James Farnham and Capt. Benjamin Maxson of Cuba. The other four acres, which lay along the east side of the road to Friendship, was bought by one of our more consequential early settlers: Hollis B. Newton. In 1833, the Wilburs sold their farmstead and their remaining seventy acres on the west side of the highway to John H. Boss, and headed for Ohio.

Trees

When Zephaniah Smith returned to his home in Otsego County, he described the area where he had been hunting as a land of forest and meadow. What he certainly also reported was that those forests and meadows were full of life, seemingly boundless herds and flocks of deer, turkeys, and passenger pigeons, whose populations were barely kept in check by a wolf pack here and there, or by occasional native hunters. Pileated woodpeckers adorned the tall pines. Bears and mountain lions prowled the ridges. Foxes and bobcats kept the rodent populations in check. That abundance had drawn Smith back for three seasons. Harvesting what nature put in front of him was how Smith had made his living.

Those of us who grew up "in the land of the deer and the derrick" probably thought wild life was and is abundant. That is true, but it is nothing like what the first settlers found when they reached the southern part of the Holland Company's lands located along the Pennsylvania state line. Deer herds could run into the hundreds. Flocks of thousands of passenger pigeons could darken the sky. Nearly every small stream was dammed by beavers. As late as the 1870s, railroad carloads of deer hides and pigeon carcasses were being shipped from Allegany County to New York City.

The forest itself would have been classified as climax growth. When eastern hardwood forests mature and develop a full canopy, slow-growing, shade tolerant species of trees take over the undergrowth, and over time become dominant. Thus, the forests these early settlers encountered were full of huge white pine, hemlock and beech trees, and to a lesser degree the maples, oaks, cherry, and chestnuts which flourish when sunlight can hit the ground. The predominant species of oak was white oak, rather than the red which is much more common today. Prized for its ability to resist decay, white oak timbers and planks could last for decades.

The southeastern part of the town of Bolivar includes some of the most rugged land in Allegany County. The road that was created running along the eastern bounds has always been known as "Stony Lonesome," and for good reason. That dirt path leads up from the valley of Honeoye Creek to the crest of the highest hills in the county. This area would be the last to be purchased, as it had little in the way of natural meadows on which a new arrivals could put in a crop. The hillsides were too steep to till, and difficult to clear for use as pasture.

But the natural meadows that did exist, in the valleys where the village of Bolivar grew, and over the hill where South Bolivar collected, were limited in scope. It was then the deeply held belief that land was there to be "improved," and there was a natural progression to be followed, to settle, plant, harvest, then to cut down trees to be used for fuel, fencing and building material. Next, the settler removed the stumps of the trees he had cut, used them to create a fence or burned them along with the branches too small to be used otherwise, and collected the ashes to make "black salts." Black salts were not a condiment. Rather, they were used to make caustic soda, which had great value in tanneries of the time, used to remove layers of fat from hides. Black salts, along with animal hides and maple products, were the first "cash crops" an early settler could gather to bring in money. But every year, the size of the forest shrank, and the size of the farms increased.

Of necessity, the earliest settlers built homes and other structures with logs. But, all knew that plank or frame buildings were much preferred. The first portable sawmill arrived in town in 1822, and it was set up on Little Genesee Creek just below its confluence with Root Hollow Creek. It was widely believed that the old Glintz service station at the corner of Main and Olive Streets was in fact the first frame home built in Bolivar, and the studs, planks and siding undoubtedly came from that mill. Other more permanent mills soon went up.

Friendship entrepreneurs Leonard & Wellman put up a sawmill along Little Genesee Creek near the south boundary of the town, which Leonard Daniels purchased in 1830. It became the site of one of the town's first great tragedies four years later, when, in April, Daniels' eight-year-old son fell off a log and into the mill pond. The boy's mother rushed to the rescue, but was soon struggling too in the frigid water. Daniels heard the cries, rushed over, saved his wife, went back in for the boy, but was overcome by the cold and drowned not far from where his son still floated face-down.

Luther Austin, a millwright, arrived in Bolivar in 1821, and in partnership with Asa, Austin and Timothy Cowles erected a mill near present day Salt Rising Road. Another millwright, Bradford Case, moved from Wirt to Lot 16 in the northeast corner of the town, near Vosburg, in 1825. Albom Lewis built his sawmill a little later over the hill in California Hollow, which he turned into a thriving business. Lewis's mill was replaced in the 1870s with one of the first mills using a circular saw, (rather than the reciprocating blades used in earlier mills), and could put out 30,000 board feet of lumber a year. The Chapel family put up their sawmill near South Bolivar in 1860.

By 1824, enough settlers were growing enough grain to justify a grist mill, which Asa Cowles built, saving local farmers trips along forest paths to Cuba or Friendship to have their grain turned into flour. Although Asa died in 1829, the mill continued to operate until 1876, when its water wheel was replaced with a steam engine.

A movement soon began to formally incorporate Town One Range One as a political entity, no longer managed as the southernmost part of the Town of Friendship. New York State formally created the Town of Bolivar on February 15, 1825. There are eight communities the United States named Bolivar, and seven of them were organized in 1825. At that time, as the United States approached its fiftieth birthday, many American looked upon Simon Bolivar, "The Liberator," who was having great success freeing South America from Spain, as another George Washington. Our town was the first town named Bolivar to be created. At the time the town was first organized, it included the south half of what would become, in 1838, the town of Wirt.

On March 21, 1825, a group of local settlers met in Hollis B. Newton's store, (on the site of today's preschool), to get organized. They chose Asa Cowles as the first town supervisor, Austin Cowles town clerk, named Pliny Evans, Jonah French and Eli LeSuer assessors, and picked Elijah Fuller and Philip Appleby as the town constables. They divided the town into twelve districts, each of which had an overseer of highways. Levi Appleby, Alvan Richardson and Ebenezer Kellogg served as the school commissioners. The clearing of land and the development of farms was a slow process, and wood and wood products dominated the local economy during these early decades of settlement. The Holland Land Company owned 276,500 acres of land in Allegany County. By 1845, 75,457 of those acres were being cultivated, and were home to nearly 20,000 cattle, more than 8,000 dairy cows, and close to 57,000 sheep. There were 118 sawmills, 113 schools, twenty-two churches, forty-five clergymen, and thirty-two doctors.

When you look at the United States census, between 1830 and 1840 the population of Bolivar decreased from 449 to 408, then began a steady increase that would last the rest of the century. The drop was not because people moved away. Until 1838, Bolivar bordered the town of Friendship. On April 12 of that year, the town of Wirt was formed, and the land located north of Town One, Range One of the Holland Company's survey became part of the new town, and the people living there appear in the 1840 census as residents of Wirt rather than Bolivar. Three hundred new settlers moved in during the 1840s, and another 276 during the early 1850s. 984 people called Bolivar home in 1855.

The population was young. Of the 449 present in 1830, only five were over the age of seventy. The route from Ceres to Friendship attracted enough travelers to goad Hollis B. Newton into converting his store into a hotel. Newton, born on a farm in Massachusetts in 1799, was the great-grandson of a Minuteman who had fought at Concord in 1775. Standing near the present-day intersection of Olean and Main streets, where the pre-school is today, his hotel, "the first hotel of note," would remain in business, most of its later years known as the Clark House, until destroyed by fire in 1915. After converting it into an inn, Newton quickly built and opened another store.

Interest in lands in the town of Bolivar was concentrated mostly along Little Genesee Creek, from the point where it crossed the north line of the town all the way down to where it crossed the western boundary into the town of Genesee.

By 1835, enough domestic livestock was being raised to prompt A.P. Stetson to open a tannery, which could count on a large supply of bark from hemlock trees, essential in the tanning process, as the settlers steadily cleared the land. The doubling of the population from 1830 to 1855 was in part due to developments outside Bolivar. Builders completed the Genesee Valley Canal from Cuba north to Mount Morris in 1841, making the Rochester area markets much more accessible. In 1851, the Erie Railroad completed its tracks from Hornell to Dunkirk, with stops in Friendship and Cuba, which made travel east and west light years faster than the old wagon trails.

There were nine "industrial operations" in Bolivar in 1855. Fisher & Gould operated a cabinet and chair factory. Daniel Kenyon tanned hides and made

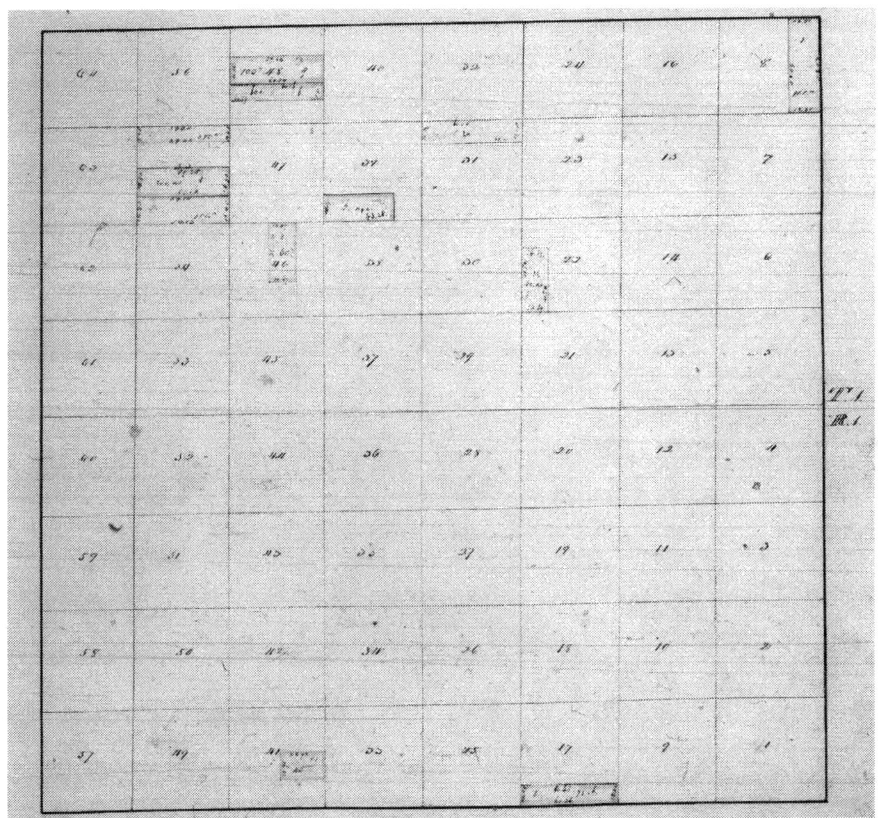

This map, in the records of the Holland Land Company, shows the parcels of land to which the company had transferred title as of 1836. Most were in the northwest corner of the town, where the village of Bolivar is located. Courtesy SUNY Fredonia

shoes. All seven others, (John Brown, Oliver Penfield, Sheldon Olmstead, John Olmstead, Abel Hosley, Allen Wightman, and Cyrus Newton), operated sawmills, three of which were powered by steam. Newton operated the busiest mill. With ten employees he had produced more than 1,200,000 board feet of lumber over the past year. The mills of John Brown and John Olmsted claimed cutting 1,000,000 board feet each. Brown had fourteen employed at his water-powered mill, while Olmstead had fifteen men working at his $1,250 steam-engine equipped operation. Combined, the output of the seven mills exceeded 4,375,000 board feet, and they employed sixty-two people, all men. John Brown & Co. had invested $23,300 in real estate ($850,000 today) to assure a steady supply of logs, nearly twice that invested by John Olmstead. Only Newton operated without investing in any timberland at all, which was becoming increasingly scarce. By that year, 1855, the Holland Land Company had left in its inventory only 1,263 acres in Bolivar, all unimproved and probably wooded, valued at about $5 an acre.

Wood was essential to life. With it homes and barns were built. It was the fuel for heat and light and cooking. But it was being cut much more quickly than it was growing. Each year the established farmers cleared a bit more land. Tree by tree, acre by acre, forest became meadow and grazing land. As the landscape changed, the huge herds of deer and flocks of birds disappeared, as did the predators which fed upon them. The last panther was seen in the county in 1850, the last wolf in 1856. Deer and bear would be gone before 1890, while crows and English sparrows increased in number.

In 1855, 157 people lived in the unincorporated Bolivar village, which boasted one hotel, one grocery, and two retail stores. Three churches had been built. The largest was the First Baptist in Richburg, (but in Bolivar town), which attracted 150 to its Sunday services. Next was the Methodist Episcopal in Bolivar village, which drew 100 to hear the sermons, and last, with fifty regulars, was another Methodist Episcopal congregation in South Bolivar, which could count on fifty regular attendees. There were seven district school houses.

One of the boys growing up in Bolivar during this time was Royal Kellogg, who went on to become a Congregational minister, who, in the early twentieth century tended a church in McHenry, North Dakota. In a letter to an old friend here, he told of his memories of the library and how it worked. It consisted of a large wooden crate, filled with books. Annually, a librarian would be elected at the town meeting, and the library would move to the house of the librarian. One year the library came to Kellogg's house, and Royal was quick to dive in. He started by reading *Thrilling Adventures Among the Indians*. He moved from that to light fiction, then to Gibbon's *History of Rome*, and then to Dick's Philosophy and Astronomy, which he read and reread, as he recalled, laying on the floor. "That little old library did more to open my dull, boyish eyes and inspire within me a hunger for larger things in this life than any other instrumentality of my early youth," he recalled fifty years later.

The 1850s were hard on Bolivar's 192 farmers. In 1854, drought was the biggest culprit, killing one-third of the potato crop, two-thirds of the buckwheat, and twenty percent of the corn. The hard winter had killed four-fifths of the winter wheat. (Perhaps as a result, Bolivar's population shrank from 984 in 1855 to 959 in 1860). One of the more enterprising farmers at that time was John Mead. His farm took up 127 acres, of which he had improved fifty. He had put the plow to twenty-four acres the year before. He had eight acres of pasture, and eight of meadow, from which he had cut seven tons of hay. He had planted 3 ½ acres of spring wheat, and twenty-two of oats, harvesting more than 1,100 bushels. He had on hand three calves, twelve head of cattle, and three milk cows from which he and his wife, Clarissa Cowles, had made 450 pounds of butter. He kept four horses and owned three pigs. They had cut ten fleeces of wool from their twenty sheep, yielding thirty pounds of wool.

Mead was by no means the biggest or most prosperous Bolivar farmer. Samuel and Lydia Carter owned almost 300 acres, and had cleared or improved 130 of them. They owned seven horses, the most of anyone in the town at that time, and had produced 150 bushels of apples, 150 pounds of maple sugar, and 400 pounds of butter. Hollis B. and Rhoda Newton owned 240 improved acres, of which they used 194 as pasture. Over the past year, they had brought in 250 bushels of turnips, and had produced 700 pounds of butter and 150 pounds of cheese. From his 130 acres, Andrew Ward collected 800 bushels of oats, and 200 bushels of corn. Oliver and Helen Penfield harvested 130 bushels of potatoes and made 450 pounds of butter. Merritt Sperry put in carrots and gathered 100 bushels. Gilbert and Martha Chapel produced 55 yards of cloth. Hollis Newton and Milton Reed both had flocks of more than 100 sheep.

In 1855, there were 189 dwellings in the town, which housed 195 families. Of those, 137 were frame construction. Thirteen families lived in log cabins, and thirty-nine lived in "shanties," usually worth no more than $10. Many of those were occupied by loggers and sawyers, the men who worked in the woods, and their families. But the forests were rapidly disappearing. Many trees were cut for lumber. The hemlocks were sought for their bark, used in tanneries. Many more trees were cut and split, some used for fences, many others to be burned in stoves and fireplaces. As the size and number of farms grew, so Bolivar village was slowly grew into a place for those farmers to shop and get supplies.

By 1860, the village of Bolivar, where the roads to Scio, Friendship, and Ceres intersected, was showing signs of the transformation from lumbering to farming. Two innkeepers were in business. Albertus A. Stevens, 33 and his wife, Emily Richardson, kept one while having three small children under foot, while Abel Frank, 46, kept the other. Darius Newton, 30, and wife Abigail kept the only mercantile establishment. Two grocers had set up shop: Alanson Clark, and Abram Voorhees. Lathrop Hendryx operated a butcher shop.

Four men worked as blacksmiths. John Lee, 69, was in business with his son, Albert, 22, and they had taken on an apprentice, a seventeen-year-old English boy named Henry Andrews. James Rohrer, Jr., 60, operated on his own. Ten others worked as carpenters or specialists with wood. S.G.S. Rowley produced and repaired wheels. Henry Blowers and Jesse Gould made cabinets. Elias Barnes specialized in making windows, sashes, and doors.

Royal Stillman made his living trading horses. Peter Ayers served as the local mason. Jeremiah Burdick operated the grist mill. George Kenyon and Edwin Smith supported their families as mechanics, repairing equipment. Sally and Alaina Ayers, Catherine Crawford, Salina Fisk and the only male, Philitus Cartwright, taught in the town's schools. The oldest of them was 23. John Fritts and his son Henry made men's cloths. Eliza Newton and Amina Weimer sewed women's garments, Amina to support her widowed mother.

The 1860s, aside from the Civil War, was a quiet time for the Town of Bolivar. Two highlights involved politicians. Richard LaGrange Andrus had been born in Tioga County Pennsylvania in 1835, and had come with his parents to the Town of Genesee about 1845, where both he and his father found work as carpenters. By the time the Civil War broke out, he had married, fathered the first of two sons, and worked as a mechanic in a wagon shop. At the county Republican convention in 1866, he received the nomination to run to be one of two county school commissioners, and he won. One of the perks of that office was having the ability to nominate candidates to attend the state normal schools, where teachers were trained. Spots in those schools were rationed; Allegany County was allowed only three openings in 1867. Andrus' wife died, and in 1883 he remarried a woman named Kate, twenty years his junior, and had two more sons. One of his grandsons from his first marriage would be named Kenyon.

Born in Bolivar in 1824, Albom A. Lewis decided to see the world before settling down. In 1844, he travelled to New Bedford, Massachusetts, and signed on as a member of the crew of the three-masted, bark-rigged whaling ship, the L.C. Richmond. In July 1845, the Richmond docked in Lahaina, Hawaii, filled with 500 barrels of whale oil, and 400 barrels of the top grade sperm whale oil. With his ship, Lewis had sailed around Cape Horn, had visited Brazil, Chile, and probably San Francisco before re-rounding the cape to make it back to New Bedford. He must have been about the most-travelled citizen in the county.

On his return, he found and married a girl from Clarksville, Mary Clark, and they raised one boy, Arthur, born in 1851. He farmed, and built and operated a very successful sawmill in the upper reaches of California Hollow. Then, (the1860s), as now, Allegany County was Republican. Of the 29 town supervisors, four were Democrats. All the rest were Republicans. Serving first as an assessor for Bolivar, Albom became active and well-respected in the county Republican Committee, and in 1864 won the nomination for a seat in the New York State Assembly.

At that time, counties were each apportioned to be represented by a fixed number of assemblymen, and in 1864 Allegany County was entitled to two seats. Lewis became the nominee of the "Republican Union Party," which was a combination of Republicans and "War Democrats," who supported the Lincoln administration's war policy. Well respected for his monetary support and his efforts in raising troops, Lewis became junior assemblyman from the county, and served in the 88th and 89th New York State legislatures. Then, based on the state census of 1865, Allegany County was reduced to one assembly seat, and Lewis's spot was abolished.

Lewis did not get to live a long life. Probably due to failing health, in the 1870s he retired and moved in with his son, who had a farm in Friendship, and there both Albom and Mary Lewis died in 1875. Bolivar attorney George Bliss ran for the assembly as a Democrat in the 1930s, but lost. So, Albom Lewis is our only resident who has served in Albany in the state legislature.

Increasing commerce was aided by the completion of the Erie Railroad, which connected Wellsville, Friendship and Cuba with points east and west. In 1870, serious discussions began at the county level to construct a road that would directly link Bolivar with Wellsville, providing a much shorter route than the one which followed the valley over to Scio, then up the Genesee to Wellsville.

The road to Scio had been improved many years before by the Scio and Bolivar Plank Road Company, which had used wooden boards to cover the roadway's ruts and mud holes. At first the proposed shorter route was controversial. The Wellsville Free Press, on March 30, 1870, with a touch of sarcasm, described it thus: *"We found the people of Friendship a little nervous over the talked of road from Wellsville to Bolivar. Of course we did not tell them so, but the fact is they need have no fears. Wellsville won't spend any money for the benefit of her people in general. She let railroads pass away on the other side of her; she won't spend money for a road that will not return an actual, feeble per cent to each of her moneyed citizens; in a word, she wants just one thing: she "wants to be alone" -and she will be. Go on, good people of Friendship, build your new bank buildings, your new brick stores, and the University of Music- if you are wise enough- and have no fear of any spasm of energy on the part of Wellsville. Just let her alone and she will you- you bet!"*

Progress was indeed slow, but in December 1871, the county board of supervisors received petitions from the people of Bolivar, Wellsville, Scio, Alma and Genesee to create such a road. A three-man commission was appointed, which laid out the route to be taken "from the head of Knight's Creek to Brimmer Brook." The route laid out avoided a direct crossing of Norton Summit, taking travelers a short way south out of Allentown on White Hill Road, then along today's Hog Brook and Bill Allen Hill roads to the crossroads that would soon become known as Petrolia, and from there along the Brimmer Brook valley floor into Wellsville.

Friendship, situated on the Erie Railroad route, remained the key mail hub. There was regular mail service Tuesdays, Thursdays and Saturdays when a stagecoach took the mail to Nile, Richburg, Bolivar, Little Genesee, and Ceres. The stage made daily trips, but only carried the mail on alternate days. The Friendship postmasters were in the habit of allowing any reputable resident of the towns to call for the mail on other days, that is until Ira Hawthorne got hold of the office and put an end to this accommodation.

By 1860, Bolivar had attracted two professionals. Joseph L. Cutler had become the area's first physician and surgeon. Dr. Cutler came to Bolivar in 1850, immediately after completing his education at New York University. To earn the money to attend college, he had taught school in his home town of Moravia, near the south end of Lake Owasco, and there he had a pupil who would become both rich and famous. The tale went that teacher Cutler "more than once warmed the jacket" of little John D. Rockefeller, during the boy's first term. Rockefeller held no grudge, and in fact formed a friendship with Cutler that lasted all the doctor's life. Cutler often traveled to New York City and visited his former pupil, who had become the world's richest man.

James M. Curtiss had set up shop as the town's only lawyer. He had come to town one year after Dr. Cutler, and had married a local girl, Huldah Root. Curtiss built his practice around a sterling reputation for fairness and honest dealing. He served for many years as Bolivar's town supervisor. In fact, the first mention of Bolivar in existing newspapers appeared in the March 11, 1863 edition of the *Genesee Valley Free Press*, which contained an account of the proceedings of the Board of Supervisors, of which Curtiss was then a part. He and Doctor Cutler took turns as supervisor, Curtiss at times in between serving as a local justice of the peace. He was again supervisor in 1882 when Bolivar was an entirely different place than when he arrived. That fall, he became a Democratic nominee for the state assembly, and succeeded in having the assessed values of the properties in the town lowered by $163,000 ($5,240,000 today), quite a feat in those heady oil-boom times. He was also the chairman of the board of elections. In 1882 he became the first president of the State Bank of Bolivar, a position he held until his death in October 1901. Curtiss would bring in a partner later in his career, Walter T. Bliss, who would also leave his own mark on the community.

One of Bolivar's most prosperous citizens before oil arrived was Alpheus G. Williams, whose home was built on what became the southwest corner of Main and Liberty Streets. Here the Williams family is seen in front of the house sometime in the 1870s.

Civil War

The contribution, in terms of manpower, of the Town of Bolivar to the cause of the Union during the nation's Civil War was enormous for a community its size. Of the 959 people living in Bolivar in 1860 just before the war broke out, 120 ended up in uniform, which was one-eighth of the total population, or about twenty-five percent of the males of all ages. Most of these men served with one of three Union regiments: the 85th New York Infantry, the 136th New York Infantry, or the 189th New York Infantry. What follows here is a short summary of each man's tour of duty, sorted by the units they served in, with a summary of that unit's tour of duty. Names of the men who died in the service are in **bold print**. Those who were wounded are shown *in italics*.

67th New York Volunteer Infantry

The Civil War broke out in April 1861. The Lincoln Administration called out the state militias, then asked for volunteers. The first men from Bolivar to step forward did so in June 1861, and they ended up in the 67th New York. Most of the regiment was raised in Brooklyn, but Company C was formed by men from Allegany County. Leaving for Washington in August, it became part of the Army of the Potomac. The early volunteers from Bolivar were:

1. Sgt. Martin Van Buren Sawyer, born Oct. 17, 1837 in Bolivar, he joined Co C, 67th NYI in June 1861. Fought at Fair Oaks, 7 Days, Fredericksburg, Antietam, etc. He came back to Bolivar at the end of his enlistment in 1864.

2. Pvt. Edward Sawyer, b 5/16/39, brother of Martin, also went to Co C 67th June 1861. Same tour, including the Battle of the Wilderness, He too came back to Bolivar.

3. *Pvt. Simon O. Sawyer,* b 6/24/41, brother of Martin and Edward, went to Co I 85th NY in Sep 1861, but transferred to Co C 67th in Dec. 1861. He reenlisted in December 1863. He was wounded in action at the Battle of the Wilderness on May 6, 1864, but recovered. He made it back.

4. *Pvt. Leander Scott*, b June 21, 1836, Bolivar. Joined Co C, 67th in June 1861. Wounded in the left arm at the Battle of Fair Oaks, May 31, 1862. Fought on at Antietam, Fredericksburg, Chancellorsville & Wilderness. At the Wilderness he wounded in the left hand and and left thigh. Mustered out with company July 4, 1864 in NYC. Returned to Bolivar.

5. Pvt. Thomas Shields, born in Ireland Nov. 25, 1840. Joined Co. C 67th NYI in June 1861. Battles of Fair Oaks, Fredericksburg and Antietam. "Has not

been heard from by his family since the latter." The regimental records list him as a deserter on June 24, 1862, the day before the 7 days battles began.

6. Pvt. Wallace T. Smith, born July 25, 1841 in Tionesta, he joined Co C 67th NY in Jun 1861. He was then transferred to the 85th (Dec 1861), and in OCT 1862 again transferred to the 4TH Artillery. He served out his enlistment and returned to Bolivar.

7. **Pvt. Stephen Wilmarth**, joined Company C 67th NYI, in 1861. Wounded at the battle of Fair Oaks, he died a few days after the amputation of his arm at a hospital in Annapolis, where he was buried.

85th New York Volunteer Infantry

Of the 120 men who enlisted from Bolivar, thirty-nine joined this regiment, which became known as the Plymouth Pilgrims. The regiment attracted so much local attention because of Bolivar resident Uriah L. Davis, a successful Bolivar farmer and lumberman when the war broke out in 1861. Davis sought and received permission from the governor to raise an entire regiment, and in the summer of 1861 set out to find 1,000 men to serve with him. He raised two companies, of about 100 men each, from the Bolivar-Richburg-Genesee area, and campaigned from Olean to Canandaigua to Wellsville to raise the rest. Succeeding in assembling ten companies, Uriah Davis became the first colonel of the 85th, and led it into training camp in the defenses of Washington DC that December.

Davis was taken ill and resigned in February 1862. Assigned to the 3rd Brigade, 2nd Division, Fourth Corps, the 85th participated in the siege of Yorktown and the Battle of Williamsburg. It was heavily engaged at the Battle of Fair Oaks, Va. on May 31, 1862.

After this it was transferred to eastern North Carolina, and was given the duty of garrisoning Plymouth, NC. There, on April 20, 1864, the regiment was surrounded by the rebels and forced to surrender. As a result, most of the Bolivar volunteers serving with it were sent to Andersonville prison, with catastrophic results. In alphabetical order, the Bolivar men who served with the 85th New York were:

1. Uriah L. Davis, born October 27, 1812 in Austerlitz, Columbia Co NY. He received permission to raise a regiment, and was enrolled as Colonel of the 85th NY Infantry on November 28. "He labored assiduously in raising and organizing the regiment, but resigned February. 7, 1862 on account of ill health contracted through exposure…"

2. Pvt. Sheldon S. Applebee, born April 13, 1843, joined Co I, 85th NY in September 1861. He was transferred to the 4th Artillery, then fought at Cold Harbor, Petersburg and Appomattox. He returned to Bolivar.

3. **Pvt. Francis E. Barnes,** born in Plymouth NY August 31, 1829. Joined Co. I Sept. 1861. Captured at Plymouth, he died at Florence SC after transfer

from Andersonville, "for want of food." A veteran volunteer, he had received a $300 bonus in January 1864.

4. Pvt. Zalmon Barnes, born Nov. 11, 1840 Bolivar. He joined Company C 85th NYI Sep 1861. He survived Andersonville, Charleston and Florence, and returned to Bolivar.

5. **Sgt. Henry Bolsover**, born in Manchester, England April 3, 1836. Assigned to Company I in September 1861. Captured at Plymouth, while being transferred from Andersonville to Florence "was wounded in attempting to escape and died in consequence." He was buried at Florence. He was a veteran volunteer, and received his $300 bonus.

6. Pvt. Elon G. Buckley, born in Bolivar Oct. 20, 1836. Assigned to Company I 85th NY Sep 1861. He was transferred into the 4th US Artillery Oct. 9, 1862, and served with that unit for the balance of his term. He returned to Bolivar.

7. *Pvt. Lewis Coon Burdick,* born in Amity September 4, 1835. He joined Company C in November 1861. Wounded in the thigh at the Battle of Fair Oaks on May 31, 1862, he was discharged on September 27, 1862, and came back to Bolivar.

8. **Pvt. Alfred Chapel**, b 6/19/1842, joined Co D, 85th Oct 1861. Fair Oaks, 7 Days, Plymouth. Captured, died "for want of food" at Andersonville 3 Aug 1864, and buried there. He had reenlisted as a VV in Jan 1864, $300 bonus. His parents received relief from the town due to his absence. His older brother Jonathan served with the 179th NY.

9. Pvt. Henry C. Chapel, born June 10, 1840 in Bolivar, joined Company D in September 1861. He survived Andersonville, Charleston and Florence, and returned to Bolivar. He was a VV, rejoining for a $300 bonus in January 1864.

10. Mus. Edgar W. Cowles, born Jan. 23, 1837 in Bolivar, swerved as a musician with the regimental band starting in October 1861. He was with regiment at Fair Oaks and the Seven Days battles, and was discharged with bands in August 1862. He reenlisted as a musician with the 1st Brigade, Harden's Division, 22nd Corps April 11, 1865, $100 bonus.

11. Mus. Orrin T. Cowles, born July 13, 1836, also joined the 85th's band in Oct. 1861. Discharged when the bands were let go in the fall of 1862, after seeing action during the 7 Days battles, he returned and settled in Nile, NY.

12. **Pvt. David Crandall,** born October. 16, 1831, he joined Company E, 85th NY in Oct. 1862. Captured at Plymouth, he died "for want of proper care and nourishment" at Andersonville, on September 10, 1864.

13. **Pvt. James H. Crawford**, born in Towanda PA on October 17, 1842. He was assigned to Company C in September 1861. He was at Fair Oaks, and the 7 Days battles, and Plymouth. He died at Andersonville on August 16, 1864.

14. **Edward Fisher Davis,** born August 27, 1843, the son of Col. Uriah Davis, enrolled as a Pvt in Co C 85th NY in Sep 1861 at Bolivar. Promoted to

2nd Lt. Nov. 28, 61, he died of dypyheria on Apr. 11, 1862, contracted at the Newport News Hospital. He was buried with military honors at Angelica.

15. Pvt. William P. Fay, born February 25, 1844 in Richburg. Joined Co C, 85th NY Sep 1861. He was with the regiment until captured Plymouth. He was imprisoned at Andersonville, Charleston, Florence and Goldsboro, was paroled Feb. 28, 1865, and returned to Bolivar.

16. Pvt. Charles H. Ferguson, born August 26, 1842, in Chemung County., joined Co. A 85th in September 1861. He fought through the 7 Days, but was not captured at Plymouth, fought also at Kingston and Goldsboro, and returned home to Bolivar.

17. **Sgt. Elijah C. Gilbert,** b 2/11/39, joined Co D, 85th Sep 1861, reenlisted as VV Jan 1864. Married, his family received help from the town, and he earned a $300 bonus for reenlisting in January 1864.. He fought at Fair Oaks, the 7 Days, and Plymouth. He died of starvation at Andersonville on July 28, 1864.

18. **Pvt. Edward B. Griffith,** Co D, 85th NY Aug 1862. Captured at Plymouth, died at Andersonville “for want of proper care,” October. 18, 1864. Buried there.

19. Pvt. Alexis L. Halbert, b 1838, joined the 85th NYI of Sep 9, 1864. Mustered out in New Berne NC June 27, 1865.

20. Pvt. Horace Hayward, b 12/17/33, Walworth NY. Enlisted Co D, 85th NY Sep 1861. Taken sick Feb 1863, saw no more field service. Discharged from Foster Hospital, Beaufort SC 7/12/1865. Came back to South Bolivar. Carried as “Haywood” on NYAG records.

21. **Pvt. Charles H. Johnson,** born in Wirt May 7, 1846. He went with Company C 85th NY September 1861. Seeing action at Fair Oaks, 7 Days, and Plymouth, he died at Andersonville July 13, 1864 “for want of proper food.”

22. Pvt. William Jones, born Feb 2, 1831, Washington ME, joined Co D 85th NY Sep 1861. At Fair Oaks and 7 Days, captured Plymouth, imprisoned at Andersonville, he was paroled at Vicksburg and discharged at Elmira June 9, 1865. Made sergeant 1/61, but reduced back to private June 1862. Reenlisted on January 1, 1864 for a $300 bonus. Returned to Bolivar.

23. **Pvt. Elmandoras (Elmer) C. Kellogg**, born in 1843 in Bolivar. Went with Company I September 1861. Fair Oaks, 7 Days, Plymouth. Held at Andersonville, Charleston, and Florence, where he died. He had reenlisted and received a $300 bonus.

24. **Sgt. William S. Moore**, born Jul 29, 1832 in Towanda PA, he joined Co D 85th NY Sep 1861 at Bolivar. Fought through the 7 Days and at Plymouth where captured. Died at Andersonville Sep 24, 1864 “for want of proper food.” Buried there.

25. Mus. Edward D. Newton, b 9/2/31 in Bolivar. Musician, 85th NYI regimental band, Oct. 1861. After muster out in August 1862, reenlisted for the Band of 1st Brigade, Hardens Division, 22nd Corps. Son of Hollis B. Newton

26. Cpl. William D. Perry, born May 7, 1841, Bolivar; Assigned to Company I in October 1861, captured at Plymouth, he was imprisoned at Andersonville, Charleston & Florence, he was paroled in March 1865. He reenlisted in January 1864, received his $300 bonus, and came back to Bolivar after the war.

27. **Cpl. Hiram Pierce,** born Nov. 8, 1837, also Co D., brother of Samuel. Captured at Plymouth 4/20/1864, he died "in consequence of ill treatment" at Andersonville on Aug. 11, 1864, buried there the same day.

28. **Pvt. Joseph Pierce,** born Dec. 3, 1844, younger brother of above, joined Co. D 85th in September 1862. Captured at Plymouth 4/20/1864, he died "in consequence of ill treatment" at Andersonville Aug. 17, 1864, buried there the same day.

29. Sgt. Samuel H. Pierce, born Jan. 17, 1836 in Warren PA, he joined Co D and fought with the regiment through the Seven Day's Battles in Virginia. Captured with the 85th at Plymouth, NC, he survived imprisonment at Andersonville, Charleston and Florence, SC, and was paroled in February 1865. Discharged and returned to Bolivar.

30. Pvt. Jonathan S. Preston, b 5/6/1842, joined Company B, in Sep 1861. Sick, he was never able to take to the field, and was discharged Sep.27, 1862. Returned to Bolivar

31. **Pvt. John Rickhow**, born in Sharon PA May 28, 1825. Went with Company E in Sep 1861. At Fair Oaks, 7 Days, Plymouth. "Carried to Andersonville and died Jun 24, 1864 in consequence of ill treatment." The Adjutant General spells his name Reckhow, and says he died September 8.

32. Sgt. Albert L. Root, born May 29, 1836, in Bolivar. He joined Company C and was at Fair Oaks, 7 Days, Campaign from Suffolk to Weldon, Kinston, White Hall, and Goldsboro. Captured at Plymouth Apr. 20, 1864, he survived Andersonville, Charleston, Florence and Wilmington. Returned to Bolivar.

33. **Pvt. Asa W. Root,** born in Aug 1841, in Bolivar. Also went with Company C in Sept. 1861. Brother of Albert, son of David & Maritta Tyler Root. He died at Andersonville on August 13, 1864 "for want of food." A friend, John Holcomb, who later settled in Bolivar, was with him when he died. Buried at Andersonville. He left a diary, which he continued to keep until shortly before his death.

34. Pvt. Ephraim Sherwood, b March 4, 1822 in Dryden, he joined Co D in Bolivar Sep 1861. Taken sick and discharged in May 1862. With $300 bonus, he joined the 179th NY in April 1864, and saw action at Petersburg. Returned to Bolivar.

35. *Pvt. Benjamin Sisson*, born September 4, 1840 in Cherry Valley NY, he went with Company I 85th NY in Sep 1861; he was severely wounded in the left thigh at Fair Oaks, and the ball not removed. He was discharged, but reenlisted in Jan 1864 in Battery D, 9th Artillery, and received a $300 bonus. He was shot in the left elbow at Cold Harbor, and was "crippled for life." He then returned to Bolivar.

36. Pvt. Erastus E. Scott, brother of Leander Scott, 67th NY, he was born May 30, 1843. He joined Company C Sep 1861. Captured at Plymouth, imprisoned at Andersonville, Charleston, Florence and paroled. Mustered out at Elmira in Feb 1865 "Has not yet fully recovered from confinement" as of November 1865.

37. Pvt. Ebenezer Shoff, born July 12, 1828 in Angelica, joined 85th Co D on Aug 26 1862. Brother of Henry Shoff, 104th NYI. He too was taken sick and never saw field action. Discharged April 1, 1863 at New Berne, NC.

38. **Pvt. Edwin R. Smith,** brother of Wallace who served with the 67th and 4th Artillery, Edwin was born July 2, 1844 in Tionesta, he joined Co C in September 1861. He came down with typhoid fever in Yorktown VA and died of it there on May 4, 1862. Brother Wallace, with the 4th Artillery, brought the body home where it was buried, "with unusual solemnity."

29. *Cpl. Uriah W. Stratton,* b Dec 2, 1839 in Cohocton, joined Co E 85th NY in October 1861. Struck with fever in March 1862, he was discharged in May. In Jul 1863, he was drafted and sent to Co H, 109th NYI. While fighting at Petersburg, VA the little finger of his left hand was shot off. He was later discharged, and came back to Bolivar.

39. **Pvt. James Vesper**, born March 13, 1831, joined Co D in Sep 1861. He died of starvation at Andersonville on June 9, 1864. The records of the NYAG say he died on May 9, less than 3 weeks after his capture.

136th New York Volunteer Infantry

In response to a call for more troops in the summer of 1862, James Woods, of Portageville, set out to raise another regiment from western New York, which became the 136th New York Infantry, members of which agreed to serve three years beginning for most in September 1862. It was assigned a place in the Second Brigade, Second Division of the Union Eleventh Corps, where it was destined to see heavy action on many of the best-known battlefields of the war, including Chancellorsville, Gettysburg and Peach Tree Creek. With the Army of the Potomac through Gettysburg, the Eleventh and Twelfth Corps were merged to form the Twentieth Corps, and were sent to Tennessee to relieve the siege of Chattanooga in the fall of 1863. They stayed there, and then went on Sherman's campaign through Georgia and the Carolinas. Twenty-four Bolivar boys went with them.

1. Pvt. Francis D. Cartwright, born Dec 11, 1843, joined Co K in September 1862. He served without injury through all the major battles and returned to Bolivar at the war's end.

2. *Pvt. Alonzo Crandall,* born in Almond May 6, 1838, brother of David, joined Company A 136th in September 1862. He was wounded in action at Gettysburg. Taken ill during the Atlanta campaign, he was in hospital in Cleveland at the war's end and returned to Bolivar.

3. Cpl. John Crandall, born June 8, 1840 in Almond, also joined Company A 136th in September 1862. He served without injury to war's end and returned to Bolivar.

4. **Pvt. Louis S. Davie,** born March 24, 1843, in Bolivar. He went with Company A in Sep. 1862. He died of dypyheria in Fairfax, Va. Dec. 17, 1862. He was buried in Bolivar.

5. *Pvt. Charles N. Finch*, born Feb. 3, 1838 in Rennselaer Co. He joined Company A in September 1862. Fought at Chancellorsville, he was wounded in the shoulder at Gettysburg. He recovered and went through Tennessee, Georgia, and the Carolinas. "Wounded severely in the left thigh near Kingston, NC May 19, 1865. Permanent disability." He returned to Bolivar.

6. Cpl. Joseph I Finch, born in Cuba May 7, 1835, joined Co A in Bolivar Sept. 25, 1862. He was with his regiment at the Battle of Chancellorsville, but a month later was struck with typhoid fever. He survived, but saw no more field service. Transferred to 49th Co., Second Battalion, Veteran Reserve Corps Sep 1863. Promoted to corporal March 1, 1865, he returned to Bolivar.

7. *Pvt. Martin Luther Finch,* born Jan. 22, 1844 in Cuba. A 136th NYI Sep 1862. Grazed in the forehead at Gettysburg, he recovered and went west with the regiment through Georgia and the Carolinas. Returned to Bolivar.

8. **Pvt. Herman C. Gardiner,** born in New Berlin, NY March 20, 1833, he joined Co A in September1862. He fought at Chancellorsville and Gettysburg, and then was killed in action at Lookout Mountain, Tennessee Oct. 29, 1863. He is buried there.

9. **Pvt. Daniel B Garthwait,** born September 29, 1843 in Almond. He joined Co K, 136th Sep 1862. Died of fever in Washington DC 1on Dec. 23, 1862, He is buried there.

10. Pvt. Harley D. Hitchcock, born Feb 9, 1841 in Wirt. He joined Company A in September 1862. He went through all the battles unharmed, and returned to Bolivar.

11. *Pvt. Hiram B. Hitchcock,* brother of Harley, born February. 20, 1844 in Wirt. He also joined Company A in September 1862. Saw action at Chancellorsville, Gettysburg, and in Tennessee. "Wounded at Peach Tree Creek [just outside Atlanta] on July 20, 1864." Transferred to the Veteran Reserve Corps Oct. 7, 1864, mustered out of the 148th Company, Second Battalion, October 18, 1865. Bolivar's last living Civil Warrior.

12. Pvt. Wallace H. Johnson, born in 1835, assigned to Company A in September 1862. Served all three years, he then returned and settled in Portville.

13. Pvt. James A. Mead, born Oct. 17, 1837 in Bolivar, joined Company A in September 1862. Campaigned from Chancellorsville to Bentonville,NC, and returned to Bolivar post war.

14. Pvt. William A. Mead, born June 14, 1841 in Bolivar. With Company A Sep. 1862, and at Chancellorsville, Gettysburg, Tennessee, Georgia, Carolinas. Returned to Bolivar.

15. Pvt. George S. Perry, brother of William, born April 2, 1842. With Company A Sep. 1862, and at Chancellorsville, Gettysburg, Tennessee, Georgia, Carolinas, returned to Bolivar.

16. *Pvt. Silas Pire*, born May 17, 1843 in Almond, joined Co A August 1862. Present at Chancellorsville, he was slightly wounded at Gettysburg. Going to Tennessee in the fall of 1863, he fought with Sherman's armies, and was badly wounded in left leg at Bentonville, March 1865, the last major battle of the campaign. Discharged in May 1865, he returned to Bolivar. His brother Oscar went with the 189th NY.

17. Pvt. Samuel A. Richardson, born Dec 2, 1842 in Bolivar, joined Company A Sep. 1862, and was at Chancellorsville, Gettysburg, Tennessee, Georgia, Carolinas. He returned to Bolivar after the war.

18. Pvt. David B. Root, b April 11, 1838 in Bolivar. joined Company A Sep. 1862, and was at Chancellorsville, Gettysburg, Tennessee, Georgia, Carolinas, then returned to Bolivar.

19. Pvt. Alanson Scott, born Sep. 30, 1831, bro of Leander, joined Co A Sep 1862. Showed signs of TB, discharged Dec 1862.

20. Pvt. David M. Stone, born Feb. 20 1820, joined Co A in September 1862. At Chancellorsville, Gettysburg, Tennessee, Georgia, Carolinas. Returned to Bolivar.

21. Pvt. Charles H. Sweet, A and K 136th Sep. 1862. Name not included in the AG reports, no other details about him other than he enlisted in Cuba, but credited to Bolivar.

22. **Pvt. Hiram G. Wakeman**, born June 24, 1827 in Walton, joined Co A in Sept 1862. Due to fatigue and exposure, he contracted dysentery, was sent to Howard Hospital in December 1863, where he died four weeks later.

23. **Sgt. Alvin White**, born Dec. 12, 1820, in Vermont. Joined Co A, Sep 1862. Killed on the battlefield of Resaca, GA May 15, 1864. "Buried on turnpike road between Resaca and Dalton, marked with a board bearing his name and regiment."

24. *Pvt. George H. White*. Born June 6, 1843 in Grove. Joined Company A Sep 1862. Fought at Chancellorsville. On July 2, 1863 at Gettysburg while defending Cemetery Hill, he was shot in the face, "causing the loss of the roof of his mouth, a portion of his upper jaw and teeth, and a portion of the teeth in the lower jaw. Transferred to the Veteran Reserve Corps, he served until mustered out in Nashville June 30, 1865. Returned to Bolivar. His life ended at the Bath Soldier's Home on Sep. 29, 1914.

25. Pvt. Henry H. Wright, b Bolivar 4/16/1830 joined Co A in September 1862. Was taken ill with fever, spent 4 months in hospital and was discharged, returned to Bolivar.

109th New York Volunteer Infantry

The 109th Infantry was recruited in the summer of 1862, asking men for a three-year commitment. Most of the recruits were from the Owego-Binghamton area. It left the state in late August 1862

1. **Pvt. William H. Stratton,** brother of Uriah, born May 4, 1842 in Cohocton. He received a $300 bonus to join Co H, 109th NY in Jan 1864. He was shot through the head and killed at the Battle of the Wilderness on May 6, 1864.

2. Pvt. William Wilcox went into Co H, 109th as a substitute for William V. Davison in July 1863 and served to the war's end. He returned and settled in Nile.

3. Musician Henry Buckley, born May 19, 1834, joined the 28th NY in Sep 1861. With Banks command until discharged in August 1862. Returned and settled in Richburg. He reenlisted, using the name Lewis Swarthout as a Pvt in Co F, 109th NYI in July 1863, and served top the end of the war.

147th New York Volunteer Infantry

Two men from Bolivar were drafted in the summer of 1863, and both were assigned to the 147th Infantry.

1. *Pvt. Martin V. Comstock,* born Sept. 17, 1840, was drafted in July 1863 and joined Co F, 147th NYI. He was shot in the right thigh at the Battle of the Wilderness, and saw no further field service. Returned to Bolivar. The ball stayed in his leg.

2. Pvt. Alvin Hughes, b Mar 14, 1842 in Almond, drafted July 1863 into Co H, 147th NYI. Discharged for disability 8/31/1864 in DC. He lived in W Shongo after the war

161st New York Volunteer Infantry

Three Bolivar boys stepped forward in early 1864 to take advantage of a $300 enlistment bonus being offered, and all three ended up as replacements in the 161st New York, which had been formed in October 1862. By the time they joined the unit, it was stationed in the Department of the Gulf, in Louisiana. All three would die in uniform.

23. **Pvt. David Cowles**, born in Bristol, MA May 29, 1821, the son of Amasa and Lucy Cowles, joined Co B 161st NYI in February 1864. While serving under Gen. Banks in Louisiana, he was struck with dysentery in July 1864. Sent towards home, he ended up in a hospital in Albany, where he was located by friends and brought home. He died in Bolivar on Jan 2, 1865 and is buried there.

73. **Pvt. Isaac Day**, born in England March 7, 1825, went with Co C 161st in Feb 1864. "Taken sick on Red River with diarrhea and died in New Orleans 8 Sept 1864. Buried at same place.

71. **Pvt. George Smith**, born Mar. 29, 1825 in Towanda, PA, he also joined the regiment in Feb. 1864. He died in Morganza, LA of "camp distemper" Oct. 7, 1864, and was buried there.

5th New York Volunteer Cavalry

Raised in 1861, Troops E and F of this regiment came mainly from Allegany and Wyoming Counties. Attached to the Army of the Potomac, in the summer of 1864 it went along with General Sheridan into the Shenandoah Valley of Virginia. Two men from Bolivar were with it in 1864:

1. **Pvt. Edgar Day**, b 6/21/46, joined Troop F 5th NY Cavalry, Feb 1864. Became sick March 19, died at Camp Stoneman, Washington July 22, 1864, buried there.

2. *Pvt. Alonzo H. Mead,* b 6/21/1846, Bolivar. F 5th NY Cavalry Feb 1864, $300 bonus. "Battle of the Wilderness. Was wounded in right shoulder severely. Never served afterwards, still disabled. Returned to Bolivar.

9th New York Heavy Artillery

The 9th Heavy was originally formed as the 138th Infantry in August 1862, but was converted into an artillery unit to defend Washington DC the following winter. Attached to the Army of the Potomac, it fought as an infantry unit during the overland campaign of 1864. Before this campaign began, three Bolivar boys were made part of it.

1. **Pvt. George W. Livingston**, b 2/28/24, listed Battery C 9th Artillery Jan 1864, he was taken prisoner in June 1864 and confined in Danville VA until paroled in October. He died of disease contracted while in rebel hands in Bolivar on Nov. 20, 1864, and is buried there.

84. *Pvt. Thomas D. Utter,* born in Friendship Feb. 20, 1822. Battery C 9th art. 2/64, $300 enlistment bonus. Wounded in the right knee at Cold Harbor, he recovered and returned to duty 7/15/64. At Petersburg on April 2, 1865, he was wounded severely in the left side of his head, sand was till disabled the following fall when living in Bolivar.

46. Pvt. Henry C. Wandover, born Oct. 14, 1844, joined Battery A, 9th Artillery in March 1863. He returned to Bolivar.

64th New York Volunteer Infantry

The 64th was raised in Cattaraugus County in the fall of 1861. In August 1864, the regiment was looking for draftees or volunteers to replenish its numbers. Two Bolivar boys took a $300 payment to serve as "replacements" for men who had been drafted and joined the regiment with the Army of the Potomac in Virginia. They were:

1. Pvt. James F. Stone, b 2/4/1847 Canada, as a substitute for H.A. Robinson G 64th NYI Aug. 1864, $200 bonus. Mustered out in May 1865.

2. *Pvt. Handy Thurber,* born Sep. 12, 1847 in Bolivar, joined Co B 64th NYI in August 1864, getting a $300 bonus to serve as a substitute for Albom Lewis, joining the regiment 1 month before his 17th birthday. He was hit in the right arm at the Battle of Petersburg in the spring of 1865, and was present for Lee's surrender, but was considered totally disabled after the war. He returned to Bolivar.

179th New York Volunteer Infantry

This regiment was raised during the summer of 1864 mainly around western New York. It became part of the Ninth Corps, Army of the Potomac, and two Bolivar recruits served with it:

1. Pvt. Jonathan S. Chapel, b 2/10/1838, joined Co A, 179th NY, bonus $300 2/14/1864. Fought at Petersburg and Appomattox, and came back to Bolivar at the end of the war..

2. *Pvt. Emery J. Millard,* b 1/21/1847 Bolivar. A 179th NYI Feb 1864, $300 bonus. He was wounded in the left thigh at Petersburg, Virginia June 17, 1864. "Not yet recovered," when the records were compiled in the fall of 1865..

189th New York Volunteer Infantry

By the late summer of 1864, it was becoming clear to the leaders of the Union war effort that the war was entering its final phase. To assure a Union victory, additional recruits were sought for a one-year enlistment, and many of them were organized into new regiments. The 189th New York was organized in Elmira, and Companies B and I were recruited mostly in Allegany County. They headed to the front in Virginia in October 1864. Assigned to the Second Brigade, 1st Division, Fifth Corps, they took a place in the line besieging Petersburg, Virginia, where they stayed until late March 1865. With the final push to end the war, they were part of the force which pursued General Lee's army from the trenches of Petersburg to Appomattox Courthouse. Their Division received Lee's flag of truce when he decided to surrender at Appomattox. These sixteen Bolivar men served with it:

1. John Jay Beers, born April 3, 1844 in Bolivar. Joined Co. B Sep 1864. Served from Petersburg to Appomattox, and returned to Bolivar.

2. Pvt. Fay Charles, born in 1847, he was 17 when he enlisted in Co. K. He was transferred to the 50th Engineers in November 1864.

3. Cpl. George Edgar Fritts, born in 1844. In Sept. 1864 he joined Co. B, made corporal March 1865, mustered out with company May 30, 1865.

4. Pvt. Charles W. Griffith, born Jul 16, 1831, joining Co B in Sep 1864. Petersburg to Appomattox, he returned to Bolivar.

5. Lt. Edwin R. Kilbury, was born Sept. 2, 1825 in Danville. Mustered in as 2nd Lt. Co. B, in Oct. 1864, he was promoted to 1st Lt. Feb 6, 1865. Mustered out with company May 30, 1865 in Washington. His abilities were quickly recognized in the Army, and he was assigned as the chief Ambulance Officer of the First Division, First Corps during most of his time in the service. E.R. Kilbury was throughout his life one of Bolivar's more prominent citizens. Although he appears in most of the censuses as a farmer, he was also a notary public served for more than forty years as a justice of the peace, and was involved in many land transfers and estate matters, often named as an executor or administrator for other people in Bolivar who knew him to be eminently trustworthy. He served as president of the board of education, town supervisor, a trustee of the Methodist Church, and as master of the Masonic Lodge. He was an active real estate trader, and a director of the State Bank. He built and lived in a very nice home at the corner of South and Main, which those of us who grew up in the mid-twentieth century knew as Doctor Hackett's house. It is now the location of the fire department building.

6. Pvt. Samuel Mead, born June 19, 1830, he joined Co. B in Sept. 1864. After fighting at Hatcher's Run, Five Forks and Appomattox, he came back to Bolivar.

7. Moses Miller, born March 28, 1843, in Almond. Joined Company B 189th Sep 1864. He served from Petersburg to Appomattox, and returned to Bolivar.

8. Oscar A. Pire, Born July 31, 1844, brother of Silas, he joined Co. B in Sep 1864 and served its tour. Returned to Bolivar. Also carried as Pyre.

9. Pvt. Albert Read, born August 11, 1835, joined Co B in September 1864. He was at Appomattox when Lee surrendered.

10. Pvt. William E. Richardson, born in Bolivar May 18, 1839, brother of Samuel A., joined Co B in Sep 1864, $600. "Was in the trenches before Petersburg and was present at the capture of Lee." Returned to Bolivar.

11. Chaplain William H. Rogers, born Oct. 21, 1834 in Willing. Joined the 189th in Oct 1864. With the regiment at battles of Lewis Farm, Hatcher's Run, Five Forks and Appomattox. He then returned to Richburg.

12. Pvt. Lyman E. Root, born Dec. 25, 1832 in Bolivar, son of Abel Root, the village blacksmith, he joined Co B, 189th NY in Sep 1864. He did the tour and returned to Bolivar.

13. Pvt. Sanford N. Scott, born Apr. 3, 1845, joined Co B in Sep 1864. Served from Petersburg to Appomattox, he returned to Bolivar.

14. Pvt. Edgar J. Scott, bro of above, b Jan. 14, 1848, he joined Co B in Sep 64, and was at Petersburg and Appomattox, then returned to Bolivar.

15. Pvt. Charles W. Williams, b April 26, 1838 in Wirt. Joined Co. B in Sep. 1864 and served with it from Petersburg to Appomattox, and returned to Bolivar.

16. Sgt. Simeon S. Williams, born in 1834. With Co. B from Sep. 1864. Mustered out with company May 30, 1865.

The following Bolivar men also served in the Union Army:

1. Pvt. William C. Applebee, born in Ellicottville Oct. 3, 1837, went with Co. B, 23rd Infantry in Sept. 61. Discharged due to a swollen neck caused by his knapsack in March 1863, he reenlisted in the 1st Battalion Veteran Reserve Corps in Sept. 1864. He came back to Bolivar after the war.

2. Pvt. Henry R. Burdick, born in Truxton NY August 2, 1823. Joined Troop B 2nd Veteran Cavalry in Sept. 1863. Served in Louisiana, Mississippi and Alabama, and was still in uniform when the town clerk's lists were compiled in fall if 1865.

3. Pvt. Melvin A. Burdick, brother of Henry, also born in Truxton NY June 16, 1825. Joining Co. I 27th NY Infantry, he transferred to the Signal Corps on Dec. 25, 1861. "The fatigues of the Seven days of McClellan compelled his discharge for disability." He reenlisted in August 1863 in the 1st NY Veteran Cavalry. After the war, he lived in Hornell.

3. Pvt. Oramel R. Burdick, brother of Henry R and Melvin, with the 2nd Veteran Cavalry, was born in Truxton May 10, 1829. He joined Co. B 42nd NY Infantry in July 1861. On Oct. 20, 1861, at the Battle of Ball's Bluff, he acted as orderly to Col. Cogswell and was sent back for reinforcements. He found it impossible to return to the command and recrossed the river by swimming. In 1862, he was taken prisoner near Harrison's Landing, carried to Richmond and soon after paroled. He reenlisted at Elmira in the 1st Vet. Cavalry, serving with it to the war's end. After the war, he lived in Hornell.

4. Pvt. Morton D. Crandall, born Madison Co. May 13, 1827. Pvt. 1st Veteran Cavalry Sept. 1863. Settled in Alfred after the war.

5. Asst. Sur. Joseph L. Cutler, born Feb. 15, 1829 in Moravia. Bolivar's doctor left to serve with the 134th NY Infantry in March 1863. "Attended wounded at Chancellorsville, Chattanooga and Lookout Valley. He resigned Jan. 5, 1864 "for physical disability," and returned to his practice in Bolivar.

6. Pvt. Richard B. Jemerson, born Aug. 8, 1826 in Owego, received a $300 bonus to join Co D, 50th NY Engineers. He returned to Bolivar after the war.

7. *Pvt. Lorenzo Dow Finch,* born April 18, 1837 in Cuba, joined Co E, 72nd NY Infantry in June 1861. Fought at Yorktown, Williamsburg, Fair Oaks, Cold Harbor during the 7 Days Battles, for which he received a medal. After, he was kicked by a horse, was permanently disabled, and returned to Bolivar.

8. Pvt. John Lang, born in Germany April 5, 1838. He joined Co. G 154th NY, a Cattaraugus County regiment in August 1862. Transferred for disability to Veteran Reserve Corps September 14, 1863. He returned to Bolivar post-war.

7. Musician Eli LeSuer, born Dec. 16, 1830 in Bolivar. Joined 28th NY Infantry band in September 1861, he was promoted to leader of the Brigade Band. Present during Banks Retreat and the Battle of Cedar Mountain in the summer of 1862. He reenlisted, and returned to Bolivar at war's end.

8. Mus. Lewis M. Raub, born 8/28/1835, son of Bolivar's dentist, joined the band of the 1st Brigade, Hardin's Division, 22nd Corps in March 1865. Honorably discharged, he returned to Bolivar.

9. Pvt. Henry L. Shoff, born Feb. 12, 1833, in Angelica. Joined Co E, 104th NY in March 1862. Taken sick, he was discharged October 6, 1862.

10. Pvt. Charles T. Wandover, b 4/17/42, brother of Henry, joined Co C, 65th NY in September 1862, and fought under Sheridan's command in the Shenandoah Valley in 1864. He returned to Bolivar.

11. **Pvt. John L. Weston,** born 1846, served with Co G, 1st Veteran Cavalry which he joined in October 1863. He was shot through the left lung and killed during a skirmish in Tennessee, and was buried near where he fell.

There were scores of other men who came to Bolivar after the war who also served. As examples, John Care served as an officer with Company I, 46th Pennsylvania Volunteers. He lived in Harrisburg, Pennsylvania when the war broke out, fought Stonewall Jackson for a solid year, was at Gettysburg, and came to Bolivar looking for work when oil was discovered. Joshua Dunning, born in 1843, grew up on a farm in West Almond. Reaching the age of twenty-one, he decided to put on a uniform, went to Mount Morris to join the 188th New York Infantry, and found himself at Appomattox when Lee sent over his flag of truce.

Bolivar was credited with sending 120 of its own men and boys off to the war. Twenty-nine of them died in uniform, just about one in four, which was far above the national average of one in ten. Another fifteen returned with wounds, and those who survived Andersonville were most often emaciated skeletons who took years to recover their strength. But, perhaps the most significant thing about the war was that it was a common experience for everyone. Nearly every family had a member who had put on a uniform. They all knew someone who didn't make it back. That sense of shared sacrifice created a bond, a deep sense of patriotism which meant far more than displaying a flag from a front porch. They had not asked what the country could do for them. Instead, they had done all they could for the country. They were justifiably proud to have done so, for the result in their minds was the preservation of the greatest country on earth. Good would surely follow such a painful sacrifice for a such just cause.

John P. Herrick, in his book, Bolivar, Pioneer Oil Town, lists forty-three Civil War veterans who became owners of oil properties in the 1880s, but many of those, such as Abijah Wellman and Rufus Scott, never lived in Bolivar. Memorial Day was established to remember those who had lost their lives in the war, and was first celebrated on a large scale in 1868. New York recognized it as an official holiday in 1873, but in the 1870s there were too few people in the town to make much of a celebration. When oil brought more people to the area, the Civil War veterans who settled in Bolivar formed the first veterans' fraternal organization known here, and it was one of the most important social organizations in town for the next half century. The H.C. Gardiner Post 247 of the Grand Army of the Republic was the second post organized in the county, in the fall of 1881, and had its quarters on Boss Street, in the building now used as the Thomas residence's garage. From the time of its organization, its members, "stalwart men in army blue, led by a mounted officer with a red sash and shining sword, marched to the music of bands or drum corps in parades to cemeteries in Allentown, Bolivar, Friendship, Richburg, Scio and Wellsville," usually followed by dinner, a patriotic address, and campfire songs.

Private Hiram Hitchcock, 136th New York Volunteer Infantry, Bolivar's last living Civil War veteran

The post was named for Pvt. Herman C. Gardiner, who belonged to Co. A, 136th New York Infantry, and who was killed in action at the Battle of Lookout Mountain near Chattanooga in the fall of 1863. Hiram Hitchcock, a member of the same company, was Bolivar's last living Civil War veteran. He died on April 26, 1935 at the age of ninety-one.

The most obvious relic of the Gardiner Post is the Civil War Monument standing in Maple Lawn Cemetery. The thirty-five ton, thirty-one foot high granite monument was erected under the auspices of the post at a cost of $2,500, (about $60,000 today), and was dedicated in September 1916.

After the War was Over

The W.H. Johnson carriage shop, as it looked in 1875

In the fifty years after Zephaniah Smith first set his traps, the town of Bolivar had been steadily transformed from forested valleys and hillsides abounding with game into farms grazed by sheep and cattle. The village had grown ever so slowly into a supply center for those farmers, dairymen and shepherds who lived nearby. Between 1850 and 1860, 250 settlers came into town, increasing the population by thirty-five percent, to 959. But the census of 1870 found exactly the same number of people as it had ten years before: 959. Enough new people had come to town during the 1860s to offset the losses occasioned by the war, but that was all. The 1870s saw only a modest increase: seventy people were added during that decade, according to the 1880 census, 1,029 being the final total. There appeared to be no reason to expect any rapid change. The forests were depleted, the farms were nearly all built. The hillsides too steep to till had been fenced to control of the herds of sheep grazing under the remaining trees. The town was not on any significant trade route. Other than the stage coach connecting Bolivar to Ceres and Friendship, there was no public transportation.

The 1880 US census listed 149 farmers and 133 housekeepers, including half a dozen girls who were listed as "assistant housekeepers." Seventy-two men said they were farm laborers, while 29 others were common laborers, many most probably working in the woods and sawmills. Twelve, mostly young, men and women taught in the district schools, while one other taught music. Nine carpenters lived in town, along with two wagon makers, two musicians, two masons, two shoemakers, two dress makers, two sawyers, and three coopers. Seven entrepreneurs were selling merchandise near the offices of two doctors and one dentist. Three cheesemakers, two harness makers, and two wagon builders lived here, as did one hotel keeper, and a solitary attorney.

The great world-shrinking pieces of technology that had transformed much of nineteenth century America had not touched the town of Bolivar. There was no telegraph office. All outside communication was done by letter, unless you traveled to Wellsville or Friendship from whence you could send a wire. There wasn't even a newspaper, nor was there much of a need for one. Everyone knew everyone else, what they did, and how well they did it. Advertising was completely unnecessary. Well attended churches and fraternal organizations gave the people plenty of opportunities to interact and catch up on the local happenings.

There were no heavy industries rising up which might justify a railroad spur. If you wanted to take a long trip, you could catch the stage to Wellsville, or Friendship or Olean, and from there ride the Erie to begin a trip to anywhere in the country. Bolivar, it seemed, was destined to be quiet and rural, off the beaten path, far, far away from the corner of Change and Progress.

If you came to Bolivar from the east, the road split at Kossuth, and you could head up the rise and then down along what we know as Olive Street and meet the road to Ceres near the tannery; or you could bear to the right, cross Root Hollow Creek and take the gentler slope down along Wellsville Street to the corner of Main. There in front of you, sitting back from the road stood the Methodist Church, its spire lit by the sun. Off a little to the right was the village school house, a single story frame building painted white, (which was unusual, most schools being red), and across the street from it stood the parsonage. To the left along Main were the hotel, known to history as the Clark House, but which was then known as Voorhees' House of Temperance, and Nelson Hoyt's Mercantile, Alpheus Williams' house, (which stood until recently at the corner of Main and Liberty), and finally the tannery and a shoe shop on the right. A few additional houses filled some of the gaps along Main, but that was all there was, and it appeared that might be about all there ever would be- unless something dramatic happened. And then it did.

Boom!

Above, pre-boom Bolivar in the late 1870s, looking north. The white house in the lower left was the Cowles house, which Al Glintz converted into his convenience store. The tall white building in the background above it is the first Masonic Temple. The steeple above that is the first Methodist Episcopal Church building, standing behind the yet-to-be-built State Bank. Also note the enormous old growth hemlock trees lining Main Street, and the well-developed orchard on the distant hillside in the upper right, probably on what would become the Casey Farm above Belmont Street.

The first commercially successful oil well in the United States had been drilled in 1859 near Titusville, in western Pennsylvania. That location had been chosen because it was near a well-known oil spring. Enterprising fortune hunters found their way to Cuba, New York, a few years later hoping for similar success near the Seneca Oil Spring, but a series of dry holes dampened their enthusiasm, and they went back to Pennsylvania. In 1875, a man named David Beatty drilled a wildcat well on his farm in Warren County Pennsylvania, and tapped into the first giant oil field discovered in the United States. Giant oil fields produce more than 100,000,000 barrels of oil, a threshold the Bradford field went past in 1884. Big, long-lived wells were drilled around Bradford in 1876, fueling the fever of treasure hunters, who by drilling test wells beyond the edge of the known producing area extended it into New York State near Limestone.

A reformed Confederate soldier working as a tobacconist in Wellsville named Oliver P. Taylor was convinced there was oil to be found in Allegany County, and he stood behind, (to the point his wife hocked her jewelry to keep him going), a series of early test wells drilled a few miles west of Wellsville looking for the precious oleaginous fluid. A company called the Wellsville & Alma Oil Company was organized in the last months of 1877, raised $5,000 by selling stock, and started drilling. Taylor was one of the investors. When the well discovered showings of oil and gas, but not enough to pay for pumping the well, the company abandoned it. But those paying attention, including Taylor, became convinced that better producers could be drilled nearby.

Taylor became the principal investor in a second well, this one located two miles northeast of the Alma post office, named the Pikeville No. 1. The drilling was completed in November 1878, but this well too failed to produce enough oil to meet operating expenses and was abandoned. After drilling one more dry hole, Taylor moved the rig another two miles to the northeast. On June 12, 1879, he completed the Triangle No. 1 near Brimmer Brook, three miles west of Wellsville, and forty miles west of the nearest producing wells around Bradford. This discovery gave encouragement to others in the area to keep looking.

At that time, Friendship was about the most prosperous town in the county outside Wellsville, and in it lived men with money in the bank who could finance exploratory drilling in the county. In March 1881, there were twenty-one rigs either up and drilling, or being built. Thirteen were in the town of Alma, near Taylor's test wells, six were in in the town of Bolivar, one in Wellsville, and one was going down in the town of Wirt.

Soon enough, the solitary well being drilled in the town of Wirt was garnering all of the attention. It was the brainchild of a Richburg shoe store owner named Crandall Lester, who had gone over to see the Triangle No. 1 and another well near Allentown, and who then became convinced the oil trend extended westward to Richburg.

On April 20, 1881, at a depth of 1,213 feet, the well he inspired encountered a promising oil sand, and the driller, John Moran, stopped operations. He sent word to Taylor, Riley Allen, and a few other significant investors, asking how to proceed. The investors immediately bought fifty acres surrounding the well for $5,000, an unheard of price per acre in the county. They then gave Moran the go-ahead, and on Saturday, April 22, he bored the well twenty-four feet into the sand. On Monday morning, the well overflowed its casing and petroleum started running onto the ground. On the twenty-seventh, a shooter exploded thirty quarts of nitroglycerin in the well. The blast sent oil spewing thirty feet above the seventy-two foot tall derrick, and the well flowed twenty barrels an hour. The Richburg Discovery Well was just 660 feet north of the Bolivar town line.

Not long after, a letter was printed in the New York Sun: "*Oil scouts who had been watching developments closely, rode with all haste to the railroad towns over the hills and the wires carried the news of the big strike to the newspaper offices. The next day people in all parts of the country knew that a new oil field had been opened. Then began a wild scramble for leases, and oil operators from the Pennsylvania regions flocked across the state line in droves, anxious to secure a slice of the new Eldorado.*"

How quickly can the world change? On April 20, 1881, a single stage coach made its daily run from Wellsville to Bolivar, via Scio and Knight's Creek. Less than a week later, four new stage lines had been established running from Eldred to Bolivar. (Eldred, on the Pennsylvania Railroad, was halfway between Bolivar and Bradford, and was the closest the Pennsylvania came to the new oil find). The coaches, pulled by four-horse teams, were jammed with fortune hunters paying three dollars each for the ride. A building boom followed on their heels, first in Richburg, but quickly flowing down the valley into Bolivar. Houses, stores, and saloons seemed to appear overnight. In a place where beds could fetch three dollars a night, (close to $100 in twenty-first century money), and a pool table could be rented for a dollar, it made real economic sense. D.A. Newton decided to put up a three story, forty-room hotel at the corner of Wellsville and Main Streets. Opening for business in February 1882, by letting out the rooms for the standard three dollars a night, it paid for itself in three months.

Most of the new housing was cheaply built, the builders thinking this was all a temporary phenomenon, so nothing needed to be made to last. Cheap, temporary buildings were all that were thought needed. Hemlock plank shacks were thrown up on short stone pilings. The walls and ceilings were covered in muslin, then wall papered. Each unit needed its own water well. Heat and light came from natural gas. Washtubs doubled as bath tubs. The wall papering cheered up the interiors, but more often than not, the exteriors went unpainted, and quickly weathered black.

They seemingly came from everywhere- Pittsburgh, Buffalo, Bradford, Oil City, and Rochester had many representatives, but as word spread, so did the number of people who came from farther away. In just ten months, Bolivar had swelled from 160 people to 4,500 "excited and industrious oil pioneers," who lived a rather sedate life, compared to the 10,000 in Richburg who kept five policemen and three town justices "busy subduing lawlessness day and night."

By the end of the summer of 1881, a narrow gauge railroad had been built, connecting Bolivar with Friendship to the north, and Olean to the west via the Erie, with three trains a day running each way. More rails were being laid, which opened up routes to Wellsville and Cuba. They too were making money. In the first month of its service through Bolivar, the Allegany Central took in $12,000 at the freight car it used as the Bolivar depot, and began paying generous dividends. The Bradford, Eldred & Cuba was soon completed running on to Wellsville. It built a little spur line from Bolivar to Richburg, powered by an engine that was "a cross between a cookstove and a fanning mill," which carried 700 passengers a day. Dividends of one or two percent *per month* went out to the shareholders who had funded the construction.

A September newspaper report told of the opening of the Alpine House Hotel, "which makes twenty-nine hotels and eating houses in Richburg." Building supplies, lumber, lath, drive pipe, casing, pipe of all sizes, iron plate, nails, rivets, engines to power new rigs, shingles, fittings, and valves all required powerful locomotives and large carriages to be delivered where they were needed.

It couldn't be all work and no play, and when there was time to take a break, it being summertime baseball became a popular outlet for both players and spectators. One paper reported, "*A return game of base ball was played Saturday evening on Dean's Flats, between the Ring-tail roarer nine of Richburg, and the Blue-bellied Blood Boilers nine of Bolivar. The game was hotly contested throughout. Several fouls were scored on either side. MJ Roach, poet, served as umpire.*" Results: Richburg 79, Bolivar 0. *"In tomorrow's letter from Bolivar these figures will be reversed to fit the exigencies of the occasion."*

Boom town excitement attracted many men of distinctive character, but few were more memorable than Samuel Boyle. Omer McQueen, the last surviving member of the drilling crew on the Richburg discovery well, remembered Boyle clearly decades later. "He wore a long Prince Albert coat, flowing tie, a broad-brimmed black beaver hat, and striped pants tucked into high, shiny, leather boots. He rode a handsome dappled grey horse, and one of his favorite stunts was to ride under a flaming open street gas flare, light his cigar with a dollar bill, then gallop away." On June 30, just two months after the Richburg well came in, Boyle hit the second great gusher in the field, a mile and a quarter northwest of the Richburg well.

By early July, in an area bounded by the Richburg well, the Boyle well, Triangle No.1, and another well drilled in Bolivar's great lot 5, between the Triangle well and Alma, eighty rigs were up and drilling. Land that had been selling for $10 an acre was now trading for $300. When August arrived, ninety-nine wells were underway. The valley became a tourist destination. Excursion trains made up of ten gondola cars left Friendship three times an hour, taking the curious and adventuresome on a tour through Richburg and on into Bolivar, so they could see the frantic activity filling the valley.

What did they see? One of the great problems being faced was what to do with all of the oil being produced. The initial answer was to build storage tanks. The biggest were thirty feet high and ninety feet across, and could hold 35,000 barrels each. Made from belts of iron five feet high and ten feet across riveted together, they seemingly couldn't be built fast enough. The United Pipeline Company had put up one of the first, while Samuel Boyle followed soon after with one of his own. In late 1881, George W. Thompson built another on the north edge of Bolivar village, painted it white, then painted his name on it in red letters four feet high.

They saw scores of oil derricks, each seventy-two feet high, built of planks, topped with a crown pulley, powered by a steam engine turning a wheel attached off center to a "walking beam," which would lift and drop and lift and drop the drill bit, which punched its way inch by inch into the earth.

Luckily, before the Richburg well came in, United Pipeline Company had been building a new transmission pipeline from Olean to New Jersey, and its route passed just three miles north of Richburg. Plans were quickly put into action to build a gathering system which would send much of the new field's production in that direction. To push the petroleum over the East Notch, United built an enormous pump station between Bolivar and Richburg. It installed an eighteen cylinder Cameron pump, and then put in another. Still not having the desired capacity, they brought in another unit, the next-to-the-largest made, weighing thirty-four tons, which had cylinders forty-three inches in diameter. With the combined units, United could push 10,000 barrels a day out through its four inch main line, and thus stay ahead of the 8,000 barrels a day being produced. But just to be safe, tanks capable of holding 60,000 more barrels were under construction on the flats above Bolivar village.

A good deal of Bolivar's production had been going into a system that was taking it toward Wellsville, where a big tank had been built earlier to handle the production from the Taylor drilling activity. So, in addition to seeing the tanks and derricks and pump station and hundreds of structures newly built or under construction, the tourists on the excursion train could listen to a confusing mess of thumps, bangs, and hisses of power machinery doing the work of modern times. All this in a valley where a year before the loudest sounds came from the morning roosters and cows needing to be milked. And of course, the smell of petroleum and unburned natural gas filled the air, foul to newcomers and tourists, but carrying the aroma of gold and riches to those involved in the business.

We have the first good, detailed description of the changes in Bolivar village itself in early 1882. On February 14, a referendum was held asking if the village should be incorporated. When the vote came back a resounding *YES*, a meeting was held the next day to get it done. Darius A. Newton was elected the first "president," which is what mayors were then called, and E.R. Kilbury took office as the first village justice. Henry D. Partridge became chief of police, and his first hire as a patrolman was a Belmont boy named Charles Hoffman, who was destined for bigger and better things. His second deputy was another memorable Bolivar character, Happy Jack Stoops.

The new village trustees faced a long list of problems. They appropriated funds to pay the police, to maintain the streets, for fire protection, for street lights, a board of health, and even authorized a census. Soon after, perhaps in lieu of the census, a business directory was published. It listed two railroads, two express companies, telephone and telegraph offices, twenty-eight hotels, seventeen lodging houses, one bank, one newspaper, an opera house, nine oil well supply businesses, thirty-five contractors, twenty painters and paper hangers, fourteen blacksmiths, eight lumber dealers, two coal dealers, ten oil well shooters, three nitroglycerin dealers, four water well drillers, (but only three plumbers), seven tank shops, four laundries including two Chinese, six livery stables, and a veterinarian.

There were six men's clothing stores, six milliners, four tobacco shops and four meat markets, three drug stores and three confectioners, two junk shops, and one undertaker. Whereas before the boom Bolivar had only James Curtis, now there were ten more attorneys hanging out their shingles, along with seven doctors and a solitary dentist.

On the other end of the spectrum were eight liquor wholesalers, two bottling works, and ten restaurants with bars, which included *The Oil Exchange*, *Delmonico's,* and *The Tivoli Beer Garden*. To emphasize the need for compliance, one unfortunate Italian saloon keeper who had failed to get a license was sentenced to one hundred days in the county jail, and another fifty in the state penitentiary in Buffalo. An Angelica editor expressed his amazement that Bolivar's only justice, E.R. Kilbury, could keep up with the case load. Richburg had three justices, and all of them seemed over-worked.

In 1880, the residents of Bolivar socialized either in church, at Masonic gatherings, or at the Grange halls. Now, with big quantities of liquor readily available, and with hundreds, if not thousands, of people looking for quick gratification of whatever desires they had, "trouble came to River City". Perhaps surprisingly, there were only two murders during the boom, and both happened in Richburg. On November 19, 1881, the first perpetrator, John McCarthy, stabbed another named named Patrick Markey. McCarthy was tried, convicted, and was hanged in March 1882, one editor commenting on the fact that the sheriff had allowed McCarthy one long drink of demon rum before he was dispatched. *"The sheriff's motive was all right- but still, there are those who think with horror of a man being cast into eternity with rum on his breath!"* The editor was even more offended that the *Bolivar Sunday Leader* had seen fit to publish a likeness of McCarthy as he appeared while hanging.

The second killing happened just two weeks later, when the owner of a Richburg bowling alley refused a drunken rig builder named Edmund Whipple the use of an air rifle on a target range. Enraged, Whipple left, only to return fifteen minutes later armed with a revolver. In a struggle to disarm him, the gun discharged, hitting twenty-two-year-old Theodore Googe in the groin. Googe died soon after. Inspired to play it safe when McCarthy was convicted, Whipple pled guilty to first degree manslaughter and went away to the state prison in Auburn for nineteen years. Other than a never-explained death of a prostitute in Richburg, those were the only violent deaths on the streets during the boom.

For whatever reason, the worst elements of boom-town society ended up in Richburg, whereas Bolivar became the location chosen by most of the new businesses coming, they hoped, to stay. The railroads, the gas utility, the tool manufacturers, the buyers for Standard Oil, all put their main offices or headquarters in Bolivar, safely away from the rowdier side streets of Richburg. In November 1881, construction began on a large business block at the corner of Main and Wellsville streets, across Wellsville Street from the nearly completed Newton House. The new building was designed to hold a bank, an oil well supply business, other offices, and a public hall. The Barse Block, as it was first known, has housed a big variety of businesses over the years, and stands there still.

In February 1882, M.J. Cain, manager of the Gem Theater in Bradford, purchased the Weaver & Williams property on Main Street, where he immediately began construction of a "temple of amusement." He was well equipped, the editor of the *Allegany County Republican* thought, "to supply what the denizens of that growing oil town demand." Thus was born Bolivar's Opera House, which stood where the Library and adjoining lot now stand, north of Olean Street.

Another active operator in town was Benjamin Ward Baum, a native of Chittenango. B.W. looked for opportunities, and was creative in his business enterprises. One of the first things he did when he arrived in the Bolivar area was to set up a skimmer on Little Genesee Creek. Petroleum was running all over the ground, from leaking wells, loose fittings, and most often from overflowing tanks, and much of it ended up on the surface of the Little Genesee. Baum's skimmer collected ninety barrels a day, better than most of the wells, which were averaging only twenty-five. With that supply, B.W. set up the Cynthia Oil Works, a small refinery not far from the creek, on the south side of the Salt Rising Road, and started selling his oil at retail prices.

B.W.'s seventh child was a boy, then twenty-five, whose passion was the theater. The refinery was owned by the company, B.W. Baum & Son. To better satisfy the boy's ambitions, the company put up an opera house in Richburg, and the son filled its stage with productions of his own creation, writing the scripts, hiring the performers, often serving as writer-producer-director and star, using the stage names George Brooks or Louis Baum. Some flopped, but one, *The Maid of Arran*, a melodramatic musical, proved such a success that he took it on the road. Many of the shows proved so popular that special excursion trains were run from Friendship and Bolivar to carry patrons to the shows. The son was L. Frank Baum, who, in 1898 would come out with the classic children's book, *Mother Goose in Prose.* Illustrated by Maxfield Parrish, it became a best seller. Baum followed that up with *Father Goose, His Story*, which was the best-selling children's book of 1899. Then, in 1900, he came out with one more: *The Wonderful Wizard of Oz.*

L. Frank Baum

The Baums were not the only enterprising operators to gather oil from the creek. Another firm, Miller, May & Co., leased a small part of the Hoyt farm not far west of the Bolivar train depot, and built a dam across the creek. Daily from 200 to 300 barrels of oil would collect behind the dam, which they pumped by hand into wooden tanks. Plans were laid to put in a mechanical pump, and to steam the oil, partially refining it so it could be sold as a lubricant. Soon enough, five men were at work collecting and processing the floating crude.

As 1881 drew to a close, drilling activity continued to mushroom. At the end of October, 392 rigs stood in the field, many of them visible either in the valley between Richburg and Bolivar, or on the surrounding hillsides. At the end of November, there were nineteen more, 189 of them drilling new wells, 222 waiting for crews to man them.

In the town of Bolivar alone, (which the *Olean Daily Herald* called, "the Land of Leeks"), fifty-nine wells had been completed in November, bringing in new production averaging 1,871 barrels a day. The best of them had been put down in Great Lot 64, the northwest corner of the town, not far from the area that would be developed into the Hilltop Restaurant decades later. Nine wells had been completed there, which averaged seventy-five to ninety barrels a day each. Another seventy-five wells were being drilled around the town, and 101 more rigs were being built, nearly twice the number of those going up in the town of Wirt.

With all this activity, the number of people in town continued to swell. The classiest place to stay in Bolivar had a new name. The inn first built by Hollis B. Newton in 1831 had taken on the name of its new owner, becoming The Clark

House, which, until the Newton House opened, was also the largest hotel in town. It housed a carved clock with "an ingenious movement" which drew lots of attention, as well as a billiard room, sample rooms where salesmen could lay out their displays, an attached barn and livery stable, and perhaps most importantly, a direct telephone connection with the Bradford Oil Exchange. A twenty-four-year-old Iowan named Charlie Winchell served as the manager.

It was far from a traveler's only option, but as cold weather returned, those options narrowed. Over the summer months, groups of twenty men had been seen crawling out of hay mows in the mornings. More than 200 had slept on the Bolivar village green, which surrounded the Methodist Church and the school yard opposite the end of Wellsville Street. Frost put a premium on tighter structures. The Bristol House, at the corner of Main and Pleasant, offered "first class accommodations" as well as a stable. The American House offered accommodations on Boss Street. The Newton House was nearing completion. The Bolivar House stood just down the street. There were dozens more whose names have faded away.

The boomtown atmosphere attracted many people intent on taking advantage of a situation where a community was completely unprepared for and overwhelmed by a huge influx of newcomers. In Bolivar's village, the 175 residents found themselves surrounded by 3,000 or 4,000 new arrivals, and, until the village incorporated, only a occasional sheriff's deputy or two to keep order. One hundred saloons opened their doors, little or no attention having been paid to securing licenses. (Yes, even back then, New York State tried to keep its finger on much of daily life). Most of the time, the people were too busy getting rich to bother about such small matters. One enterprising saloon keeper's stock arrived before his building was ready. He stood two whisky barrels on end, laid a broad plank over the top of them, and began business at the side of the street. His first day's receipts amounted to $72, $2,200 in modern currency. Money flowed like water… or was it like whiskey?

And it was the same way with the gambling houses. They ran wide open Games of every description flourished. Even the best of men could be lured to a table covered in green felt. Samuel Boyle, who had drilled the second big well, decided to cash in, sold his oil interests, and used a chunk of the proceeds to remodel a building in Friendship, converting it into "a swank two-story gambling house with a colonial entrance." Perhaps the first omen that the place might be unlucky happened when a veteran gambler bet his last dollar, drew a fourth ace, and collapsed at the table, killed by a heart attack. Not long after, Boyle himself sat down at one of his tables, and entered into a poker game that ebbed and flowed for two full days and into a third night. He lost everything he had. Loaned $300 by a friendly neighbor, he left town never to return- but two years later, he repaid the loan!

About the same time, "a handsome bachelor and man-about-town," by the name of John Preston, got into an argument with his business partner over their lease, which had six wells on it. Preston suggested settling the argument by rolling the dice, winner take all. His partner accepted the challenge, and they retired to "the long mahogany bar" of the newly-opened Newton House to settle the matter. They rolled the same number on the first toss, but Preston lost the next two and his share of the lease.

Where money and whiskey flow freely, other forms of vice are quick to spread, like mold on freshly baked bread. The winter cold and more and more people looking for beds and opportunities only worsened the situation. The *Allegany County Republican*, an Angelica newspaper, called its readers' attention to the fact that while Bolivar had become infested with dangerous gamblers, and women were now being seen drunk walking along the streets, Wellsville's revival meetings were doing a brisk business.

The winter of 1881-82 was unexpectedly mild, which was good for both the drilling of wells and the construction of buildings of any type. The news was both good and bad. In February, the Allegany Central Railroad completed its track all the way to Angelica. During February, 190 wells were completed, 206 more were being drilled, and 203 more rigs were up waiting to drive pipe. Half a dozen new wells drilled on the Reed farm between Bolivar and Richburg had come in at more than 200 barrels a day each.

On the other hand, Baum's Opera House burned to the ground, touching off demands for an immediate replacement. As a Cuba paper put it, "Richburgers shudder at the idea of having to journey down to rival Bolivar for entertainment." In its ashes were scattered a number of L. Frank's Baum's early manuscripts.

Despite the fresh news about the hanging of John McCarthy, reports began to appear in the papers of lesser crimes. One safe was broken into, but the thieves, believed to be four in number, got away with just eleven cents. A wallet containing forty dollars disappeared. Then, on May 3, 1882, a twenty-eight-year-old ne'er do well named John Golden was reading a newspaper in the first floor center parlor of "Madame Stewart's Bagnio" in Bolivar, where he was engaged as a piano player. Mattie Pierce, one of the girls working for Madame Stewart, walked in through the open door, raised her arm, pointed a small seven-shot revolver at the back of Golden's head and pulled the trigger. Hearing the gun's report, another man ran in from an adjoining room and saw Golden getting up while Mattie aimed her second shot. A third man appeared, tore the pistol out of Mattie's hand, but then turned his attention to Golden, allowing Mattie to flee into the night. Doctors Latham and Cutler arrived, examined Golden, and found that he had only been grazed above his right ear.

Golden was well known in "the sporting circles" of Bradford, having played his piano tunes for a time there at the Erie Beer Garden, but he had spent at least part of the summer of 1880 in the McKean County jail. Mattie Pierce was apprehended a few hours later, and on June 10 was indicted for "shooting with intent to kill," and soon after pled guilty.

At Pierce's preliminary hearing before Justice Kilbury, Golden had been a very reluctant witness. "One of the more important witnesses was Nettie Yockey, who is said to have been the cause of the jealous woman's shot." Addressed as "Mrs. Kindorff" by the D.A., it took her "some time to recognize herself under that title. Nettie is described by the Echo as the only woman who had any preten-

Looking east out over boomtown Bolivar, probably in the early months of 1883. In the original photo, the author counted thirty-five drilling rigs circling the village. Not a single hemlock tree was left standing along Main Street. Store fronts fill not only Main Street, but also most of Railroad Avenue

sions of being passably good looking in the crowd, which will give Wellsvillians a fair idea of Richburg's standard of female loveliness." Nettie was "well known in this village (Wellsville) as one of the refugees from the recent law and order prosecutions."Golden too had been held in custody, his reluctance to cooperate and testify indicating he might be a flight risk. The judge sentenced Mattie to just one year of hard labor.

Despite the constant building going on, in April 1882 papers started reporting that people were being driven out of Bolivar and Richburg by the high rents. Little did they suspect how quickly that problem would be solved, for production in the Allegany Field peaked that month, a 22,438 barrel a day. On May 18, 1882 a well called the 646 was torpedoed. Drilled near Cherry Grove in Warren County, Pennsylvania, it came in at 1,000 barrels a day, more than double the best wells in Allegany County. (The Big Injun well, drilled on the Reed Farm that month, came in at *only* 400). The price of oil fell through the floor, from 75 cents a barrel to less than fifty. Drilling contractors tore down their rigs and loaded them on trains heading to Warren County. The drilling crews left next, and so did thousands of their camp followers. There were vacancies again at the hotels and in the rooming houses.

The exodus hit Richburg the hardest, for it had been home to the majority of the field labor force and to those who catered to their hopes, needs, and desires, whereas Bolivar had become more of the commercial center, where people had businesses to tend to and greater incentive to stay put.

Although the population of the valley dropped as fast and farther than the price of oil had, it by no means emptied out. For the whole of 1882, the Allegany Field produced on average more than 17,600 barrels of oil a day, a total of 6,450,000, and 1,605 wells were completed. 1,207 more would go down in 1883. The Empire Gas & Fuel Company, which had been able to sell a $1,000,000 bond issue on the same day as the Cherry Grove news arrived, proceeded to lay pipe connecting the field's prolific gas production to lamps, stoves, boilers, and street lights in Wellsville, Allentown, Bolivar and Richburg, bringing central heat and light to everyone who wanted it, and cheap power to those who had ideas for factories.

The ever increasing volume of oil production led the Tidewater Pipeline to build an additional pump station south of Bolivar on the LeSuer farm, and more and more of Bolivar's production was pumped east to Wellsville. There, on the flat valley bottom along the road to Elm Valley and Andover, seventy-nine 35,000 barrel tanks went up, all painted red, which together could hold 2,765,000 barrels. Around Olean, 300 of these tanks could, and did, collect more than 10,000,000 barrels, most of that coming up from Bradford.

The collapse of Richburg's population meant that the vice market shrank in proportion. Many of those who did not pull out for Cherry Grove, instead relocated to Bolivar, and Railroad Avenue was soon labeled, "Bolivar's Bowery." In Wellsville, where local citizens still easily outnumbered the newcomers, a "Law and Order League" had launched a campaign to clean up the streets and back rooms. This led to numerous arrests, including that of a Carrie Mills for keeping a house of ill repute. The papers were quick to report that no one would pay Carrie's bail.

But, Wellsville was not made spotless. In November 1883, the press complained about the presence of another bagnio, "in a brick block over business places" where "its denizens ply their avocation without regard to the rights of respectable people or public decency." In frustration two years later, a gang of self-righteous citizens took matters into their own hands, and decided to rid Wellsville of another house of ill repute housed in a tenement on lower Main Street. They called in the fire department and started to kick in the door. The proprietor, one Dan Wilder, started shooting to drive the firemen away, slightly wounding one. But, the door went down, and the firemen, "turned an inch and a half stream of water on the soiled doves, who were literally washed from the building."

The tightened economic circumstances brought on by the Cherry Grove exodus strained nerves and tempers along with pocket books, and reports of crimes increased. In late May 1882, just a couple of weeks after the exodus began, a James Nailan was charged with stealing money and a watch from a drunken customer of Daisy Smith. Daisy testified on his behalf. In February 1883, Joel Shoff, a "boarding house" keeper on Railroad Ave., was poisoned and robbed of forty dollars and his watch. No arrest was made, but it was believed that the woman with whom he had been seen had skipped town.

The following July, two Italians appeared on the streets of Richburg with a pair of dancing bears. They wandered about the town until they crossed paths with four drunken drillers, the three Boyd brothers and a man named Rogers. The foursome started hurling beer bottles at the men and their bears, which brought on a fight where the Italians and the bears come out the worse. A black woman tried to intervene and was in turn attacked, which she brought to an end by pulling out a revolver, causing the foursome to sprint down the road to Bolivar.

Sheriff Elliott happened to be in town. With two deputies, he set out to find the Boyds, and located them in a bagnio near Bolivar's depot. When he tried to arrest them, "a general free-for-all fight ensued," in which the officers were badly handled, Deputy Manning ending up with two black eyes, (and probably a broken nose), and the sheriff himself well bruised. The Boyds might have escaped, had not the sheriff pulled out his revolver, shoved it into the face of one of the Boyds, and called out, "Hands up, or off goes the top of your head!" At that, they surrendered, and were carted back to Richburg for arraignment, with the thought being floated that they would be bailed out by their employer. "These desperados have tyrannized this community for a long time, and there is great rejoicing over the prospect of them getting to state prison."

Just a week later, fresh headlines appeared:

> *"Row at Allentown! In a House of Ill Fame. A Dentist of Bolivar, and an Allentown Driller in a hand to hand melee. The dentist's nose bit off!"*

The article relates how "a noted courtesan by the name of Madame Sergeant" with her "soiled doves" had moved her business from Richburg to Allentown, bringing along her "bleary-eyed, depraved creatures." On Sunday night, July 22 at her place, a fight broke out among many of the drunken customers. Among them were a dentist from Bolivar and a driller from Allentown, both of whose names the paper chose to withhold. They started a war of words, and when it escalated into the "brothel vocabulary," it quickly grew to an exchange of blows. "Stairs, stands and furniture were sent flying" and "the combatants roared and struck at each other like demons". The Madame tried to break it up, but failed. "The driller was the boss of the situation and in the rough and tumble encounter he got firm grip on the dentist's nose, and off went the gentleman's proboscis into the driller's mouth, who spitefully spit it out on the floor." Still, they kept at it. Officer Gigee arrived, the dentist calmed down, but the driller, "bellowed like a mad bull, and swung his ponderous arms with the force of a walking beam". Before Gigee succeeded in arresting him, the driller made use of his teeth one more time, nearly biting off one of the officer's fingers. The dentist swore out a warrant for the driller's arrest. The driller anted up $100 for Gigee's finger, but the price of the nose was yet to be determined.

That episode seemed to mark an end to the headline-making rowdiness associated with the boom. Richburg shriveled into a near ghost town, the main excitement coming every now and then when an abandoned building caught fire. Bolivar cooled down, but retained a population more than double that of the 1870s, and continued to serve as a distribution center and supply base for the operators of oil and gas leases. But the boom town atmosphere left a permanent mark. For the next century, Bolivar had a disproportionate number of establishments offering alcoholic beverages. And, although houses of ill repute were by no means commonly found, they were not eradicated until World War One.

The most famous local madam was Nellie Dwyer, who was born into unfortunate circumstances in Ellicottville in 1867. In the 1890s, she was living as a "hotel keeper" in Allegany, but by the coming of the Twentieth Century had moved east, to Olean and Bolivar. As small as Bolivar was then, (not much bigger than it is now), it had a rough neighborhood: Railroad Avenue, which paralleled the Shawmut Railroad track, was still our "Bowery."

Nell decided to set up her house of ill repute on the avenue, and gave it a name which would appear innocuous enough to passersby, but which also conveyed a clear message to those in the know: hers was the "Hornell House." Appropriately enough, her husband, who spent most of his time raising rabbits, hatching chicks, and going fishing, painted the place red. There was a famous incident in the early 1900s when a group of Bolivar's women paraded en masse down to Nell's front door, demanding that she close up and move on. Nell appeared on her front porch, and listened patiently while she sized up the opposition. Then, she spoke with great authority: "Well, if it wasn't for your husband, Mrs. Jones, and your husband, Mrs. Smith, your husband, Mrs. Brown, and your husband, Mrs. Green, I wouldn't have much business here anyway." The protesters retreated in silence. They pressured the village board to take action, the board in turn would feel the pressure, and every couple of years would order the chief of police to do something. He would walk down to railroad Ave., arrest whoever was on premises, (one time that being only Mr. Dwyer), and watch as they readily paid the five or ten dollar fines, which was all the law allowed.

For a time, there were at least two other such establishments in Bolivar, and both Nell and a woman who called herself "Billie Burke," after the then famous stage actress, had similar business setups in Olean. Perhaps one of them operated the house which then stood on the southwest corner of Clark and East State Streets, across the street from what became the Olean Tile plant.

The front of the Hornell House peeks above the stock cars, while John C. Bradley and an unknown friend seal a deal with a handshake, about 1916.

There is a legendary tale about an old Bolivar boy, one of the Williams Brothers, who knocked on the door at that address late one morning. When the madam opened the door, he meekly asked, "Was I in here last night, and did I spend a twenty-dollar bill?" When told, that yes, he had been, and yes he had, a big smile lit up his face and he exclaimed, "Thank God! I thought I'd lost it!" Nell Dwyer died, at the age of fifty, in 1917. The Hornell House stood until the1980s. When it was torn down, Mike Schaffner salvaged the knob from the front door and had it mounted in a frame, with a small plaque explaining that more satisfied customers had turned this knob than that of any other business in Bolivar. Perhaps.

After the Boom was Over

One of the principal differences among oil fields is what is called the "drive mechanism," the natural process that moves petroleum through rock and into the wells, sometimes pushing the oil all the way to the top and more. Some, like the great East Texas Field, are water driven. There a gigantic aquifer slopes down from west to east most of the way across Texas, then slopes abruptly upwards. Petroleum is lighter than water, so a huge amount of it accumulated above the level of the water at the eastern end of the formation. Anyone drilling into this at the point where it slopes upwards had themselves a powerful artisan oil well, out of which a steady stream of oil flowed for decades before it suddenly turned to water.

The Bradford and Allegany oil fields are gas driven. Through natural processes, large amounts of methane gas were compressed into the petroleum. When a well was drilled into the Richburg sand, it provided an outlet from which this pressure could be released. When the pressure was released by the drilling of a well, much like opening a pop bottle, the bubbles of methane expanded, pushing the oil through the rock toward the well, and sometimes out of it. But as more and more gas escaped and the pressure decreased, the amount of oil flowing into a well steadily declined. The decline is most pronounced early in a well's life, and then does so at a regular and predictable rate, until not enough oil comes to the well to pay for its maintenance..

In 1882, production in the Allegany Field peaked at 6,450,000 barrels, an average of 17,671 barrels a day, after the completion of 1,605 new wells. In 1883, 1,270 more new wells came on line, but total production fell to 4,800,000 barrels, or 13,151 barrels a day, a decline of twenty-five percent. Thirteen years later, in 1896, daily output for the field stood at only 2,013 barrels a day.

The other side of the oil coin is the price you can get for it. In 1884, the producers banded together, and in an attempt to raise the price of crude from 79 cents a barrel to $1.00, an estimated eighty-seven percent of New York and Pennsylvania producers quit drilling new wells. The moratorium lasted four months. In the interim, a big gusher was drilled in Butler County, Pennsylvania, and the price fell to 74 cents.

To understand what happened when the boom ended with the exodus to Cherry Grove, I asked two questions. First, who left? And second, who stayed? It is easy to understand how Richburg nearly folded up, its hundreds of quickly-built shelters and stores either burned or torn down for the lumber, its population, which had been made up mostly of oil field workers and camp followers, shrinking back to the level before the boom happened.

So, who left? The fortune hunters, the gamblers, the camp followers, those with short-term outlooks and dreams of quick riches. They had seen the hardships of working in the fields, and in the process had started to dream of easier

President Grover Cleveland and Allan Thurman were the Democratic nominees in 1888, but Cleveland lost his re-election bid to Benjamin Harrison. This photo is of the west side of Bolivar's Main Street, at the intersection with Boss. The village green has disappeared, the State Bank and a grocery taking up the portion nearest the corner. Mrs. O'Brian's BonTon shop is hidden behind the tree. The Cutler Brothers served as the town's physicians, and as the pharmacy. Taken during the campaign season, the sign on the Democratic headquarters says "they meet every night!"

going, higher returns, and better times somewhere else, undoubtedly the same dreams they had when they flocked to Richburg after the discovery well came in.

The declining production and shrinking income stream which held sway from 1883 right up until World War One created an intensely competitive atmosphere in which to carry on business, whether that was in a restaurant, a barber shop, or selling oil well supplies. The people who were looking long term, who had the determination to take a stand and make a corresponding success where they were with what they had, and who could best pay attention to their business pursuits, those were the people who prospered and stayed. Those less determined, less skilled, or less fortunate, were forced to make their way somewhere else. As oil production shrank, the fierceness of the competition steadily intensified.

Many of the old names in town, Cowles, Williams, Andrus, Richardson, Voorhees, Hoyt, Root, Scott, and Davidson, as examples, were still represented, and many were active in community affairs, but the boom had brought to town a number of other families whose names are familiar to nearly everyone living in Bolivar in the twenty-first century. O.T. Cowles kept his grocery business, but expanded his inventory to include crockery, silverware, sewing machines and thread. E.W. Cowles became the undertaker. The oldest person in town was Uncle Ben Cowles, who had lived through just about the entire history of Bolivar to that time.

C.M. Williams served as the clerk of the board of education, as secretary of the Bolivar Track Association, and was Democratic candidate for mayor in 1893. J.P. Williams was busy in the lumber business. Samuel Richardson was a candidate for commissioner of excise taxes. G.A. and Ira Root served respectively as the candidates for tax collector and treasurer of the village.

But the newcomers had among them people of grit, who were determined to make a success of themselves no matter the conditions, no matter unforeseen circumstances of an oil field providing steadily diminishing returns. No one better epitomized that grit and determination than a man who arrived in Bolivar in his early twenties with a skill much needed at that point in time. Boilermaker Daniel S. Dempsey was tall, thin, handsome, and determined.

Daniel Dempsey was raised on a farm near Fenton, New York, along with a string of brothers, and virtually all of them became boilermakers, probably learning that trade in or near the rail yards of Binghamton, not far from their home. When the Allegany oil field was discovered, every derrick erected was powered by steam, which required a boiler. Once the well quit flowing, if it ever did flow, it needed to be pumped, and that same derrick and steam engine were needed to power the pump and lift the petroleum out of the ground. Literally thousands of boilers were needed, and once installed, they had to be repaired and maintained.

When the Dempsey brothers first arrived in the area, boilermakers were in high demand. But as the field developed and production declined, drilling activity dropped off, and the demand for boilers declined as well. But, this technology was the best available, and if you drilled an oil or gas well, you needed a boiler too drill it, and if oil, to pump it. Dan Dempsey proudly put a sign on the front of the company shop: *"We Like to Work."* It was an eye-catcher, expressing the attitude of a man determined to succeed, and telling potential customers this was exactly the sort of man they should hire. The Dempsey name became well established, and the Dempseys soon found themselves building boilers and smokestacks from Shinglehouse to Swain.

But new technology can have drastic and unexpected consequences. In 1900, the Bessemer Engine Company introduced a large, single-cylinder internal combustion engine fueled by natural gas, which was soon known by its popular nickname, the "one-lunger." The engines were designed so they could easily be installed on the same bed as the steam engines they replaced. Bolivar businessman Alexander C. McDonell brought these engines to town, and Erie Wilson, always on the forefront of modern technology, became the first lease operator to equip his property with one. Wellsville's McEwan Brothers came out with a model of their own in 1901, as did Clark & Norton, soon to be Clark Brothers, in 1902.

One of the more important things about one-lungers was that they could be set up in a central location, and one of these engines could be used to simultaneously pump six, perhaps a dozen, wells. They were a game changer, drastically reducing the cost of operating a lease, thus prolonging the producing life of the wells they were used to pump. Suddenly, powerhouses containing the engine and a large belt-driven wheel, connected by wooden or steel "rod lines" to the wells surrounding the power, sprang up everywhere on the hillsides around Bolivar. The air was filled with a new sound, the "ka-thug, ka-thug-thug" of the powerhouses, a sound that would resound around the hillsides for the next sixty years. Two years later, natural gas-powered engines became available for use in drilling rigs, and that spelled the death knell of steam in the oil field.

The effect of this change was clear enough on the Dempseys. Between 1900 and 1910, one by one, the Dempsey brothers headed west; all but Daniel S. He adjusted to the changing times, and kept his reputation as the go-to man if you were dealing with steam, while the company expanded into the pipe business, something that was always in demand in an oil field. Steel pipe would not be replaced as an oil field staple until the 1980s, when spools of plastic finally pushed it aside. In 1910, Daniel Dempsey was chosen as Bolivar's fire chief. In 1914, he was endorsed by the *Bolivar Breeze* to be the postmaster, but the post went instead to another of the town's stalwarts, Bernard Dunn.

Daniel S. Dempsey

Daniel Dempsey died in his home on Liberty Street in July 1932. But the business he started lived on into the twenty-first century, owned and operated by his great-great grandsons. Dempsey Pipe held itself out as a leading supplier of steel well casing for water and geothermal well drillers throughout the northeast; and it was the only business born in the boom times of the 1880s which was still owned and operated out of Bolivar, New York in the twenty-first century. Dempsey Pipe outlasted them all.

The oil boom brought others to Bolivar who weren't part of the oil business. One of the best examples was Bernard S. Dunn. Bernard was born to Irish immigrant parents in 1860. He completed his schooling in Owego, then headed west to see what all the excitement was about. He found a job with the railroad, and arrived in Richburg in 1881. The following year, he became the station agent for the Central New York & Western Railroad in Bolivar. He would keep that job after the railroad was converted to standard gauge and became the Pittsburgh, Shawmut & Northern.

Bernard was an accomplished telegrapher, and quickly gained a high reputation for the lengths he would go to accommodate a customer's needs. As a consequence, on a number of occasions he was offered promotions, but he always declined because accepting meant he would have to move away from Bolivar, and he was very happy where he was. In 1896, he married his wife Regina, and by the end of 1900 they had a daughter and two sons to house. Two more daughters would follow the first three.

Bernard S. Dunn

Bernard was enmeshed in the Bolivar community. He was a charter member of the Citizens Hose Company, and of the Holy Name Society of St. Mary's Catholic Church. As early as 1888, he had become active in Republican politics, had been Bolivar's delegate to the Republican County Committee, and served as a village trustee and treasurer. In 1910, President Taft appointed him Bolivar's postmaster, a post he held for four years. Like Joshua Dunning, both of Bernard's sons, Louis and Gus, and two of his grandsons, would make meaningful contributions to the Bolivar Community during the twentieth century. He stayed with the railroad until he retired in 1929, at which time he had worked for the railroad longer than anyone else. He died in his home on South Street five years later, in 1934. Bridget died in 1950.

Another enterprising young man attracted to the oil fields was Joshua Dunning. Dunning started life in the 1840s on a farm in West Almond. At the age of nineteen, in 1862, he went west into the forests of Wisconsin, working one end of a cross-cut saw. In 1864, he returned home, and collected a $900 bonus for enlisting in the 188th New York Infantry. The regiment went with the Army of the Potomac to capture Richmond, and was engaged at Hatcher's Run twice, along the Weldon Railroad, the assault at Petersburg, and in the Appomattox Campaign. Joshua's regiment formed the guard around the McLane house when General Lee arrived to surrender to U.S. Grant.

Joshua Dunning

Joshua came back to New York state, but had no intention of going back to the family farm. He spent three years rafting on the Allegany River, carrying goods to Pittsburg, then tried a farm of his own. In 1880, he began working as a teamster for Standard Oil around Bradford, and arrived in Bolivar in 1882. About 1890, he started a produce business, shipping potatoes to Pittsburg and hay to New York City. Along the way he saved up enough money to drill oil wells of his own, and in the late 1890s controlled more than 130 acres of oil property. His energy was quickly recognized, and his comrades chose him to lead the local branch of the Grand Army of the Republic, the fraternal organization for Civil War veterans.

Dunning first became interested in politics in 1895, when he ran for assessor. He was appointed to the town board of health, and by 1899 was active on the school board, of which he became president soon after. It was Joshua Dunning who led the drive to build the town's first high school, in 1904. He remained active in village affairs until his death in 1924. His many years of active civic engagement would be carried on by two of his sons and a grandson.

The main difference between Justin Bradley, Daniel Dempsey and Joshua Dunning was that J.B., as he was usually called, was no longer young. When he arrived in the town of Bolivar in 1881, he was fifty-five. Born on a farm located about thirty miles south of Erie, Pennsylvania, he was the son of a Connecticut Yankee who had pushed his sons to march their cattle all the way across Pennsylvania to realize a higher sale price in Philadelphia.

When he came of age, J.B. decided to make his living as a huckster, driving a wagonload of goods around the backroads of western Pennsylvania, selling household wares to farm families who were far away from the nearest store. Then, in 1859, less than forty miles away, Colonel Edwin Drake drilled the first commercial oil well in the United States, and J.B. thought there might be a better way to become a financial success. He enlisted his kid brother Edwin, "E.C.", to come along, and together they drilled their first well in 1860 in Ohio, using their stirrups hung over a sapling tree and their own body weight to pound the rock. Not very far down they encountered an oil-bearing formation, but the oil was too thick to flow. They looked at the map, saw a place called "Petrolia" in western Ontario, and headed north.

Justin Booth Bradley

In January 1862, using the same method, at a depth of sixty-two feet, they opened a well which flowed 1,500 barrels a day. It was in Ontario, Canada, in January. There were no barrels to put the oil in, no lumber to make barrels, no pipelines, no railroad tank cars to haul it away. The ground was frozen hard, so they couldn't even dig pits to collect the oil. They got nothing from the gusher. But, they rounded up the backing to build a small refinery. It burned to the ground a few months later.

The brothers returned to western Pennsylvania and struggled to get a foothold in the rapidly developing oil field there. J.B. gave up, sold out, and put up a grain elevator in Salina, Kansas. But, in October 1871, the great Chicago fire turned much of the city to ashes, and J.B. saw an opportunity. He sold the elevator and put his money into rebuilding Chicago. By the end of 1872, he had made a small paper fortune. Then the financial Panic of 1873 struck, all his loans were called in, and he was bankrupt.

He returned to western Pennsylvania, and made a meager living dealing in oil leases. But when he and his seventeen-year old son, George Hiram, arrived in Bolivar, in 1881, he brought with him all the experience he had gained over the last twenty years, 2,000 feet of two inch pipe, and an idea. When a driller hit a well that made primarily gas, J.B. would offer to buy it for very little, since there was no market for the gas, then use his string of pipe to supply that gas as fuel for the drilling rig working on the next location. In a fairly short period of time, (less than a year), he had acquired enough gas wells to realize his dream of setting up a natural gas utility company that would bring central heat and light to Wellsville, Allentown, Bolivar, Richburg and Cuba. The Empire Gas & Fuel Company, which he and E.C. formed, did just that: transformed those communities with the modern conveniences of light and heat, which are so much taken for granted today. In the process, Empire Gas & Fuel became one of the major employers in the area, hiring men to maintain the supply system, install new service hookups, keep the wells producing, and, a little later, women to work in the offices collecting the monthly revenues and accounting for the same, (which in the beginning was simply a flat rate for each stove and light), and to handle customer complaints.

J.B.'s son, George H. Bradley, built both of his homes at the corner of Boss and First Streets, the first in 1884, which he moved a short way down First Street so he could build the second, which still stands, in 1907, while J.B. and his wife Naomi lived over the gas company office on Boss Street. J.B. and Naomi were active in the prohibition movement during the 1890s. Naomi died in Bolivar in 1900. J.B. died in Chicago, where he gone for medical treatment, in 1904. The company he and his brother started served the area until 1962, when it was sold to the Iroquois Gas Company of Buffalo. George Hiram spent his entire life in Bolivar, helping run the gas company and investing in the field, forming his own July Oil Company. He and his wife, Sarah Care, raised a family of five. She passed away in 1930. George H. left the scene in February 1938.

Another father and son duo who would be important to Bolivar's development and prosperity were the Moores. Martin B. Moore was born in Manchester, New York, less than ten miles north of Canandaigua, in 1855. He heard about the Richburg excitement, and arrived in the valley in 1881 when the boom was in full swing. He met a local girl, Sarah Gavin, and they married in Richburg in 1882. In 1883, she delivered a baby boy, which they named Raymond B. Martin became actively engaged in the oil business, and collected over the years seven hundred acres of producing oil property, on which were drilled more than 400 producing wells. He did not limit his operations to the Allegany Field, and managed to acquire 225 acres and ninety wells more in McKean County.

Raymond B. Moore

Martin Moore was generous. Known to be wealthy in his later years, "he did not hoard his money, but gave liberally of it to charity… He was a good citizen, always ready and willing to do anything for the betterment of Bolivar." His son, Raymond, grew up and lived his life in Bolivar, and was known through his business career as R.B. R.B. Moore followed the example set by his father. He built his own collection of oil properties, which he operated under two business names, Moore Producing, and New York Oil. He also started the R.B. Moore Oil Well Supply Company, with a large and busy store on Railroad Avenue in Bolivar.

Martin Moore sold his oil properties in 1927 to Penn Petroleum, and he died in 1929. R.B. conducted secondary recovery efforts on his properties, and in the 1930s enjoyed life, touring Europe, taking an around-the-world cruise for nearly a year, and developing the home and property on South Main which would become Schaffner's Funeral Home, the Parochial School, and Moore Memorial Park. He followed his father's example as a doer of good deeds, and he and his wife did many generous acts for Bolivar. R.B died, on February 15, 1945. His wife, Helen, built and gave the swimming pool to the village in memory of R.B.

One of the youngest men to venture off to Bolivar during the boom was a seventeen-year-old farm boy from Lamartine, Pennsylvania, named Albert L. Shaner. He was born in 1865, the eldest of ten children, on a farm near Lamartine, Pennsylvania, about twenty miles south of Oil City. As a boy barely seventeen, A.L. arrived in Bolivar at the height of the boom, and found his first work cutting cord wood to feed the fireplaces and campfires heating the dwellings filling the valley. Not long after, he found another job, working as a teamster moving drilling rigs from one location to the next. In four years, he managed to save up $507, which he loaned to a drilling contractor. The contractor never paid him back.

He found another job, hired as a pumper on the Garthwait Farm. The Garthwait Farm was 157 acres on a hillside just a half-mile or so east of the village of Bolivar. On it were twenty-eight wells, which had been drilled into some of the best sections of the Richburg oil sands. Wells drilled there in the early 1880s had started off producing hundreds of barrels a day each. By the 1890s, the average daily production of the entire Garthwait Farm was about 460 barrels a month, or just a little more than half a barrel per day per well; enough to pay A.L.'s wages and operating expenses, but leaving very little left over for the owner.

Albert L. Shaner

In January 1894, the owner struck a deal with A.L., and sold him the Garthwait Farm. Using his own thrifty business sense, Albert was able to drill additional wells, the production from which more than offset the declining amount of oil produced by the wells which came with the farm. That allowed him to pay off his debt on the property and to invest in additional holdings. Today, we know the Garthwait Farm as Shaner Hill. His organizational skill would lead to his successful involvement in many business ventures which would be important to Bolivar as the twentieth century progressed.

Walter T. Bliss was a native to the area, born in November 1860 in Little Genesee into a family that had come to the area in 1830. Walter was studious, and enrolled at Alfred University in 1880. He had an uncle, Edwin Bliss, who was one of the promoters of the Richburg discovery well. Uncle Ed owned a store in Richburg which became so busy during the early boom years that Walter dropped out of college to help man the store during the hectic summer and fall of 1881, but he returned to his classes in 1882, and graduated from Alfred in 1886. From there, he spent a year at the University of Michigan Law School, then came back and clerked in the law offices of Kruse & Kruse in Olean, while still helping out at his uncle's store when he had spare time.

Walter T. Bliss

In 1887, Edwin Bliss decided to sell the store. While helping conduct the inventory prior to the sale, Walter met Minnie Mitchell, the daughter of the buyer. Four years later he married her, and set up a law practice in Alfred. After one year, he moved his practice to Bolivar, and began a long and successful career centered on the oil business. He had a tremendous memory, and his experience in the store had given him a detailed knowledge of chains of ownership of hundreds of properties during a time when attention to detail and the recording of papers had not always been closely adhered to. This knowledge base would prove invaluable twenty years later when leasing activity blossomed again. In the meantime, Walter and Minnie would establish themselves as integral members of the Bolivar community, and would start raising a collection of sons who would do the same in their time. A touch of Walter's sense of humor can be found in an advertisement he ran in the Bolivar Breeze: "Do your swearing before W.T. Bliss, notary public."

Alfred and Archie MacDonell were Canadians. Alfred C. was the older of the two, born in 1850. He found his way to Titusville, Pennsylvania in 1868, and there learned the machinist's trade. He set up his own shop at Parker's Landing, Pennsylvania in 1876, about twelve miles south of A.L. Shaner's birthplace, and stayed there until 1882, when he made some big changes. First, he married a widow named Ellen Brannen, and brought her and her young son, William J. Brannen, to Bolivar, where he took charge of the Boviard & Seyfang machine shop.

A few years later he established his own machine shop at the west end of Liberty Street, and brought in his stepson as a partner, establishing the firm of McDonell & Brannen. As the firm prospered, he began investing in oil properties and timberland. After the machine shop burned, in 1919 the firm purchased the LeRoy Jordan machine shop on Main Street and changed its name to the Bolivar Supply Company, although in later years a big "McDonell & Brannen" sign went up, on the building that would become Hall's Department Store. He was elected a director of the Union Pipeline Company, and had enough gas wells that he laid his own line into town to supply his shop and a number of private homes.

Arriving not long after A.C came his kid brother, Archie. He began his career as an oil field worker, and a few years later he established a grocery business at the corner of Main and Friendship Streets. He earned a great reputation as a very popular shopkeeper, thanks in part to his hiring of the equally likable Abner Marchesi as his chief clerk. In 1908, in order to devote more time to the oil business, he sold the store to Ira Dillie. (The store building is still there, known for much of the twentieth century as Neill's five and dime). However, Archie MacDonell died in 1912, at the age of fifty-six. His son, Leon, took over the operation of the oil properties, and went on to have a long career in local politics.

A.C. continued with his business operations and investments, eventually joining the Motor Age by becoming a dealer of Paige motorcars. He died August 15, 1920. Ironically, his wife, Ellen, died of injuries she suffered when she was run over by a Ford commercial automobile while crossing Main Street near the corner of Boss and Main streets on December 8, 1920. She died in her home the following morning, and is, as far as the author can discover, the only traffic fatality who lost her life in the village of Bolivar.

In doing the research for this history, I planned to do a section on people who have called Bolivar home who have made it on to the national stage, and brief biographies of such people are found where appropriate. But what struck me as unusual is that of the fewer than ten people who have made it to the big time, three of them grew up in Bolivar during the post-boom years, two of them as close boyhood friends.

One man was undoubtedly essential in helping two of them develop the necessary skills and confidence to successfully venture out into the world. His name was Alexander J. Glennie. Glennie was a Scot, born in Scotland in 1866, brought to America by his parents in 1871, who settled that year in Geneseo. Starting his education in the primary department of the teacher's college, he continued there, enrolled in the college, chose teaching as his profession, and graduated as president of his class in 1889. His first job was as principal of Arkport's school. A year later, he took the job of principal of the Union school in Alexander. He left at the end of his first year there, and came to head Bolivar's school in 1891. He arrived with a mission: to turn Bolivar's into an enviable institution. He spent two years assembling his faculty of five, and in 1893 raised the school's classification to a regents degree-giving

SKETCH OF PROF. A. J. GLENNIE.

high school. He could keep discipline "without friction." His objectives were clear: He wanted to give his students "the power to think for themselves, act for themselves, and control themselves." His efforts clearly paid off starting that year, when Bolivar put forth its very first high school graduating class, a class that included two young men who would make it on to the national stage in two very different fields of endeavor: baseball, and publishing.

A photo from the grandstand of an 1890's ball game

Patsy Dougherty

Anthony Dougherty was born in Ballintoy, on the north coast of Ireland not far from the Giant's Causeway, in 1830. He came to America in 1860 and found work as a section hand for the Erie Railroad. His work brought him to Andover and Wellsville, where he met and married his wife, Ellen Kane, also an Irish immigrant, in 1871. In 1882, they moved to Bolivar, where he worked as a section boss on the railroads leading into town, bringing with them two sons and one on the way. The eldest, born in 1876, was named Patrick Henry, Patsy for short.

The Dougherty's placed great emphasis on the education of their children, and Patsy Dougherty was one of the members of Bolivar's Class of 1893, at the time an unusual achievement for a boy. (A majority of high school graduates then were women wanting to attend college in order to teach). At graduation that year, each graduate was expected to give a short speech demonstrating his or her degree of learning, and Patsy spoke on "American Aristocracy," his point being that he believed Americans were always "quick to appreciate and always to honor one's true worth, the only thing that makes a genuine aristocracy."

While he was growing up, there was a town baseball team, and there Patsy first picked up a bat and glove. Playing alongside him at catcher was Frank Gannett. Playing ball, usually at first base or in the outfield when not pitching, was where Patsy felt most at home, and as he grew into a generously sized, powerful man the level of his play steadily improved. When mature, he stood six feet two inches and weighed 190 pounds. After his high school graduation, he stayed in Bolivar, filling in for Bernard Dunn at the railroad station when needed. When the weather warmed, he worked on drilling rigs and led the town baseball team on weekends.

The town team, called the Ponies, was organized in 1895 with Sandy Wertman as its manager, and its first outing was on its new home field against the Pikeville Pirates. Dougherty took the mound and fired off a no-hitter. "His superb pitching was backed up by fine support and the Pikeville's were never in the hunt." The Pikeville team managed a run in the fifth inning of what was a seven inning game. Bolivar began its scoring in the second, when Dougherty, batting sixth, came to the plate. He led the team with three hits in five at bats, scoring three of the team's eighteen runs.

J.P. Herrick, who played center field, wrote, "Dougherty fields his position finely, and 'cool as a cucumber' fits his case exactly. You might as well try to rattle the Sphinx as to unnerve Sir Patrick." A few days later he pitched again, striking out seventeen and scoring two runs himself, as Bolivar beat Portville 11 to 5. A week later, the team played Portville again. Patsy allowed five hits, while getting four hits, two doubles and two singles, and scoring twice when at bat, leading Bolivar to a 9-1 victory.

In the next game, Patsy faced a much tougher team from Olean, who arrived in town taking rooms at the Clark House, registering under assumed names, using those of then prominent professionals. "One curly-haired youth registered as McGraw, although on the diamond he moved about like an ice wagon drawn uphill by two lame mules." The Oleanders outhit Bolivar seventeen to thirteen, but thanks to Olean's shortstop, who registered five errors, Bolivar again carried the day, winning 15-11, scoring seven of those runs in the last two innings. Patsy struck out twelve, including striking out the side in the seventh inning.

The following week the Ponies went to Friendship, accompanied by fifty Bolivar fans. Dougherty went hitless in four at bats, but held Friendship to seven hits, and, scoring one run in the top of the ninth, Bolivar went away winning again, 5-4. Friendship came to Bolivar the next week, and at the end of three innings Bolivar led 7-0. Then the wheels fell off. In the fourth, Friendship scored twelve unearned runs. Bolivar committed a total of twelve errors, (eleven Friendship players reached first on errors), and Bolivar went on to lose their first game of the season, 11-21. In the next game, against Portville, Patsy struck out fourteen, had two hits and scored two runs, leading to an 18-9 victory. In a return match at Friendship, Dougherty was unable to play, and the Ponies went down 14-2.

The final game of the season saw the Friendship nine return to Bolivar, providing "the most exciting game ever seen on home grounds." It took Patsy two innings to warm up, with the score at that point 7-7, but after that he allowed only two runs, while the Ponies scored three in the fourth and five in the fifth, winning the game 17-9 on a perfect October afternoon, with a hot prospect from Shingelhouse named Fielder Jones playing shortstop, hitting a triple, a double, and scoring five of Bolivar's runs.

The 1896 season started with wild swings, the Ponies losing at Angelica 18-3, but defeating Portville 31-6. Angelica came to Bolivar for the third game of the season, and both team settled down, Bolivar taking the contest 4-1, Patsy striking out eight batters, J.P. Herrick stealing two bases, with 400 spectators taking in the game. Patsy trained in part by riding his bicycle far and wide. Herrick reported that by mid-July, Dougherty had ridden more than 1,000 miles. On one occasion early in the season, while riding in the company of Claire Jordan, Jordan's sprocket wheel and chain broke as they were going through Main Settlement. Patsy found a piece of rope, and managed to tie Jordan's bike to his own to form a sort of tandem, but only Dougherty could peddle. He proceeded to tow Jordan and his bike all the way back to Bolivar.

In a twelve-inning "comedy of errors" where three of Bolivar's starting nine, including Dougherty, were unavailable, Bolivar lost to Belmont 13-12, then traveled to Angelica, where Manager Wertman pulled the team off the field in the seventh inning, then leading the game 9-7, when a completely incompetent umpire made one more blatantly bad call than Wertman could stomach. Olean came to town for the next game, and went down to the Ponies 8-6, with Dougherty striking out ten. Allegany provided the next competition, and Bolivar pulled out another win, 13-12, Dougherty as always on the mound.

In August, Bolivar pounded Cuba 23-3, edged past Belmont 9-8, flew past Wellsville 30-11, even though Dougherty left the game after the third inning, and beat Olean again on the Bolivar home field 11-8, for the championship of Allegany and Cattaraugus Counties. 1,000 people watched from the stands and grounds who had come both for the game and for a series of bicycle races that preceded it, the largest crowd yet to attend an athletic contest in Bolivar. What they saw was the end Patsy Dougherty's amateur career.

In March 1897, Patsy signed with the Springfield, Massachusetts Ponies in the Eastern League, which had won the league title in 1895. He resigned his position with the Oil Well Supply Company in Bolivar and left for Springfield in early April. In the lineup with him was Dan Brouthers, who batted .415 in the 1897 season, and would go on to win a spot in the Cooperstown Hall of Fame. In Patsy's first season, the Ponies finished fourth of eight teams and did not qualify for the playoff. Dougherty was sent to a team in Bristol, Connecticut, a team that was being run as a cooperative by the players. Soon after, he went with a team in Brooklyn, where he finished the professional season. On his return, he took to the mound for Bolivar one more time, and shut out arch rival Friendship while scoring three runs himself in a 20-0 rout.

In the spring of 1898, Patsy left to play for the Dayton Old Soldiers, and was sent by them to the Mansfield Haymakers. That didn't work, so in June he joined the Olean team in the Iron and Oil League. It was reported later in the month that he struck out twelve of the Meadville side, nine in the Dunkirk lineup, and owned a one-half interest in Olean. He won seven of the first eight games he pitched for Olean. He still found time to play for Bolivar when the schedule allowed, and in July he scattered four hits to Angelica, with only one opponent reaching third base. In the eighth inning, with two men on base, Patsy drove a line drive right over the head of Angelica's center fielder, hitting a home run that was one of the "longest hits ever recorded on home ground." Bolivar won, 5-0.

For the 1898 season, Dougherty led the New York State league with a .400 batting average, and in 1899 he returned to Bridgeport. In the spring of 1900, he again signed to pitch for Bridgeport, which was part of the Connecticut State League. In 1901, during the regular season he stayed with Bridgeport, but in the fall he went west and played for a team in Los Angeles, and that got him noticed. Now twenty-five years old, he received offers from several major league teams. It was assumed that he took advice from his old companion Fielder Jones, who was now with the Chicago White Sox, and decided to sign with the Boston Americans, which in a few years would be better known as the Red Sox. In fact, Boston's manager had been with the LA team, and liked what he saw.

During that first season in the majors, Dougherty was plagued with a series of minor injuries that kept him out of thirty games. But when he was in he played well. He led the team with a batting average of .342, which was fourth in the American League that year. He also led the team in on-base percentage, posting a .407, which was second in the league. His performance kept Boston in the pennant race, despite the team's loss due to injury of three of their better players for much of the season.

Then came 1903. The Boston management expected much from Patsy, based on his stellar rookie season- and Patsy expected the same of himself. He delivered. Placed in left field, he connected for 195 hits, and accounted for a league-leading 107 runs scored. He led the team with a .331 bating average, and 35 stolen bases, both of which placed him third in American League standings. On June 1, the Americans had a record of 20 wins and 15 losses, moving into the league's top spot. After a short slump, they regained the lead on June 23, and stayed there for the rest of the season, ending with a 91-47 record. The top offensive player was thought to be Buck Freeman, who hit 13 home runs and 104 RBIs. The team's top pitcher was Cy Young, who had 35 starts, 34 complete games, and 28 victories.

On June 21, Freeman hit for the cycle, the first Boston player to ever do so. Not to be outdone, Dougherty matched the feat on July 29, in a losing 14-15 effort against New York, which was Boston's highest scoring game of the year. At season's end they were 16 games ahead of the second place Philadelphia Athletics. They had a winning record against every other team in the league, their closest competition coming from the Detroit Tigers, who they beat ten times and lost to nine. They beat the A's 13 times, losing only six.

At long last, the managers of the American and National Leagues had decided to have a season ending championship playoff. Boston took the American League Pennant and headed to the very first World Series ever played. It was set to be a best of nine game event, with the first three games to be played in Boston, the next four in Pittsburgh, the last two, if needed, back in Boston. Boston was led by Cy Young, and Pittsburgh by Honus Wagner.

The 1903 World Series was played by the Boston Americans, seated, and the Pittsburgh Pirates, seen standing behind them. Seated fifth from the right with his auburn hair bulging out of his cap is Patsy Dougherty. Two to the left of Pat sits Cy Young. Standing on the far right is Honus Wagner.

The Americans lost the first game 7-3. Dougherty had hit only four home runs all season, but he came to life in game 2, knocking a ball out of the park in the first inning, (the first home run ever hit in a World Series), and doing it again in the sixth, accounting for all of Boston's runs as they took the game 3-0. 18,801 fans came through the gates and another 10,000 were turned away in anticipation of game three. In the eighth inning, with the Pirates ahead 3-1, Patsy caught a high fly ball, then made a stellar throw to third, allowing the tag that retired the Pirates. But his bat was cold, and he struck out for a second time. Each side scored one more run, and the game ended with the Pirates again on top, 4-2, leaving Boston trailing the series two games to one. The Pirates kept it up in game 4 in their home park, winning 5-4, leading the series 3-1

Then Patsy again came to life. In game five, he singled once and tripled twice, batted in three runs, and inspired the team to their second win, 11-2. Game six was all about Boston's pitcher, Cy Young. The largest crowd to ever come to a Pittsburgh home game, 17,015, watched "Uncle Cyrus, that grand old man of the game" (he was 37) who was never in better form, according to the reporter for the Pittsburgh Gazette, lead Boston to a 6-3 victory, evening the series three games to three.

Boston won three in a row, taking game seven 7-3, after which they headed back to Beantown. In the second inning of game 8, Patsy pulled down a long ball hit by Wagner, but he never got to first base himself. With Boston leading 3-0 going into the ninth, Patsy made a sideways catch of a fly ball for the first out. Honus Wagner struck out to end the game and the series, which Boston took five games to three.

After the season ended, the Boston Globe publisher took over ownership of the club, and turned it over to his "business failure of a son" John I. Taylor. John I., who knew little or nothing about baseball, soon was at odds with Patsy about how much the team's best hitter should get paid. The matter was settled going into the 1904 season, but neither man much liked the other. On May 2, 1904, Dougherty led off the fourth inning with an infield single, Boston's first hit of the game played against Philadelphia. He was the last Boston base runner that day, as the A's pitcher threw a one-hitter and walked away with a 3-0 win. But at the end of the contest, the A's pitcher, Rube Waddell, taunted Cy Young, daring him to pitch against him when the A's came to Boston.

That day arrived on May 5, and Old Cyrus accepted the challenge. In the seventh inning, Patsy ran head long into the left field fence in order to catch a foul fly ball for an out, his main contribution to "Cy Young's perfect game," the first perfect game of the modern baseball era, which Boston took 3-0. But Patsy's tenure in Boston was nearing its end. On June 17, he was sent to the New York Highlanders, formed just the year before, perhaps at the instigation of league president Ban Johnson, who wanted New York to develop a strong team that would attract more fans. While the Boston newspapers panned the trade, (in return, Boston got a utility player hospitalized with alcohol poisoning), the Boston *Herald* ran a headline, "Dougherty as a Yankee," which was the first time the New York team was called by that nickname in print, a name that would be commonly adopted by the press by 1913, although the Highlanders have never formally changed their name to Yankees.

Patsy made his presence known eight days later when the New Yorkers ventured to Boston. Patsy had three hits off Cy Young, and New York won 5-3. Two days later Dougherty again had three hits, New York winning 8-4. And on July 11, he had four hits helping New York win its third in a row against Boston, 10-1. At season's end, Boston and New York were neck and neck. On October 7, with New York trailing by half a game, Patsy doubled in the fifth inning, bunted for a single in the seventh, and scored both times allowing New York to carry the day 3-2. But the teams then travelled to Boston, where the Americans swept a double header and took the pennant. For the season, Patsy led the league again with 113 runs scored, on 181 hits and 21 stolen bases.

In 1905 he and the rest of the Highlanders went into a deep slump. Patsy hit only .263 and scored just 56 runs. Never a strong fielder, he tallied an .898 fielding percentage, at the bottom of the league. Things did not improve in 1906. He had contract issues with management, which heated things up to the point he got into a fist fight with team manager Clark Griffith. Hitting just .192 at that point in the season, he skipped town after just twelve appearances, and joined an outlaw team in Lancaster, PA, which led to league president Johnson suspending him.

Word spread fast, and one who perked up his ears was Fielder Jones, who had played with Dougherty back on Bolivar's diamond. Jones had also turned pro, and was in 1906 the player/manager of the Chicago White Sox, who were then known derisively as the "Hitless Wonders." On July 6, he bought Patsy's contract from New York, smoothed things over with the league, and sent Dougherty a ticket to the Windy City. His team started to gel.

That year, Patsy would bat only .233, the lowest of his career, but that number put him in the top half of all the White Sox players. His fielding shot up to .987. He committed only two errors all season, nineteen better than the year before. In early August, the White Sox stood fourth in the league. But Dougherty and teammate Ed Hahn's bats got hot, as did pitcher Ed Walsh, and the White Sox set off on a nineteen game winning streak, a major league record that would stand until 2002, when the "Moneyball" Oakland A's had a string of twenty-one. The streak shot them from fourth to first in the league, and they took away the pennant from New York.

The 1906 series was the first "subway series" between the White Sox and the Cubs, (who were then known as the "First Nationals"), and was a best of seven game event, just as it is now. The Cubs, who had won 116 games, were heavily favored. Patsy had only two hits in twenty at bats. In the third game, leading off in the seventh inning, he reached first on a error, got to second on a sacrifice fly, and to third on a long ball to right field. But he was left stranded there when the next batter struck out. The Sox, who had scored three runs in the sixth, won the game 3-0. In game four he had one of the only two hits the Sox were able to get off of Three Finger Brown, and the series stood tied two games to two. Then the Sox got hot, won game five 8-6, and game six 8-3. Patsy Dougherty then became the first player in major league history to win a world series with two different teams.

In 1907, he proved his worth in Chicago, leading the team in batting at .270, in slugging with a .315, and with 33 stolen bases, which kept the Sox in contention, but never able to catch up with Detroit. His numbers improved in 1908, batting .278, slugging .326, being on base with a .367 average, and leading the league with 47 stolen bases. The White Sox battled for the pennant right into the final weekend, ending up a game and a half behind Detroit. On September 24, Dougherty scored the only hit against New York's Joe Lake, the second of four times he would ruin a pitcher's attempt to get a no-hitter by getting the only hit for his team.

In 1909, he was the offense for the White Sox, leading the team again with a .270 batting average, (the second highest for the Hitless Wonders was a .240), and also leading in slugging with a .391, runs scored with 71, 55 RBIs, 23 doubles, 14 triples 140 hits, 36 steals, 51 walks, and home runs- with just one! One noted event of that season took place on August 28 in a game against Washington. The Senators' pitcher was Dolly Gray. Patsy came to the plate in the second inning and bounced a ball over the first baseman in what would be Chicago's only hit of the game. But Gray proceeded to walk the next eight batters, still a major league record for walks in a single inning, putting six runs on the scoreboard for the Sox, who ended up winning 6-4.

The poor performance of the team for the season led to a total remake of the White Sox lineup for 1910, with the result that, at 33, Patsy was the oldest man in the lineup. He still led the team, but with a .248 batting average, 43 RBIs, and 110 hits. He missed twenty-games to what were called "malarial attacks," and the Sox finished sixth in the league standings. He came back in 1911, but saw action in only 76 games. That year cork-centered baseballs were introduced and his batting average rose back up to .289, but Patsy was worn out. At season's end he retired, and brought his wife, Florence, and growing family back to Bolivar.

He invested and worked in the oil business, but the hardest time ever to make a living in the oil business in New York State was during the 1910s. In 1917, he became the assistant cashier of the Bolivar State Bank, and kept that position until he retired at the end of 1939. During most of the 1920s, he served on the school board. He enjoyed the great outdoors, "and was never happier than when hunting, fishing, or playing golf." Baseball remained his favorite pastime. He was last seen on a diamond in 1938 when he played several innings in an old timers game in Bolivar. He was sixty-one. His heart was wearing out. He never left his house on South Main after December 21, 1939. In the early hours of April 30, 1940, Patrick Henry Dougherty suffered a fatal heart attack. He was survived by his wife Florence, three sons, and two daughters, Helen and Mary, both of whom were members of the BCS faculty. He lies in St. Mary's Cemetery. In 1942, Cy Young was asked to make up his personal all-time All Star Team. Cy put Patsy back in left field.

Patsy Dougherty, 1910

Main Street as it looked in 1911, when Patsy Dougherty returned home to stay.

Frank Ernest Gannett

by Tom Manning

Frank Gannett was a newspaper publisher who founded the media corporation "The Gannett Company." Young Frank and his three siblings first lived in South Bristol, N.Y., (near Rochester), with parents who struggled at farming and later as hotel operators. His interest in newspapers began as a delivery boy for Rochester's *Democrat & Chronicle. W*ith his profits he bought his own clothes — with spending money left over.

The Gannetts moved to Bolivar in 1889 for another try at the hotel business, leasing the Clark House that stood near the corner of Main and Olean streets. Frank began high school and soon became a community stand-out. John Herrick, founder of the *Bolivar Breeze* weekly newspaper, took note of him and later wrote these praises: "He was diligent, ambitious, personable and intelligent, and as a student he had an infinite capacity for study, passing the Regents examinations with the highest rating of any student in the state. He delivered papers, worked in a local hotel, played cornet in the band and was the local baseball team's catcher, playing with Fielder Jones and Patrick Dougherty" — future major leaguers.

To speed his delivery of 200 evening newspapers, Frank acquired Bolivar's first "safety bicycle," sporting wheels of equal size, hinting at his lifelong passion for efficiencies and timesavers. After graduating from the Bolivar Union School & Academy in 1893, he worked in town for the next year with the hope of funding a college education. At the Newton House, Bolivar's other hotel, he waited on tables, tended bar and did various chores. In his spare hours he mastered a correspondence course in bookkeeping that led to more part-time income. Urged on by his school principal, in the middle of 1894 Frank sat for a special exam and his scores earned him a state scholarship to Cornell University.

Turning down a U.S. Army education at West Point, that fall he entered Cornell where he carried a varied course load while working on the side to help fund his studies. As a reporter for the "Ithaca Journal" covering Cornell news, he also sold articles to other inquiring papers and magazines, hiring other student writers to help meet the demand. Upon graduation in 1898, Frank departed with $1,000 in his bank account. There followed a stint with a Syracuse newspaper, his return to Cornell to pursue a master's degree, and renewed demands for stories from his news-craving previous customers that derailed his post-grad plans.

In early 1899, Gannett signed on as the secretary of President McKinley's Philippines Commission, spending a year in that island nation. Returning stateside, he held editorial positions at publications in Ithaca and Pittsburgh through 1905. By 1906 — eight years out of Cornell — Frank Gannett was ready to plunge into media ownership. He bought into the *Elmira Gazette* and soon merged Elmira's *Star* with it to create the profitable *Elmira Star-Gazette*. Business in Elmira was fine, but in 1918 Frank and his partner were watching a three-paper fight for market share in Rochester. Moving to buy two of them, they raised $250,000 through bank loans and personal borrowings, acquired both and effected the merger that created the *Rochester Times-Union.*

While his partner pursued advertisers, Gannett pursued newsworthy content for their newspapers. By the early 1920s they were pumping profits, and in 1923 Frank's co-owner was ready to cash out. So Gannett acquired full ownership and moved the enterprise's assets into his new Gannett Company. Along the way in Rochester he had also acquired a wife, the ambitious Miss Caroline Werner. (Over time they parented a daughter and son; Caroline became a 17-year member of the state's Board of Regents, focusing on early childhood education.)

In 1922, the ultra-wealthy William Randolph Hearst's nationwide newspaper juggernaut came to Rochester. Hearst, a politically erratic print media despot whose views dominated within papers bearing giant page one headlines over lurid stories, tried to crack Gannett's near-monopoly in the city. Oppositely, Gannett was known for granting editorial autonomy as he focused on management. If he sent his printable political views to his editors they came with a note, "For your information and use, if desired", and editors were free to ignore them. He disliked sensationalism and his publications played down crime and scandal, even rejecting liquor ads. Hearst finally gave up on Rochester, and to the east in Albany, Gannett fought him to a draw, merging his morning paper into his evening *Knickerbocker Press*, while Hearst switched his evening one to mornings.

Over his 50 years in newspaper ownership, Frank Gannett acquired 30 papers (plus a string of TV and radio stations), merged ten of those, and sold off just three. He acquired more papers unaided by inherited wealth than any other publisher of his era.

Well established in the media world, Gannett turned to politics. He was an unsuccessful Republican candidate for New York governor in 1936. In 1940 he tossed his hat into the ring of presidential prospects but, along with others, lost out to Wendell Wilkie. Still, Gannett was rewarded with Republican Party leadership posts in the 1940s. More important were the Gannetts' roles in charitable causes and philanthropy. His name is on the campus libraries at Utica University plus Elmira and Ithaca colleges, the Cornell student health center and an academic building at the Rochester Institute of Technology. As a Unitarian Church member and denomination leader, Frank with Caroline generously supported charitable causes, including the United Negro College Fund whose Rochester unit he chaired.

Frank E. Gannett

The Gannett Corporation remains a major media empire to this day with a fleet of ninety daily newspapers led by *USA Today*. In 2015, to the benefit of stockholders, its collection of tv stations and digital platforms was placed in a separate company — TEGNA, Inc.

The last time we know Frank Gannett returned to Bolivar was when he accepted an invitation to serve as the commencement speaker in June 1936. The *Breeze* anticipated "one of the most colorful and happy events the town has known for many years." Since Frank planned on flying down in his private plane from Rochester, principal J.F. Whitford proposed a temporary landing strip be set up for him near the new refinery, but Frank opted to land at an established strip near Portville. He noted in his talk the contrast between his thirty-five minute flight that day, and the first time he arrived in Bolivar, in 1889, after a buggy ride from Wallace, in Steuben County, a sixty-mile trip that took nearly twenty-four hours. His address focused on national politics, in which he commended some aspects of the New Deal, such as the bank reforms, bank deposit insurance, and Social Security, but strongly disagreed with others, saying "I was forced to draw the line when the administration invaded the field of personal and economic liberty". Sounds familiar ninety years later.

Frank Gannett died in 1957, concluding eighty-one years that influenced and benefited life in America in multiple ways. He had greatly advanced his education and come of age in Bolivar. And growing into an adult among its people created lasting friendships and taught him life lessons that later served him well. If the National Honor Society for high school academics could encompass all graduates throughout Bolivar's history, that "fifth candle" reserved for one of high national achievement — the candle that has never been lit — should instead be glowing in honor of Frank Earnest Gannett, the "can-do" kid from Bolivar High.

W. D. Stevens

There was a third Bolivar boy who was educated and grew up in Bolivar in the post-boom years who also reached national prominence. William Dodge Stevens was the eldest of the three, born in Tidioute, Pennsylvania on September 13, 1870. His father, Captain Stevens, had caught the oil bug early and followed the trend north. In 1880, the family lived in Olean. The boom brought the Stevens family to Bolivar, including William's maternal grandmother, the Countess de la Dernia.

W.D. Stevens

In the mid-1880s, before Professor Glennie came to town, there was a schism in the school system. The principal at the time was "Professor Blackman," who was probably "Capt." George H. Blackman, a man born in Chenango County in 1841. He volunteered at the outbreak of the Civil War and started out as a corporal with Co. E, 93rd New York Infantry. He went through a couple of cycles of rising in rank, then being broken back. During the Battle of the Wilderness, on May 6, 1864, he was severely wounded and lost his right arm. Blackman followed his father into the legal profession, and in 1880 became the Allegany County Clerk, but did not stay there long. When the spot opened, he applied to become the principal in Bolivar, got the job, but in a short time found himself at odds with the school board. He quit, and then opened his own competing academy on Liberty Street. He offered to teach only boys and limited enrollment to twenty students. Among them were William J. Hogan jr., and William D. Stevens.

Stevens demonstrated at a very early age a great aptitude for art. The son of a Civil War veteran who celebrated by mounting his horse to lead Bolivar's Memorial Day parades, William would spend his spare hours doing pen and ink sketches of his teachers and classmates, sketches which impressed everyone who saw them. In 1889, he headed to the Art Institute of Chicago to better hone his skills. He stayed in Chicago all through the 1890s, and was joined there by his kid brother, Dalton, eight years his junior. When Dalton finished his training in 1902, the brothers headed off to see if they could make it in the Big Apple. They landed in Greenwich Village in New York City, living together in a flat on West 23rd Street. By February 1907, they had established themselves so well that a newspaper article appeared about the two of them and their working methods. Ten days later, their mother died, and their father recruited them to accompany him on a prolonged tour of Europe. They were gone eighteen months.

William used the time abroad to better develop his skills, and on his return made regular contributions to many large-circulation publications, including the *New York Tribune, McClure's Magazine,* and *The Saturday Evening Post*, as well as lesser ones like *Physical Culture* and *Liberty*. (Dalton's work was most often rather lurid covers for pot-boiling dime novels). W.D.'s reputation grew. He was mentioned as one of the prominent New Yorkers vacationing at Saratoga Springs in the summer of 1920. The New York Tribune offered a regular feature they called "illustrated songs." The Trib would publish the sheet music for a new song, accompanied by an attractive illustration, often a picture of a beautiful young woman, and frequently the illustration was provided by William Stevens. He published at least one cover for the Saturday Evening Post. He was married to his art, stayed in New York drawing and painting for the rest of his life, which ended in a New York hospital in 1942. (Dalton, having gone blind, committed suicide in 1940).

While the village of Richburg withered back to little more than it had been before the boom occurred, (375 souls remained there in 1890, and the population of the town of Wirt was slightly less than it had been before the boom occurred) the population of Bolivar in 1890 stood at 2,233, more than double the number living in town in 1880. There was a decline of nearly 200 during the 1890s, with only 2,035 calling Bolivar home in 1900, but the next ten years saw that loss more than made up, with 2,282 residents in Bolivar in 1910. Darius Newton, the first mayor of the village, died in 1890, leaving as his legacy the ban on the drilling wells within two hundred feet of any residence, which set Bolivar apart from Richburg. In June of that same year, a man named Sandy Wertman arrived and established a cigar factory in the Opera House block. It was the start of a fifty year business career in Bolivar, the last decades of which he spent operating a popular billiard parlor and news room in a building on the north side of the State Bank. Sandy was a sportsman, promoted the rod and gun club, which had a shooting range at the end of Pleasant Street, and many times managed the town baseball team

Railroad service continued from Bolivar to Olean throughout the 1890s, bringing in the loads of pipe, tankage, boilers and engines needed in the oil field, keeping the oil well supply businesses in operation. In 1892, William Sawyer built a small, (fifty barrels a day), refinery west of Allentown, not far from the present-day Baldwin sawmill, thinking he would sell his crude oil when prices were up, and refine it when prices were low. However, the rail line from Bolivar to Wellsville shut down in 1893, which shrank his marketing area to that which he could reach by horse and wagon. Other refiners cut the wholesale price of their kerosene to two cents a gallon, and the Sawyer refinery closed its doors in 1900.

In 1891, enterprising local talent brought to life the Bolivar Race Track Association, and built a half-mile track and a grandstand on the east end of the village. *(See the photo on page 117)*. The grandstand, rebuilt at least twice, still stands overlooking the school baseball diamond, which then was located just across the way on the infield of the race track.

As the newcomers who had come to town during the boom settled down and became permanent residents, the 1890s saw a profusion of social groups which drew people together. The Masons had been in town for decades, established here in the spring of 1852. In the mid-1890s their membership stood at 115. The cornerstone to the brick lodge building they still occupy was laid in 1891. Its sister organization, the Order of the Eastern Star, came into being at this time, in June 1895, with twenty-five charter members.

The International Order Odd Fellows' Bolivar lodge, formed in 1884, sported forty-three members, and was growing rapidly. In 1906, they built their own headquarters, the cast stone building which stands at the corner of Boss and Main. The Knights of the Maccabees, a fraternal organization which also acted as an insurance company, boasted more than 100 members. The town's first fraternal organization of veterans, the H.C. Gardiner Post 247 of the Grand army of the Republic, open to Union veterans of the Civil War, chartered in 1881, had forty members and its club building stood on Boss Street.

Old Home Week, 1910

Although originally limited to twenty-five members, by 1925, when this photo was taken, membership in the Bolivar Sorosis club had grown to more than fifty. They are shown here in front of the Bolivar Free Library, which the group was instrumental in creating.

Our Better Half

The women who had come to town during the 1880s and 1890s were essential in creating the close-knit community which they then called home. Virtually every fraternal organization eventually had an attached organization for the wives and daughters of its members. The Order of the Eastern Star, the auxiliary of the Masons, was perhaps the best known. The ladies whose men were Odd Fellows joined the Daughters of Rebekah. But by far and away the most influential group of women in Bolivar were those who, in 1895, organized the Bolivar Sorosis.

The Sorosis was originally exclusive, limited to twenty-five members. (Probably this was because of limited meeting space, not snobbery). Angela Cowles, then fifty-five, the wife of undertaker E.W. Cowles, was one of the most important founding members. The group devoted itself to the study of music, literature, and education. They began meeting in 1895, and quickly gained a great reputation for organizing "delightful socials," open to the public, which centered around musical performances and literary readings. The first such social we know of was held in January 1896, at the Cowles home on South Street. Their programs were seasonal, usually held during the academic school year, and in the early years the events were also fundraisers. These ladies wanted to establish a free lending library in Bolivar.

Progress was rapid. They raised $50 with their "dime socials," (about $1,900 in today's money), then sent out a fundraising letter looking for $150 more. That amount came in quickly, and New York State matched the $200 raised so far. On March 21, 1898, Bolivar's first free library opened, in a room at the back of the State Bank at the corner of Main and Boss. The ladies raised the funds to wallpaper and carpet the room, "improvised divans and sofa pillows," acquired 500 books and the needed bookcases, and hired Minnie Kilbury as Bolivar's first librarian. The new library was open Tuesday and Saturday evenings, illuminated by four incandescent lights, and on Friday afternoons. J.P. Herrick commented in the Breeze, *"The work has been a labor of love on the part of the members of the Sorosis and in creating the Bolivar Free Library they have builded better than they knew."*

The ladies of the Sorosis did not stop there. Soon after opening, they organized a bazaar at the Newton Hall, selling lemonade, candy, popcorn, fruit, and ice cream. They had a craft booth, and a "fish pond" where for a nickel you were guaranteed to catch something. There were "cake walk" competitions, first prize being a cake, (of course). Two local orchestras and the Hearons sisters provided music. Soon after, a fresh group of officers took over, Bertha Cook becoming president, with Kate Andrus, Leonora Furnald, Jenny Nichols and Ellen McDonell filling the other leadership positions.

In 1899, the Sorosis organized a colonial dinner as a way to celebrate Washington's birthday, the ladies serving dinner dressed as their great-grand mothers might have, the Hearons providing the entertainment, and they raised another thirty-seven dollars for the library fund. The 1899 bazaar featured an expanded menu, which included oyster stew and sandwiches.

The Sorosis met monthly during the school year. Each year, all meetings focused on a single theme. In 1898, that theme was France. In 1899, it was United States history. They decided in 1900 that the bazaar was more effort than it was worth, and instead divided the town into districts and had the members make door to door appeals for funds to buy more books. The ladies also inspired girls in the high school to organize their own literary society along similar lines, Donna Reynolds (Chipman), being one of the more important students who got it going.

In just two years since opening the first reading room, the Sorosis tripled the size of the book collection, to 1,452. The library's circulation, (number of books loaned) was 5,811, meaning every book had gone out on average four times- and, on average, every townsperson had taken out three books! Herrick commented in the Breeze that since the establishment of the library, the sale of cheap, ten cent "yellow backed" novels had ceased entirely in the village, which he considered a very positive development.

By 1903, just five years after opening, the library had outgrown its space in the bank building, and it moved into the Nickel Plate block at the corner of Main and Plum, expanding into two rooms, one for book storage, the other for reading,

and open every evening of the week, except Sundays, staffed mostly by Sorosis volunteers. Angela Cowles remained an officer through those years, along with Bertha Cook, Ellen McDonell, Minnie Bliss, Ida Coon, and Inez Cranston. The Sorosis kept hard at work, raising more funds, adding more books, and organizing cultural events. In 1904, there was a special "Eugene Field Entertainment," which featured the recitation of many of Field's popular children's poems, such as *The Duel*, *Little Boy Blue*, and *Winken, Blynken, and Nod.* On another occasion that year, the Sorosis served as part of a five-day event aimed mainly at raising funds for the fire department. One night there was a dinner, on another a humorous play entitled, *The Confidence Man*. There was a masquerade ball, and on the fifth night a "grand dance" ending at midnight.

On June 14, 1910, the Sorosis realized its goal, thanks to a grant from the Carnegie Foundation, with the laying of the cornerstone and the beginning of the construction of a real library, the one which stands today at the corner of Main and Olean Streets. The ceremony that day included the community band, the village board, the Sorosis members, and all citizens of the town. They assembled near the corner of Kinkaid and Olean Streets on the grounds of the high school, and, carrying scores of flags, (it was Flag Day), paraded around town to the library site, where they listened to speeches by Mayor James. B. Gray, President of Alfred University Boothe Caldwell, Reverend Dolan, school principal Vandegrift, as well as R.L. Andrus and Walter T. Bliss.

For the first sixty years the library existed, it was managed by just two women. Ella Williams became the first librarian in the new building, assisted and succeeded by her daughter, Florence Williams Smith. Ella Williams retired as librarian in 1933 at the age of 80, after twenty-three years, and lived another fifteen. Florence took over for her mother, and served nearly until she died, in 1974.

For many years after, Jenna Mae Cossaboon served as Bolivar's librarian. She was succeeded by popular, retired English teacher Betty Cornelius. I, the author, was the president of the library board who recruited Betty. I asked her if she would like the job, and that was all I needed to do. I had two teachers in Bolivar who turned me into a scholar. The first was my sixth grade teacher, Jim Watkins. That year I wanted nothing more than to please Mr. Watkins, and we became lifelong friends. The next year, I had Betty Cornelius for English. At the end of the second marking period, she singled me out as the only member of that section whose grade had gone up from the first marking period. I was hooked. Two decades later, my friends and I spent many a rollicking evening up at The Hilltop, singing along to the big band era songs Betty played on their piano. The other junior high teacher who got, and kept, my attention was Bernice Baldwin, whose energy didn't seem to have ebbed since she arrived, the year the school building opened.

Bolivar is very fortunate in that the library has a substantial endowment. About 1940, Bolivar resident and one-time mayor, Clyde Witherspoon, gave two hundred shares of Standard Oil of Indiana stock to the library. The certificate was placed in a safety deposit box and was then nearly forgotten for close to 40 years. Over than time, the stock split three times, and appreciated substantially, meaning the 1,600 shares owned by the library in 1980 was the cornerstone of the endowment. Other citizens of Bolivar have made contributions to the library's endowment over the years, and starting in the 1980s, the portfolio became professionally managed, with the goal, set by the trustees, of putting the library in a position where it could operate without the need for any funds from New York State.

Until the 1960s, the library was overseen by the Sorosis club, but changing times led to the disbanding of the Sorosis, and the oversight of the library was taken on by a board of trustees. The internet age has been a challenge to libraries nationwide, but Bolivar's facility has developed into a mecca for young readers and students, thanks in no small part to the efforts of our current librarian, Cathy Fuller. The building had remained substantially unchanged for 114 years, and offered the challenge to modern minds and elderly bodies of having the stacks and reading room on the second floor, at the top of a substantial staircase. At this writing, the library is closed while an elevator is installed, which will make the Bolivar Free Library twenty-first century compliant, and an asset to the community for decades to come.

The Sorosis was an important women's organization, but it was only one element in a web of social groups the ladies of Bolivar put together at the end of the nineteenth century. The local Buttrick Chapter 109 of the Order of the Eastern Star was organized in 1894, just three years after the "new" Masonic Lodge opened its doors on Main Street. It was initiated by women who had organized a chapter in Allentown, but which had folded as Allentown shrank along with the local oil economy. Prominent Bolivar ladies who joined were Emma Hulbert,

Elizabeth Garthwait, and Ella Dunning. Emma Hulbert was also the commander of Bolivar's Ladies of the Maccabees, which had 45 members in 1895. Naomi Bradley headed up the local branch of the Women's Christian Temperance Union, which met in its quarters on Boss Street every Friday afternoon. Also helping run the chapter were Augusta Wood, and treasurer Mrs. D.C. Hoyt.

In the 1890s, there were three active church groups in town. The largest was the Methodist-Episcopal Church, which during the boom had moved out of its old building on Boss Street to a much nicer structure on Friendship Street, where it remains today. It had functioned since the founding of the town. With the Boom came the Free Methodist Society, which was struggling in the 1890s as many of its members moved on in search of employment. The Catholic Church arrived in Bolivar in 1882. Parishioners quickly raised $2,000 to build a church on Wellsville Street, and boasted 200 members. All of these were maintained, financially supported, and kept running through the efforts of the altar guilds or similar ladies organizations who made those churches part of their lives.

A fourth church was established in Bolivar in 1909, when the Church of Our Savior Episcopal Church was built on Olean Street, thanks in great part to the financial support of Ida and Alonzo McKee, who donated the lot where it was built. It became the spiritual home of many of Bolivar's families, including the Shaners, Morrisons, Ferrises, Bradleys and MacDonells. But like all the other churches in town, it operated mainly due to the efforts of its altar guild, which held regular rummage sales and suppers to raise funds. It never grew large enough to support its own ministry, but was instead tied to either the Cuba or Wellsville Episcopal churches, where a priest resided.

While all of these activities were important to the people of that time, none of them provided much in the way of fun or entertainment. One of the great innovations of the age which came to Bolivar with the boom was the telephone; and the telephone made it much easier to talk and make arrangements for social gatherings. The result, combined with a craze for playing cards, was almost magical. Seemingly everyone in town became part of a "club" which met regularly to get together, kibbutz, and play their favorite card games. The Dempseys were at the heart of the Pedro Club, and would gather together as many as twelve couples to play "pedro," a partnership trick-taking game, somewhat like bridge, but where certain cards have point values. There was a whist club which also attracted a couple of dozen players to its evening gatherings.

The Current Events Club was one of the longest lived of these social clubs, where the couples gathered in each others homes to give presentations and to play games of various sorts other than cards. Organized before 1909, it survived into the 1960s. The W.W. Club, whose purpose remains undiscovered, hosted a masked ball which attracted fifty couples from as far as Olean and Wellsville. Georgiana Bolender, wife of the owner of the local grain mill, hosted the "U-Know Club." Bolivar had a "Progressive Club," which held a New Year's dance attended by ninety people, with music provided by Maire Williams, Stanley Dempsey and two others making up a quartet. The numbers they played ranged from waltzes to square dances, those called by Will Brady. That party lasted from nine until two the next morning.

Another interesting social group in town in the early twentieth century was the Ladies of the Maccabees, the local branches of which were referred to as "hives." The LOTM was born in Michigan in 1886, and it was the first fraternal insurance benefit society controlled and operated by women. In 1915, the Bolivar hive was presided over by New Jersey native Carrie Swachamer, assisted by Mary and Ada Parker, Julia Maine, Clara Tracey, and Hattie Hazzard. The hive's organist was Goldie McMurdy.

This group of ladies called themselves La Douze Amis, French for "The Twelve Friends," just right for three tables of bridge. They are seen here one sunny afternoon on the porch of Van Curen's house on South Street.

Organized groups of card players would persist for decades. The Monday Club played bridge, as did the Les Huit Amis Club and the 150 Club, at which Genevieve Jennings was a frequent winner. The Pinocle Club played that game. Another popular card game was 500, which could be played by three or four people at a time, and which was regularly played by the Elliotts, Smiths and Salzers. Another group of 500 players called themselves the Jolly Jokers, and met at the homes of Helen and Floyd Dunning, or at Calvin and Maude Best's, or at Willis and Sophia Neely's.

And there often were large card parties which could be used as fund raisers, or simply as an excuse to gather together a large group who could catch the others up on the goings on in their lives. In the mid-1930s, a committee composed of Leona Reeland, Sylvia Matson, Donna Chipman, Florence Smith, Edith Bradley and Evangeline Brannen hosted a bridge party at the Bolivar Hotel for nearly ninety women. Bolivar resident Betty Davis was the only local prize-winner.

One of the most renowned bridge players to come from Bolivar was Daisy McDivitt. Born in Bolivar in 1903, Daisy made short work of the coursework at Bolivar High School, and for the 1921-223 school year was hired as the teacher for the Daggett Hollow school, and was congratulated at the end of that term for her success. She went on to St. Elizabeth's Academy in Allegany, then to Buffalo State for formal teaching credentials. Daisy had a sharp mind, a quick wit, and an independent streak. She left teaching when the one-room school houses closed, and became, in the early 1930s, the chief office manager for Bolivar's Monroe Motors.

Her organizing skills were such that in 1937 she became the president of the Bolivar American Legion Auxiliary, even though she had never married, and all of the other officers of the Auxiliary were wives of veterans. The Legion Auxiliary was another large women's group, with committees devoted to soldier rehabilitation, children's welfare, the health camp in Cuba, and to other matters of community service. She remained active in the Auxiliary until at least 1953, when she helped organize and attended a dance for the veterans at the Bath VA Hospital.

Daisy's passion became bridge, (her mother, also Daisy, was an avid card player), and she travelled far and wide to enter duplicate bridge tournaments. (In duplicate bridge, the players at each table are given exactly the same hands of cards, testing which pair of players can make the most of what they have). On one occasion in the early 1950s, Daisy decided she would like to make a grand entrance at a weekend tournament being held at Cuba Lake, and she asked a young John D. Bradley if he would be willing to be her "chauffeur." John obliged, and Daisy pulled into her host's driveway riding in the backseat of a vintage 1920s Rolls Royce with a divider window. Literally rolling out of the car and on to the host's lawn, she made the entrance and impression she wanted to make.

Daisy spent most of her working life as the Bolivar office manager for the Empire Gas & Fuel Company. There she got to know everyone in town, since bills were paid in person at the company office on Boss Street. In 1962, when the extended Bradley family sold the gas company, one of the customers asked Daisy what it meant, that the Bradleys had sold the company. Daisy replied: "I'll tell you what it means. It means there will be two more guys coming in here next month to bitch about their bills!"

When she died, in September 1967, twenty-three books were donated to the Bolivar Free Library in her memory. Three were about playing bridge. One was a Random House Dictionary. And one other, the one which she would have liked best, was "The Groucho Letters" by Groucho Marks. She was one of a kind.

All this card playing and socializing was in addition to the more formal groups which attracted support. Bolivar had its own Grange Hall and Grangers, with male and female officers. The Order of the Eastern Star was the women's branch of Masonry. For the wives of higher degree Masons, there was the Order of the Amaranth, whose members focused on one's duty to God, truth, faith, wisdom, and charity. Some of the most prominent Bolivar members over the years were DeEtta Bascom, Mary Ingalls, and Madeline Walchli.

In the 1930s, another committee of Bolivar's women joined in the "fresh air" movement, to give city kids a chance to escape the heat of New York City and relax in the countryside for a couple of weeks during the summer. Among those active in organizing this and finding hosts for the children were Suzie Shaner, Gladys Nichols, Eileen Dillie, and Grace Sackinger. But all in all, it is important to keep in mind it was this constant, personal interaction which made this small town such a tight knit and supportive place to raise a family. If it was late on a Saturday night, and you didn't know where your kids were, one of your friends did!

Laura Albert

The 1890s saw a series of other developments. The railroad to Wellsville shut down, taking with it Sawyer's refinery. Plans to rebuild the Central New York & Western as a standard gauge line had to be delayed because of the financial panic of 1893. The work started in 1895. That same year, a stage line was set up to run from Bolivar to Wellsville. In 1894, a group of ten, including J.P. Herrick, A.C. MacDonell, Bernard Dunn and Charles Munich, banded together to buy and refurbish the Opera House at the corner of Main and Olean. That fall, they brought to town Laura Albert, a well-known Canadian actress who performed in two plays, *An Arabian Night,* and *The Clemenceau Case.*

In 1896, sixteen village property owners banded together and planted more than eighty trees along the streets. The operators of the race track attracted more than 1,000 spectators to bicycle races, with William J. Hogan, (we assume the father of the Bill Hogan many of us knew), acting as the starter. Professor Glennie left Bolivar at the end of that school year, to take up the reins in Monticello, New York. He would move on and finish his career as a principal in the Newark, New Jersey schools.

In 1898, Reverend W.W. Manning of Bolivar led a memorial service for Frances Willard, founder of the Women's Christian Temperance Union. He filled every pew, turning it into a standing-room-only event. At the start of that year, there were two operators of stage lines connecting Bolivar with Friendship. Carl Rice bought them both and immediately shut one down, running only the stage with the mail contract.

War With Spain

The Spanish-American War broke out in April, 1898, triggered by the explosion of the battleship Maine in Havana Harbor in February. Five Bolivar boys were belatedly swept up by the war fever, and all of them ended up in Captain Ward's Company of the 202nd New York Infantry Regiment. The regiment left Savannah on the transport ship Minnewaska and arrived in Havana harbor on December 9, 1898, the first American regiment to arrive in Havana by sea. The very next day the Treaty of Paris ended the war with Spain.

The troopship Minnewaska, decks crowded with volunteers

The regiment mustered out of the service on April 15, 1899. The first of Bolivar's soldiers to return home was Tom Murphy, who reported that he had enjoyed the country of Cuba and would like to return. Terrence O'Brien arrived next. He had spent several weeks in a hospital fighting malaria. Although not crazy about the idea of returning to Cuba, he said he was considering enlisting in the Regular Army. He died in 1901 of the lingering effects of the malaria, and never had the chance. Albert Rapp and Corporal Stanley Furnald did not come straight back to Bolivar, instead stopping to visit relatives on the way, which left Jesse Swarthout as the last Spanish American war vet to return home in a timely manner. Jesse, Irv Swarthout's older brother, spent his life as a shopkeeper around Bolivar, and was also the last of our Spanish-American War veterans to leave the scene, passing away in 1962 at the age of eighty-five.

World War One

One of W.D. Steven's best known posters promoted the United States war effort

The United States entered what we now call The First World War on April 6, 1917. Although Washington had expanded the size of the Navy, it had made no preparations to fight a land war in Europe prior to the declaration of war on Germany, brought about by the decision of the Germans to start sinking any merchant ships headed for England or France. Thus, significant numbers of American troops would not arrive in France for some time, after they had been recruited, sorted, organized, and trained. In all fifty men born in Bolivar joined the United States armed forces to serve during the First World War. Unlike World War 2, no one from the town jumped up to volunteer on April 7, the day after the declaration. Most of those who served were drafted, and they waited for the call, which came for most of them in 1918.

When the war arrived, one Bolivar boy was already in uniform: Lewis Holder, born in Bolivar in 1888, had walked into the Rochester Recruiting Station on June 15, 1916, and joined the United States Navy. He was first assigned, as a Fireman, to the USS Hartford, perhaps the most famous of all Navy ships of the 19th century, other than Old Ironsides. She had been built as a steam-powered sloop of war, meaning she also carried three masts fully rigged for sail. She had served as Admiral Farragut's flagship when he took Mobile in 1864 during the Civil War. When Holder climbed aboard, she was a station ship in Charleston

Harbor. After eight months there, he became a machinist's mate on one of the Navy's newest boats, the submarine K-5. Along with two sister ships based in the Azores, she was the first American submarine to patrol European waters. He left the service in June 1920, having spent his post-war tour in New London. There he stayed, raised his family, and worked steadily as a submarine "engine man" for his entire career, passing away in New Lindon in 1975.

After war was declared, Bolivar boys trickled into the service. Albert Hassard went first, on 27 May, assigned first to the 23rd Cavalry, before being transferred to the 81st Field Artillery. He didn't get to France until mid-October 1918. Stanley Dempsey joined on 13 July, Thomas Hungerford on 22 August, and Bill Apgar and Clarendon Streeter on September 5.

Dempsey joined at Gettysburg, PA, and started his military career as a musician with the headquarter's company of the 7th Infantry. He was accepted into Officer's Candidate School in May 1918 and received his commission in mid-October at camp Hancock, Georgia, where he remained until discharged in January 1919.

Tom Hungerford, an uncle of Bolivar's well-known petroleum engineer of the same name, served as a private with the 15th Field Artillery, Battery D. He departed with the unit for France in December 1917, arriving on Christmas Day. He remained in Germany and France until July 1919. When discharged, he was considered ⅓ disabled, the victim of a gas attack, from which he would never completely recover. He spent his life as an oil producer around Bolivar, passing away in his home on First Street on Christmas Day, 1965 at the age of 67.

Another casualty was Ray Miller. On August 8, 1918, shrapnel from and artillery barrage hit him in the left arm. That October, when his parents heard the news, he was still recovering in a military hospital in France. Corporal William Shannon became a German prisoner of war and was held at Rastatt, twenty-five miles north of Strasbourg on the banks of the Rhine. He wasn't repatriated until December 18, 1918, more than a month after the war had ended.

Apgar and Streeter were both assigned to Battery C, 307th Field Artillery. Apgar worked his way up to sergeant, and Streeter received a lieutenant's commission near the war's end. With the 307th, as part of the 153rd Field Artillery Brigade, 78th Division, they reached the front lines in June 1918, near Baccarat, and saw action along the Vesle sector in August, as part of the Oise-Aisne Offensive from August into September, and in the Argonne from late September to war's end in November. Both returned to Bolivar after the war ended. Streeter lived most of his later life as an oil producer around Bradford, passing in 1972. Bill Apgar, who spent his life selling oil well supplies here in Bolivar, was the town's last surviving World War One vet, leaving the scene in 1978.

Numerous other Bolivar boys were assigned to various field artillery units. Harry T. Baker went with Battery B of the 34th; Burton Bliss went to France with the 81st. Bernard Gavin, who opened the Gavin & McCarthy clothing store in Olean after the war, served in the Argonne with the 304th. Henry Hitchcock served with both the 4th, and then the 81st, Field Artillery with Bliss and Hassard. Ned Hungerford served as a musician with Battery B of the 4th, but never left the states. Finally, Bolivar's oldest recruit, Clyde Witherspoon, served as a wagoner with the 24th, and like Ned, never left this country.

Only four Bolivar-born boys ended up in the US Navy. Marion Benedict was one of the few local men to become an officer, commissioned as an ensign in May 1918. He was in the Navy Reserves, and made Lt. jg in 1919. Neil Crandall signed up in July 1918, and spent his tour at the Great Lakes training center as a machinist's mate working on airplanes. Lewis Holder served as a fireman and machinist first class at New London, then as part of the twenty-eight-man crew on board the USS K-5, one of the Navy's first submarines, based in the Azores for six months. He was then transferred to the sub tender USS Bushnell to war's end. (The Busnell, rechristened the Sumner, was in Pearl Harbor on December 7, 1941).

The next group of boys to leave were John C. Bradley, Harley Loop and Maire Williams, on September 27, 1917. Bradley, whose leg had been crushed in an accident a few years before, limped so badly on the parade ground at Fort Dix, New Jersey, that he was sent home after just two weeks. Loop was assigned to Battery B of the 307th Field Artillery, but was discharged by an order from the Secretary of War on 12 Jan 1918. Maire Williams went to the 307th with Apgar and Streeter, as a musician. Working as a violinist in a local orchestra before the war, he became the regimental band leader of the 307th beginning in July 1918. He was in France with the unit from 26 May 1918 until 14 May 1919, and was discharged a month later. He continued to work as a musician after the war, but died in Bolivar in January 1929, aged only 39.

Another cluster of Bolivar boys joined the Army on February 27, 1918: Erie Munich, Ralph Hill, Frank Dougherty, and Kenyon Andrus. Munich and Dougherty were assigned to Co. L of the 308th Infantry, Hill and Andrus to Company M. On April 6, 1918, the regiment left for France, destined to become one of the most famous American units in the war. In early October 1918, during the Meuse-Argonne advance that broke the back of the German Army, a large part of the regiment moved through a gap in the German defenses and became trapped and surrounded behind the German lines when the gap closed. They became known as the *Lost Battalion* , which suffered sixty percent casualties during the next four days, holding out until a relief column broke through.

None of the Bolivar boys were with the "Lost Battalion," their companies not being the ones which drifted past the German barricades, but they were very much part of the relief effort. Munich, a blacksmith, had been reassigned to the headquarters company. Both Dougherty and Hill had been hit by machine gun fire, (Dougherty three times), in mid-September during an earlier advance, but luckily neither had been seriously wounded. Andrus was in the hospital suffering from the great Spanish Influenza outbreak that had spread at a breakneck pace through the Army's camps.

Andrus died from the flu on October 5, for many years thought to be the only man from Bolivar who died in uniform during the war. A few months before he left for the war he had married a professional organist, Florence. She never remarried, but did change careers, training as and becoming a registered nurse in New York City, before joining the Bolivar school system as the school's nurse when the new central school building opened in 1929.

Kenyon Andrus was not the only Bolivar-born boy to die in uniform as a result of the First World War, but he was the first to die in France. Corporal James C. Root, age 18, was in Colorado when he entered the service in March 1918. He died two days after Andrus, on October 7, 1918. Charles Kreiner died on October 8, while John C. Velie lingered until January 28, 1919. They all succumbed to "bronchial pneumonia," the Army's diagnosis for influenza.

Kenyon Andrus's cousin, Lowell, was actually the first Bolivar boy to die in uniform. Lowell, BHS '10 and Cornell '15, enlisted in October 1917. In July 1918 the Army sent him to the Great Lakes Naval Training Station to become an aviation mechanic. While there, influenza killed September 29. The influenza pandemic resulted in a flurry of government actions. It was illegal to cough in public without covering your mouth and nose. In Bolivar, the schools, saloons, pool rooms, churches, theater, and other public places were closed on Monday, October 14, by the order of health officer Dr. Charles Hoffman.

There were no protests. Everyone covered their faces and worked together to quell the epidemic. The first local death was reported on Oct. 17. The saloons reopened on November 7. The epidemic neared its end by Christmas, and mentions of locals suffering from it disappeared from the paper in March 1919.

At the time, it was called the Spanish Flu, because of the belief that it had originated in Spain. It didn't. That impression arose because of censorship in the countries fighting the Great War. Spain being neutral, its press was free to report. It is now believed that the outbreak began in Fort Leavenworth, Kansas.

Looking east over Bolivar, about 1910, home to 3,600 town and village people

Bolivar's Hearons Sisters

The Hearons Sisters singing to the 101st Machine Gun Battalion
Bois de Rohanne, France 1918

Fifty Bolivar boys ended up in uniform, and many of them in France, due to the outbreak of World War One. But what about the women of the town? Clara Stimson, Trina Williams MacDonell, and Bernice Williams, packed their bags and took jobs in Washington DC, in May 1918. But three Bolivar sisters got to France before many of the Doughboys arrived. Thomas and Anna Hearons, themselves the children of Irish immigrants, arrived in Bolivar from the Pennsylvania oil fields in 1882, right at the height of the excitement. Thomas was not a fortune hunter. The son of a trusted employee of Standard Oil, he had started his working career as a gauger, and came to Bolivar to work for the Tidewater Pipeline Company, first as a gauger keeping track of how much of whose oil was making it into the gathering system, and quickly becoming the company foreman for the Allegany Field, in charge of all of the gaugers and roustabouts who kept the system operational. He brought with him his wife and four daughters, adding one more girl shortly after they arrived in town, and he made his home on Wellsville Street, near and across the street from St. Mary's church.

There has always been a strong presence of music in Bolivar. We produced band leaders during the Civil War, and boasted at least a couple of professional musicians in nearly every census. But just who developed the Hearons sisters' interest in and skill performing music is now unknown. Surely their mother played an important role, but their is no mention of her ever performing herself, or of her teaching other people. The Baxter University of Music was a well-respected academy set up in Friendship, but it faded out of existence not long after the Hearons arrived in Bolivar, so that is not the explanation.

People like to be entertained. In nineteenth-century America, there were three traveling entertainment circuits that catered to various markets. Most remembered is Vaudeville, where you might see magicians, jugglers, animal acts, comedians, and dancers. The performances could be risqué, the humor sometimes blue. Liquor might be available. At the opposite end was the Chautauqua circuit, which aimed to educate and uplift, where you might take in lectures and sermons, and listen to prominent orators of the time, including Robert LaFollette, William Jennings Bryan, Russell Cowell, and Jane Adams.

Preceding the Chautauqua movement was the Lyceum, the first movement seeking to provide a form of adult education around the country. Among the early speakers were Ralph Waldo Emerson and Henry David Thoreau. As the century moved on, the big names on the card could be Mark Twain or Susan B. Anthony, but slowly the emphasis turned to lighter fare, to more music and entertainment. There would be a slate of speakers and entertainers who would travel from town to town. Virtually every community boasted an opera house. If there was none, or even if there was, many churches contained hundreds of seats and decent acoustics where speakers could be heard and music enjoyed.

However the sisters acquired their musical skills, they were extensive, and never attracted, so far as I could discover, a negative review. The oldest sister, named Anna after her mother, was born in 1878. She became "a skilled pianist and mandolinist." Second sister Mae had no apparent musical interest. She married and settled in West Virginia. The third sister, Frances, came into the world in May 1880. She became a "violinist of rare ability." The fourth sister, Charlotte, born in December 1881, specialized in the clarinet. The youngest, Winifred, who joined the family in 1883, after they arrived in Bolivar, played the coronet, and acted as the group's "reader."

Their first mention in the press was in 1894, when they provided the musical entertainment at the monthly meeting of the Allegany County Farmer's Club. Next came an appearance at an elocution contest in Belmont, in which Winnie was entered, and then a program for Bolivar's Memorial Day "of a character that is not often to be found in a small town." They listed themselves in the 1900 census as "professional musicians," when they ranged in age from sixteen to twenty-two, and that year they were the featured musical entertainment at the annual temperance assembly in Cuba, which was no small deal: invited speakers included Confederate General John B. Gordon, and Booker T. Washington.

Their career took a significant turn in the winter of 1901, when they signed their first contract to go on a six-week tour on the lyceum circuit. To prepare, Anna and Frances signed up to spend the fall at a "leading conservatory." J.P. Herrick commented, "They are hard-working, conscientious young women and have fairly earned their success." That tour took them up the Mohawk Valley, then to Rochester, Buffalo and into Ohio. They proved so popular that the tour was extended, and they quickly signed a contact for twenty weeks in 1902.

The exposure gained on tour led to frequent return bookings in the communities where they had been seen, often hired as an attraction at church fund-raisers and the like. Their 1902 tour took them for two months around northern New York. They came back to Bolivar for two weeks, then were off again to "start a southern trip." They took their earnings and invested it in additional music training at a conservatory in Cincinnati. In 1907, they took their extra time and money and spent it studying in New York City.

In the summer of 1904, the concert company left Bolivar for an extended tour through North and South Dakota, Iowa and Illinois, after which they spent a week at the St. Louis World's Fair. A review given in 1905 paid credit to Winifred in particular: "Their music blends the classical with the popular. Miss Winifred Hearons is a talented reader who introduces variety and humor into the otherwise musical program." The most common word in reviews was "delightful." They combined classical, "high-brow" music with popular tunes and humor. Even as their popularity grew, they were never too busy, it seemed, when home, to play for the locals, at Memorial Day gatherings, at church socials, at high school graduations. And when traveling, their popularity had grown to such a degree that they were usually booked into mid-sized cities, like Rockford, Illinois or Janesville, Wisconsin, for a full week. In January 1908, they came home, but put on a show in Salamanca which sold out, standing room only. The program, which included readings, orchestra, violin and string quartet numbers drew wild applause and calls for two encores- not your usual ending for a string quartet!

Perhaps tired of the constant touring, they moved to New York City, found plenty of work in Gotham's hotels, and in the summer of 1910, hit the big time, carrying out a "very successful" concert tour of England, Ireland and France, where, it was said, they performed before royalty. The tours became seasonal, often during the summers, taking them to the Panama Canal Zone and the West Coast. At the end of the summer of 1912, "after closing a most successful midwest tour," Anna and Francis came back to Bolivar for a "few weeks rest" before heading back to New York to prepare for their fall engagement. In the fall of 1917 they toured in the South before beginning their New York season.

But by then, the war had drawn America in. In World War Two, the USO organized entertainment for the troops. In 1917, that job was taken up by the YMCA. That winter, the sisters were approached to see if they would accept an appointment from the National Work Council to entertain in France. They did. Well, three of them did. Frances has fallen for a promising-looking salesman names Morton B. Chace. Rather than go to France, on August 12, 1918, in Manhattan, she married him.

Anna, Winifred and Charlotte went off to the war. They applied for their passports in January 1918, and were soon on a French transport taking the YMCA entertainers to LeHavre. The sisters spent the next fifteen months in France, doing their part to keep up Doughboy morale. They returned to New York in July 1919 on the SS Antigone, a single-stack transport ship built in 1900 for a German company. The ship had taken refuge in Baltimore at the outbreak of the war and had been seized and converted shortly after America became involved.

After the war, the sisters went their separate ways. Frances had already left the act. Her husband made a modest living in sales, and died in Albany New York in the spring of 1939. She returned to New York City, took up residence in the Roosevelt Hotel, and left this life on May 31, 1941. They are buried in Bolivar.What had made the Hearons Sisters Concert Company different from so many other groups playing the Lyceum circuit was Winifred, with her spirited and often humorous readings. She too saw a man she wanted, and on May 20, 1920, she married Francis Flahive. To replace Frances, the remaining sisters recruited a niece, Rosalee, and for a time Winifred remained with the act. But her husband's business interests were in New England, and they settled in New London. In 1933, they bought an 1812 farmhouse on four acres in Brookfield, Connecticut, and there lived out their lives. After her husband died, in 1958, Winifred moved to Santa Clara, California, where she passed away on June 15, 1962.

Anna and Charlotte kept the act alive for a time, hiring others to fill the gaps. In 1923, they worked as part of a quintet, with a new violinist who "played gypsy airs," another who did child impersonations, and a soprano, who sang and also was part of the comedy sketches. After the touring ended, Charlotte kept busy in New York, and remained single into her fifties. Just when she met Henry Fletcher Godfrey is a detail we do not know. His family, based in New York, had money. At the time he married for the first time, in 1910, Henry was thirty-six. He was a Harvard grad, a prominent stock broker, and by profession a banker, his father a partner in Drexel Morgan. He had two step daughters with the last name Tiffany. When he left for the war, he lived at 1 East 49th Street, Manhattan, today the site of Saks Fifth Avenue. He was also Master of the Hounds of the Meadowbrook Hunt. He traveled to France in the spring of 1918 on YMCA work, so perhaps he met Charlotte Hearons while "over there."

Henry's first wife died in 1925. He married Charlotte on July 14, 1936, at the St. Vincent Ferrer church, and she moved into homes filled with servants and pleasant times. It was not a long marriage, for Charlotte died at her sister's home in Brookfield on January 29, 1939, but her marriage gave Charlotte the means to help her sisters when and if they needed it. Henry died in June 1940.

While back in France in 1926, Anna married a Russian civil engineer named Alexander Turin; not just any Russian, but Prince Alexander, one of dozens of Georgian princes looking for fortunes or tickets to America. He had made headlines in December 1926, when a previous wife sued for divorce. She said she was Princess Nadepda Troubelkoy, who claimed to have been a member of the Battalion of Death, an all-female Russian Army unit formed prior to the Revolution, about the time she married Turin, who had abandoned her after eight months. Saying she thought Turin had died in the war, the princess married an American army captain, only to receive a $20,000 demand from Turin to keep quiet. She left husband number two to search for Turin. The captain had the marriage annulled. When she finally found the prince, she sued for divorce.

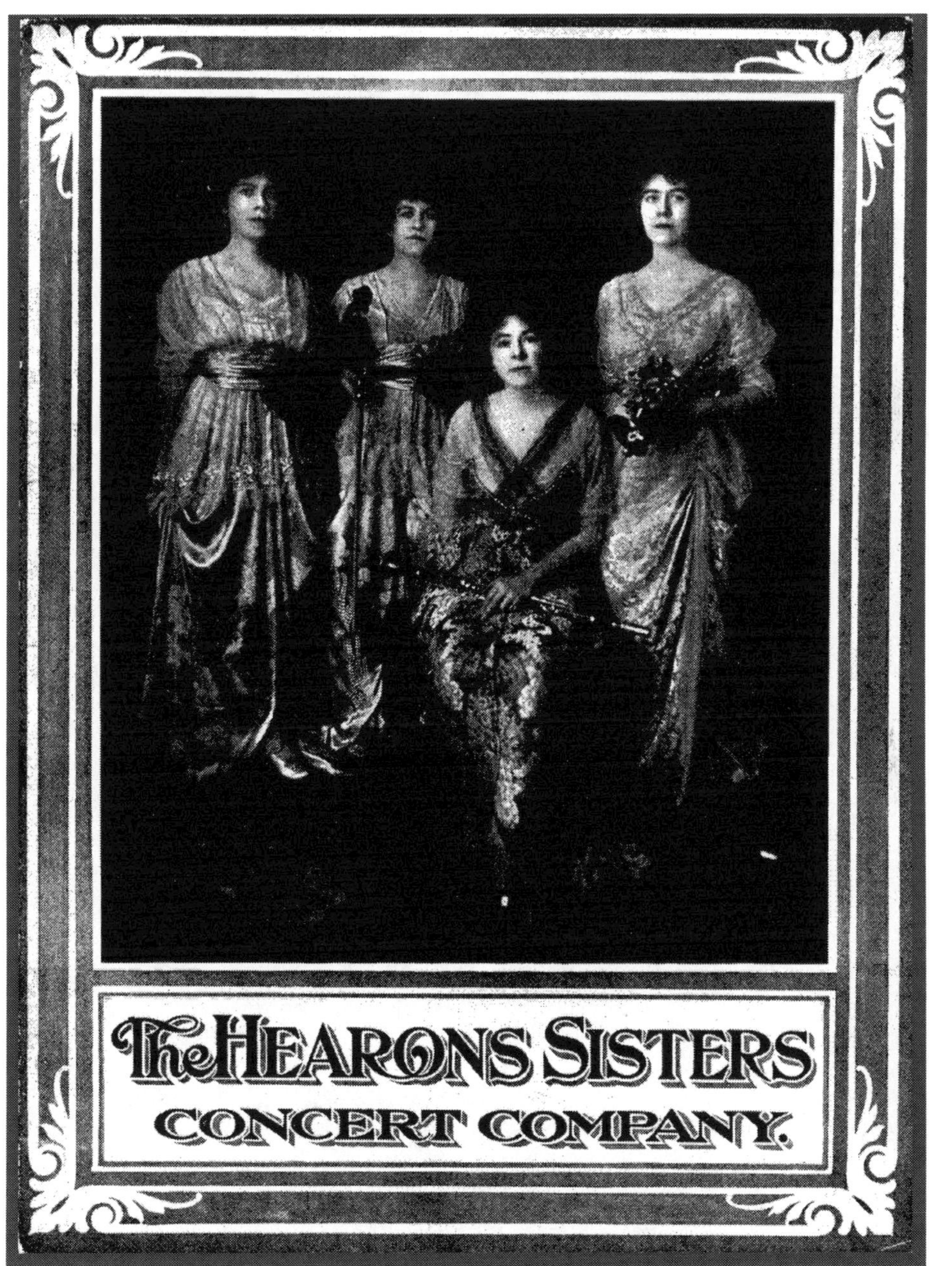

The sisters: Anna, the pianist, Frances on violin, Charlotte clarinet and Winifred with her coronet.

Anna and Alexander returned to the USA in the fall of 1927, questions about the legality of their marriage never seeming to arise. It must have been a tumultuous time. They toured the east, including a stop in Bolivar to see her parents, and worked their way back to New York City, where the "prince" reverted to his old self. On October 11, 1928, the New York Times reported his death in the apartment of a woman he had met at the Plaza Hotel a week earlier.

Anna never remarried, kept Turin's name, but never called herself a princess. For a time she lived again in Bolivar, caring for her father and helping to organize the Christmas pageants at St. Mary's. Then in the 1950s, she moved near her niece, Rosalee, in California. She died in a convalescent home in Redwood City on July 27, 1972, the last of the fabulous Hearons Sisters Concert Company.

Arrival of the 20th Century

There was a flurry of activity around town as the nineteenth century drew to a close and the twentieth began. 1899 saw the organization of the Pittsburgh, Shawmut & Northern Railroad, which promised improved transportation service. With 1900 came the arrival of the one-lunger engines that kept the declining oil production economical, and the arrival of the first automobile seen in Bolivar. Erie J. Wilson was born in Cherrytree Township, near Titusville, Pennsylvania in 1854. An uncle had been one of the promoters of the Drake well, the first commercial oil well drilled there in 1859. Erie arrived in Richburg in 1880, settled in Bolivar in 1884, became a busy drilling contractor and the owner of a number of good producing properties in the oil field.

He was the first operator to install a one-lunger engine on a lease. He was the first person in Bolivar to have electric lights and appliances in his home, on Wellsville Street. And in June 1900 he brought to Bolivar the first automobile, a Locomobile, powered by a two-cylinder steam engine with a twenty-one gallon boiler riding on four, heavy-duty bicycle wheels. On Friday June 13, a brave W.L. Nichols climbed in beside him, and they set off for Olean, "covering the eighteen miles in an hour and a half." The car created as much excitement in Olean as it did in Bolivar, and Erie played to the crowd, happily giving twenty of "the society women of that city" rides around town, before heading back to Bolivar.

But the question loomed, was this horseless carriage really a practical advance, or was it just a rich man's toy and novelty? The quickest way to settle that argument, it was thought, would be to have a race; and when better to have a race of such importance than on the afternoon of July 4, 1900 on the racetrack in the town park on the east side of the village. And so it was a that a match race was arranged between Erie Wilson and his blue locomotive, and a fast, white horse owned by Grant Williams.

July 4 was set up to be a banner day. It began at 8:30 in the morning with a "Grand Fantastic Parade." At 9:00, there was a "free-for-all" horse race with a $25 purse, and at 9:30, the Locomobile and horse race, "the first of its kind in Western New York." Those would be followed by a hundred yard dash, sack races, wheelbarrow races, chasing a greased pig, a firemen's parade, hose cart races, a shooting match between the Bolivar and Allentown gun clubs, ending in the evening with a band concert.

The great race was scheduled not as a sprint, but as a four-mile run, a much longer distance than horses were normally raced. Wilson did not push his vehicle. Williams, perhaps a little anxious, pushed his horse and built up a huge lead. But going through the third mile, the horse became winded and slowed to a trot, then to a walk, and the Locomobile just kept chugging along. As the fourth mile came to an end, Erie caught the horse, and the Locomobile crossed the finish line a single yard ahead.

The Great Race, July 4, 1900, between the future and the past

Erie touched off a craze. He took his car everywhere, often being the first to drive a horseless carriage into a town, as he was in Belfast that October. The race also inspired others. Wellsville's summer fair featured automobile races, locomotive races, and mixed races with cars and horses.

Trolley systems became popular in the 1890s, Washington DC having the first underground electric trolley system operating in 1894. A line from Olean to Bradford began operation in 1897, and plans to expand began almost immediately. It wasn't until December 1899 that a trolley line connecting Bolivar and Wellsville was proposed, but that never came to be. In August 1901, the Olean Street Railway Company, which had already extended service into Portville, asked for a franchise to serve Bolivar, and the idea met with strong opposition. Those against were concerned about the effect a trolley line would have on the success of the Shawmut, which was just then being built all the way through the county to Angelica. However, by the summer of 1902 opinion had swung the other way, and the village trustees approved the granting of a franchise.

Construction began almost immediately. The proposed trolley track had to cross both the tracks of the Pennsylvania Railroad and of the Shawmut, and both companies did their best to frustrate its progress. In August there were fights between the laborers working for the Shawmut and the trolley company when the trolley men tried to build a crossing of the Shawmut near Ceres. In August, after a battle that involved stone throwing, swinging picks, shovels, and crowbars, as well as fists, the outnumbered trolley company men were forced to retreat. The crossing wasn't completed until November. By November 20, 1902, the trench was being dug along Main Street, so that the tracks would rest at street level, and within the week the line began operations. The round trip fare for a trip to Olean was $.60, whereas it cost a full dollar to take the Shawmut. The result was that four out of five travelers were filling the trolley.

The first decade of the twentieth century was labelled the Motor Age, and the transition from a world of horse ownership to automobiles was steady, but in Bolivar it was not particularly swift. The second town resident known to own a car was Asa Root, who spent $750 to buy a twelve horsepower, yellow 1905 Cadillac. Soon after he bought it, he picked up W.J. Hogan, and they made good time on a run to Olean. A.C. McDonell followed suit, buying a runabout. George H. Bradley got on the bandwagon that August, bringing home a seventeen-horsepower Haynes-Apperson five-passenger touring car. Will Scott bought a 1906 Rambler, and promptly took Fred Williams on a two-day jaunt to Alfred Station. The first advertisement of a car for sale in Bolivar was run by the Herrick Agency in August 1907, offering a used 1906 Buick. (It's owner wanted something bigger).

Starting in the summer of 1908, the firm of Beatty & Jordan began advertising automobile supplies, gasoline, and automobile repairs. The first advertisement run by a Bolivar automobile dealer appeared in the February 18, 1909 Breeze. Will Scott, who had been born in the town of Wirt and who was now forty-four, had obtained the Oakland Agency for all of Allegany County, and parts of Potter, McKean and Cattaraugus. Oakland offered two models, a two-cylinder twenty horsepower, and a four-cylinder forty horse. That same year, General Motors acquired the Oakland company and set it up as their entry level automobile, meaning it would compete with the offerings of Henry Ford. Scott's ads took advantage of the fact that Oaklands had been made since 1896, more than ten years. His line was "Don't Buy an Experiment! Oaklands Make Good."

On June 17, 1909 Michael Haeley announced his intention to build a fireproof garage and automobile storage warehouse, and to act as an agent for Buick. The article said that Haeley had sold more cars than Buick could deliver to him. Therefore he wanted to be able to have an inventory in stock so that problem would not happen again. Things were picking up. "Right here in Bolivar, a village of 1,400 population, over $50,000 is invested in automobiles. More than 30 machines are owned by Bolivar men." On June 1,

1909 Oakland

1911, signs went up at the village limits which said, "Incorporated village of Bolivar. Slow Down! 15 miles per hour."

Turn-of-the-century Bolivar saw more than its share of excitement. When I wrote my contributions to the sesquicentennial history of Bolivar, I was rather proud to conclude that there had never been a murder in town that involved town residents. In May 1905, there was a fight among members of the Italian work gang building the new school. Guinsippe Churuso shot and killed Filipo Fanghi. Fanghi's brother then shot and and severely wounded Churuso. Recently returned Spanish-American War vet and former policeman Jesse Swarthout pulled a pistol of his own and ended the melee. That, I thought, was the only killing which had happened here.

I was mistaken. In 1900, Edward Mead and his brother-in-law, Bert Wixson, were in business together operating a carriage shop on Main Street near Root Hollow Creek. About 8:30 a.m. on the morning of March 1, Joseph Wasson, a drayman, went to the shop to have some small repairs made to his wagon. Wixson was able to do the repairs in a short while, and Wasson drove off back into town. He crossed paths with Ira Voorhees, who was on his way to the carriage shop on a similar mission. When Voorhees entered the shop, he saw Wixson laying lifeless on the floor in a pool of blood, with a bullet hole through his head. He summoned a doctor and the coroner, who quickly determined Wixson was dead. Soon after they decided to search for Mead. Handy Thurber found him laying at the top of the stairs. Beside his body was a .32 caliber pistol with two

The first trolley to roll into Bolivar was a big shock to this team of horses

empty chambers. It was known that the two men had been quarreling over seemingly petty matters over the past few months. This murder-suicide was the only such incident in the town for nearly the rest of the century, until another occurred while Rick Whitney was the chief of police.

The other major crime that took place during those years happened in 1902, when burglars blew open the safe of the Bolivar Post Office. Although no one was apprehended, it was widely believed that the crime was the work of a well-known burglar named Tom Hughes, who was fatally wounded in a shootout with police in Limestone in 1905.

There was a flurry of building activity in the first decade of the century. The prosperity that underlay it was the result of the installation of the one-lungers, the opening of the Sinclair refinery in Wellsville in September of 1902, and the solid, and slowly increasing price for a barrel of oil. The community was busy enough that the village installed its first street signs in 1903, and various homeowners contracted to install 16,000 feet of concrete sidewalks. In 1904, the thermometer touched an all-time low of -37, and the Bolender grain mill went up on Boss Street. In 1905, the high school at the corner of Olean and Kincaid opened, as did St. Mary's Catholic Church on Wellsville Street. A few doors to the east, in 1906 the Reynolds house went up, the first in town built with blocks of cast concrete. The store building at the corner of Main and Friendship, built with the same blocks, went up almost at the same time, as did the Odd Fellows hall at the corner of Main and Boss. In 1907, the new Bradley house was built at the corner of Boss and First. In 1909, the Episcopal church opened on Olean Street.

The Dreamland Theater had been in operation before 1909. In July 1910, A.L. Merritt, the owner, installed an electric generator, which included a twelve horsepower gasoline engine hooked to a dynamo. With electricity available, Merritt installed ceiling fans, lighting around the theater, and ran power to his new, bright, motion picture projector. One could now watch the modern marvel of "the movies," while the air circulated around you, the images brightly flickering on the screen, and you could find your way out after the show was over. The shows changed three times a week, but he rarely advertised. In September, he ran a three-reel edition of Uncle Tom's Cabin, for both matinee and evening performances.

John P. Herrick

His "Bolivar Breeze" newspaper recorded area life for 73 years.

by Tom Manning

A dapper John P. Herrick, as he looked when he launched the Bolivar Breeze

In 1872, at the age of four, John Pierce Herrick moved with his family from Michigan to northwestern Pennsylvania where his father entered the lumber business. He attended a one-room school was at Sterling Run, south of Emporium, until age fifteen when his father fell ill, forcing John to help with the business. The Herricks moved to Costello (near Austin) and for two years he helped his father sustain operations there. Then a work injury caused John to switch to clerking at the local tannery store. As an accomplished student he passed the state exam for a teaching certificate and at eighteen was conducting classes at another area schoolhouse. On the side, he wrote news stories for a Coudersport paper.

He planned to become a doctor. In March of 1886, however, a relative wrote to tell John of a defunct newspaper in Shingle House (a two-name town back then) whose equipment was for sale. He thought John could be a newspaper success, so they inspected the setup and made an offer, but it was refused. By the following Saturday John was packed up and ready to leave for college on Monday. Making a last visit to the post office, he was handed a letter from Shingle House – a reconsidered acceptance of his offer. Bolivar, New York, came that close to missing the future benefits of John Herrick's adoption of the town and its enthusiastic adoption of him.

That Monday, he rode the train to Ceres then the stagecoach to his new home to begin his newspaper career. The first issue of his weekly *Sharon Leader* appeared on May 4, 1886, but in a matter of weeks John concluded that Shingle House was too small to support the enterprise. He surveyed nearby Ceres – a thriving village with 300 residents straddling the state line, served by two railroads, with two sawmills, two hotels, an opera house and a number of stores. John concluded that adding a Ceres newspaper, well supported by a larger advertising base, would wring more revenue from his printing investment. He moved the bulk of the "plant" to Ceres, continued publishing the "Leader" and in August came out with the first issue of his "Ceres Courant." Covering the Oswayo Valley thusly, his venture succeeded beyond "break-even." After a few years John merged his two papers to create the "Oswayo Valley Mail."

In 1891 a group of Bolivar citizens urged him to establish a newspaper in their village, population 1,100 or so. They had lacked one for a year and were impressed by his success in Ceres. John canvassed the Bolivar business community, decided the ad revenue potential was good and launched "The Bolivar Breeze" on August 31, 1891, with its motto atop the front page: "All things come to him who hustles." As he later recalled, "Oil country folks were friendly and hospitable and I liked them." Thus began a long relationship of mutual admiration between John Herrick and the people of his new hometown. "I worked long hours to merit their goodwill and approval," he said.

The *Breeze* steadily grew in circulation, content and influence, and in 1900 John sold his Ceres newspaper to his brother Charles to fully focus on the Bolivar area for twenty-plus more years. Along the way, he noted, "As rapidly as I made a dollar in newspapers I invested it in oil leases and royalties" in the Allegany field. (His financial acumen and diligence would serve to compound his wealth.) Meanwhile, John's Bolivar-boosting "Breeze" editorials helped spur local economic benefits and civic improvements: bringing the standard gauge P.S.&N. Railroad through the valley; making Bolivar the eastern terminus of the regional trolley system; creating a village water system and area telephone network; and building a high school and a village park. He was Bolivar's postmaster for several years and was also president of the Bolivar Free Library, and was instrumental in securing the Andrew Carnegie grant that funded the new library building. (John and Carnegie had become personal acquaintances aboard an ocean liner.) And John's *Breeze* writings on wider issues were often quoted in other papers.

As the new century progressed, so too did John Herrick's role in the petroleum industry, summarized as follows:

- his group of royalty holdings eventually became one of the region's largest

- he was the operator of some Allentown area leases
- at its peak, his portfolio of interests in the Allegany Field involved about 150 wells
- he helped organize the Penn Grade Crude Oil Association in Ohio and West Virginia, serving terms as an officer
- he helped establish the N.Y.S. Oil Producers Association, served terms as its president and was honored as a "President Emeritus"
- he contributed articles to petroleum industry publications
- his industry studies took him to every U.S. producing region and twice to European fields
- he became a valued consultant to executives of major oil companies, even making a presentation in his eighties to the Standard Oil Company of California's board of directors.

In 1912, the Herricks relocated to Olean where John could better manage his growing business enterprises and keep tabs on his oil and gas holdings. Olean's mayor appointed him in 1926 as the Fourth Ward's representative on the city council. The new *Breeze* editor was his brother Frank. John scoured his weekly copy to keep up with all things Bolivar.

While based in Olean and managing his business interests, John Herrick continued writing. With the means to travel extensively, he related his foreign observations in articles published by metropolitan newspapers. And by 1952's close he had penned three books. The first, in 1938, was the slim *Founding a Country Newspaper Fifty Years Ago*, John's reminiscences about starting his Ceres and Bolivar papers but also about local personalities, social customs and entertainments, farm life and business practices. From extensive research and his own experiences, in 1950 he published *Empire Oil*, a history of the petroleum industry in New York State. Last came *Bolivar, New York – Pioneer Oil Town* (1952), demonstrating his enduring fondness for his old hometown. Very few small towns have been honored with such a volume. It describes Bolivar's general history, economic highs and lows, schools and social organizations, notable businesses and noteworthy residents from all walks of life.

At age 83 in 1951, Herrick relocated to Los Angeles. Twice he had become a widower, Nellie (Young) and second wife Margaret (Brown) having predeceased him. The move may partly have been made to be near his namesake son. (John had also fathered two daughters.) His endeavors had brought him substantial wealth and now he would focus more on an activity he had long enjoyed: charitable giving. Some major highlights of the Herricks' philanthropy are these:

• Funding for fourteen full scholarships to Alfred University; contributing $525,000 to build the Herrick Memorial Library; and other major donations to help build other campus structures. (In 1945, Alfred U. bestowed on John an honorary Doctor of Laws degree. He served on its Board of Trustees for three decades).

• The Herricks endowed scholarships at St. Bonaventure U., Pennsylvania State U. (where his extensive collection of historical notes, documents and more is now secured), and the University of Missouri.

• To the Boy Scouts, they gave a donation that built the "Herrick Lodge" at Wolf Creek Scout Camp.

• They also created an endowment underpinning the Olean Association of the Blind, and made a donation used to acquire the parcel where the Olean YMCA was built.

The *Bolivar Breeze* later said of its founder, "He was most happy while giving." Having just turned 93, John Pierce Herrick died in Los Angeles in 1961. After reviewing his life to report in print on his passing, the *Breeze* editor concluded, "Mr. Herrick came to look upon the Bolivar area as his home, even after moving on to Olean and California." John was put to rest just twenty miles short of "home:" his grave is in Olean's Mount View Cemetery, off South Union Street. His newspaper motto of long ago had declared, "All things come to him who hustles." John P. Herrick hustled and much came his way. But best of all, he gave back.

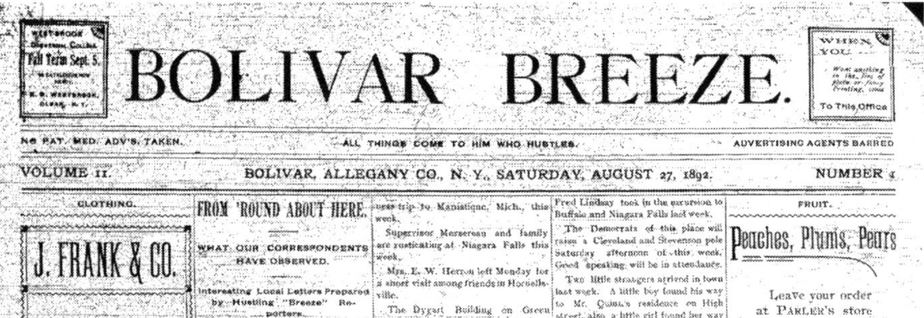

BOLIVAR BREEZE.

NO PAT. MED. ADV'S. TAKEN. — ALL THINGS COME TO HIM WHO HUSTLES. — ADVERTISING AGENTS BARRED

VOLUME II. — BOLIVAR, ALLEGANY CO., N. Y., SATURDAY, AUGUST 27, 1892. — NUMBER 1

CLOTHING.

J. FRANK & CO.

FROM 'ROUND ABOUT HERE.

WHAT OUR CORRESPONDENTS HAVE OBSERVED.

Interesting Local Letters Prepared by Hustling "Breeze" Reporters.

... trip to Manistique, Mich., this week.

Supervisor Mersereau and family are rusticating at Niagara Falls this week.

Mrs. E. W. Herron left Monday for a short visit among friends in Hornellsville.

The Dygert Building on Green ...

Fred Lindsay took in the excursion to Buffalo and Niagara Falls last week.

The Democrats of this place will raise a Cleveland and Stevenson pole Saturday afternoon of this week. Good speaking will be in attendance.

Two little strangers arrived in town last week. A little boy found his way to Mr. Quinn's residence on High street, also a little girl found her way ...

FRUIT.

Peaches, Plums, Pears

Leave your order at PARLER'S store

The masthead of J.P. Herrick's Bolivar Breeze. This issue, of August 27, 1892, is the earliest known, although it began the second year of its publication. With the exception of the first year's issues, and those from August 1912 to July 1913, all issues of the Breeze from 1892 to October 1965, when it ceased publication, can be accessed on line by going to ***nyshistoricnewspapers.org***

School

Austin Cowles was thought to have been Bolivar's first school teacher, who gave his lessons in a little log building between Bolivar and Richburg. In 1828, a new, frame schoolhouse with a bell tower went up on the Wilbur farm on the south side of the village, where it was more centrally located, many of the earliest settlers, such as the Rowley's, Roots, Davies, Cowles and LeSuers, having settled where the valley widened closer to Horse Run. The second teacher was Asa Cowles, who also preached and used the school as his church. His tenure was short, as he died in 1829 at the age of thirty-five.

In 1842, the town elders divided Bolivar into eight school districts, and erected small school buildings in each, the largest being in Bolivar village near the present-day site of the post office. Its first teacher was Rogers Crandall. During those years, the teachers in the various schools usually boarded with one of the families whose children he or she taught.

With the large influx of new people during the boom, the school on Main Street was replaced with a much larger, two-story frame building with seven rooms at the corner of Olean and Kincaid streets. It opened for the fall semester 1882. Stephen Pollard, who had grown up on a farm near Belmont, was hired that year as Bolivar's first principal. His stay in Bolivar was short, but it was probably through his efforts that Bolivar gained the title of having a Union Free School in 1885. He returned to Belmont and lived out his life there, serving for many years as the town clerk. He died in 1926.

Pollard was succeeded by "Professor Blackman," who could not get along with the school trustees, quit, and set up his own school for boys on Liberty Street. Despite this schism, enrollment in the village school grew so quickly that the Olean Street building was enlarged in 1887. There was a rapid turnover in principals in the late 1880s. Pollard was followed first by Blackman, then by professors McCartney and Benedict, before Alexander Glennie arrived in 1891. Glennie's efforts led to Bolivar having its first accredited high school, and its first high school graduating class, in 1893. Glennie left Bolivar in 1897. He was succeeded by a man named McDowell, who lasted only to 1900. His departure resulted in Bolivar doing something revolutionary. The school board hired as Bolivar's next principal Ella Crandall. Born in Alfred in 1866, at the time Ella was thirty-four, held degrees from the normal school at Geneseo and from the University of Chicago, and was a charter member of both the Bolivar Sorosis and the Bolivar Grange. She was the daughter of Alonzo Crandall, a Civil War veteran who had served with the 136th New York, who had the good fortune to have acquired a prime piece of oil property about two miles east of the village. Her tenure as Bolivar's principal was three years, typical of the times, but her departure was probably due in part to economics. Professor Glennie had been paid $1,200 a year. Ella, certainly in part because she was a woman, was paid only $450. She went to work with her father operating the farm and the associated oil lease. She would live in Bolivar until she died in 1934. Ella Crandall is still the only woman to serve as the head of the Bolivar school system.

The 1882 school had been built in a hurry, and like many of the buildings thrown up during the boom, it was cheaply and poorly constructed. By the time Ella Crandall took charge, despite efforts to shore the building up with steel reinforcing rods, people were becoming increasingly concerned about the building's safety. After three years of people about town saying, "we need to do something," someone finally stepped forward and took charge.

That someone was Joshua Dunning. As president of the school board, he searched for an architect, developed a plan of action, and stated as the only constraint that the new school be built for no more than $25,000, (close to $900,000 in twenty-first century currency). Working with him on the project were R.L. Andrus, Louis Seibert, George Wilson, Elmer Garthwait and William J. Brannen.

The old school building was moved off of the corner lot, and construction of the new building began on the northeastern corner of Olean and Kincaid streets. It, "the finest and most modern high school building in Allegany County," opened on December 21, 1905. Designed by J. Mills Platt of Rochester, and built by the firm of Warden & Rail from Dansville, the walls were put up with red brick made at the Hanley factory in Bradford. The window and door trim was of cream-colored terra cotta. The sound proof interior walls were concrete, the floors hard maple, the roof green slate. The interior trim was of Norway spruce, and the twelve-foot ceilings were pressed metal. The building was two stories tall, with a basement, of nearly 24,000 square feet, with a single story 1,400 square foot extension that housed half of a 500 seat auditorium.

A wide central corridor made it easy to move about. A fire drill, the first ever conducted in Bolivar, showed that the building could be emptied in two and a half minutes. Although always called "the high school," the building in fact housed all twelve grades. First through fifth grades were located on the first floor. Kitty McBride's first grade classroom had 48 seats, as did Theresa Davitt's room where she taught second and third. Nellie Hovey's room was slightly smaller, holding forty fourth and fifth graders.

The new building's second story contained a "high school room" that could seat eighty pupils. There was a small laboratory room for chemistry and physics experiments. The principal, Charles D. Hill, served as the high school science teacher. There were two more classrooms seating twenty-four pupils each, used by Florence Graham and Jeanette Deal for courses in English, history, and other upper level courses. At the rear of this floor were four more classrooms. Bessie Wyvell's seventh grade room seated forty. Mary Manchester's room could hold forty-two sixth graders. Christine Pride's "grammar school room" was also set up for forty-two. At opening, a fourth room was left vacant.

The basement ceiling was nine feet tall. The heat plant, made up of eight gas fired hot air furnaces with fans that could exchange the air in four minutes, took up much of that space. Since the loss of the Opera House, which had burned to

The new Bolivar High School opened in 1905

the ground on March 15, 1901, there had been a desire to have another performance hall available. The new school's 500 seat auditorium filled the gap.

Over time, an expanding curriculum pushed the limits of this building too. A homemaking department began, and was set up in the basement, in rooms poorly lit and not well heated. By the late 1920's the second floor, the high school, had become so crowded that the school office had become a class room, the library room was used as a class room, a drawing room, physical director's room, and as the faculty lounge. The lower grades then had close to forty children in each level, more than one teacher could manage, but there were no additional rooms where the classes could be divided.

Bolivar's principal during most of the 1920s was Professor Ray C. Witter, a handsome, athletic man who was popular with the students and faculty alike. Getting his first education in Warsaw, he had graduated from Alfred U., where he was a star fullback on the football team. He left a post in Fillmore for a much better $2,100 salary in Bolivar. He replaced Clifford Grimm, a popular teacher who had accepted a position in Portville. "Chief" Witter oversaw numerous innovations at the school, including the publication of the first yearbook in 1924, which was called the Blizzard. Chief Witter also put in his time as the coach of the football and baseball teams, and taught history.

Witter was a fascinating man. He loved to travel. In the spring of 1923, he accompanied the senior class on a trip to Washington, DC, which included side trips to Mount Vernon, Annapolis, and Philadelphia. He had toured Europe in 1922, and lectured about it and his other travels, which in 1937 included an extensive trip through the Soviet Union. In the summer of 1924, he led a two-month tour through England, France, Belgium, the Netherlands, Germany, Switzerland and Italy.

Between 1905 and the late 1920s, there had been a revolution in transportation. The village streets had been paved, and the major thoroughfares connecting villages were being rapidly converted from dirt to concrete, if they hadn't been already. Gasoline powered busses were available that could quickly transport two dozen or more people at one time. New York State, with these developments in hand, in 1928 began pushing the idea of using busses to consolidate rural, one-room schools, into "central school districts," where all could be offered a uniform, widened and improved course of instruction. And the state put its money where its mouth was, offering big increases in state aid. New York would put up twenty-five percent of the cost of a new building, and half the cost of the busses. Those incentives got people not just thinking, but acting.

A new central school district was proposed that would include all of the towns of Bolivar and Genesee, and part of the town of Clarksville. To make it happen, the idea had to be approved by the voters in the school districts in each town, and there were eight in Bolivar alone. The voting was set up, and most of the districts overwhelmingly approved the formation of the central school. (The Horse Run school remained independent until 1938, when the voters finally decided to close it and send their fifteen pupils to Bolivar. Ceres held out until 1943).

The 1931 Bolivar Central student council. Clarence "Mike" Schaffner stands to the right of Prof. Whitford, who is wearing the bow tie.

As part of the approval process, a new school board was elected. Albert Shaner of Bolivar, who had gone from humble origins to prominence with his oil investments, was chosen as the board president. Charles Chipman, another oil operator and Shaner's neighbor on Wellsville Street, was also elected. Lucien Lewis had a farm in Mead Hollow. Nelson Wightman was a drilling contractor who lived in Kossuth. Mary McDermott had taught in the local system, but by

1928 was busy managing family oil properties. Clair Rigby was a rural mail carrier who also lived up Mead Hollow. The final member of the new board was Lewis Champlin, a drilling contractor who lived on Salt Rising Road in the town of Genesee.

Another man who played an interesting part in the development of the new school was Harley Loop. Harley, a World War veteran, was Bolivar's furniture dealer, undertaker, and resident socialist. He had the idea that the district should be able to assess and tax the oil and gas revenue which was mushrooming as water flooding was becoming widespread, and he took that idea to Albany, arguing that the hydrocarbons were part of the real estate, and that local governments should be able to assess and tax the same. He won the argument, and the law was changed to allow oil and gas production to be assessed on local tax rolls. The projected revenue allowed the new board to think big, without worrying about increasing the taxes levied on the average homeowners in the area. (For comparison, in 1933, the Cuba School district had properties with a total assessed value of $1,500,000, Portville $1,000,000. Bolivar? $8,250,000).

Prof. J.F. Whitford

A $650,000 project was proposed, about $12,000,000 today, a new big building, with both a dedicated gymnasium and auditorium, situated on twelve acres that could be developed into athletic fields. It would be built on the race track property, an easy sell since the track had been little used when horses gave way to autos. After an expansion project completed in 1939, the new school building contained eighty-four rooms, a gymnasium, auditorium, a music room, metal and wood shops, a homemaking room, and two cafeterias.

Making such a big change to the system begged the question, should there also be a change of administration to run this new central school district? We don't know exactly what happened. Perhaps Chief Witter saw this as a great opportunity to look for a fresh pasture for himself. Perhaps the new school board didn't think he was up to the job. Whatever the reason, Principal Ray Witter moved on, taking the post of principal in Salamanca, and the search for a proper leader for the new district began.

They hired John Ferris Whitford, the head of the Milton College department of education. Milton College was a small school in Wisconsin, which had a renowned music department. Whitford had been raised on a farm near Friendship, but had gotten his teaching education, worked in the Buffalo area, then in

It was all new in 1930, the school, the busses, the uniforms for the drivers. Even School Street was brand new.

1923 had headed to Wisconsin, where he became the dean of the education department. When they came to Bolivar, the Whitfords rented a house at 123 Friendship St. (Their home was two doors away from that of Belle Streeter, on the northwest corner of Friendship and Davis streets. Mrs. Streeter had a parrot that whistled at and conversed with students as they came down Friendship Street after school; it was a big star for decades).

Prof. Whitford, as he was most commonly called, wanted to find an avenue to put Bolivar Central School on the map, drawing attention from around the area, and he decided, logically enough based on his experience at Milton, to do it with music. What the new school needed in Prof. Whitford's estimation was a really good band; and to have that the school needed a really good band leader. Shortly after his arrival, J.F. found Umberto Clavelli.

In early 1935, Whitford enrolled BCS in the National Spelling Bee. One of the events in school at that time were "posture marches" for the grade school, and Whitford served as one of the judges. In 1936, he was the main speaker at the first Supervisory District Teacher's Association convention, which was held in Fillmore. He spoke on "The Teacher's Job in 1936." He was sought after, speaking more than once to the Shinglehouse PTA, the Richburg Literary Society, and to the Olean Kiwanis. He was active in the Masons, in 1937 being in charge of the "degree team," which went to other lodges to show them how it was done. He spent the summer of 1937 on an extended trip through "the Gulf States" and on to Yellowstone.

The booming economy, supported by the drilling of thousands of new wells to water flood the oil field, had the happy consequence of the student body outgrowing the new building less than a decade after it was built. The original building had been made in the shape of a L. With the help of WPA funds from the government, a new wing, of three stories including the basement level, was added to the south side of the building, turning it into a symmetrical U.

Part of the expansion was to accommodate a popular agriculture program, and Whitford was awarded an honorary FFA degree at the annual awards banquet of six participating schools held in the BCS gym, an obvious nod to his support of the program.

The expansion came none too soon. In September 1939, the announcement was made that Bolivar Central had the largest registration in its history with 811 pupils, 366 in grades seven through twelve, (which included twenty-five post-graduates), and 455 in the grades. The two largest classes were the junior class (Class of '41) with sixty-five, and sixty-six in kindergarten, an overall increase of twenty over the year prior. Kindergarten had been made possible by the construction of the new school building, and had not existed before it was built. That same year, Richburg's enrollment jumped from 352 to 425.

In the middle of October 1939, John Babcock of Ceres was diagnosed with polio, and other cases had cropped up in Belmont, Bradford and Olean. Whitford decided to ban children from Ceres from the school for the last three school days of that school week. At the time, there was still a grade school operating in Ceres, and it too closed. (The Ceres School did not join the Bolivar Central district until after World War Two). In 1943, Whitford received a letter of commendation from the state department of education for the development in Bolivar of a course in pre-flight mathematics taught by Dean Thompson, which was approved for credit, being "of value to students who are soon to enter the armed services."

He presided at the 1945 graduation. The graduation speaker was Lt. Governor Joe R. Hanley, who served in that office from 1943 to 1950. And with that, the professor decided to change course. He took a position as Milton College's personnel director, and lived another twenty years, passing away in December 1965. An inspection of Bolivar's school just before he left placed the Bolivar Central School in the top five percent of all schools in the state.

Our Music Man

Umberto Clavelli

The man who would fulfill Prof. Whitford's dream of creating a great band for Bolivar Central School arrived in the United States in 1906. Umberto Clavelli was born in Ancona, on Italy's Adriatic coast, on July 7, 1883. At the age of eighteen, he became a bandmaster at an Italian military school in Naples. Three years later he became a musician with a traveling band. He stayed with it two years, then decided to seek his fortune in America, bringing with him his deep and genuine enthusiasm for music and marching bands. He arrived in New York City, stayed there for eighteen months, "struggling to keep alive," and working hard to learn English.

In 1909, he heard there were jobs available doing railroad construction in western New York. He came to Hinsdale, where an overhead bridge was being built north of Olean. Hearing about his background, the foreman hired him to play his mandolin and sing to the work crew. His job paid so little that three months later he took a job on a dairy farm, where he learned to milk, plow and drag. The couple he lived with suggested he head to the Ontario Knife Factory in Franklinville, and there he landed a position as a blacksmith and worked his way up to edger. But, his heart remained in his music. Whereas many factories in the area fielded baseball teams, in 1912 Umberto decided to start a company band, and it quickly earned a reputation as a first-class outfit. In his spare time he led a community effort to organize a drum corps, and in 1926 he put together a school band for Franklinville. For two summers, he directed a boys band in Arcade.

Clavelli's possible career as a school band instructor was limited by the fact that he had no teaching credentials. But Principal Whitford saw in Umberto exactly the sort of man he wanted, and he had a solution to the credentials problem. He offered Clavelli the job of bandmaster, selling the school board on the idea that the school's bandmaster could appear on the payroll as a custodian. Knowing he was being offered the chance he had always hoped for, Umberto Clavelli arrived in Bolivar in August 1930, telling Prof. Whitford that he would produce a prize-winning band within the year. Initially only eight students signed up, but Clavelli's kind, enthusiastic and encouraging manner quickly attracted students to his side. The following spring, the BCS band took first place in Class D at the Western Zone Music Festival, and won a $75 first prize at an event in Jamestown. During the March 1932 Bolivar PTA meeting, he unveiled his new twenty-four piece madolin-guitar-banjo orchestra, the third large musical group he had created during that school year, the others being the junior and senior high school bands.

In 1933, the Senior band grew to include forty-seven musicians. They appeared at the County Firemen's Convention in Cuba, and took second place at the Ellicottville homecoming parade, losing to Jamestown's eighty-member group. Clavelli worked on the bands and the performers seven days a week. A letter sent to the Bolivar Breeze in 1936 by Bolivar grad Dick Jordan explained much of Clavelli's success: "I wish I were still playing in your band because we had so much fun playing in it." C.J. Hughes wrote, "no matter how far I get in music, I'll never forget your very kind patience and generosity in teaching me what I know." So many alumni felt that way forty of them formed a community band. It was managed by Dana Williams, but Umberto Clavelli was the "musical director."

Although the students enthusiastically supported the band, the same was not always true of the school board. There was a time, probably not long after Clavelli's arrival, that the board balked at buying the band new uniforms, which Clavelli thought were sorely needed. To make his point to the community, at a school concert he had the band appear dressed in burlap bags. Most in the audience laughed at the prank, and the band got their new uniforms.

Student appreciation of the band master was best expressed when the 1937-38 Gusher was dedicated to him. At the 1938 annual concert, a 4th and 5th grade drum and trumpet corps, a middle school band, the Senior Band, and a trumpet trio, (made up of Gene Salzer, James Wasson, and Karl Thomas), all performed, all of them taught and led by Umberto Clavelli. Seven of those students had qualified for the state competition as soloists.

That summer, Umberto volunteered to lead the Junior, Senior and Community bands, with two rehearsals a week for the each of the school bands and one for the community band. He also offered to give free lessons to any BCS student or graduate, beginner or advanced. He found a way to supply instruments to those who needed them. He led these bands at weekly public concerts, often held on the grounds of the old school on Olean Street, the three bands taking turns. Marching while playing was often practiced on Friendship Street, where the traffic was light. Mary Ingalls Briggs said that Clavelli had the patience of a saint. It was this selfless devotion which spurred so many to put in the practice required to master their instruments and the compositions he asked them to play, which ranged from marches to operatic overtures to more popular tunes, so that the bands themselves functioned at the highest level.

In the spring of 1939, the band included fifty-one members. The district music festival of 1939 was held in Olean. The trumpet trio stayed together, and Alyn Shaner, Richard Barnes, James Shaner and Floyd Neely formed a saxophone quartet for the competition, (which had already been selected to appear during the choral concert portion of the event). Daniel Dempsey, Gerald Hulbert, James Reeland, Kenneth Root, Bruce Maxson, Keith Jordan, and Thomas Ackerman formed a brass sextet. The band placed first of seventeen at the Snyder Music Festival, which qualified them to appear at a national festival to be held in New York City May 25-27. They left Bolivar on Thursday, May 23, after a pep rally led by Bolivar's cheerleaders, escorted to the Erie train station in Wellsville by street commissioner Sam Ryan on his motorcycle. They pulled into Jersey City at 12:30 a.m. on the 24th, and were bussed to the Imperial Hotel at the corner of Broadway and 32nd Street.

The Imperial Hotel

The 24th was a free day. As a group, the band, chaperones, and a few parents were given a morning tour of the New York World's Fair. In the afternoon, some returned to Manhattan to shop and sightsee, while others spent the entire day taking in the sights to be seen at the fair. Saturday was competition day, and everyone was at their best. The band received a rating of 1, the best you could get, and as a result was the only Class C school band asked to perform as part of a massed-bands concert at the Court of Nations at the World's Fair itself. But, they were not given the chance to celebrate after appearing at the fair. Instead, they caught an 8 o'clock evening train and pulled into Wellsville at 5:30 Sunday morning. Clavelli himself sent a letter to the Bolivar Breeze, in which he expressed his "heartfelt thanks" to the people of Bolivar for the treats showered on the band members before they left and after they returned, and thanking them also for the "great spirit" the people of Bolivar had demonstrated in supporting his efforts. All true, but that spirit had been fanned by the hard work and leadership of Umberto Clavelli.

During the summer, the Olean Oilers baseball team held a "Bolivar-Richburg" night at Bradner Stadium, with an appearance by Larry McPhail, president of the Brooklyn Dodgers, and the Bolivar community band led the parade, and Umberto led the band. The Community Band made seven appearances that summer and won prizes five times. The Senior Band brought home a trophy from the Erie County Fair. In recognition of the accomplishments of the Bolivar school's instrumental music program, the Fifteenth Annual Southwestern New York School Competitive Music Festival was held in the Bolivar Central School Auditorium on April 11 and 12, 1940.

In organizing the event, Clavelli was assisted by Doris Bain, the newly arrived music director who had charge of a sixty member chorus. Both the band and chorus qualified for the state competition held in Canandaigua, where the band scored a 2 rating, and the chorus a 1, meaning both qualified for the National School Music Festival to be held in Albany in mid-May. Told that competing in Albany might not happen unless they could raise most of the money needed, parents went out and raised $500 in donations, students sold trinkets that brought in another $120, and a well-attended fundraising concert topped off the effort, with the school board agreeing to put up the small balance needed to make it happen. At states, the a cappella choir scored a 2, and the band a 3. That summer, the members of the Senior Band voted to put on a series of evening concerts on the old school lot, Clavelli never giving up his hope that a bandstand might someday be built there,

In 1940, the band again appeared at the Erie County Fair. Parents provided the transportation, and in return were given free admission. The band and a cappella choir again qualified for the state competition, the choir with a II+ rating, and the band a I-, the highest given any class C school. Robert Whitford qualified as a soloist both as a tenor, and as a piccolo player. That year, the Southwestern New York School Competitive Music Festival was held in Bolivar. Both band and choir qualified again for the national competition to be held in Albany, after attending the state music festival in Canandaigua. Needing funds to make the trip, a concert was scheduled for May 9. As usual, the money came together, part of it coming from Sam Gandel who gave a special showing of *Mr. Smith Goes to Washington* at the Lyric, and the 60-member band headed to Albany in two chartered busses. The band included many enterprising members who would take the chance on these trips to have some fun. Bruce Maxson would pack his instrument case with bottles of elixir, and would board the bus first to have privacy in the back seat. In Albany, flute-player George Ninos donned a cape and ran around the hotel roof. That year, the junior a cappella choir, with ninety-two members, went to Houghton to compete. During the summer of 1940, the senior band again gave a series of evening concerts at the old school lot on Olean St. The Community Band, now the official musical organization of the Bolivar Fire Department, won the prize as best band in the convention parade held in Belmont.

In the spring of 1941 the band and choir were again off to the State competitions, that year held in Jamestown. Then winter and the war came. With the war came gasoline rationing, and rationing put an end to traveling competition for the high school's musicians. The Clavelli's son, Dean, went into the Army.

There was one poignant mention of the band, when it performed for a service at Maple Lawn Cemetery on Memorial Day 1943. Thus far, four Bolivar boys had died the war. Seven more were leaving that week to be inducted, five of them headed for the Navy. *Destination Tokyo* was playing at the Lyric. The band opened the service by playing, "Abide With Me," and a vocal quartet closed it by singing "Tenting Tonight."

All through his tenure, Umberto's champion had been Prof. Whitford. But Whitford too was aging, and had passed the retirement milestone of sixty-five in 1943. He remained on the job until the war ended, then went back where he had come from. After the 1945 school year, he and his wife packed up and returned to Milton, Wisconsin, where he enjoyed nearly twenty years of retirement, passing from this life on December 5, 1965.

Umberto plugged along for seven more years. The musicians he trained in the 1930s were his biggest fans. When the servicemen returned, they jumped at the chance to form the Bolivar Veterans Band, and asked him to be their leader, which of course he did. And the Veteran's Band, who had Dan Dempsey as its first president, won more prizes. They put on their first public performance on June 19, 1946. That July, more than 1,000 people showed up for an open air concert, which they put on as the start of a multi-year fund-raising effort to buy uniforms. They played in firemen's parades and before ball games in Olean and in Wellsville. In the fall of 1946, the Clavellis personally put on a spaghetti dinner at the Legion hall on Friendship Street, which Mrs. Clavelli cooked, for the thirty-two band members, their wives and dates. For the Clavellis, it was a big family gathering.

The Veterans won more prizes during the summers of 1947, 1948, 1949 and 1950. But the school concluded that Umberto needed help. In 1947, they brought on board Orven Hess, a Houghton College graduate, one of a couple of faculty members Bolivar shared with Richburg. Hess became responsible for orchestra and junior high instrumental music programs, while Mr. Clavelli continued in his role of band master. During the 1948-49 academic year, the New York State School Music Festival returned to the Bolivar auditorium. But little was heard about the high school band as the 1940s drew to a close.

In 1950, the Genesee Country Music Festival came to Bolivar. The first day was for choral groups, led off by Yolanda Questa's all girl chorus. The second day was band day. Umberto Clavelli took up his baton and led the Bolivar High School band through three numbers to start the day-long program, and he ended it by leading a 600 member massed band on the school lawn that evening.

He stayed with the school, and in his position until 1953. That year, his second and youngest child, Anita, graduated from high school, and Umberto reached the age of sixty-five, meaning he could collect Social Security and retire. In October, they sold their home and moved to Washington DC, near where their son was then stationed, and where their daughter was continuing her education, and lived out their lives in sight of the capital of their adopted country. The bandmaster passed away ten years later, on November 3, 1963.

In the summer of 1954, Bolivar's new band instructor, Dick Sailor, issued a call to the veterans to come out again to be the core of a community band. They did, and the Veteran's Band played one more time for a ball game at Tullar Field in Wellsville, and were never heard from again. Umberto Clavelli had been there for them; and they had been there for the bandmaster, Bolivar's Music Man.

The Bolivar Veterans' Band at Bradner Stadium, Olean.
Mr. Clavelli is seated in the lower left.

Richard Dougherty

The Whitford Era produced two more Bolivar-raised personalities who appeared on the national stage, again in very different fields of endeavor. The oldest was a member of Bolivar Central's Class of 1939. That class contained a number of members who would become familiar faces to me and those of my generation. Ralph Best, Bob Buell, Jack Cooper, Dan Dempsey, Dutch Dunning, Bill Nagle and Fran Paffie were all '39ers.

Richard Dougherty in 1962

And so was Anthony Dougherty. His full name was Richard Anthony, called Anthony or Tony during his Bolivar years in honor of his grandfather, the first Anthony. The first Anthony Dougherty, born in Ireland before the Civil War, was the father of ball-player Patsy, and of John P. Dougherty, six years Patsy's junior. John P. worked in the local oil field as a driller. He, his wife Elizabeth, daughters Elizabeth and Maureen, and sons John and Richard lived together on Olean Street.

In the 1939 Gusher, the editors said this about "Tony"- *"In spite of his 'devil-may-care' attitude, Tony possesses a brilliant mind and the ability to offer a decision worthy of mature judgement when sought."* Such attributes made him indispensable to his senior class. Soon after graduation, Anthony left Bolivar and his "Tony" nickname behind, making his way in the world as Richard Dougherty. The war drew him into the Army Air Force where he made sergeant, serving with the 57th Fighter Group through North Africa, Sicily, and Italy. He returned to the states in August 1945, enrolled in the Columbia University School of Journalism, and graduated from it in 1948.

He landed a job as a New York City deputy police commissioner and was given public relations assignments. That led to a position with the *New York Herald Tribune,* first as a city hall reporter, then as their Washington political correspondent. In his spare time, he spun out five novels. The most successful of those was *The Commissioner,* which served as the basis for the movie and subsequent television series, *Madigan*, starring Richard Widmark.

When the *Herald Tribune* went out of business in 1966, Dougherty became the New York bureau chief for the *Los Angeles Times.* He covered and wrote on many important events, including the assassination of Robert F. Kennedy, the administration of New York's Mayor John Lindsay, the Apollo moon landing, and the presidential campaign of Nelson Rockefeller in 1968. In 1971, he left that position to become press secretary for George McGovern, a position he held throughout McGovern's presidential run in 1971 and 1972. (It may be just coincidence, but his grandmother's maiden name was McGovern).

In 1974, Dougherty became a vice-president of the Metropolitan Museum of Art, where he was involved with fund raising, public relations and membership. During his tenure, the museum's membership more than doubled. Among his outside interests was croquet, and he was a member of the New York Croquet Club, which held its matches in Central Park, where he competed in the 1980 national championships. He was remembered as "an urbane, witty journalist, who wrote with insight, style and humor," and as "outrageously charming, funny, outspoken, and so often right." Married twice, he had one daughter, Elizabeth. He died of cancer in 1986.

Herbert MacDonell

The other Whitford graduate who went far was a member of the Class of 1945. Margaret "Mugsy" Sherwood was the valedictorian of that class, a class that included future Mayor Buzz Dunn, Betty Ferris, Buck Reeland, and Pru Kuhn, the wife of future principal George Kuhn. It also included a kid who had skipped a grade: Herbert Leon "Bud" MacDonell. Herb was a science prodigy who spent as much time in the family's basement with his chemistry set as he probably did anywhere else.

He was born July 23, 1928, and after high school headed to Alfred University where he received a degree in chemistry in 1950. His unique abilities had caught the attention of Prof. Whitford, and it is likely that this connection landed him a job as professor of chemistry at Whitford's Milton College in Milton, Wisconsin nearly as soon as he received his undergraduate degree, starting at Milton in 1951. Herbert remained in Milton for three years, then decided to seek an advanced degree. He gained a master's degree in analytical chemistry from the University of Rhode Island in 1956.

Even as a boy, Herb was fascinated with crimes and criminology. He was a fan of both Charlie Chan and Sherlock Holmes, and of Perry Mason. He carried out innumerable experiments in the family basement, and played often with homemade explosives. There was a tree on the bank of the creek near the school that served as a gathering place for students sneaking a smoke. One day Herb decided to surprise the smokers, planting one of his bombs at the base of the tree. When he set it off, he not only surprised the smokers, but toppled the tree into the creek.

Herbert & wife Phyllis MacDonell in front of the McDonell home at the corner of Shaner Ave. and Plum Street, 1940s

On another occasion, he decided to show Bolivar the power of "atomic weaponry." Up on Shaner Hill, he buried a five gallon oil can up to the lid, which was removed, filled the can with gasoline, set the surface of it on fire, and tossed in a cherry bomb. The result was a glowing red mushroom cloud a hundred feet high. Anytime there was a BANG heard around town in the late 1940s, there were two quick explanations- a nitroglycerin magazine had exploded, or "Bud" MacDonell had touched off another of his bombs.

His first deliberate attempt at mystery solving was in the fall of 1949, when a rumor spread around town that his father, Town Supervisor Leon, had hung himself, after having embezzled some town funds. Herb was told about this rumor by his father. It was an election year, and Democrat Leon was running yet again for town supervisor. Through methodical questioning of people around town about where they had heard the rumor, it became obvious that its original source was the town's Republican chairman, attorney A.J. Matson, whom Herbert confronted. Leon was reelected handily.

MacDonell's contributions to the discipline of forensic science include his invention of the MAGNA Brush in 1960. This device, which used carbon dust covered iron filings dragged around with a magnet to highlight fingerprints, revolutionized crime scene investigation by allowing the detection of latent fingerprints on surfaces that before had not easily yielded such evidence to investigators. Manufactured at the MAGNA Brush "Factory" on Friendship Street in Bolivar for many years, MAGNA brushes are still used by police agencies around the world.

In 1963 MacDonell was the first expert witness to get the Breathalyzer accepted in a New York State County Court. (Later in his career he was also accepted as an expert on drinking beer!) In 1964 he became a Fellow in the American Academy of Forensic Science. He founded the Bloodstain Evidence Institute in 1973, and through 2011 conducted seventy-six educational programs for over two thousand law enforcement professionals, attorneys, and students from thirty-one countries.

Under the auspices of a grant from the United States Department of Justice in 1971, he published his research in bloodstain pattern interpretation in a booklet entitled, "Flight Characteristics and Stain Patterns of Human Blood." This work was the forerunner of many follow-up textbooks and led the way in what is now recognized as a significant forensic discipline.

In 1983 Herbert founded the International Association of Bloodstain Pattern Analysts, a professional forensic organization which today has over one thousand members around the world. He was a recognized expert in not only bloodstain evidence, but also firearms identification, ballistics, and fingerprint identification. His testimony as an expert was accepted in courts throughout the United States and in many other countries including Canada, Australia, New Zealand, Germany, the Netherlands, Italy, and the United Kingdom, among others.

In a career spanning over 60 years as a professor, forensic scientist, and expert witness, Herbert MacDonell taught and inspired hundreds of students and consulted on hundreds of criminal cases locally, nationally, internationally and testified in innumerable courtrooms.

Some of those cases were widely-known and notorious. He testified at the trials James Earl Ray for the assassination of Martin Luther King Jr. and of Sirhan Sirhan for shooting Robert F. Kennedy in 1968, at the Chicago Black Panther case in 1969, the Jean Harris-Scarsdale Diet Doctor murder case in 1980, and, in the "trial of the century," of O.J. Simpson for the murders of Nicole Simpson and Ron Goldman, in 1995.

MacDonell prided himself on objectivity and the application of the scientific principles of chemistry, biology, and physics. He was retained by both prosecutors and defense lawyers. He did not pick sides. He had no interest in motives, or in emotional pleas for or against a defendant. He was interested in the scientific analysis of the evidence found at a crime scene, in the truth as revealed by the application of the scientific principals discovered through his research and experience. MacDonell's philosophy and ethos is best captured in the introduction to his 1984 book, *The Evidence Never Lies*, co-authored by Alfred Allan Lewis:

"You can lead a jury to the truth, but you can't make them believe it. Physical Evidence cannot be intimidated. It does not forget. It does not get excited at the moment something is happening – like people do. It sits there and waits to be detected, preserved, evaluated, and explained. This is what physical evidence is all about. In the course of a trial, defense and prosecuting attorneys may lie, witnesses may lie, the defendant certainly may lie. Even the judge may lie. Only the evidence never lies.

Dr. Myrtle Collins Dineen
BCS Class of 1933

There is one more standout student of the Whitford era who should be remembered. She never got so far as the national stage, but she certainly stood out far above the crowd in her time. Playing saxophone for Mr. Clavelli, Myrtle Collins graduated with the class of 1933 as its salutatorian. But when she took the state regents examination she scored the highest of anyone in western New York, and with that landed a full scholarship to the University of Rochester. She did not let up there, graduating in 1937 Phi Beta Kappa, and left for Ann Arbor and the University of Michigan School of Medicine, where she became secretary of her graduating class.

Her medical career began at the Mount Morris Tuberculosis Hospital. Next, she taught clinical laboratory science at Alfred State College and then did her internship at Philadelphia General. Her formal training completed, she was hired as a staff physician at Kent State University. In 1955, she became the first woman to be appointed as the physician for the Kent, Ohio public school system, and was appointed the university's physician in 1958. She was the assistant director of their health system from 1962 to 1966. Perhaps we know little of her because she died at the age of fifty-three, in 1968. Married and divorced, she was the mother of three. Women becoming doctors in the 1930s were rare. Myrtle Collins was one of those who bucked the odds and the system, and made the most of the time she had here. (At least four other Bolivar Central graduates from this era headed to medical school: the Ciampa brothers, George Ninos, and Bill Hughes).

A Second Coming

The mania for automobiles brought with it a demand for vastly improved roads. Above is a shot of the work crew charged with paving Main Street in 1914. The flood of new automobiles created an enormous demand for gasoline, and for the petroleum from which it was made. Crude prices climbed, and local producers began looking for ways to get more of it out of the ground.

As previously mentioned, from 1882 on, oil and gas production in the Allegany field very steadily declined, despite the fact that more and more wells were drilled. The use of one-lunger engines and central powerhouses helped keep the pumping of wells economically profitable, but there was a second factor which helped even more: the coming of the automobile. In 1900, about 8,000 cars were owned in the United States. In 1920, there were more than 9,000,000. The demand for gasoline grew a thousand fold in just twenty years, and as a result, despite significant discoveries, the price of crude oil steady climbed. In 1900, the average price was $1.19; in 1920, despite the discovery of many major fields in Oklahoma and Texas, the price per barrel had climbed to $3.07, and the US Geological Survey predicted that the United States would run out of oil by 1930. The hunt was on.

The history of the oil business has been consistent. There are a relatively few periods where demand exceeds supply and the price of oil goes up, sometimes dramatically. These periods are followed by prolonged periods of oversupply, and the price falls or remains stagnant. The second decade of the twentieth century was one of those times when demand got ahead of supply. For local produc-

The interior of a pressure plant. To the left are two sand filters. It was essential that the water pumped into the oil-bearing formations be as clean and pure as possible, so as not to fill and close off the tiny pores in the rock with impurities. To the right is a pump. Small plants might have but one. The largest pressure plant in the area, near Allentown, housed seventeen. Although engineering opinions varied, most producers pushed the water into the oil sand at pressures exceeding 1,000 pounds.

ers, it was known that the vast majority of oil in the ground under Allegany County when the Richburg well came in was still there. Modern estimates are that only about seven percent of the oil originally in place was recovered before 1917. So, the question became, how can we get more of it out?

Many small oil producers in the area at the time had noticed something. If the tubing and casing were pulled from an old well, or if the casing of an old oil well developed a leak that allowed ground water to flow into the well, oil production at nearby active wells would show a modest increase. A man who took full notice of this phenomenon was Forest Dorn. Forest was the son of a Bradford, Pennsylvania oil producer. In 1916, when he was twenty-five, he came to Bolivar with a proposal. He was forming a new company, The Forest Oil Company, which would use scientific engineering methods to build on the observations of the old producers, and use water to recover more oil.

In return for a one-third interest in his new company, he picked up two prime pieces of real estate; the five-hundred thirty acres controlled by the July Oil Company, which included the three-hundred acre Reed Farm across Dean's flats, and an adjoining thirty-eight acre property owned by A.C. Smyth. On these properties were more than 190 wells. Dorn immediately set up a "circle flood," letting water flow down a series of wells in a roughly circular pattern around a central producing oil well. He achieved modest results, but he faced a substantial obstacle. It was illegal to pump water into oil bearing formations. After two years of lobbying, on April 17, 1919, New York State legalized the water flooding of oil bearing formations. The difference water flooding would make to local fortunes was seriously underestimated.

1919 came in with a bang in other ways. A powerful squall line passed through the area on June 16. Lightning set oil stock tanks on fire in both Olean and Bolivar, hit the McMillan home on Olean Street, killed a cow owned by Walter Bliss, and killed a man in Black Creek. Late in the year, returning veterans organized Bolivar's Kenyon Andrus Post of the American Legion. In 1920, the village elders decided to build a new village hall, and the search committee, headed by W.J. Hogan, decided to place it at the corner of Olean and Main Streets, on the site of the Clark House which had burned in 1915.

Meanwhile, Forest Dorn was busy thinking and experimenting. In 1921, the Forest Oil Company began a "line flood," drilling twenty-six new water-injection wells in a long row on the Reed Farm. In the process, one of those wells turned out to be a dry hole, completely surrounded by producing wells. Another of the line wells encountered 177 feet of oil sand, the top eighty-seven feet saturated with oil, the bottom ninety feet having the appearance of bituminous coal. It being the thickest section of the Richburg Third Sand even encountered, the well was shot with nitroglycerin and started out producing 125 barrels a day. During the boom in 1882, another well drilled on the Reed farm had encountered sixty feet of sand and had started off at 400 barrels a day.

John Casey's team of Percheron horses, here near the top of Belmont Street, moved tons of equipment around the oil field, alongside others using trucks.

As production from these properties increased, the profits were reinvested in acquiring additional acreage, and in additional experiments with water flooding techniques. In 1928 the engineers concluded that a "five spot" pattern was the most effective and cost efficient. Four water injection wells were drilled on the corners of a square, and a fifth producing well was drilled in the center. From that date to September 1944, Forest Oil recovered more than 4,000,000 barrels of oil from its Allegany County leases, at which point in time it sold the leases to Quaker State.

The distance between the wells drilled was a function of how porous and permeable the oil sands were. The Richburg sand is considered a "tight sand," with an average porosity of fifteen percent or less. As a result, the wells on the corners of a five-spot were only 240 feet apart, meaning that five wells would be drilled on just 1.3 acres of land. To develop the original 568 acres Forest Oil owned around Bolivar required the drilling of more than 430 wells. There were 60,000 acres of oil production around the southern tier, most of it suitable for water flooding.

What this meant for Bolivar was that there were jobs available everywhere you looked. The placement of all these wells required the services of surveyors and their helpers, to map the leases, set the stakes marking well locations, and establishing the boundary lines. Engineers were needed to study the progress of wells, map the oil formations, compute and project production. Road builders came in to bulldoze trails through the woods, clear rights of way for water and oil lines, and to clear and level locations on which to erect rigs. Teamsters, draymen, and truck drivers were needed to move rigs, deliver pipe and tankage. Standard drilling rigs required rig builders, and all drilling rigs needed drillers, tool dressers and roustabouts to make hole. Completed wells created the need for pumpers, roustabouts, electricians, mechanics, welders, and carpenters to build pressure plants, powerhouses, tool sheds and garages to keep the leases operating, and gaugers to keep track of how much oil was being sold from each property. Office staff was needed to account for all of the oil and gas sold, make sure it was paid for, to make out the payroll, pay the taxes, procure and pay for the equipment and supplies.

Lawyers were needed to prepare lease agreements, handle property transfers, and to resolve disputes. Abstractors were required to trace the titles to the properties and the mineral interests beneath them. In the 1930s, Bolivar had four attorneys: Albert J. Matson, and the Bliss firm of Walter T., whose encyclopedic memory was a great asset when tracking down owners of mineral interests, and his sons Chester and George.

People socialized. Bolivar had two billiard parlors, Sandy Wertman's next to the State Bank, and Irv Swarthout's, in the Odd Fellows Hall. There were three barber shops, one owned by Dick Guise, a second by Leland "Squeak" Dickerson, who usually had another barber in the shop, and another in the Bolivar Hotel, last operated in the 1950s by Louis Schiralli before he bought a building of his own. People could afford to eat out, and workers on the road looked for a hot breakfast and lunch. Meals could be obtained at the Hotel, at the Washington Restaurant, operated by the Ninos family, or the Sugar Bowl, operated by the

A young Irv Swarthout stands behind the counter of his pool room, about 1924 in the Odd Fellows Hall. Generations played there.

Cretekos clan, both Greek immigrants, and after 1940 at Maxson's Lunch Room, better known as Marie's, or at the Walker's Diner, at Elliotts next to the Hotel, and at the Main Street Restaurant on Main across from South Street, where smart alecks who pestered the waitress, Edie Greene, got back as good as they gave.

One of the busiest lunch counters was located in Allentown. Mildred's was a famous gathering place, especially for those who made daily runs to oil well supply stores to pick up the valves and pipe fittings constantly in demand. Mildred's pies were well known and well liked. When asked what kinds were available, she was famous for replying, "peach and apple." Some would order peach, others apple, only to find out there was only one pie, which was a mix of peaches and apples.

All this activity created a demand for vehicles that could move through mud, and mechanics to keep them running. Over time, Bolivar supported car dealers selling Fords, Chevrolets, Pontiacs, Jewetts, Marmons, Marquettes, Buicks, Overlands, Chryslers and Nashes. Four service stations sold gasoline and performed oil changes, did lube jobs, changed tires, and performed other routine maintenance. There were two pharmacies, four groceries, two banks, Dillie's men's clothing store, two dress shops, and Fagouris for clothes and shoes. There were beauticians ready to style ladies' hair and to do your nails. Between 1920, when 3,125 people called Bolivar home, and 1930, 1,413 people moved in, swelling the population by forty-two percent, to the highest point it would ever reach of 4,538 residents in 1930. Dozens of new homes were built. The student population swelled, bringing about the construction of the new central school. (Population numbers add together the town and the village censuses).

A "double-header" of two steam locomotives pushes a line of cars up the grade across Dean's Flats towards Richburg and the horseshoe bend at Cadytown, during the heyday of steam in the early 1900s. Bolivar would enjoy rail freight service for a little more than forty years, ending after World War II. Passenger service ended in the 1930s.

New homes going up on Plum Street circa 1930

Putting the Boom in Boomtown

Since the 1860s, oil and gas wells were routinely "shot," a tube full of nitroglycerin exploded at the level of the oil or gas formation, which would make a cavity under the earth, and expand the surface drainage area for oil or gas to flow into the well. The technique usually dramatically increased the flows, and quickly paid for the effort. But nitroglycerin was powerful, notoriously unpredictable, and dangerous to handle, and thus the lives of shooters could be tense, to say the least. A trick often played on neophytes was to dip a needle or nail in the nitro, lay it on a tree stump, then challenge someone to hit it with a sledge hammer. The challenge was to hang on to the sledge after the strike had been made. Few could.

The first Bolivar shooter to lose his life to a nitroglycerin explosion was Lorenzo Garthwait on October 14, 1881. He had a job working for the Roberts Torpedo Company, and was killed in an accident near Duke Center. (Roberts had patented the method of lowering an explosive charge into a well and setting it off). Lorenzo's death did nothing to get the Garthwaits out of the shooting business. They would still be shooting wells in the 1930s. Three months after Lorenzo died, Charles Berridge, "an exemplary young man" of twenty-six, shot a well on the Root farm, near Richburg. He returned to the company magazine, and while there a pile of recently used, empty cans exploded, "turning Berridge to atoms and mangling his team."

Two months after that, on March 1, 1882, John Grant, an experienced shooter, and William Orcutt, new and wanting to learn the business, took one hundred pounds of nitro from Roberts' Bolivar magazine to shoot a well on Lot 48, not far from Richburg. They arrived at the well only to be told that a decision had been made to postpone the shooting. Grant and Orcutt turned around, heading back to the magazine. When they were quite close to home, something touched off the load, killing both Grant and Orcutt, and knocking down the magazine building-but not touching off the 2,400 pounds of nitroglycerin inside.

The shooters became more careful, and there wasn't another report of a glycerin explosion for fifteen years, when a magazine outside Wellsville blew up, killing no one but breaking $2,000 worth of windows and lights along Wellsville's Main Street. Just a a week later, 300 quarts in a magazine near Orchard Park went up, killing two. Two weeks after that, an "expert well-shooter" named Henry Young, of Bolivar, was "blown to atoms" when several hundred pounds of the stuff ignited, again outside Wellsville. "Shooter, team, wagon and magazine disappeared in a cloud of smoke." All three of these events occurred in the month of March, and it appeared that most of these unexpected explosions took place in the cold weather months. Nitro was notoriously touchy when frozen, and keeping a fire going to keep it thawed didn't significantly reduce the incidence of accidents.

In December 1899, a magazine blew up outside Bradford, Pennsylvania. It killed no one, but the shock was felt in Ceres, New York. Two month later, two magazines containing 3,200 pounds of explosives blew up six miles east of Wellsville, making a big crater, but doing little other damage. Then on March 3, 1900, a Bradford Torpedo Company magazine located a mile and a half east of

Mel, standing on the left, and older brother Warren Van Curen aboard their delivery wagon, stopped on Main Street about where the Manor Apartments stand today, loaded with torpedoes ready to head out to shoot a well, about 1905. Both worked as shooters themselves, but gave their occupations as oil producers. Both died natural deaths.

Bolivar, (probably near Black and George Hollow), containing 500 quarts went off at one in the morning. The flash was seen in the village, but damage was confined to houses near the blast.

Over the next twenty years, as drilling subsided, there were reports of a few magazines being lost around Bradford and Titusville, Pennsylvania, but none in the Allegany Field. Then came secondary recovery and the drilling of thousands of wells, all needing to be shot. 1923 was a banner year for accidental explosions. One of the premier shooters in our area was Mel Van Curen. The Van Curen magazine was kept in a deep gulley 3/4 of a mile southwest of the village on the Bartlett farm. On April 14, about 8 o'clock in the morning, it exploded. It was believed Leo Root, a shooter, had been killed, since it was known he had headed there shortly before it went up. His wife was certain he had been vaporized. A desperate search for scraps of Leo began.

Leo had been lucky. He had taken a load of 40 quarts shortly before the explosion, preparing to shoot a well up Horse Run Road. He heard the bang just as he came to the corner of the state highway. Quickly going back to see what had happened, he returned to his wagon, and went off to shoot the well up Horse Run as scheduled. When he returned home later that day, his wife fell into a faint which it took a long time to bring her back from. The explosion had been felt as far away as Coon Hollow and Shinglehouse.

Five months later, on September 6, the Van Curen magazine blew up again. This time, Leo's team and wagon were found a short ways from the magazine, but there was no sign of Leo anywhere. An initial search of the area didn't turn up a single scrap, but about a week later a piece of cloth was found in a tree some distance away, and Mrs. Root identified it as part of Leo's undershirt. His obituary appeared, and the area grieved for his widow and five children, all under the age of ten.

A little over two weeks later, on September 23, Leo walked back into his house and shocked his wife again. So, just what had Leo been doing all this time, everyone asked? Leo had been shell shocked. A short time before the first explosion at the magazine, he had dropped a can of nitroglycerin while walking down the street, but it did not explode. Then, on September 6, the magazine had exploded just after he left it. Close call number two. And finally, on September 23, the magazine blew yet again, just before he got to it.

He had spun on his heels and ran for dear life. In his panic, he made his way to Olean and hopped a freight headed east. He rode it all the way to Binghamton where he had a sister, and he crashed at her place for two weeks, trying to catch his breath and settle his nerves. Then, after his fortnight of rest, he rode back to Friendship on the Erie and walked to Nile, where he encountered Paul Wardner and Albert Moyer from Bolivar. Both recognized him. Wardner was surprised; Moyer about fell out of the car. But they gave Leo a ride home, and soon enough he was back at work as a shooter. (Eventually, Leo found a job as a pumper. A veteran of world War I, he served again briefly at the end of World War II. He fathered three more children and died in the Bath Soldiers Home in 1961).

All was quiet for four months. On January 10, 1924, the Van Curen magazine blew up a third time, eighty quarts flattening the new concrete block magazine just built. No one was hurt. A number of windows were broken in Bartlett's house, and eighteen windows in the high school building on Olean Street. The last man to visit the magazine had been Wayne Hulbert, who said he had turned off the gas to the stove in the building before he left. But Hulbert was cursed. Just three days later, he witnessed a train collide with a car in Scio, killing the two occupants. And in June, Hulbert himself died in a nitroglycerin explosion near Franklin, PA.

One of the scarier incidents for the people of Bolivar happened in April 1926. The year before, village voters had voted down a proposal to pave Olive Street, a popular bypass for trucks headed east and west. On April 27, a truck loaded with 500 quarts of nitro sank into the mud while headed up Olive toward Kossuth and to the magazine kept there by Pringle Powder Company. Other truck traffic had made the street impassable. The load of nitro was safely extricated, but the *Bolivar Breeze* wryly noted that the paving question would undoubtedly appear on the ballot again next year. In March 1929, Charles Mansfield, manager and shooter for the Bolivar Glycerin Company died in an explosion which happened on the highway four miles north of Emporium. His load of 400 quarts blew a crater in the Macadam highway eight feet deep and sixteen feet across.

Mel Van Curen built his nitroglycerin factory along Wilson Brook in the town of Genesee. On April 2, 1930, it blew up, but the employees had spotted trouble and safely escaped. They moved their magazine to Foreman Hollow, but it wasn't any more stable there. Filled with 100 quarts, it blew up again in the early hours of December 4, 1930. The blast woke up almost everyone in the village, broke numerous windows, and knocked some goods off of store shelves. But, no people were hurt.

Two years later, on May 5, 1932, the magazine of the American Torpedo Company, also located up Foreman Hollow, filled with 400 quarts of nitro, blew up at 10:20 in the morning. It created a crater five feet deep and thirty feet across, broke windows all around the village, knocked off one of the organ tubes in the Methodist Church, and stampeded a herd of cattle, but again injured no one. It was considered the most severe nitroglycerin accident to occur near Bolivar. It was on the location that later became Al Glintz's "Cloud 10" camp. In March, 1934, Pringle Powder's magazine, also filled with about 400 quarts, but located outside of Bradford, blew, injured two people, and killed John Riggs of Bolivar.

One of the great characters to inhabit Bolivar for fifty years after the boom was Charles Melvin Van Curen, seen at left, known to all as Mel. Born in Belmont in 1868, in his younger days he went adventuring in Dakota Territory, but after seeing the sights there he returned to Allegany County, where he became "one of the pioneer manufacturers and shooters of nitroglycerin." He is seen here with a tight grip on a can of nitro, carefully pouring it into a torpedo. But Mel was no roughneck. He was an active member of the Methodist Church on Friendship Street, and went through the steps to become a 32nd degree Mason. Not only that, he had a literary bent. He wrote his first novel, *The Waif of the Wreck*, in 1919. He loved his story so much he took it to Hollywood and turned it into a movie with the title, *Glory of Youth*. In 1927, he came out with another novel, *The Russell Millions*. He always considered himself an oil producer, not a shooter. He died after a short illness

Melvin Van Curen

on Dec. 3, 1935 at home on South Street. But with his passing, the incidences of nitroglycerin magazine explosions around Bolivar became increasingly rare.

In fact, there was only one. On June 24, 1936, the rebuilt magazine on Foreman Hollow Road, now owned by DuPont, blew up yet again about 10:00 that Sunday night. The 350-400 quarts broke windows from Miller Hollow to Main Street and was heard in Eldred, twenty miles away. About two weeks later, the news spread that Mark Smith, a seventy-four-year-old retired shooter, had not been seen since the magazine had gone up. He had left a short, suicide-like note at his brother's, where he had been staying, and a number of witnesses said that they thought they had seen him walking up Foreman Hollow Road the morning before the explosion.

A thorough search of the site uncovered no flesh or body parts, but the *Breeze* commented that this proved nothing. "The magazine was lined with 1,200 bricks. No piece of a single brick larger than a small chip was found following the explosion." A piece of shirt front, believed to be his, did turn up. Smith, an expert shooter who had worked for Van Curen, American Glycerin, and DuPont, was never seen again, and the conclusion was that he had indeed been blown to atoms along with the magazine.

The last fatal nitroglycerin incident in the Bolivar area happened on June 18, 1937. William G. Shannon had come to Bolivar as a boy of eleven. He went to Ridgeway, Pennsylvania to enlist in World War One, becoming private in Company H, 112th Infantry. He was slightly wounded on August 7, 1918, and on August 27, while engaged in the Battle of Chateau Thierry, was captured and held by the Germans as a prisoner of war until after the war's end.

On his return to Bolivar, he met and married his wife, Marjorie, and began work as a pumper for R.B. Moore. As the years passed, Bill became well-known for his diligence and became Moore's lease superintendent. On June 18, 1937, he took his oldest boy, Bill Jr., and headed for California Hollow, where a well was scheduled to be shot. A torpedo containing sixty quarts of nitro was lowered into the well to the appropriate depth. To set it off, a separate canister filled with four quarts was lowered in after it. Thinking that too had reached the correct level, Jack North, the winch operator, started to pull the cable back out. As the cable came up, Bill heard a clanging inside the tubing, and realized that the small canister had not released. He yelled to Bill Jr. to run out to tell North to stop the winch, but it was too late. Bill turned back and saw the canister coming out of the well, about to be drawn into the pulley leading to the winch. He reached to grab it before it hit the pulley, and it went off. The explosion killed Shannon and badly injured Angelo Tower, one of the workers on the rig, who ended up in the Wellsville Hospital in "grave condition." The entire town mourned for the Shannons.

The last blast felt in Bolivar happened on the morning of Oct. 18, 1939, when the gelatin packing plant of the National Powder Company located just outside Eldred, Pennsylvania, blew Up. In killed eight employees at the site, and broke a plate glass window in Sawyer's Kendall Station on Main Street in Bolivar.

Finally, on Sep. 21, 1941, former Bolivar resident Clarendon Streeter was on his way from Bradford to Oil City with J.C. Martin, executive secretary of the

Pennsylvania Oil Producers. As they started up a hill heading out of Bradford, Streeter came up behind a slow-moving nitroglycerin truck and decided to pass. Just as he got beside it, the truck exploded, killing the truck driver and Martin. Streeter lost an eye, but kept his life. That was the last nitroglycerin accident involving someone with ties to Bolivar. Over the years, methods had been developed to make the handling and transportation of nitro much safer, and as the re-drilling of the Bradford and Allegany fields neared completion in the 1940s, the number of wells shot decreased accordingly. In the 1960s, fracking became the method of choice to stimulate production. Karney Cochran, field superintendent for the Bradley Producing Corporation, discovered that the oil sands, due to under-surface stress, always cracked in the same direction. This allowed for very systematic and effective drilling patterns which made leases developed using fracking much more productive.

Fracking has advantages over the use of nitroglycerin, other than it does not require the handling of temperamental explosive liquids. The objective in using any of these methods is to create a bigger surface area along which oil and gas can flow into a well, or to ease the delivery of water into the formation. The use of an explosive, such as dynamite or nitroglycerin, shatters the rock near the well, accomplishing that goal. However, the high temperature created by the blast fuses the face of the rock, partially defeating the goal. Fracking does not use explosives or anything generating a high temperature. At that time fracking involved pumping either water or crude petroleum into the well to create high hydraulic pressure on the oil-bearing formation. When the pressure gets high enough, it will create a long, deep fissure in the rock, penetrating much farther into the oil sand than a shot of nitroglycerin ever would, and without damaging the surface of the rock with high temperatures. The drainage area, held open by pumping loose sand into the fissure, is much greater as a result. It is a much more effective method, but well shooting did not entirely die out.

So far as I know, the last wells shot in the Allegany Field were on the hillside behind Hahn & Schaffner, by the Ebenezer Oil Company in 1982. For the most part, the drilling of the input wells to waterflood the Allegany field was completed in the 1950s, with some small development carried on through the 1960s into the 1970s around Alma Hill in the town of Alma, and in the town of Independence. Those wells were fracked, not shot.

This photo of the wellhead where Bill Shannon died appeared in the Buffalo Evening News.

Prohibition

The campaign in the United States to ban the manufacture and sale of alcoholic beverages began in the early nineteenth century. Although Bolivar was home to a few ardent proponents of prohibition, the community at large was not. Naomi C. Bradley was "the pillar" of the Allegany County Women's Christian Temperance movement, and her husband, J.B. was an avowed member of the Royal Templars of Temperance, the men's auxiliary of the WCTU. Walter Bliss was active in Prohibition Party politics, and in 1918 was their candidate for New York State attorney general. But the issue was basically of rural communities in favor, and of urban areas against, and the urban areas usually had the votes. Many of those votes came from the German immigrant community, but World War One effectively suppressed the political clout they had.

With a sixty-eight percent super majority in the House of Representatives, and with seventy-six percent support in the US Senate, the Eighteenth Amendment to the Constitution was passed in 1919, and was quickly ratified by forty-six of the forty-eight states. Congress passed the Volstead Act to enforce the ban on the manufacture and sale, and the United States went dry on January 17, 1920.

I was told by many who lived through the era before prohibition went into effect, that it was impossible to buy a drop of alcohol anywhere between Bolivar and Olean. But once it took effect, you could stop at every other farmhouse on the way and get some gin or whiskey, or cider, all depending on what crops the farmer had that he could let ferment. It is estimated that by 1925, there were between 30,000 and 100,000 speakeasies operating just in New York City. So, every other farm matches up statistically with the concentration found in the city.

New York passed its own law so state law enforcement could take action, and that law became effective until April 4, 1921. The first mention in the Bolivar Breeze of a prohibition-related problem appeared that February, when it was said, "a Bolivar man had a close call when he took a drink of wood alcohol. It is a poor substitute for whiskey." Three days after the law took affect, a Bolivar man was seen gazing into an empty beer keg, and sighing, "A mirage."

Ceres often appeared in the news. A hotel there had been built straddling the state line, which the owner painted onto his floor. He built a portable bar on casters. If New York police raided, he would roll his hooch into Pennsylvania, and vice-versa. There was a sheriff's raid on Tony Candadoria's place in Bolivar during June 1921, which uncovered nothing illicit. This was Tony's second raid. The first had come away with a keg of "raisin jack," which was said "to have a big kick in it, and a smell that is strong enough to kill a hog."

Bolivar's Dr. Hulett was making a house call in Ceres in August 1923, when a drunk driver was involved in an accident, and the doctor was summoned. The doc immediately grabbed two bottles of whiskey from the driver. The driver, thinking quickly, grabbed two other bottles from his car and heaved them across the state line into Pennsylvania. The *Breeze* commented, "thereby helping to break the drought in that state."

There were a series of raids in the summer of 1924, which started with five arrests in Canaseraga and Cuba. It was known at that time that bootleggers were making "several trips a week" to Bolivar, but it wasn't until October when one was caught. John Hord, of Olean, was arrested on Saturday night, October 19, for selling whiskey from his car, which he had parked on a side street near Main.

In 1926, Anthony Sanzo, Angelo Sanzo, Charles and Lewis Ross operated the Bolivar Ice Plant, located near the Shawmut railroad station. According to the Friendship Register, quoting Bolivar people, "it was anything from a cold business, and it is alleged some rather hot stuff has been dispensed from the ice plant, while the place is said to have borne an unfavorable reputation." Charlie Ross was caught in Bolivar, the other three were arrested in Olean, and all were able to post $1,500 bail each. The arrests were made by Undersheriff Birney Wilson, and three deputies. At the time of the raid, they found only a few bottles of beer at the ice plant, but that group earned themselves the label, "Bolivar's Ice House Gang."

Another major raid of Allegany County was organized in August 1928. The biggest haul was seized at the Bradley Hotel in Cuba, where the agents uncovered more than 850 bottles of beer, and a cache of "white mule, a decoction of some sort of alcohol and other stuff." The raid started at the Barbecue Inn near Bath. Their second stop was at "the establishment of Mrs. Carrie Jones in Bolivar," where they seized Mrs. Jones and fifteen pints of hooch, before going a short ways to "the establishment of James Torrance," (who also operated a boarding house in Rochester), where they located a store of gin and wine.

The Sanzos had a hard time finding another line of work. Tony and Francis plead guilty to charges of maintaining a nuisance in October 1929, and were fined a total of $500. Francis and Angelo were charged with peddling beer in Salamanca in the spring of 1926, and also swept up at that time was future Cuba Lake ranger Jacob Geyer. Besides supplying others, the Sanzos had place of their own on "the back road to Allegany." One result of the 1929 arrests was a court order to close down their soft drink bottling business.

The next raid on Bolivar occurred on July 3, 1930, when federal agents seized a quantity of beer, "of exceptional quality." Asking questions to locate the supplier, they uncovered an Olean brewery which they raided at the end of the month. In early March, 1933, the G-men returned, this time raiding 278 Main Street, (which in later years would become Stoll's Dry Cleaning), but which was then occupied by Anthony DeFusto. They seized a collection of "alleged" whiskey, gin, creme de cacao, and two and a half barrels of beer. DeFusto, who had come to town six months before, was arrested, but was able to post $1,000 bail and was released. The *Breeze* noted that his establishment "was not closed."

After that, all remained quiet due to the election of Franklin Roosevelt, who took office at that time, in March 1933. Keeping his campaign promise, he introduced a constitutional amendment to repeal prohibition. New York put the matter to the voters. Repeal was approved by the voters of the town of Cuba by a mar-

The interior of the Washington, 1950s

gin of 98 votes, in Wellsville by 147, and in Bolivar by a margin of 183. All the other towns in the county voted to stay dry, making Allegany County one of only six in the state to so vote. Overall in New York, the amendment passed 2,000,000 to 250,000. (The margin in New York City ran 40-1 in favor).

Prohibition was over, but you still needed a license to make whiskey. In 1936, federal agents in Buffalo uncovered unusually large shipments of sugar going to a farm in the town of Wirt. One day, they followed the delivery truck to the farm, owned by a tool dresser named Frank Speta, where they found a 1,500 gallon still, 25,000 gallons of mash, 125 barrels of sugar, and 800 gallons of alcohol. Frank lived until 1972, and lies today in Maple Lawn.

New York was the ninth state to ratify the end of prohibition, and the sale of alcohol became legal again on December 15, 1933. Bolivar opened up. Just a week later, the Washington Restaurant advertised *free* fish fries on Wednesday and Friday nights from eight to midnight, but, "you pay for the beer."

The owner of the Washington in 1933 was its founder, Stephen Ninos, who offered the free fish with your beer. However, Steve hadn't waited for the official end of Prohibition to offer beer, at least not for certain special customers. On

June 29, 1933, the enormous Italian heavyweight boxer, Primo Carnera, knocked out Jack Sharkey in Madison Square Garden and took the Heavyweight Championship and the belt he is seen wearing in the photo on the right. He then did a series of exhibition matches. On August 18, he held one in Erie, Pennsylvania, and the next day headed for Troy, New York to conduct another. On the way, Primo, his trainer, and four companions, walked into the Washington to get "a light lunch." The Champ ordered some soup, a tomato and lettuce salad, roast beef, a piece of pie, and three glasses of beer.

Primo Carnera

During World War II, Steve managed another restaurant in Lockport, and left the Washington to be managed by Michael Ninos, a relative. The Ninos family sold the Washington, and in the 1950s, it was operated by Dick Smith, seen on the previous page draining a long neck, and his brother James. When operated by the Ninos family, there was a back room where you could sit and drink in privacy. On Saturday nights, you could usually find Doc Hackett and his nurse/assistant, waiting patiently there, rather than be woken from sleep, for the inevitable call to attend to the victims of an auto accident, one of the downsides to the end of prohibition.

One of the casualties of prohibition in Bolivar was Edward Hungerford, who had come to town in 1904 to set up a bottling works where he packaged Dotterwich Beer, which was made in Olean. The bottling works was built behind the houses on the west side of Main, near the village line. Hungerford also had an ice business and oil property near Rixford, Pennsylvania, at the time he brought his family here. Prohibition put an end to the legal operation of the beer bottling business. Regardless, Edward Hungerford became a well-regarded citizen of the village, and served as a village trustee during most of the 1920s.

He, and his wife, Mary, brought with them to their new home on First Street three sons, Francis or Frank, and his younger brothers, Edmond or Ned, and Thomas. One has to wonder about what a happy place the Hungerford home must have been to have come from it such a collection of friendly, fun-loving boys as the Hungerford boys were. Legend has it that their antics started at home. In those days, dogs were pretty much free to roam about town. The boys would watch for a bitch in heat, and when they found one, they would take their father's overcoat and rub the female dog all over with it. Then they would put the coat back on the rack, and wait for their father to put it on and walk up town, where he would be closely followed and harassed by every loose male dog in the neighborhood.

The brothers went into the oil business when they got out of school, their principal lease located near Vosburg, on the north side of Baldwin's sawmill, running up to the Phillip's Hill Road. At the end of the 1930s when big game hunting resumed, Ned would offer his services as a guide for the hunters from Buffalo who were anxious to get their deer. One of his favorite tricks was to walk into the property with his clients along the lease roads. He would walk very slowly and quietly, admonishing the city boys to do the same, closely examining the ground as he moved along. Ned would act a little surprised, whisper to his hunters to stand still, and go to the base of a nearby tree where all could see a pile of small, brownish lumps. Ned would pick up a few, put them up to his nose, then pop them into his mouth, and chew a bit, inevitably declaring, "Yes, its deer!" What it was was chocolate M&Ms, or Raisinets that he had planted there himself. Such acts built Ned a fine reputation around town, and he served as a village trustee and vice mayor. He was also asked on many occasions to serve as a parade judge, once, during the second Old Home Week in1936, for a "pet parade" where he gave the prize to a duck pulled in a wagon.

Oldest brother Frank graduated from Bolivar High School and went off to the University of Michigan to study law, but he stayed there only a year. The twinkle in his eye and his kind, warm demeanor won him a wide circle of friends. Despite not completing the course, Frank remained for the rest of his life a devoted fan of Michigan football, leading biennial trips to Ann Arbor with a group of Bolivar friends to attend the Michigan-Michigan State games. In the 1930s and 1940s, Frank would regularly send humorous, but thoughtful, letters to Clint Bowman, a popular newscaster and performer on WGR radio, and Clint would often respond to Frank over the airwaves, much to the delight of those listening in Bolivar. Frank was the perpetual emcee at most large public gatherings in town for decades, at alumni banquets, boy scout dinners, sports banquets, whatever, it was Frank who warmed the crowd. One of his last such assignments was as the Honorary Chairman of the Sesquicentennial Celebration in 1975. He passed at the age of eighty-seven in 1982.

Frank Hungerford, about 1975

Depression

The era of prosperity which Bolivar saw all through the 1920s began its end in October 1929, when the stock market crashed. I have a good friend from Wellsville, whose mother was the daughter of a prominent drilling contractor, and whose father worked his way through Syracuse University carefully counting every nickel. His joke was that for his father the Depression was a traumatic experience. His mother never knew there was one. The market crash led to a huge slowing of the national economy. That slowdown, coupled with the discovery of huge oil fields in Oklahoma and Texas, caused the price of oil to collapse, from its peak of $6.10 a barrel in 1927, to less than $2.00 in 1933. (It could have been worse- the price of oil in Texas dropped to ten cents a barrel). With the price drop, and the decision of local refiners to limit their purchases of crude oil to a percentage as low as one-half of what they bought in the past, drilling activity and the redevelopment of the Allegany field slowed to a near halt. Hundreds of rig workers were left to sit on their hands. Suppliers of oil field goods and equipment saw their sales plummet from where they had been. Everyone was much more careful with what they spent.

In 1930, there was nothing resembling a "social safety net," to help people carry on when times got tough. Virtually all help was local. It took a while for the depth of the depression to really strike home. Wells in progress were completed, leases continued to be pumped and operated, but rig after rig was disassembled and parked, and the drillers and tool dressers were left to try to find other ways to feed their families.

In 1931 people started to get organized with attempts to help. In April of that year, Bolivar's American Legion sponsored an advertising campaign asking for *a Declaration of War on Unemployment*. They asked every employer in the area to commit to hiring just one more person. Working on the committee to get the ball rolling were Bill Apgar, Joe Dempsey, Sherm Maxson, and Leon MacDonell. They argued that this path was a "shortcut to prosperity." Few took it.

In June, Neil Sullivan, then secretary of the Oil Producer's Association, wrote a detailed report, where he said there were now 18,000 wells in the field, representing an investment of $36,000,000. The assessed value of the oil properties was thirty percent of all property in Allegany County, but seventy-four percent of the real property in Bolivar. Now, producers were limited, by proration agreements with the refiners, to selling only half as much oil as they had in the past, and at half or less of the price. Who, he seemed to ask, could afford to add anyone to their payroll?

Nerves frayed, tempers shortened, and radical solutions were seriously considered. In September, the new school was broken into and vandalized, interior doors smashed, plate glass windows shattered, locks torn out, requiring $1,000 in repairs, ($21,000 in today's dollars). The school nurse, widow of Kenyon Andrus, organized a Charity Ball, "one gala evening of entertainment," to raise money for needy children. There was music for dancers, other entertainments for those who didn't, supper, cool drinks, and dainty refreshments with twenty girls, including Rita Sherwood, Veryl Casey, Clara Milgate and Anita Herrick, working as waitresses and coat checkers. Sponsors included the Olean and Wellsville Elks Clubs, the Fire Department, the Sorosis and the Odd Fellows. It drew a crowd of 400, raised more than $350, ($6,400 in modern money), all contributed to the school's health fund for needy students.

In September, Robert Stohr brought in from Buffalo a speaker named A. Kline, who delivered his message at the village hall, (upstairs in the old fire hall), which drew a crowd of eighty people. The topic was "the cause and remedy of

When built at the corner of Main and Olean streets, in 1922, this structure was called the Village Hall, but soon enough became known for its principal use, as the Fire Hall. The upstairs was open, used for public gatherings until the mid-1930s, when it was turned into

the depression." Kline set out in detail the Soviet system of five year plans, claiming that Russia was then prospering because of this system of planning. He thought the United States would be much better off if it followed the Soviet's example. About thirty of the attendees were from Olean, and Klein encouraged them to go home and get organized there.

Robert Stohr was at the time an unemployed rig worker, who had started looking hard for alternatives and solutions. He had settled on Communism. He was then nearing sixty, born in 1874, the son of German immigrants. A year and a half later, in March 1933, he and Burr Root formed the Unemployment Council. At that time, 1,200 Allegany County men were looking for work. The only help the County could offer were construction projects, and they laid out plans to build eighteen more miles of highway and two major bridges, as well as maintaining the 113 miles of county roads already built. What Root and Stohr hoped to stop were tax sales of real property, evictions, and foreclosures of mortgages. That same month, the Sorosis brought in a speaker, John LaWall from Rochester, who also spoke on Soviet Russia. He championed the idea that the United States should recognize the Soviet government, which it had yet to do, and work to develop a trade relationship, despite differences about government and economic policies, "none of which," he correctly pointed out, "work any too well at present." Ralph Ressler's going out of business sale was proof enough of that.

Stohr's and Root's efforts made the New York Times, which focused on their call for a moratorium on tax sales, saying it "caused anxiety lest violence should develop. The Village of Bolivar was a particular center of protest." The Times went on to report that the county tax sales had gone ahead as scheduled without disturbance, accompanied by a last minute rush to redeem more than 300 properties. At the village tax sale, held in February, twenty-one properties went up for sale. Only one attracted a bid. Newly installed President Franklin Roosevelt, as one of his first moves declared a "bank holiday," which Bolivar's banks honored by staying closed from March 4 to March 15. The area banks used the time to form a joint "clearing house association," as a step in offering each other mutual support. The Bolivar School band reduced the price of admission to concerts from twenty cents to a dime. Conditions were slow to get better. In 1934, forty-four parcels in the village went up at the tax sale, and 149 in the town, by far the most in any town in the county.

There were a number of significant events in 1934. Johnny Messer and Roy Strickland had a dog kennel at Hilltop. They took five dogs to the National Dog Show in Madison Square Garden. Their pointers took first, second and third, and a setter took first. Gus Dunn moved his drug store into the north half of the Odd Fellows Hall, taking the space vacated by Ralph Ressler's dry goods. Al Glintz left his job as the meat manager at the A&P store to open his first service station selling Eldred Gas, his location on the west side of Main, opposite the intersection with Olive.

Monroe Motors, which had been one of the larger automobile dealerships in town, closed, and its property on Main Street, located between the village hall and the movie theater, was sold at a foreclosure sale in 1935. McDonell & Brannen filed for bankruptcy in 1936, and the bank bought both the store location on Main Street, and the parcel on Liberty Street where the original McDonell shop had been when it burned. But a new landmark business arrived in Bolivar that August. The Magneto Repair Company moved its operation from Friendship to the former Severson & Shaner building on Wellsville Street. The next year Jesse Pounds bought the business, renamed it the Bolivar Magneto, and began building a business reputation that would spread all around western New York. Jesse, who had been a lieutenant in the Army during the Great War, came from Chicago. He had worked at a foundry in Chicago before the war, and after got into sales, in 1927 selling leather in Bradford.

The Magneto Repair Company was already well established, and had some patented parts that came with it. Jesse and his partner, Homer Smith, added B.F.

Goodrich belting to their offerings. Every powerhouse in the field used many feet of ten or twelve inch rubber belting to carry the energy from the engines to the eccentrics to pump the wells. It was tough stuff, but it wore out. The original name of their business, in fact, was the Bolivar Magneto Repair and Belting Company, but in time it became simply the Magneto. Two employees came with the business: Claude Murray, and Edward "PeeWee" Greisch.

The municipal water system for domestic use was privately owned, the residents having voted down a proposal in the 1890s to build one. (The fire hydrants were on a separate system). In June 1936, the village bought the domestic system, and immediately enlarged it, installed hydrants on Second Street and Railroad Avenue, built a new control plant, drilled two supply wells, installed an aerator, built a 640,000 gallon tank on the hill above Wellsville Street, and began installing water meters. The village also passed an ordinance forbidding the painting of class year numbers on the new tank. And they hired Sam Ryan to operate it.

Slowly, the ravages of the Depression ebbed away. It wasn't until 1938 that New York set up a program of unemployment insurance, which one local declared "a great victory for labor." But it was too late for most. Those who were again at work on the drilling rigs might rest a little easier if hard times came again, but they were no longer in need, and those who hadn't found work had moved elsewhere. (More than 500 people left town between 1930 and 1940). In 1939, the price of oil rose from $1.68 to $2.50, rig counts climbed, and people started speaking of the Depression in the past tense.

The 1930s brought some memorable people to Bolivar. One of the most colorful was a young Canadian butcher named Royal Allen Glintz. Born in Ontario, Canada in August 1909, in 1929 in Buffalo, he married Lillian Hardman. He worked as a butcher for the Great Atlantic and Pacific Tea Company, better known as the A&P. Sent to Florida to work in a store there, he quickly decided he did not care for the South, and in 1930 he became the manager of the meat department of the company's Bolivar store.

J.P. Herrick said that good things come to those who hustle. Al Glintz hustled. He was quick witted, outgoing, and hard working. He made friends quickly. He entertained in a man's man sort of way, and became good friends with scores of people across generations, in his early years often guiding people like R.B. Moore and Johnny Messer on fishing trips to Canada.

His time with the A&P was short. Al was ambitious, and he wanted to work for himself. In 1934, he leased Bolivar's Eldred Gas Station, on the west side of Main opposite Olive Street. He would be in business there or across the street for the rest of his working life. Al was fiercely competitive, and he frequently switched brands and suppliers. At one time, he was the highest volume Atlantic gasoline retailer in western New York. He got into a row with Atlantic, bought the old Cowles house across the street, converted the house first into a sandwich shop, then into one of the very first convenience stores in the area, put in new gasoline pumps, and to start with sold Sinclair gasoline.

The new operator of the old station across the street didn't stand a chance. Al watched happenings over there with an eagle's eye. When old customers pulled into the old location, Al would run out and call them over to the new one. He used his binoculars to read the price on his competitor's pumps, and would consistently set his price just a cut lower. Within five years, Atlantic realized their mistake, and Al started selling their brand again. The location across the road closed and became part of the Ferris and Forbes complex. His convenience store was popular in and of itself. There was always a wheel of Shinglehouse cheese ready to yield up a pound to two, and shotgun and .22 shells behind the counter. During hunting season, he would put out a sign on the corner saying, "Beer Hunters Welcome," and would sell case after case of Genesee Cream Ale. Al was busy with community affairs from the time he went into business for himself. He sat on the merchant's committee of the Chamber of Commerce, served for a time as the fire chief, and later as the fire warden. He became active in Republican politics, and won renown for the number of signatures he could collect for candidates on their nominating petitions.

But most of all, Al Glintz liked to entertain. In the 1940s, he had a hunting camp on Bell's Brook called "The Dirty Shame," and the parties there gained a wide and wild reputation. He recruited Joe Meek to provide music for many of these soirees, and thus was born the Dirty Shame Camp Band, a trio comprised of Joe on fiddle, Walter Hinman on drums, and Shorty Nolan playing the accordion and providing vocals. (The band also provided entertainment at MacDonell's camp on Beers Hollow). In the late 1950s, Al sold the Dirty Shame and set up camp closer to home on Foreman Hollow, buying the property where the DuPont magazine had exploded, calling his new camp, Cloud Ten. There on Sunday afternoons would be hilarious card games, where Al would run out on the porch to welcome late arrivals with a blast from his French horn.

Al Glintz about 1935

Al did impersonations, the most commonly recognized being his portrayal of Groucho Marx, whom in later years he resembled, which began when he played Groucho in the shows put on by the Bolivar Mens Club and the American Legion as fund raisers. In the mid-1950s, Louis Whaley, owner of Genesee beer, was nominated to be the New York State Game Commissioner, and a large dinner was arranged to celebrate, to which Al got a ticket. Showing up early, he found his way to the private suite where the commissioner was to be before the evening began, but Al arrived before Louis. The phone rang, Al answered it by saying "Yes, this is Commissioner Whaley." No one there actually knew Whaley, so Al spent the next half hour pretending to be the Commissioner, disappearing before Louis came in. A few years later, he recognized Whaley at a restaurant in Florida, went over and introduced himself as Frank C. Resch, the Genesee distributor in Cuba, and got a free dinner! During the Arab oil embargo of the early 1970s, he donned a white robe and headdress and went to the Cameo Restaurant acting the role of a sheik looking for new deals. Al retired in 1974, sold the station to his son Pete, and had twenty years to relax before his time expired. He took up skiing at age sixty, and had fun stopping half way down a slope wearing a long blonde wig, facing down hill. Inevitably, a man would ski over to see who the blonde was, only to be greeted by Al spinning his head around to offer a view of his goatee and glistening gold teeth. They don't make 'em like that anymore!

Mattie Dellone arrived in Bolivar in the 1920s, a middle-aged widow with a young son. She moved to Bolivar from San Antonio, Texas after her husband

Al's Sinclair, in the 1960's, with Al's DeSoto parked under the roof. "Beer Hunters" were welcome!

died, to be near her sister, Elizabeth Dougherty. She worked as a bookkeeper for Monroe Motors, which paid the bills. Her passion was Democratic politics, which she inherited from her father, who had been prominent in the Democratic party in Kansas where she grew up.

She went right to work, in 1926 taking a spot on the county Democratic committee, and she began circulating with the upper echelons of New York Democrats. In 1928, she was an alternate delegate from New York to the Democratic National Convention in Houston, where Al Smith was nominated to run for president. Perhaps it was at the convention that she first connected with Franklin Roosevelt, candidate for governor to fill Smith's spot in Albany. Connect she did. On August 14, 1929, she escorted Governor Franklin D. Roosevelt on a tour which took him from Alfred State College to Allegany State Park, and she made certain he literally went out of his way to come through Bolivar. Running two hours behind schedule, FDR stopped briefly on Bolivar's Main Street to shake hands, but lacked the time to make a speech. He promised to come back, saying he wanted to learn more about the oil business. Other job opportunities kept him from keeping that promise, but he is still the only President of the United States who has stopped in Bolivar, NY.

In 1930, Mattie scored another first. She opposed western New York's Representative Dan Reed, and ran for Congress. She lost handily and unsurprisingly, but in the process became the first woman to run for Congress on a major party ticket in New York. In 1934, Mattie was one of the state party's traveling speakers promoting candidates in the fall campaign. Mattie was rewarded with the position of postmaster of Bolivar in 1936, and was immediately elected the Allegany County director to serve on the board of the New York State Postmaster's Association. FDR's aide, Jimmy Farley, referred to her as "one of the best party workers in the state." Because of her, the county Democratic committee sent its first monetary contribution to the state party. She earned a reputation as "Bolivar's militant Democratic leader," while working with future Governor Herbert Lehman on the state party's finance committee.

After the war, she found work in Buffalo and moved there. Her son, Ted, lived in Bolivar working for Jones & Laughlin until 1955, when he was transferred to New Mexico. She died in 1964 in Dunkirk, but rests with her family in St. Mary's Cemetery in Bolivar.

World War Two

No event, except perhaps the Civil War, has had a deeper and longer effect on the people of Bolivar than did the coming of World War II. No one wanted it, but everyone watched its slow and steady arrival. The Japanese had been fighting in China since 1931, and launched their full scale invasion in 1937. In July 1941, to pressure the Japanese to stop, the United States imposed an oil embargo and froze Japanese assets. At the time, Japan bought eighty percent of its petroleum from the United States.

In 1939, Europe exploded when Britain and France came to the defense of Poland, which had been invaded by Germany from the west and the Soviet Union from the east. America stood by as Germany took control of nearly all of Europe, and as the British RAF won the battle of Britain, stopping Germany's push to invade the island.

Then, on December 7, 1941, the Japanese struck back, crippling America's Pacific Fleet by attacking Pearl Harbor. The next day, Hitler declared war on the United States. On the afternoon of December 7, after hearing the news, three Bolivar boys stood near the door of Swarthout's billiard parlor, talking about what they should do. Concluding that the draft would be coming for them soon enough, they decided to enlist. The next morning, high school students Gerry Wight, Tony Sallazzo and Ken Cummings, appeared at the recruiting station in Olean, ready to enlist in the Army. They waited and waited for someone to show up, when finally a man in a uniform with a bright red stripe down the sides of his blue pants walked up and asked them why they were there. They told him. He said he could help them out. But, he signed them up as US Marines, not as GIs. Two more Bolivar boys, James Maxson and Gordon Hughes, enlisted shortly af-

Roy Schaffner, second from the right, in the Pacific

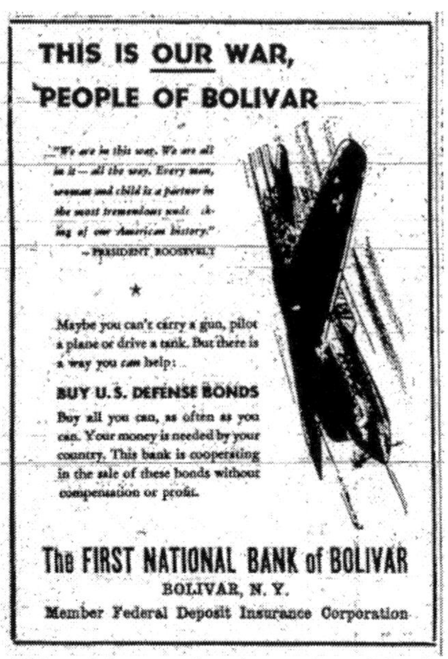

This ad for war bonds ran in a March 1942 edition of the Bolivar Breeze. At the top, it quotes President Roosevelt: "We are in this war. We are all in it - all the way. Every man, woman, and child is a partner in the most tremendous undertaking in our American history."

terwards. They were the first five of the 344 men and women from Bolivar who would put on uniforms to play their part in the war after Pearl Harbor. Eleanor Wilson, daughter of Forest Wilson, was offered and immediately accepted a secretarial position with the headquarters of the Army Air Corps post in Victorville, California. Roy Schaffner, who had put on his private's uniform the summer before, was stationed at Fort Riley as a medic. Roy was destined for things other than a private's stripe. He decided to apply for a spot in the Air Force, qualified, and earned a commission as a bombardier in November 1942. I recall Roy one crisp morning sitting on the pew at Hahn & Schaffer's store. I am unsure of what prompted him to relate the tale, but he allowed how when he was in the South Pacific, he had enjoyed the most serene and spectacular view he had even seen, which was from his unit's latrine overlooking a lagoon and other South Pacific islands. He did not relate how he had risen to be the lead bombardier for his group of 36 planes, meaning his drop signaled all the other planes in the formation to drop their loads of bombs, or that he had flown fifty-seven combat missions. Roy was not one to boast.

On December 8, 1941, the rest of the middle and high school students gathered in the auditorium at 12:30, and listened to a live broadcast of President Roosevelt's address to Congress, hearing him say that December 7 would be a day that would live in infamy, and asking for a declaration of war. The assembly closed with the Pledge of Allegiance, the singing of *America*, and, as the students filed out, singing *Onward Christian Soldiers*, which teachers Clare Lawler and Betty Reinhardt pounded out as a duet on the piano.

The draft had been enacted in September 1940 in anticipation of the war. As a result, four Bolivar-area men were in Hawaii on December 7. Wayne Stimson was serving on the USS Vestal, a Navy repair ship that was moored next to the battleship Arizona that morning. It was hit by two bombs, but managed to cut loose from the Arizona and run itself aground to prevent sinking. She was repaired and ready to go in February. Jim DeGroff worked in the boiler division of the battleship Pennsylvania, which was in dry dock when the Japanese struck. Damage to the Pennsylvania was minor because she was not in the water. Homer Baldwin was attached to the cruiser USS Louisville, which was returning from a cruise to Borneo on December 7, and was not in the harbor that morning. After a brief stop at Pearl, he continued on to California. Staff Sgt. Frank Schwan was attached to the 11th Field Artillery at Schofield Barracks. None of the four were hurt in the attack.

As the days passed, war was about the only topic of conversation. Clayton Dunning was again serving as mayor, and was responsible for organizing locally to meet the directives of the National Defense Program. One of the first moves was to stop the burning of waste paper and cardboard. The Boy Scouts were enlisted to conduct paper drives, collecting the accumulated waste, and the mayor appointed a committee to oversee the gathering and shipping out of the material. The local Boy Scouts were also charged with distributing their share of 5,000,000 posters containing air raid instructions.

In anticipation of the war, the previous September, Bolivar Central had been designated a National Defense Training Center, one of sixty-eight in the country. The training center was aimed at men from seventeen to twenty-eight and out of school, teaching skills that could be used either in the service or in the defense industry.

Three Bolivar air raid observation posts were immediately activated, the American Legion organizing the staffing. Gilbert Winterberger took charge of the one near Little Genesee, Frank Clark of the one on White Hill, and Sam Ryan of the third on Jordan Hill. Jack Hay was placed in charge in the fall of 1942. Legion Post Commander Clyde Witherspoon coordinated the effort with the instructions he was receiving from Mitchell Field in New York City, where a thirteen-state air raid precaution system was controlled. Each observation post was set up in a newly constructed six by eight wood frame shanty, with a tin roof. Each had three windows and a door, and had a direct telephone connection to Mitchell Field. Volunteers were recruited to man the posts twenty-four hours a day.

Stephen Ninos immediately erected a red, white and blue illuminated "V for Victory" sign in the window of his Washington Restaurant near the corner of Wellsville and Main. Ninos had led a fund raising campaign the previous winter to help the people of his native Greece. Red Cross branches in both Bolivar and Kossuth immediately became active, attorney George Bliss heading up the Bolivar chapter for a month, until he enlisted in the Army, when Bob Mills took over. Although he enlisted as a private, Bliss was almost immediately made provost marshall of Fort Wayne, Indiana, where he was stationed. In the fall of 1943, he received a commission in the Air Force. In Richburg, 112 people volunteered for the Red Cross, in Bolivar 152, and all of them, with Wilkins Newell, Wins Davis, Jack Hay, Max Richardson, and Paul Donnelly listed first, got their names in the paper. Leona Reeland organized Bolivar's women Red Cross volunteers, many needed to sew and knit. Red Cross rooms were initially open nine hours a week.

The Allegany County Defense Council met on December 10. Set up in two divisions, Bolivar's Trina MacDonell was chosen to lead the women. The governor requested that all adults in the county report for volunteer service at offices set up in each town, Bolivar's at the Town Hall. By mid-January, 248 people had stepped forward. On Sunday, December 21, the Lyric featured the film, *March of*

Time's Our America At War, a "graphic confirmation" of President Roosevelt's assurance that we would be victorious. In the school, fire drills were initially replaced with air raid drills. Fire drills required everyone to evacuate the building. Air raid drills sent everyone into the gymnasium.

The Legion undertook the registration of all firearms and ammunition held by private citizens, to serve as an inventory of available firepower in the event of an "emergency." Bill Apgar served as the registrar. The Legionnaires also organized a scrap metal drive, brass, lead, and copper at the head of the list, to be collected at Oil Well Supply, the Spang machine shop, or at the Bolivar Magneto. A defense savings campaign was started before Christmas. William F. Hogan led the committee, which included Frank Hughes, Clifford Wing, and Frank Dougherty. The Shawmut Railroad posted guards on its three most important bridges, at Belvidere across the Genesee, at the Allegany River, and at Stoney Brook Glen.

Tire rationing started on January 5, 1942, and the town appointed a committee of three, James Milgate, Bill Apgar, and Ned Hungerford, to supervise the program in Bolivar. For that month, the town of Bolivar's quota was seven tires and six tubes for trucks, and two tires and two tubes for passenger cars. In February, the quota dropped to four tires for trucks. Apgar was also named the village and town Civilian Defense coordinator. He appointed Doc Morrison as the chief air raid warden, with Sherm Lyons and Chester Jacobs to head up the bomb squad. In early 1942, Oil Well Supply moved its Bolivar machine shop, set up in 1923, to Oil City. It was said the move was occasioned by the war effort, and its need to consolidate machinery and manufacturing in one location. C.A. Schaffner, age 62, was the only machinist still at work. He had come when the shop opened in 1923. Three sons, Clarence D., Roy, and Joseph, were still living at home, Clarence D., "Mike," working as a salesman for the company, Roy in the service, Joe in college.

Special defense-related courses were offered at the school as part of the Defense Training Center curriculum. A ten-week metalworking course had been offered during the previous fall, and was repeated in February, this time with an emphasis on farm machinery repair, and a new course covering elementary electricity began at the same time.

Tony Sallazzo arrived at Paris Island in mid-January 1942, and immediately encountered a problem digesting the food, which was plentiful, loaded with lots of meat, potatoes, and gravy. He went to the post doctor, who uncovered Tony's Italian background, and his upbringing on spicy Italian food. His prescription? A bottle of Tabasco Sauce! It worked. Tony felt a lot better. Gerry Wight, who played trumpet in the BCS band, joined the Marine band at the base in New River, North Carolina where both he and Tony had been assigned.

The *Bolivar Breeze* published sample Civilian Defense questionnaires, one for men, another for women, which asked everyone to describe their health, occupation, educational attainment, special skills, (the list included house wrecking, morse code and public speaking for men, and cooking, driving, child care, and stenography for women). The form did not ask for telephone numbers.

A Junior Defense Organization came together in late January, an outgrowth of the Boy Scouts. Its first goal was to organize the waste paper drive. They divided the village into three districts. Shirley Ferris had charge of the first, Bill Neely of the second, and Lewis Baker the third, and they collected the paper on Saturdays. A "Victory Book Campaign" was launched to supply libraries being set up at the many new military bases, books to be dropped off at the Library, Florence Smith in charge.

First aid courses became popular. Twenty-five signed up for the first one offered. To make certain everyone who wanted to could help the war effort, the government offered both victory bonds, and victory stamps. Postmaster Frank Hughes appeared at the school Tuesday afternoons at 3:00 so students could add to their collection of war stamps. Every dime available would be accepted and put to use. Dr. Leonard Claflin took on the post of Chief Air Raid Warden, and appointed more than sixty men in the village as neighborhood wardens. They had the duty of becoming completely acquainted with their neighbors, where they worked or could be found, if anyone handicapped lived in the home, help homeowners select and supply their "safe rooms," help them reduce fire hazards, especially in their attics, learn where gas and electric shutoffs were located, and offer other suggestions to the neighbors about complying with blackouts and the like.

The first practice blackout was held on Friday, April 24, 1942. It was designed as a practice run for the civil defense organization, and it was not meant as a test of civilian cooperation. The first full practice run, requiring that all homes either have their lights off, or windows blocked so no light was visible outside the home took place a week later on May 1. (At my grandparent's home on Boss Street, my grandfather had special plywood covers made for the windows in the basement around the safe room set up there). A county-wide blackout test happened on the evening of May 8.

Town clerk Maude Maxson became responsible for the Bolivar branch office of the draft board to make registration more convenient, one of eight in the county. Eight other community members were placed on a committee to help her have the office open for three full days from February 14th through the 16th, 1942. All men ages 20 to 44 were required to register. Helen Dunning headed up a local committee charged with preparing plans to house people fleeing the East Coast, in the event of an invasion. She was in charge of conducting a survey of all housing in the town, and determining how many evacuees could be accommodated in each.

Daylight savings time went into effect on February 12. Prof. Whitford decided to move the opening of school to 9:40, meaning the sun would be just as far up as it was before the change when school began. On March 1, rules for the conservation of natural gas went into effect, so there would be all the gas required in defense plants. It did not affect domestic heating and cooking appliances already installed. It did prohibit the conversion of any appliance including space heaters, to burn gas, and forbade utility companies from accepting new non-residential customers without cutting a lot of red tape.

To train personnel, the government called for the production of 500,000 model airplanes, 10,000 of each of fifty different types of planes flown both by the allied forces and those of the enemies. They wanted all of them on hand by June 30. The models were wanted for use in aircraft identification programs in all branches of the service and for civilians manning air raid lookout posts. Pupils in Bolivar's industrial arts program, supervised by their instructor, Philip Caflisch, were given the task of making fifty 1/72nd scale models for the program. The scale was meant to simulate seeing a plane half a mile away, when the model was but thirty-five feet away. Anyone making ten approved models received a certificate giving him the rank of Captain Aircraftsman.

Coach Donnelly arranged with the American Legion for the use of twelve rifles to begin teaching the manual of arms. In March 1942, as an incentive to get that program going, PFC Anthony Sallazzo, home on leave, demonstrated the Marine manual of arms for several classes. At the same time, a motion picture about incendiary bombs and how to fight the fires they cause was shown in the auditorium, once during school hours, and again in the evening. Over the next six months, Bolivar went through five nighttime blackout drills, and one daylight alert.

In anticipation of a gasoline rationing system, in mid-March 1942 the War Production Board ordered a twenty-percent reduction in gasoline deliveries to all gas stations in the northeast, and limited the hours the stations could be open to twelve hours a day, six days a week. The third drawing of the military draft took place that month. Bill Tapp drew the second spot. Fran Paffie's name was 36th, Bob Buell 76th, Alvin Wallace 132nd, Paul Neely 140th, and George W. Bradley 149th. The full list filled two columns in the Bolivar Breeze.

In a move to promote oil production, the War Production Board allowed an increase in the price of crude oil to $3.00 per barrel. On top of that, if local producers could lift production levels even further, they were promised a second increase to $3.25. In Bolivar, the Bolivar Machine Shop won an order to manufacture parts for the Army's 28-ton M3 Lee tanks. Sugar rationing took effect the first week of May, with a limit of eight ounces per person per week. Despite that, the Odd Fellows hosted a spaghetti dinner for some of the early draftees and their families, letting them know the entire community appreciated what they were about to do.

Gasoline rationing started on May 15, with ration books determined and issued May 12-14. Your ration was based on how much gas you needed to get back and forth to work, and maybe a little extra for other necessary trips. I was told many years ago of one Bolivar man's experience. Ivan McKay tried too hard to be honest and conservative, and he ended up shorting himself, so that he could not buy enough gasoline to get him to and from work through the week; and no matter how hard he appealed for an increase, it was denied. He ended up sneaking around town at night, draining the hoses of the numerous gasoline pumps in the village into a can that he could get to his car. The extra gallon or two he got that way usually made up the difference for what he actually needed.

The ladies of the Firemen's Auxiliary started sending packages to men in the service. Forty-one had been sent out by the end of April 1942, and the ladies looked for donations of candy, cookies, nuts, tobacco, cigarettes, "and other suitable articles," so they could keep up their work. At the same time, the *Bolivar Breeze* carried news of the war's first casualty with Bolivar ties. Franz Rosebush had been Bolivar's school principal from 1910-1916. About the time his tenure ended here, the Rosebushes had a son they named Richard. Richard, an Army Air Corps flight instructor, died in a crash on April 18, 1942. His name was the first on a list that would steadily grow longer.

President Roosevelt said, "we are all in it." It was almost impossible to find anyone who disagreed. When anyone in uniform arrived back in town, he couldn't pay for a haircut or a shoe shine. They could hunt and fish without a license. The teachers in the school wrote hundreds of letters to keep up the morale of their former students. Others bought gift subscriptions to the Breeze, where some of the letters written home appeared for all to see. The model airplane project was taken over by the Boy Scouts, who turned them out by the hundreds. The Auxiliaries loaded more and more boxes of treats to let the boys know they were appreciated. Everyone was in it. They all found ways to help. Absolutely everyone was a partner in ensuring the Allies came out of the war victorious, and that the totalitarians who had brought it on were no more.

It is easy to do a history of a local area's participation in the wars America participated in up through and including World War One. That is true because of the way troops were raised and records kept. Beginning with the Civil War, when the federal government needed troops it assigned a quota to be raised by each state. The states in turn assigned a quota to each county, and the counties did the same for each town. Town clerks kept a record of every soldier or sailor credited to the town to prove that they met the quotas. Those records are now readily accessible on line.

That is not true for World War II and later. Allegany County does have records of all those who joined the armed services from the county, but they are not sorted by town, and are not available online, or otherwise, to the public. So, even if there was room in this book to describe the service of all 344 men and women who served in World War II from Bolivar, the information cannot be compiled to write it. What I have written about the war to this point is a description of what was happening in town on the home front as the nation prepared for war. I hope readers get the sense of how this was a war that involved everyone, not just those who ended up in the service. But it was the service of those who wore uniforms which counted most.

It is possible to catch glimpses of many of those who served through the pages of the *Bolivar Breeze*. One of those most often mentioned was Keith Wilson, BCS '33. From there he went to New York University to study aeronautical engineering. He did well, was the cadet colonel of his Reserve Officer Training Command unit, and received an officer's commission before the war began, made major in October 1942, and spent much of his time conducting or in charge of bombardier training. He then went to Wright-Patterson Field in Dayton, Ohio.

In early 1945, on a trip from Dayton to Buffalo, he buzzed Bolivar in a small two-passenger plane to signal his father, Forest Wilson, to come meet him. Forest went, and was treated to a ride in a new Bell Helicopter, probably the first person from Bolivar to have a ride in one. Keith made the Air Force his career, ending up as a colonel and director of the research and analysis branch of the Directorate of Flight Safety Research, based in Dayton. After the Air Force, he worked for a time for Lockheed in Marietta, Georgia. When fully retired, he returned to Dayton, and passed away there in 2014, three months shy of his 99th birthday.

People from Bolivar served all over the globe. Lawrence Ackerman went aboard the battleship New Jersey, which fought its way through the two largest naval battles in history, as well as every significant amphibious landing of the Pacific campaign. Gunner's mate Vern Baldwin spent ten months in the South Pacific. Karl Best served as a parachute instructor at Fort Benning, and Bob Buell worked as a gunnery instructor for the Navy. PFC Neal Clark spent six months campaigning through northern Europe with the 9th Army in an observation battalion.

Staff Sgt. Jack Bullock served with the ground crew of the 467th Bomb Group. After spending sixteen months in England working on B-24 bombers, he was called back to Sioux Falls, South Dakota to learn how to keep B-29s in the air. PFC Albert Bunt spent twenty months in the European theater. Dean Clavelli ended up with an assignment in the Air Force with the weather predicting squadron in the American northwest. Bob Crowley went on the USS Tarbell, a World War One vintage destroyer, doing carrier escort and target ship duty in the Atlantic. When the war ended, he was at code school in Norfolk.

Larry DeRock spent four years as a US Marine aircraft mechanic. Sgt. Richard Dougherty served with the 57th Fighter Group as it crossed North Africa, Malta, Sicily, Corsica and Italy. Patsy Dougherty's son, Lt. William Dougherty, served with the 13th Corps Engineers as it campaigned across Europe. Major Robert Dunning flew with the 20th Air Force in the Pacific. He flew over Nagasaki the day after it had been hit by the second atomic bomb. PFC Daniel Ford was discharged in March 1943, because he had aged out of the Army Air Force, as did PFC Leon Jones. Sgt. Francis Griswold, who put on his uniform in December 1940, spent two years in the European theater. His brother, Marvin, spent his time on board an LST in the Pacific.

Bill Hogan was commissioned a lieutenant in the Navy in early 1943, and went to Harvard as his first assignment. Sixty people attended his sendoff party. Sgt. Jack Pounds spent two years as an airplane mechanic in China. Sgt. Harry Hull received the Purple Heart for wounds he received near Buschen, Germany on Feb. 27, 1945. PFC Augie Johnson served with the 504th Bomb Group, 20th Air Force. Originally equipped with B-17s, the group switched to B-29s, and had the distinction of flying the last combat mission of World War II, to Japan on August 15, 1945, the day the Japanese surrendered.

Malcolm McDivitt, was born in Bolivar in 1908, and graduated with Bolivar High's Class of 1925. He went on to attend St. John's College in Indianapolis, and was working as a retail manager at the time he enlisted in the US Air Force on January 8, 1942. He received his officer's commission in Miami, Florida the following September. During the War, he rose to the rank of Major. After the war ended, Mac (as he was known to his friends), decided to change careers, and he spent the rest of his working life as a teacher in the Olean school system. Mac never married. With a keen mind and a subtle wit, he was a memorable friend to many. He died in Bolivar on July 30, 1993.

Edward F. Mergler, Sr., born in Buffalo in 1916, had completed law school before the war started. He enlisted in the Army in June 1942, standing all of 5'6" tall, and weighing only 122 pounds. Ed saw service in the European theater, and in a staff position took part in the planning for the D-Day landings in Normandy. Because of this, after the war Ed was contacted by author Cornelius Ryan during his research for his best-selling book, "The Longest Day."

William Nagle. Born July 13, 1922, Bill graduated with Bolivar's Class of 1939. He became part of the original crew of the Fletcher-class Destroyer Albert W. Grant, (DD 649), and sailed with her on her maiden voyage from Charleston, SC to Bermuda in November 1943. In February 1944, the Grant escorted the new carrier USS Hornet (CV12) through the Panama Canal to San Diego and then on to Pearl Harbor, Hawaii. In April 1944, the Albert Grant supported the invasion of Hollandia, New Guinea, and provided part of the screen protecting Task Group 58.3 during the raid on Truk.

In June 1944, the ship used its guns in support of the landings on Saipan and Tinian. In October, it supported the landings at Peleliu and Anguar.

Bill Nagle

On October 24, 1944, the Grant was engaged in the naval surface Battle of Suriago Strait. The destroyers went in advance of the battle group to launch a torpedo attack on the main Japanese naval force. (The Grant was equipped with ten 21 inch torpedo tubes). During this fight, Bill's ship suffered 22 hits, many from six inch shells, which killed 38 and wounded 104 of the 329 men on board.

For a time, the Albert Grant lost all power and began to list severely to port. The crew was able to restore power, and after sailing through a typhoon, made dock in Leyte, Philippines. It was towed back to Pearl Harbor, then sailed to California for full repairs. For good reason, Bill Nagle came out of the action being considered a hero. One need imagine nothing more than Bill's constant desire to put a smile on your face to know he would have been an ideal person that day to help the wounded or put out the fires, all the while keeping everyone's spirits up.

No one looked upon him more as a hero than did his maternal grandmother, who bought and gave to him a new Buick convertible when he arrived home on leave. Bill and the Albert Grant returned to service with the Pacific Fleet in March 1945, and escorted General MacArthur on his tour of the Philippines before providing support for the landings at Brunei Bay. It was on its way to Adak, Alaska when the war ended. Bill, who had risen to Torpedoman 2nd Class, returned to Bolivar, worked in the Post Office. He had a hobby of collecting old, unused postcards, which he used to carry on his personal, very humorous, correspondence with friends in his later years. He died April 22, 2004.

PFC Bob Nugent served with the 346th Infantry Regiment, landed in France in October 1944, and went through Luxembourg, Alsace-Lorraine, Belgium, and Germany. Cadet and future doctor George Ninos ended the war at Duke University in the Army's medical training course. One of his brothers, Staff Sgt. William Ninos, worked as a company cook for the 1st Mobile Radio Broadcasting Company in Italy, having managed the Washington Restaurant in Bolivar before he enlisted. On October 14, 1944, when near Rome, a spark of static electricity touched off some spilled gasoline. Ninos won the Soldier's Medal for quick thinking, grabbing a fire extinguisher and putting out the flames before they reached a collection of 1,200 more cans of gas. A third brother, Johnny was assigned to the aircraft carrier USS Franklin.

Ray Payne

Machinist Mate 1st Class Ray Payne joined the Navy in October 1940, serving on the cruiser USS Quincy. The Quincy spent nineteen days shelling Normandy, was used as President Roosevelt's transportation from Malta to Yalta, and then went to the Pacific, where it shelled Okinawa, before firing on the Japanese mainland in July 1945.

Richard "Bud" Pounds - BCS Class of 1940, was an Army Air Corps bomber pilot whose B-17 was hit and lost engine power over Germany during a bombing run in World War II. Bud was the pilot (and the youngest crew member) on a B-17G assigned to the 422nd Bombardment Squadron, 305th Bombardment Group, 8th Air Force, based in England. On December 5, 1944, his was one of 451 B-17's, escorted by 630 P-51 fighter planes, sent to attack factories and airfields around Berlin. The Air Corps lost 12 B-17's and 15 of the P-51's in the raid. Bud and his crew were among the 115 men missing with the bombers.

Bud Pounds

According to his brother, Bill, Bud gave his crew the option of bailing out or crash landing with him at the controls. (Their B-17 lost an engine to AA fire, then lost two more trying to keep in formation.) His entire crew stayed and Bud crash landed his badly damaged bomber safely with no fatalities.

German civilians arrived at the scene and had plans to execute the crew, when German troops arrived and saved them from the vigilante mob. However, after arriving at the German POW camp for processing, their radio operator, TSgt. Robert L. Phillips, was shot and killed when the pistol being waved about by a German officer telling them about the dangers of escape accidentally discharged, hitting Phillips in the head.

After the war, Bud returned home where he and his brother Jack continued operating the Bolivar Magneto Co. with their father. He also served on the BCS Board of Education while spending a lifetime with his wife Glenna at their home on Streeter Brook in Little Genesee.

James Reeland joined the Army Air Corps in January 1943, and went first to Canisius College for his elementary flight training. Six-feet-three-inch Bob Richardson joined the Army in July 1942, and drew an assignment to SHAEF Headquarters (Supreme Headquarters, Allied Expeditionary Force). As a result he occasionally acted as a driver for Generals Eisenhower and Montgomery.

Harry Sackett made corporal while serving in the Air Force. Pvt. Vince Sallazzo did not get in uniform until the summer of 1945. He spent his first year in the Philippines and the second in Japan. Tech. 3g Dallas Seamans joined up in 1941, before the war started, and went to Ireland with a medical unit in 1942. He went on to manage a PX in England, then another in France. His brother, PFC Donald Seamans joined the service in December 1943. When they met in Paris in July 1945, Dallas said that his brother was just the second person from home he had seen since he left civilian life.

Sgt. Jack Matylas was stationed at Fort Benning in the spring of 1942. On his way home on a two-week leave, he managed to see that year's running of the Kentucky Derby, won by a horse named "Shut Out." 2nd Lt. John Bradley got caught up in an oversupply of pilot candidates in late 1943, went through basic training in Miami Beach three times, before flight training. Awarded his pilot's wings in March 1945, his first assignment was instructing Free French pilots at Maxwell Field in Montgomery, Alabama. They did not speak English, and he did not speak French, so their rides in B-25s were somewhat *exciting*.

Private Manley McQueen served with the 261st Medical Battalion. With his unit, he landed on the Normandy beaches two hours after the fighting began, and in the next six hours worked to clear the area of mines, set up tents, carry the wounded to where they could get treatment, or surgery if needed. Cpl. Morrison Swain was attached to the 108th Infantry, which did not see heavy action until they landed on Luzon in the Philippines in January 1945, fighting for possession of Fort Stotsenburg and Clark Field. He ended the war on garrison duty in Korea.

William Monroe received his commission as a 2nd Lt. after graduating from OCS in Fontainebleau, France in June 1945. He had been in Europe since August 1944. On graduation, he went to Worms, Germany. His wife, Seaman 1st Class Marjorie Graham Monroe, was stationed at the Naval Air Station at Ottawa, Iowa. Sp. Q 1c Josephine Bush had joined the Navy in 1944. She spent much of her tour at the US Naval Communications Annex in Washington, DC, and was discharged in 1946. Bosun's Mate Earl Potter, in the Coast Guard, won a medal for "fighting the blazing munitions ship USS El Estero" in the harbor of Bayonne, NJ in the spring of 1944.

1st Lt. Bill Shannon served as a navigator in the Army Air Force, and was wounded in action flying over Europe. He was awarded a Silver Star, Purple Heart, and a Distinguished Flying Cross. He became a pilot before he was discharged in October 1946.

Bob MacDonell went into the Army as a private, and declined every offer of promotion, happy where he was, riding from St. Lo in France to the Elbe River in Germany with the 823rd Tank Destroyer Squadron, collecting souvenir Nazi flags and uniforms he sent home to his kid brother, Herb.

Bob MacDonell, right, with a Russian comrade he met near the River Elbe near the end of the war.

Marine Carl Wilcox was hit by shrapnel on Iwo Jima. Cpl. Everett Shaner was wounded in action on Feb. 27, 1945, also on Iwo Jima. Tech 4g Daryle Harris served with the 27th Infantry and spent much of his time as a cook, turning out bread and cake, but more than once he stepped in as a platoon leader during combat on Okinawa, and "dodged from hole to hole and position to position," building a strong defensive line from which a successful attack was later launched. Wounded slightly by shrapnel from a mortar burst on April 25, he returned to his company a few days later. A veteran of the fighting at Makin, Saipan and Tsugen, China, he wore the Infantryman Badge "for exemplary conduct in battle." He was also awarded the bronze star.

The closest Bolivar itself came to real action came on November 7, 1944, when a tow rope broke and a military glider landed near the refinery. Its pilots were welcomed as guests at Bolivar's annual football banquet.

These men left for the war and never came back. They appear here in the order they were lost.

November 13, 1942: Mitchell Leland Jordan, born in 1924, was the sixth of the seven children, and fifth of the six sons, of Percy and Hazel Jordan, who made their home in Bolivar at 145 Friendship Street. Percy was a well-known and successful drilling contractor. Mitch graduated from Bolivar in 1941 and joined the Navy. He trained as an electricians mate, and went to serve aboard the new light cruiser, the USS Juneau, which was commissioned on Valentine's Day, 1942 at the Brooklyn Navy Yard. After a shakedown cruise along the Atlantic Coast, and a patrol in the Caribbean, she left for the Pacific on August 22.

There she fell in with Task Force 61. Juneau first saw action at the Battle of Santa Cruz on October 26. During the engagement, the Juneau provided antiaircraft gun support for the carrier Hornet, but the Hornet was severely damaged and sank the next day. The Juneau then joined the group protecting the USS Enterprise.

On November 8, 1942, Juneau escorted transports carrying reinforcements from New Caledonia to Guadalcanal. The convoy arrived at Guadalcanal early on November 11 and began unloading. The next afternoon it fought off an attack by 30 Japanese planes without loss on the ship. However, just before 2:00 a.m. the next morning, Nov. 13, during a spell of bad weather, two Japanese battleships, one light cruiser and nine destroyers moved into position undetected and attacked the Juneau and the convoy.

The battle, one of the fiercest surface naval battles of the war, was fought in pitch darkness at point-blank range. The Juneau was torpedoed on the port side, which caused it to list heavily, and it withdrew from the action. Later that morning the Juneau, with two other badly damaged cruisers, the San Francisco and Helena, turned and headed for repairs at the US base on Espiritu Santo. About 11 a.m., Japanese submarine I-26 spotted the stricken ships and launched two torpedoes at the San Francisco. Both missed, but one went on and struck the Juneau in the same spot it had been hit the night before. There was a tremendous explosion, breaking the ship in two. It sank in just twenty seconds.

The crew on the San Francisco assumed there were no survivors. Not wanting to make itself a sitting target, it steamed on. In fact, more than 100 of the 698 men on board came to the surface. They were not located by search planes for eight days, when only fourteen were still alive. The five Sullivan Brothers went down with the Juneau, as did Mitchell Jordan. The destroyer named in their honor is now a museum ship in Buffalo. Jordan was the first Bolivar boy lost to World War II.

Feb. 20, 1943: Sgt. Kenneth E. Brenneman enlisted Nov. 26, 1940 in the regular Army. He was with the 26th Inf. Regiment, 1st Infantry Division (yes, The Big Red One). The 26th led the first amphibious landing in North Africa, and fought at Kasserine Pass, the first meeting of the US Army with Erwin Rommel and the Africa Corps. Brenneman was killed in action there, on the second day of the battle, Feb. 20, 1943, probably defending the line between Bordj Chambi and a hill called DJ Semmama. He is buried at the North African Cemetery & Memorial, in Carthage, Tunis, Tunisia.

March 10, 1943: Lt. Earl Stillman Monroe was the only son and eldest of the three children of Lewis and Bertha Mix Monroe, who lived at 87 Wellsville Street in Bolivar in 1930, where "Louie" supported himself as an auto mechanic and car dealer. Earl, born October 9, 1916, was greatly admired around town, serving for time as Bolivar's Scout Master.

He enlisted on January 22, 1942. A year later, he was attached to the 473rd Bomber Squadron, 334th Bombardment Group, which was training in twin-engine Mitchell B-25's near Greenville, SC. On March 10, 1943, Earl was the ranking officer aboard, but serving as the co-pilot of a B-25 on a training mission north and west of Greenville over the mountains of North Carolina. At a point very near the border of North and South Carolina, twenty-two miles north of Walhalla, SC, the plane passed too low over a mountain ridge. It sheared off tree tops for half a mile while the pilots fought to pull up, but they lost the battle, the plane crashing on a remote, forested hillside. Ten days later, a local boy riding his horse through the woods happened upon the wreck, which had killed everyone on board, including Earl Monroe. His was the first funeral held in Bolivar for someone who died in the war.

March 30, 1943: Pvt. Willard Bean, was sent off with a big farewell party in June 1942, complete with singing and dancing for entertainment. He went with Company A, 109th Engineer Battalion, attached to the 34th Infantry Division, which was the first American division to land near Algiers late in 1942. He was killed fighting around Jebel Ain El Rhorab in Tunisia on March 30, 1943, battling the Africa Corps.

January 11, 1944: Staff Sgt. Donald Brundage. Star Bolivar football player Donald E. Brundage enlisted in the Army Air Corps on September 30, 1942, at the age of twenty. After his training ended, he reached the rank of staff sergeant and flight engineer, attached to the 353rd Bomber Squadron, one of three squadrons forming the 301st Bombardment Group. The Group was initially deployed to England, but was soon transferred to North Africa. When the war moved to Italy, the heavy bombers were regrouped into the15th Air Force, and in December 1943 the 15th Air Force relocated from North Africa to the southeast coast of Italy, in and around Foggia, equipped with B-17s.

On January 11, 1944, four bomb groups, about 144 planes, were dispatched to attack Piraeus, the port city of Athens. Don flew with pilot 1st Lt. Joseph Dunbar. The weather was awful, and as the planes reached the Peloponnese Peninsula they began climbing to their bombing altitude of 19,000 feet. As they did so, they passed through a layer of clouds at 18,000 feet, which iced most of the planes, including the windows.

Elements of the 97th Bomber Group flew ahead of the 301st. As it began to make a right turn to line up on the target (still about 40 miles away), one of its squadrons ran into heavy turbulence, perhaps caused by the the dozens of bombers flying ahead of it. The lead ship in that formation was knocked into a steep left turn, and disappeared into the clouds. The two planes on either side of the lead plane became confused and decided to follow their leader. In doing so, they turned and flew directly into the path of the oncoming 301st Bombardment Group.

The groups met head on. Both of the planes that turned back were destroyed, although three of the 19 men aboard them survived. They, and the debris from the initial collisions, took down six other B-17s, including two from the 353rd Bomber Squadron. The tail gunner, James Raley, of the plane piloted by Capt. Robert Goen was trapped in the tail when it broke off, but the tail did a revolving flat spin and slowly fluttered the entire 18,000 feet to the ground, where it landed in a clump of trees. Raley lived, nearly unhurt. Everyone else aboard those two planes died, including Don Brundage.

Feb. 22, 1944: Staff Sgt. Howard Bessey, from Richburg, was aiming at becoming a potato farmer. On Washington's Birthday, 1944, Howard was in the ball turret of a B-17G with what seems to me to be a real western New York name on its nose. It was named *"Blow It Out Your..."* Piloted by Lt. Fred Melzer, they were on a mission to Olching, Germany from Foggia, Italy, as part of the 429th Bomber Squadron, 2nd Bomber Group. The plane developed mechanical problems while flying over the Adriatic. It caught fire, and the pilot ordered everyone out. Eight chutes were seen, for ten men in the plane. Bailing out over the water, all were lost. Howard received the Air Medal with two oak leaf clusters. His name appears on the Tablets of the Missing at the Florence American Cemetery, Via Cassia, Italy.

March 5, 1944: PFC Herbert Wood. Herbert F. Wood was the son of Hollis and Mae Wood, who were living in Kossuth at the time of their son's death. Herbert, born September 8, 1919, had attended school in both Bolivar (his father, a mechanic, owned a home on Leather Street in 1930), and Friendship, and had enlisted in the Army on March 5, 1942.

Attached to the 104th Combat Engineer Battalion, he trained in the US for the next year. In July 1943, the Battalion was part of the operation that retook the Aleutian Islands, after which they were shipped to Oahu, Hawaii, building facilities near Koko Point. Beginning in January 1944, the 104th provided support to the Army's 7th Infantry Division and to the 4th Marine Division in the taking of the Marshall Islands, which fell in February. On March 5, (exactly two years after he had enlisted), PFC Wood was killed while helping build a water purification unit on Eniwetok, one of the Marshall Islands. He was hit in the head by a piece of shell. His body was returned to Bolivar in 1948.

May 18, 1944: Pvt. Arthur G. Stoddard was born 1922 in Bolivar. In 1940, he lived in Clarksville. Serving with the Army in India, he died of disease, a "fever of unknown origin" for which he had received blood transfusions, on May 18, 1944.

June 11, 1944: Momm2c Andrew Pockalny, or Pocklny, lived in the town of Genesee. Born in 1921, one of twelve children, he had left school after the 8th grade, when his father died. He joined the Navy in July 1942 and trained at Great Lakes. Rated as a Motor Machinist's Mate, 2nd class, in early 1944 he was serving on LST 314, (Landing Ship Tank) which was sunk in the Seine Bay on June 9, 1944, going down with 67 officers and sailors. Many others were saved. The records say he died "in action" on June 11, 1944, and is buried in the Cambridge American Cemetery. My guess is he was mortally wounded when his LST was attacked, and that he died two days later.

June 15, 1944: Master Sgt. Richard Childs, Bolivar '40, enlisted straight out of high school. In 1942 he made Staff Sgt. at Fort Bragg. He died June 15, 1944 at Camp Gordon, Georgia after suffering a serious, but unnamed, illness. He had made Master Sergeant and was the chief surveyor at the post where he died.

June 17, 1944: 2nd Lt. Merritt Pequeen. The family of Merritt Pequeen moved around quite a bit. He was born in Pennsylvania in 1923, lived in Olean in 1930, attended Bolivar High for a time, but about the time the war broke out in Europe his family moved back to Pennsylvania, settling in

Union City, and Merritt finished his education at the Corry Area High School.

He enlisted at Corry on February 17, 1941, giving as his occupation "actor." He rose through the ranks to become an officer, and by 1944 was a 2nd lt. attached to the 165th Infantry Regiment, which was part of the Army's 27th Infantry Division, known as the "New York Division." The 165th trained at Fort McClellan, Alabama beginning in October 1941, and arrived in Hawaii on April 8, 1942. It first saw action on Butaritari, part of the Makin Atoll, in November 1943. After quelling all Japanese opposition there, the regiment returned to Hawaii, where it remained until May 1944. The regiment, along with the rest of the division, landed on Saipan on June 17. The 165th immediately undertook the capture of the island's airstrip, known as Aslito Field. This area fell quickly, and they moved on to assault a ridge beyond, which fell to them the next day, June 18.

The regiment was then sent to attack some of the last remaining positions on the south end of the island, at Nafutan Point, beginning the attack there the next day, June 19, while offshore the largest naval battle of the war was taking place, the "Marianas Turkey Shoot." Merritt Pequeen was killed near Nafutan Point that day. He had three brothers, all of whom were on active duty at the time.

June 21, 1944: T Sgt George B Thornton, served in the Army Air Force with the 28th Squadron, 60th Troop Carrier Group, flying C-47s, known to civilians as the Douglas DC-3. In June 1944, their mission was to fly supplies to partisans in the Balkans from their base in Italy. Thornton died on June 21, 1944, in a plane piloted by Capt. Robert H. Snyder. These flights were usually flown at low-level and at night. Thornton was the in-flight engineer. The only description in the Missing Air Crew Report is that the plane "crashed and burned in Albania."

June 22, 1944: George Hickey, born in 1909 in Silver Lake, worked around Bolivar as a driller before the war broke out. He entered the service in December 1942. Stationed at Camp Chafee in Arkansas, he was transferred to Camp Campbell, Kentucky. He was killed in an accident while his unit was practicing maneuvers on June 22, 1944. An unidentified soldier walked into a trip wire, which set off a flare that hit Hickey in the face, killing him. He was buried at Maple Lawn on June 29.

June 23, 1944: 1st Lt. Joseph Matson. Bolivar lost a number of boys serving in the Air Force during World War II: Earl Monroe, Don Brundage, George W. Bradley, Joe Matson, Alvin Wallace, Jim Gray, and William Pelton among them, but only Gray and Brundage went down in action. The others died in flying accidents.

Through much of the war, Air Force pilots trained in three levels of planes: PT's, or primary trainers; BT's, basic trainers; and AT's, the advanced trainers. As you moved up through the levels, more and more features, including more powerful engines, were introduced.

Joe Matson is seen here standing beside a Vultee Valiant BT-13, a widely used basic trainer during the first three years of the war. Officially called the Valiant, Air Cadets referred to it as the "Vibrator." It was notoriously underpowered and could easily stall, spin, and crash. If a pilot was transitioning back into it after flying something more powerful, such as an advanced trainer like the AT-6 Texan, accidents came easily.

Joe, an honors graduate of Notre Dame, was a talented pilot, good enough to be chosen to stay stateside as a flight instructor. (Usually, the top ten percent of a pilot class qualified for duty as flight instructors). Assigned to put on a performance for a graduation ceremony, on June 23, 1944, Joe and another instructor climbed into a BT-13, took off, stalled and crashed. Both men died. It was witnessed by Joe's wife, and by his parents, A.J. and Sylvia Matson. He was their only child. They left their estate to Joe's alma mater, Notre Dame.

Sep. 10, 1944: Tech5 Harold O. Lafferty, was the middle of the five children of Theron, a driller, and Esther Lafferty, who lived on the Pleasant Valley Road north of Richburg in 1930. Harold dropped out before he got into high school, and with his big frame quickly found work as a tool dresser, probably alongside his father. By the time the war came, the family had moved into a home at 185 Olive Street. Harold enlisted in the Army on September 1, 1942, and after basic training became a member of the Army's oldest operational division, the First Infantry Division.

The First Division was made up of 24 separate units, including everything from the headquarters company and medical detachment to tank and antiaircraft battalions. Harold Lafferty was assigned to the 1st Cav Recon Squadron, a unit that more often than not found itself out in front of the rest. The Big Red One landed on Omaha Beach on D-Day, June 6, 1944, taking 30% casualties in the first two hours of the assault. Following the Allied breakthrough at St. Lo, the division attacked the area around the town of Marigny on July 27, and then was engaged in a fast-moving, continuous drive across the north of France, which took them to the Belgian border by the beginning of September.

On September 10, patrols went out across the Belgian-German border to scout the approaches to the German city of Aachen. It was during this action that Harold Lafferty became one of the 4,280 men who died serving with the Big Red One. (More than 15,000 others were wounded). He was buried in the cemetery at Henri-Chapelle in Belgium.

Sep. 12, 1944: Staff Sgt. James Gray, born April 6, 1925, was the oldest of the four children of Daniel T. and Helen Gray, who made their home at 211 North Main. Jim graduated from BCS at the age of 17 with the class of 1942, PG'd with the class of 1943, and joined the Air Force that summer. He did his basic training in Miami, Florida in the fall, then went off to gunnery school. He was a warm and personable man, a close friend of Joe Matson, four years his senior, as well as of his classmates.

The Air Force assigned Jim to the last Bombardment Group activated to be part of the 8th Air Force based in England, the 493rd, nicknamed "Helton's Hellcats," activated on November 1, 1943. The crews received final proficiency training at McCook Field, Nebraska, before heading overseas. Initially equipped with B-24 Liberator bombers, the transfer to Britain began in January 1944. Some of the air crews traveled by ship on the USS Brazil, leaving from Boston on May 12, arriving in England on May 26. Others flew from McCook, with stops in New Hampshire, Labrador, Iceland and Northern Ireland, on the way to their base in southeastern England at Debach, where today there is a museum dedicated to the unit. The first of 160 missions made during the course of the war, an attack on the crossroads city of Liseux, France on the morning of D-Day, was aborted because of cloud cover over the target. They continued flying B-24s until early September 1944, when the group received B-17Gs. They flew their first missions in the 17s September 8.

On September 12, 1944, the 493rd went to attack a German munitions plant in the city of Magdeburg, located in the center of the country, 440 miles away from their home field. That day, Jim, who served as a waist gunner, flew on a plane piloted by George Owen from Chicago. From an altitude of 23,000 feet, at 11:10 that morning, they made their run, dropped their bombs, and turned for home. That's when the Messerschmits arrived. Pilot Owen announced enemy fighters were incoming. Radioman Trunzo moved back to the other waist gun opposite Jim.

The 493rd Bomb Group was composed of four squadrons, the 860, 861, 862 and 863. On this day, the German fighters focused on the 863rd Bomb Squadron, in which flew Jim Gray. The action started about 20 miles west of the target, just north of a little hamlet named Uplingen. As the ball turret gunner underneath the plane, Charlie Gialloretto, looked for targets, he saw the B-17 on their left take a heavy volley in its right wing, and it "immediately turned into a puff of smoke." It exploded in mid-air, instantly killing everyone on board. About the same time, machine gun fire started ripping apart Jim's plane.

Probably because pilot Owen had been killed or wounded, co-pilot Blades gave the order to bail out. The navigator and the seriously wounded bombardier, dropped out the front hatch, along with the flight engineer. The tail gunner opened his hatch and dropped out the tail. The guy with the most difficult escape route was ball gunner Gialloretto, who, to make it back up through the tiny hatch in the turret, he had to take off his oxygen mask. When he popped up into the fuselage, he saw radioman Trunzo and Jim Gray on the floor of the plane laying side by side, both choking, and unconscious from oxygen deprivation. In the thin air, Gialloreto passed out too. The next thing he knew, he was falling through space. Their plane too had exploded, taking with it both pilots, Trunzo and Jim Gray. The rest of the crew were captured and survived the war in German prison camps. In all, the 863rd Bomb Squadron lost seven of its 12 planes that morning, leaving the half-empty mess hall a grim and gloomy place that night, exactly the atmosphere the Germans thought would help them win the war. Of the ten planes lost by the 493 Bomb Group, four exploded in mid-air. Jim Gray's body was so badly burned that only the last name on his dog tags could be read by the Germans who found him. He was 19.

Sep. 26, 1944: PFC James L. Nichols, born in the town of Genesee in 1917, was drafted into the Army on June 1, 1942 and served with Co. D, 16th Infantry Regiment. The 16th was also part of the Big Red 1, the First Infantry Division. With it, beginning in November 1943, Nichols campaigned across Africa from Morocco to Tunisia, then across Sicily. The division was then withdrawn, and underwent extensive training in England for an amphibious assault.

They took part in the landings at Omaha Beach on June 6, and it was this regiment which broke through the German defenses on D Day. After D-Day, the regiment was placed in reserve until late July. In June 1944, (we don't know which day), Nichols was hit by artillery shrapnel in his leg, and made it to a hospital where the shell fragments were extracted. The 16th then took part in the breakout at St. Lo, and chased the retreating Germans all the way to Mons, Belgium. Beginning in mid-September, the 16th became part of the drive from Mons to Aachen, and the grueling combat in the Hurtgen Forest. In September 1944, PFC Nichols was again under artillery bombardment, was hit in the chest, and died Sep. 26, 1944.

Nov. 29, 1944: PFC Clark J. Hughes, born in 1915, BCS '34. In the 1930s, he and Richard Common organized a jazz orchestra to play at local events. He went on to work as a professional musician on tenor sax and clarinet with orchestras in Syracuse and other cities. When the war came, he served with the 180th Infantry Regiment, 45th Infantry Division, which went through Sicily and into Italy. The 45th then became part of the invasion force sent into southern France in August 1944. His regiment endured 86 consecutive days of combat as they pushed their way north. On November 9, they were relieved and had fifteen days to relax, going back into the fray on November 24. They then moved through the Saverne Gap, and protected the division's north flank as it pressed ahead through Strassburg and on toward Pfaffenhoffen, which fell on Nov. 30. Hughes was killed in action during this push, on November 29. He is buried at the Espinal American Cemetery, France, on the banks of the Moselle River, about 35 miles from the Rhine.

Feb. 2, 1945: 1st Lt. Alvin O. Wallace was born in Sweden Valley, outside Coudersport, on July 28, 1920. His family moved to the Bolivar area in 1923, and for a time in the 1930's they lived in the former Wilbur Cook home on the north side of Boss Street. In school, Al joined the band, sang in the glee club as well as the Methodist Church choir, and made the basketball and football teams. He was warmly remembered by his classmates for one very chivalrous act. When it came time for his senior prom, Alvin asked a girl who had never had a date before to be his for prom night. After graduating in 1940, he worked at the Bolivar Hotel and the Main Service Station. In early 1942, the American Sales Book Company of Niagara Falls hired him and he moved there.

He joined the Army Air Force on July 1, 1942, and originally trained as a bombardier. As such, he was in the first class trained specifically in low altitude bombing, and received his bombardier's wings in March 1943. Soon after, he qualified for pilot training, and did his flight training in Texas. He received his pilot's wings in February 1944, and four days later married a girl he had met in Niagara Falls named Maxine Cairns.

Of all of Bolivar's boys who joined the Air Force, Al was the only one to achieve what was probably a common dream - of piloting the hottest fighter in the arsenal, the P-51 Mustang. He served with the 4th Fighter Group, 336th Fighter Squadron, going to England in July 1944. He was promoted to 1st Lt., and in January 1945 was credited with destroying two German fighters: a Messerschmidt Me109 in air to air combat on New Year's Day, and a Focke-Wulf Fw190 on the ground during a January 16 raid near Ulzen. He was awarded the Air Medal and Oak Leaf Cluster. On February 4, 1945, while practicing low-altitude slow rolls near his home base in England, his plane slid out of the roll and crashed. He died instantly.

Feb. 11, 1945: Lt. Ralph G. Lester, was born Jan. 10, 1918, son of Onnalee and Paul Lester. He was working as a forest scout for the US Forest Service when the war broke out. He enlisted in the Naval Air Reserve in 1942, trained in Virginia, and took a commando course in Iowa. He then applied for flight training, and received his wings January 15, 1944. He did training in dive bombers, but requested a transfer to a spotter squadron and was attached to VMO No. 1, Quantico. He left the states for the Pacific in December 1944, and was killed on Feb. 11, 1945 on Guam, flying a Stinson OY-1 Sentinel, used by the Marines as an artillery spotter. His unit, VMO-1, (Marine Observation Squadron 1), also included the first enlisted Marine to win the Medal of Honor, Gunnery Sgt. John Basilone. Notice of Lester's death appeared on the same page of the *Bolivar Breeze* as that of Alvin Wallace.

Mar. 16, 1945: Lt. William B. Pelton grew up around Bolivar and Richburg, but graduated from Olean High with its class of 1942. He joined the Air Force on January 23, 1943, and qualified as a pilot. He became a B-25 pilot, assigned to the 488th Bomb Squadron of the 12th Air Force. (Also serving in the 488th at this time was Joseph Heller, who wrote his best-selling novel "Catch 22" based on his experiences. Although a best-seller, the book was despised by the men who served in the 488th.) They were stationed on the island of Corsica.

In January 1945, the entire bombardment wing with which Bill flew was assigned to repeatedly bomb the rail lines leading into Italy through the Brenner Pass and down the Italian Alps on a route north of Venice. On January 21 Bill was piloting B-25 with tail number 8P. High winds, gusting to 60 miles per hour, and heavy flak caused the formation to pull out of two bomb runs before lining up for a third attempt, which finally allowed them to drop and head for home.

As another plane in the formation, "8U", piloted by Lt. W.Y. Simpson, turned to the new heading for Corsica, he was hit by one of these blasts of wind, and "became unbalanced." The plane slid across the sky and its left propeller struck the tail of Pelton's plane, cutting off the right stabilizer, the right elevator, and chewing up the tail gunner's compartment. The tail gunner, Aubrey Porter, was seen falling through the sky without a chute.

8U lost a wing, immediately went into a spin, and crashed into the hills near Trento, Italy with all five crew members on board. Pelton's plane also went into a spin, but Pelton, and his co-pilot, Harry Shackleford, managed to regain control and keep their ship aloft, slowly climbing back to 13,000 feet, embarking on one of the most famous flights ever flown by any of the pilots of the 12th Air Force. These planes had no hydraulic assists on the control surfaces, so Bill and Harry had to push and pull with all their might to steer the plane and adjust altitude with the one remaining stabilizer and elevator; and they had to do so for a flight that under normal conditions took three and a half hours. The fact that they made a successful, and even smooth landing astonished the hundreds of onlookers who witnessed it.

Bill won the Distinguished Flying Cross, but the stress of the flight, combined with the DFC, turned into a curse. According to other members of the group, he began flying as though he was invincible, and took ever increasing risks; so much so that the veterans of the group would no longer fly with him. His plane filled with green replacements. The runways on Corsica launched the planes quickly out over the waters of the Mediterranean. Good practice was to immediately begin climbing to assigned altitude. Pelton would instead stay "on the deck," flying as low as he could over the water, then pull back and climb quickly up to join the formation. On March 16, 1945 (just as the articles about his famous flight were finding their way into the local papers, including the *Bolivar Breeze*), Bill skimmed the waves after taking off, but caught a wing tip on a wave just as he started to climb out. The plane disintegrated, and only one body, that of the radioman, was ever found.

Mar. 19, 1945: Fireman 1st class Herman E. Lewis, was serving on board the aircraft carrier USS Wasp, CV 18. The Wasp, the USS Franklin, and fifteen other carriers were all part of the Fast Carrier Task Force, Task Force 58. In mid-March 1945, the task force was sent to support our forces at the Battle of Okinawa, and to reduce Japanese air fields within range of the island. The *naval-history.net* site says the Wasp was engaged in support of "Okinawa Gunto" operations on March 19. At 7:10 in the morning, it was hit by one 500 pound armor-piercing bomb, which penetrated the flight deck, the hangar deck, and detonated in the crew's galley, where many of the men were having breakfast. It also wrecked one of the fire control rooms. 102 men were lost, including Herman Lewis. Lewis's wife, Margaret, lived at 491 Beach St., in Boston, MA.

Mar. 19, 1945 Petty Officer John Ninos, son of Mr. & Mrs. Stephen Ninos, graduated from Bolivar with the class of 1943, and joined the Navy on July 12. In high school he was the sprinter on the track team, running and often winning the 100 and 220 yard dashes. He did his basic training at Sampson Naval Base on Seneca Lake. He then attended radar school at St. Simons, Georgia and was assigned to the carrier USS Franklin when it was commissioned in Norfolk, VA. The Franklin was hit during the Battle of the Sibuyan Sea on October 30, 1944,

and returned to Puget Sound in the US for repairs. This allowed John to spend Christmas 1944 at home with his parents, and he returned to duty on Jan. 5, 1945. He brought home a piece of shrapnel from the kamikaze that had struck the ship. His last letter home was written on February. 26, in which he told his family not to worry.

Just after 7:00 a.m. on March 19, 1945, a lone Japanese dive bomber hit the Franklin with two 550 pound bombs, at a time when thirty-one fueled aircraft armed with fifteen tons of high explosives were warming up to take off. Those planes burned, as did others in the hanger deck, where gasoline vapors exploded.

On board a ship pulling alongside the Franklin to lend it aid as it drifted and listed without power was Bolivar's Lance Cpl. Anthony Sallazzo. Close enough to call across to a sailor on Franklin's deck, he yelled, "Johnny Ninos! Johnny Ninos!" The sailor heard him, stared back, raised his arm, and gave Tony a thumbs down. Johnny Ninos was one of the 807 men killed that day, the heaviest damage and highest casualties suffered by a US fleet carrier that survived the war. Only the crew of the battleship Arizona suffered more men killed in action.

A ship pulls alongside the USS Franklin seeing if it can be of help
March 19, 1945 *Photo credit, National Archives*

May 21 1945: PFC Junior F. Stoneham, born April 12, 1926. He enlisted in 1944 at Buffalo. Junior F. Stoneham, son of Isabelle Stoneham, 105 Olean St., died in Magdeburg, Germany on May 21, 1945. He was poisoned, probably by German partisans who could not accept the fact that Germany had lost the war and surrendered on May 8. He had attended Richburg school and joined the service in 1944. Only 19, he was given the bronze star posthumously. His body was returned and buried in Bolivar in July 1949. His mother posted this poem in the *Breeze*: "When all is still and silent, and sleep forsakes my eyes, my thoughts are in the silent grave, where my dear son lies."

July 13, 1945: 1st Lt. George W. Bradley, born September 6, 1920, grew up in a house located at 91 First Street which was torn down in 1960. When Charles A. Lindbergh flew from New York to Paris in 1927, George became fascinated with flying and became a passionate builder of model airplanes. After high school he spent the money he earned on flying lessons with pilot Stretch Kane at the old Wellsville Airport. When the war broke out, he had accumulated more than 50 hours of flight time. He joined the Army Air Corps in November 1942, and did his training in Arkansas and Texas, receiving his fighter pilot's wings in August 1943.

Because of his skill and experience, he became a flying instructor in P-47 Thunderbolts, America's largest and most-produced fighter of the war. He spent most of 1944 training pilots in Winfield, Kansas. In late 1944, the Air Force acquired a modified version of the P-47, the P-47N, the longest-range fighter we had, to escort B-29 missions to Japan. George was assigned to one of these new units, the 463rd Fighter Squadron, training at Dalhart, Texas.

The 463rd left for the front in late April 1945, via Hawaii and Eniwetok, arriving at their forward base on the island of Ie Shima, just off the coast of Okinawa, on June 26, 1945. The 463rd launched its first combat missions on July 1. George led a flight of four planes that took off for a routine patrol late that afternoon. His radio stopped working, and he relinquished the lead position to his wingman. They returned to land as night fell. The new flight leader lined up to land, but was waived off because of an accident on the runway. He led the flight on a circular path around the island as darkness descended, and lined up on a line of lights he thought was his runway. It wasn't; he had lined up on the taxistrip leading away from the far end of the runway, along which was parked another group of fighters being readied for their next flights. The flight/leader wingman was again waived off, via radio. George, having no radio, was unaware of the mistake, thought his wingman had done him a favor by lining him up, and proceeded to land. Witnesses said it was picture perfect; the wheels barely made a sound when they touched the ground. Within 100 yards of touchdown, he hit a fuel truck, a communications pole, and two parked P-47s. His plane erupted in fire. He threw back his canopy, stood up, but stunned by the collisions, collapsed back into his seat.

The soldier who pulled him out of the burning wreckage won the Silver Star, but he was only able to do it after the fire crews made a third approach to quell the flames. George was taken to a hospital on Okinawa, where he remained unconscious for five days. He briefly rallied and dictated letters to his wife and parents saying he had burned his hands, but would be home soon. He died in the hospital listening to his chaplain recite the 23rd Psalm on the evening of July 13. He was the last Bolivar boy lost in the war. He left a wife in Olean and a three-month-old daughter he had never seen. The war ended thirty-three days later.

We hear much today about PTSD, which had other labels in other times. Tony Sallazzo and my father, John D. Bradley, were Bolivar's last two surviving World War II veterans. If you were around Tony, he was warm, funny, outgoing, seemingly unchanged by the four years he spent in the Marines. But in private conversation, he might tell you how he still had nightmares, forty years later, provided by the memories of the battles he had lived through, the foxhole he had abandoned just before a grenade dropped into it, and the horrors of Iwo Jima.

My father never got out of the United States while in the Army Air Force. According to him, the man who was most changed by his war experience was his classmate, Gerry Wight, who had joined the Marines with Tony on December 8, 1941. Before he left for the service, Gerry was one of the high school stars, setting the record for running the mile, scoring touchdowns as an end or as the fullback on the football team, while my Dad blocked for him. They both played in the band, but Gerry also played the guitar and would serenade his classmates, imitating Gene Autry and Roy Rogers, sometimes leading sing-a-longs. After the war, Gerry kept a much lower profile. He gained a reputation as the best man in the area to repair rusted out sections of a car body, especially rocker panels, but the Gerry Wight I remember was very quiet, the last person I would have ever thought to have been a center of attention in high school. I know there must have been many others like Tony and Gerry, upon whom the war had dramatic, personal effects.

The war certainly had a profound affect on my life, even though I didn't come along until it had been over for two years. Because of my uncle's death, I came to fill, to the extent I could, the holes made in my grandparents hearts by the loss of the uncle for whom I was named. I spent far more time with my grandparents as a child than I did with my parents, not realizing until I had the benefit of decades of hindsight just how lonely they were because he never again sat at their table. I am sure that was true everywhere, in each of the twenty-five Bolivar area households where a son didn't come back. They fought and died to make the world a better place. And the world the rest of them came back to was in fact a better place. The post-war United States was better than the pre-war country had been. The dictators and autocrats were gone. The Depression was over. Jobs could be found. Educations could be afforded. Families could be started. And they were.

Bulldogs

Up until the mid-1930s, the Bolivar sports teams had no nickname or mascot. In the newspapers they were referred to as the *Blue Blazers*, or the *Donnellymen*, or as the *Centralites*. In 1936, two cheerleaders, Mary Prue Chipman and Helen Hogan, started a community-wide drive to raise funds to buy equipment for the football team, including "football togs, Eskimo cloaks and other equipment." They raised $200 from the Bolivar business community for the school Athletic Association. In the process, they thought the teams should have a proper nickname, and so it was that the *Bolivar Bulldogs* were born.

The 1936 season was notable for the Wellsville game. Bolivar had not beaten Wellsville in a football game since 1924. The 1936 game took place in Wellsville, and late in the game Bolivar was ahead as Wellsville put on a drive looking to take the lead. Instead, a Bolivar guard, George W. Bradley, intercepted a pass, and ran it back ninety yards for an apparent touchdown. However, a referee called a clipping penalty on Bolivar during the runback, which nullified the game-sealing touchdown, and he then imposed a twenty-five yard penalty based on an old rule, rather than the fifteen which current rules required. Infuriated, coach Paul Connelly pulled the Bulldogs off the field, went home, and forfeited the game.

Football seasons for Bolivar in the 1930s were short, sometimes as few as four games appearing on the schedule. For the 1937 season, Bolivar played away at Hornell and Portville, and lost both, Portville pulling out their 7-6 win in the last minutes of the contest. Led by 110 pound Fran Paffie, the team beat Coudersport 20-0, but at the cost of injuries to key players Bronco Reeland, Jim Ford, and their "hippo-sized" tackle named Jones. The last game of the season, against Bradford's St. Bernards, was a loss, 20-0.

The 1938 season started better. Thanks to a thirty-yard pass play from Bill Monroe to Phil Richardson, Bolivar upset Portville, 6-0. St. Bernards came to Bolivar and led at halftime 7-0. Richardson passed to Dan Dempsey to start the second half scoring, and in the fourth quarter Bolivar put on a long drive, capped off by Tom Ackerman crossing the goal line, putting Bolivar ahead 13-7. But those wins were followed by a 0-6 loss to Cuba, and to Port Allegany 0-27. To determine second place in the league, a second game against Portville was set up, and this time Portville won easily, 20-0. That game is notable as the first game ever started by Robert, then called "Buster", but later "Dutch" Dunning.

In 1939, New York State decided that New York schools could only play other New York schools, so Port Allegany and St. Bernards could no longer appear on the schedule. With Dunning, Fran Paffie, Ralph Best and Bill Nagle in the backfield, Bolivar beat Lakewood 22-6. In pouring rain at home, the Bulldogs rolled over Allegany 33-0. Allegany never crossed the fifty yard line. But then came Cuba, and Cuba won again 14-6. The final game was against the Thomas

Indian School, who had beaten Cuba 20-0. Dunning returned the opening kickoff fifty yards, Ackerman scored twice, and the Bulldogs won 14-0.

"Buster" Dunning was voted captain on the 1940 team. They won their opening game against Lakewood 25-0, with "an unbeatable aerial attack," but it was Johnny Ninos who threw two touchdown passes, and Gene Salzer who threw the third. Alden fell next, 24-0, with Salzer scoring twice on end runs, while throwing for a third, and Bill Nagle pounding over for the final score of the game. They won the southern division of the Tri-County League, but tied in the title game against Blaisdell, 6-6, Nagle making the tying touchdown.

In 1941, the Bulldogs won an opening game against the Olean JVs. When Bolivar was about to score, Olean intercepted a pass, but the player who caught it bobbled the ball, and Gerry Wight grabbed it and ran in for the game's only touchdown. They went on to lose to Lakewood 6-13, tied Allegany 6-6, then beat the Thomas Indian School 19-6, Wight, playing fullback, scoring twice and Johnny Ninos the third.

Wartime conditions and gasoline rationing truncated the 1942 season. The Bulldogs beat the Olean JVs and Cuba, but lost to Allegany and Portville. After that, the state said busses could not be used to get players to games, and the parents did not have enough ration tickets to go the extra miles. There were two games played in 1943 and 1944, Bolivar beating Cuba in 1943, but losing in '44. The only other game that year was against Bolivar alumni.

In 1945, assistant principal Tony Perrone took the reins as coach, and with the war over they had a full seven-game schedule. Bolivar lost the opener to Portville 0-6, but then ran off four wins shutting out Cuba, Lakewood, Canisteo and Allegany, before losing decisively to Wellsville 13-38. The season ended with a 45-12 trouncing of St. Bernard's in Bradford.

There had been a change in ownership of the Bolivar Breeze in November 1946, when Frank Herrick, brother of the founder J.P. Herrick, retired and sold the paper to a World War II veteran from Chicago named Glenn McCoy. Perhaps that was a factor in the drastically reduced mention of the high school band in the years that followed, but so too, I assume, must have been the declining energy of Bandmaster Clavelli.

There were other substantial changes to the Bolivar school after World War II came to an end. Professor Whitford's replacement was W. Cecil Davis. Dr., or Prof. as he was known locally, Davis had a collection of advanced degrees. He had started his career in education as the principal of the Shinglehouse school in 1918, when just twenty-one. A member of the lay faculty at St. Bonaventure, before coming to Bolivar he had been Portville's principal. Prof. Davis brought with him a fellow member of Portville's pre-war faculty.

During the 1930s, the head of the boys athletic program at Bolivar had been Paul Donnelly. Donnelly was well liked by the players on his teams, and kept on at his job until the war came, when he, like everyone else, went off to war and was assigned the job of conducting physical training for new Air Force recruits. But Coach Donnelly had developed a problem with alcohol before the war, and it

Milt Latimer, 1950

only got worse while he was in the service. When the war ended, he was not offered his old job back. Instead, Prof. Davis turned to a coach who had worked for him before the war in Portville, whose teams had won championships. His name was Milt Latimer.

Latimer had made the varsity club at Cortland State when only a freshman, and graduated from there in 1936. His first job had been at Portville, where he stayed until he went into the service in 1942. He joined the Bolivar faculty in 1946, and would be with the school for eight years. Milt Latimer did for sports in Bolivar what Umberto Clavelli had done with music fifteen years before.

The five win and two loss 1945 season had re-instilled interest in football in Bolivar. The season ended with a football banquet attended by 135 people. Neil Sullivan served as toastmaster, and there were a wide variety of speakers, including Sarah Morrison, Doc's wife, whose topic was "the Mother's Role in Football." Undoubtedly, the hundreds of returning veterans, who had spent the last two or three years staying in shape and focused on winning a great contest, also explains the deep interest and support given new coach Milt Latimer.

He got off to a great start. To open the 1946 season, the Bulldogs ran over Bath 41-6, leading 27-0 at halftime. The ease of the win may have gone to their heads, because they lost to league rival Portville the following week, 6-16. They then squeaked by Cuba 7-6, only to lose to Canisteo, 27-28. Two more losses, to Wellsville 7-14, and St. Bernard's 6-19, closed out a losing three wins and four loss season. But the community was closing ranks behind Latimer and his men on the gridiron.

To kick off the 1947 season, the Bolivar merchants sponsored a contest, something like the final four ladder. You entered by giving your guesses as to the scores of each of the seven scheduled games. Bath got even for the embarrassing outing the year before by edging out the Bulldogs 6-7 in the season opener in Bath. The Bulldogs then won three in a row, defeating league rivals Cuba 19-0, and Portville 32-0, before beating Lakewood 20-12. The Lakewood game was costly, four of Bolivar's starters knocked out with injuries. The next week, the game ended in a 6-6 tie with Canisteo.

With most everyone back in the lineup, Bolivar faced Allegany for the Alle-Catt league title, winning easily 38-0. They had won the league while holding all of the other teams scoreless. The last game was against arch-nemesis Wellsville, and they went down 6-19. For the season, the Bulldogs had scored 127 points, while allowing only 44.

Two of the emerging stars for the Latimer teams were Jerry Codispoti and Wayne Torrey. Expectations for the 1948 season were high, but were quickly dampened when they lost the opening game to Wellsville, 6-39. But with that defeat things began to click. In the second game, they defeated Allegany 20-6, but at the cost of Codispoti, who was knocked out with a knee injury. When they played Canisteo, his loss wasn't noticed as the Bulldogs rolled to a win, 25-0. But it did when Portville came to town, and the game ended in a scoreless tie. The Bulldogs next took on Cuba, winning 13-6, and Franklinville 26-6. After that they faced newcomer Otto, which again ended in a scoreless tie, and with a cost: Wayne Torrey broke his collar bone. That game completed the schedule, but left the league championship tied with Portville. The coaches agreed to a playoff game, and there Bolivar pulled it out once again, defeating the Panthers 12-7, and keeping the Alle-Catt trophy in Bolivar for the second year in a row. Perhaps more telling about future success: the JV team went undefeated.

The 1948 Bolivar Bulldog football team. After losing the opening game to Wellsville, this team did not lose again, starting a five-year-long streak of never losing a game. That record of success instilled an expectation of winning that would carry over in the school sports programs for decades. Coach Latimer sits in the back on the far right. Sitting second and third to Latimer's right are future stars Jim Bentley and Herb Claflin. In the second row on the left end is Don Lounsberry and nearby No. 11, Jerry Codispoti. Wayne Torrey wears number 8, front row, fourth from the right.

Prospects for the 1949 season looked bright, so bright that it touched off a landslide of community support. Back in the days when there was no other ready way to communicate, in late August Coach Latimer sent a letter to all the players he hoped would return, letting them know that the first practice would be held on September 1, giving them three weeks to get ready for the home opener against Wellsville. If they were aiming for an undefeated season, that made it a tall order. Bolivar hadn't beaten Wellsville in a football game since 1924, although there were eight years when they had not played one another. Of the fourteen games they had played, Wellsville had scored 316 points, and Bolivar just fifty-three. Only once had Bolivar scored more than once in a game, and that had been a loss of 13-38.

But this was 1949, and the Wellsville game would be played immediately after the dedication of the brand new, $9,000, 90,000 watt lighting system, which allowed night games. Half the money had been raised by J.F. Dunning and the Fire Department. For Dunning, it "was a dream come true." Not only were there lights, but there was also a public address system, which meant that there could be a play-by-play announcer. The school board's clerk, Soupy Campbell, quickly grabbed hold of the microphone, and held on to it for the next twenty-nine years. The field was wet that night, and the action was slow. In the second quarter, Lounsberry broke around the end and crossed the goal line from fifteen yards out, only to have it called back. But in the second half, both Lounsberry and Wayne Torrey scored, while the defense held solid. Bolivar finally defeated Wellsville, 12-0.

Fifteen hundred spectators had taken in that game. 2,000 showed up the next week to see the Bulldogs take on Portville. The Bulldogs fumbled on their own twenty-five yard line, and Portville took full advantage, leading 7-0 at halftime. But Latimer proved inspirational in the locker room. In the second half, Bolivar defender Russ Lewis blocked two Portville punts deep in Portville's end, and both times Bolivar scored. On top of those, the Bulldogs put on a sixty-yard drive to score a third time, walking away with a 21-7 victory. The next week, Franklinville came to play in the last home game of the season. Torrey scored twice, and Lounsberry, Schnettler and Davis each scored once. Final score, Bolivar 30, Franklinville 6. Allegany fell 26-0. Traveling to Canisteo, Herb Claflin started the scoring with a fifty-yard pick-six interception return, and the Bulldogs led 27-0 at the half, final score 47-6. The next week, they similarly rolled over Cuba 45-13, and won the league for the third year running, without losing a league game.

In those times, eligibility rules were much looser than they would be just a few years later. Wayne Torrey, Larry Paffie, Jim Schena and Neil Dempsey were all post-graduate students. The last game of the year was away at Otto, and Otto said no to post-graduate players. Without those four starters, the game ended in a 25-25 tie, but the Bulldogs had finished the season unbeaten. For the season, Torrey had scored eleven touchdowns and four extra points, averaging almost twelve points a game. He wasn't through.

Torrey returned for the 1950 season, and Latimer ran the boys through practices using two alternating formations, one a box, the other a single wing. The first game was at Wellsville. Three minutes into the first quarter, Torrey picked up a Wellsville fumble and ran it home. Bolivar led 20-0 at halftime, and went on to win 32-7. The season before, the lights on the field went up. This year it was the bleachers. They had been built, but were left unpainted for the first home game, against league rival Allegany. The exact count of spectators for that first home game was confused; some thought it was 2,000, others 2,500. Announcer Soupy Campbell received special commendations for his work as Bolivar won 33-6.

Cuba came to play under the lights the next week and fared no better. Wayne Torrey broke free for a ninety yard touchdown, and shortly after broke away again, running eighty-two yards for a second score. Bolivar led 21-0 at the end of the first quarter. The reserves made the final score 42-6. In the Canisteo game, Torrey scored two more, as did Lounsberry, while Harry Cummings and Claflin added one each. Bolivar 40, Canisteo 0. The team had a rhythm. In the final league game, Bolivar played Portville. Torrey scored three times, Lounsberry twice, and Cummings once, and the Bulldogs walked off the field winning 37-0.

Football mania had seized the town, and the Bolivar Men's Club sponsored what it billed as the First Oil Bowl Invitational game, inviting the Bishop Duffy School to come down from Niagara Falls for a season ending game. Duffy accepted. Presale tickets went for sixty cents, game night for $.75. An overflow crowd expected a close contest. Because Duffy's school color was also blue, the Bulldogs donned bright, yellow jerseys with black numerals. The first time Torrey was given the ball, he broke away for an eighty-yard touchdown. Then Lounsberry scored from the forty-nine. Then Cummings broke away for sixty-five yards. Duffy did hold Bolivar to a season's low number of points, but the game still ended up 32-0 in favor of the Bulldogs. For those thinking about the long-term prospects for the program, the JV team again finished its season undefeated. Two hundred and fifty parents and guests feted the team at the annual football banquet, and looked forward to 1951.

For the 1951 season, prospects originally seemed dim. Although sixty boys came to tryouts, only two of them had been starters the year before, Herb Claflin and Jim Bentley. The twenty-one game unbeaten streak appeared to be under serious threat as Wellsville came to town for the season's opener. But the more than 2,500 fans who came to see it saw Bolivar edge by the Lions 14-12. Portville fell next, 14-0. Bolivar then journeyed to Cuba, where the score stood 7-7 at halftime, but the Bulldogs pulled together, put one more on the board, and won 13-7. The next week, Bones Chadderton scored twice in the first half, while Bentley and Claflin both scored in the second, carrying the team past Salamanca 25-0.

The next game was the Second Oil Bowl, on October 20. St. Bernards came over from Bradford and held Bolivar scoreless through the first half. The Men's Club had decided a halftime show was in order. With Alyn Shaner acting as the MC, Bob Crowley, Bob MacDonell, Don Saunders and Sam Shaner pulled onto the field in John Bradley's 1910 Cadillac, threw up a makeshift derrick, and set off "a startling display of fireworks." Thus fired up, the Bulldogs went on to win 19-0. Over the following three weeks, Allegany, Canisteo and Franklinville all fell. The undefeated streak stood at 29.

The 1951 team had been made up of mostly seniors and post grads, so there were only three starters who came back for 1952. But, by now Latimer was seen as a miracle worker who could mold a new winning team year after year. The challenge, as usual, was to get by Wellsville in the opening game. The two teams fought to a draw, 6-6, but the unbeaten streak remained in tact. 2,300 came to the home opener, and the Bulldogs held on to in, beating Canisteo 6-0. The third game of the season was the Third Oil Bowl, and Shaner and his committee returned to do the halftime show. Bolivar won again, 19-7 over Randolph.

Interest in the team, and in how far the unbeaten streak might go, ran high, especially among former players. Many would call home long distance, a major expense back then, shortly after the games ended to get the scores. 2,000 paid to see the Bulldogs sneak past Portville 12-6. George Holdridge was the star of the Allegany game, which Bolivar won 27-7. Rich Ryan scored the third touchdown as Bolivar defeated Franklinville 19-0. The next week it was Cuba's turn to fall. Bolivar won the game 20-0, which meant it also clinched the league championship for the sixth year in a row. In the last game of the season, Holdridge scored the last touchdown in a 28-0 blanking of Salamanca. The streak stood at thirty-seven games. The Men's Club hosted the team and coaches at a banquet held at the Country Club.

And then it ended. In the opening game for 1952, Wellsville came to town and won for the first time since 1947, 0-7. The sense of communal loss might be best expressed by the Bolivar Breeze, which made no mention at all of the game or its outcome. The team went to Canisteo and lost again, 0-13, but Latimer was in the process of developing new talent. In the third game, Randolph was ahead 7-0 going into the fourth quarter. The Bulldogs scored twice, the second a sixty-yard pass caught by Brad Pohlig, and the Bulldogs went back to winning, 12-7. They beat Portville 20-12 the next week in the Fourth Oil Bowl game, again coming from behind, the final score set up by another pass from Jack Root to Pohlig. To end the season, they lost to an undefeated Allegany team, but beat Salamanca 21-6, and Cuba 14-0.

In 1954, Latimer's boys lost two games and won five, including the Fifth Oil Bowl, 28-12 over Cuba. One of the losses was to Portville, who won the league. More importantly, key players were coming along. Pohlig, Root, Wayne Hollister and Cleo Fisk were among them. But Milt Latimer was looking for a fresh start. The last game of 1954 was at home against Canisteo. Early in the week, the coach was stricken with a severe pain in his lower back, which was so bad he couldn't leave his house. Was it nervous tension? Had he pulled a muscle or just had a bad attack of sciatica? We don't know. While assistant coach Lou Foy ran practice, the Men's Club got wind of the problem.

Latimers lived in a house on Wellsville Street overlooking the football field. The club paid to have a direct telephone line run from the house to the field, so Latimer could still direct the team while looking out his kitchen window. Thanks in great part to the heroics of Brad Pohlig, who recovered two Canisteo fumbles, both on the Canisteo thirty yard line, Bolivar carried the day, winning 25-6. That was the last football game Milt Latimer coached for Bolivar. The following February, he tendered his resignation, saying he had been made an offer he did not think he could turn down. He finished the school year in Bolivar, then left to take his position as the first physical education director at the new Iroquois Central School in Erie County, where he would remain for the rest of his career. He died in 1966 at the age of fifty-five.

Milt Latimer's lasting legacy in Bolivar was instilling the idea that if you participated on a Bolivar sports team, you could, should, and would win. The school has been fortunate in having other coaches since who have been able to

Edward M. "Soupy" Campbell was born on July 24, 1900 and grew up in Belmont. He attended Alfred University, and was the starting quarterback for the Saxons all four years he was there. This is how he was thought of in his playing days: "Hardly large enough to be noticed by an opposing team 'Soupy' has, by means of his speedy feet, made himself a powerful factor on the offense, while many an opposing backfield man has come to grief after breaking through the line and, feeling well on the way to a touchdown, suddenly brought down by the terrific tackling of the little quarterback."

He came to Bolivar in the 1920s to manage the Belmont Lumber Company's Bolivar branch location, located on Railroad Avenue, which he operated for thirty years, until the 1950s when demand for its products declined. from the 1950s until the end of his life, Soupy served as the clerk of the Bolivar Central School Board

"Soupy" was a childhood nickname that stuck. He picked up the microphone to call the action for the Bulldogs in 1949. He liked the job so much, he assisted in broadcasting Alfred games for twenty-five years, and for Bolivar until 1977. He enjoyed golf, and became a charter member and president of the Bolivar Country Club. He often held the starter's pistol at Bolivar's track meets, and officiated at many track and field events. We lost him on May 20, 1978. Bolivar's gymnasium now bears his name as a memorial, along with the coach he first called the play by play for, Milt Latimer.

reinforce that idea. Sherman Craumer replaced Latimer, and in his first season oversaw the Pohlig-Hollister-Root combination as they led the Bulldogs to another undefeated season. Bob Cawley took his basketball teams to sectional titles. Lou Foy had success with the baseball teams he worked with. Bob Dunsmore left a lasting legacy too for the teams he developed in the 1970s and 1980s. I had the privilege of playing on the 1961 football squad, coached by Dutch Dunning. That team, led by Bobby Codispoti, Bear Hogan, Roy Boser, Phil Childs and Dennis Cole, among others, also went undefeated. What I remember most about that team is how much fun the seniors had that year. Codispoti and Boser would practice trick handoffs to use when receiving kickoffs. They would take Bear Hogan, who played center and nose tackle, and put him in at fullback. They had a ball, and so did the rest of us.

Korea

The price America paid for Russia's declaration of war on Japan in the summer of 1945 was the division of the Korean peninsula into two zones, North Korea, being occupied by the Russians, who installed a communist regime, and South Korea, who the United States and its other allies tried to set up as a democracy. On June 25, 1950, the North Korean Army invaded South Korea, igniting the Korean War. 1,789,000 United States soldiers served in that war, while we still had 5,720,000 in uniform in all branches of the service. It is estimated that more than 3,000,000 people died as a result of it. 33,686 of them were Americans who died in battle, 2,830 who died of other causes during the conflict, and 7,586 who were reported missing.

Many men from Bolivar were already in uniform when the war broke out. Jesse June had joined up in 1949, and was with the 89th Tank Battalion. Leland Blakeslee had gone in about the same time, and was serving with Company B, 1st Provisional Infantry Battalion. Wilbur Rinker drove a half-track for the 2nd Armored Division. Don Gardner and Fay Kinney were serving together in the 35th Infantry Regiment.

The front page of the August 17,1950 Bolivar Breeze carried the headline, "Two Bolivar Youths Named Heroes in Korea." Gerald Wescott, son of Harold, the R.F.D. mail carrier for Bolivar, had enlisted at age seventeen in 1946. When the Korean War broke out, he was already in Korea, attached to a special intelligence unit known as Kelly's Boys, which operated behind enemy lines assisted by South Korean guerillas. He was nominated for a Silver Star in August 1950, for carrying a wounded comrade out of harm's way. Word arrived in early September that Corporal Wescott had been killed in action, the first soldier from Allegany County to fall in the war.

Life was only slightly easier for Lt. Fay Kinney. Lt. Kinney had been assigned command of another group of South Koreans, who carried he nickname, "Kinney's Marauders." Kinney's wife did not know he was in Korea until she read a newspaper article about the unit sent out by the AP wire service. Kinney's unit had been in the front line, and fought off four North Korean attacks in three nights, when his unit was ordered to withdraw. As they prepared, a column of tanks pulled up to cover the retreat, and, as Kinney wrote home, "who should pop out of one of the tanks but Jesse June from next door! He seems as delighted with his tank as a ten-year-old boy with a new Buck Rogers weapon." Just a few hours later, Kinney was hit by shrapnel, but was back on duty within two weeks.

Although dozens of Bolivar boys served in the Korean "conflict," Bolivar only lost four who were directly connected to the community. Wescott was the first. Donald Kuhn, who lived in Little Genesee and attended Bolivar Central, was sent as a replacement to the 27th Infantry Division in May 1951. He was killed in action on June 2. A memorial service was held for him at Loop's Funeral Home. Gordon Hahn, Fenton Yehl, Merle Hollister and Everett Shaner formed the firing squad. Bob Paffie played Taps.

Sgt. Leland Blakeslee had been born in Bolivar on June 28, 1931. He played in the band for six years before he graduated with the class of 1949. One month later, he joined the National Guard, and one year later, found himself in Korea. On September 5, 1950 he used his automatic weapons to hold off a grenade attack carried on by "overwhelming forces," and was awarded the Bronze Star for his heroics. Five days later, he was wounded in the hands and face by shrapnel during the fighting for Hill 314, which was part of the battle of Tabu-dong, eventually won by the Americans thanks to McArthur's landings at Inchon. However, he was caught up in the collapse of the "Home By Christmas" Campaign when the Chinese intervened, and was declared missing in action of November 2. Never located, Blakeslee was "presumed dead" on December 31, 1953.

The last was PFC Ross Roe. An only child, he attended Bolivar Central, and on February 1, 1952, while still a senior in high school, he joined the US Marines. He arrived in Korea on August 10, 1952. He served as a radioman with Co. E, 5th Marines, 2nd Battalion, 1st Marine Division, and was caught up in six battles. On February 23, 1953, he was hit by shrapnel from a grenade and was hospitalized for a month. During the build up for the Battle for Outpost Vegas, which the Chinese and North Koreans launched to better their bargaining position at the peace talks which had already begun, on March 23, Roe was wounded again, this time severely. He was successfully evacuated, but died of his injuries on March 28. His body was returned home, and on May 25, 1953 all the businesses in town closed while his committal service was conducted at St. Mary's, and all students who wished to attend were excused. Every flag flew at half staff. Although commonplace when a soldier's body was returned to Bolivar for burial during World War 2, Roe's funeral service marks the last time that this was done.

The Korean War ended on July 27, 1953. Knowing that Bob Sortore would be home soon, but not in time for Christmas 1953, his family postposed their Christmas celebration until he arrived, which was in mid-January. Marine Cpl. Lewis Jordan sent a letter of thanks to all the many friends and neighbors who had thought of him that holiday season, and who had sent him cards and gifts. The war was over.

PFC Ross Roe is seen here receiving his Purple Heart, on board the hospital ship USS Haven. While recuperating, he had the chance to meet Red Sox great Ted Williams, and also ran into two friends from Bolivar: Zola Goodrich and James Champlin.

Watering Out

When the secondary recovery effort began, most people familiar with the process knew that only about ten percent of the oil under Bolivar had been pumped to the surface in the twenty-five years since the field had been discovered. Engineers also told them that with water flooding, they could hope to recover another forty percent of the petroleum there when they began. But, the recovery would follow similar characteristics with the original flowing wells. After the pressure had built up in the formation, the amount of oil being produced would dramatically increase, but would soon begin a steady decline year to year as the producing wells disgorged less and less oil, and more and more water. Eventually, the value of the flow of oil would not cover the considerable expense of keeping the lease equipment operational and paying the necessary salaries of lease workers, meaning the wells would need to be plugged and the leases abandoned.

One of the earliest and most aggressive water-flooding operators was the Messer Oil Corporation, financed by the Duesenbury and Yahn families from Olean, but managed by Johnny Messer, who lived in Bolivar. One of the properties they developed first was ninety-nine acres in the southwestern corner of the Town of Wirt, which the company bought for $1,500 an acre in 1925. They drilled a line of 38 water-injection wells, another of twenty-eight producing wells, and cleaned out and shot a number of old oil wells that had been previously drilled there. By 1927, the property was producing 176 barrels of oil a day, and over the next ten years gave up over 3,800 barrels per acre. The money rolled in. The company decided to turn part of the property into a lavish corporate retreat, spent $100,000 to bring redwood logs from California to build it with, and created Hilltop.

But in 1938, the oil property watered out, meaning it could no longer be operated at a profit, and the Hilltop lease became the first water-flooded oil property in the field to be plugged and abandoned. The last oil run from its storage tanks went into the gathering system on November 10, 1938. Four years later, the Forest Oil Corporation announced that it had completed the drilling of all the wells it required to fully develop its 530 acre block of acreage which straddled the road from Bolivar to Richburg. They would still employ the pumpers who kept the machinery running, but would no longer need the services of drilling crews.

As more and more properties were fully developed, the demand for drilling rigs ebbed. Oil prices climbed and remained strong, in the $3 to $4 range all during World War II, which both prolonged the producing life of developed leases, and made the development of thinner sands potentially profitable, but what that did was to postpone the inevitable. The demand for drilling rigs and crews still shrank. The demand for oil well supplies shriveled in step with the decline of drilling. This trend was aided by the abandonment of wells, creating a steady supply of used pipe and fittings which could be had for much less than new. Some suppliers could adapt. Murray Bascom had started a supply business to the west side of the railroad tracks in Bolivar. When he died, it was taken over by the Bradford Supply Company, and they got into the business of refurbishing and selling used pipe. So did the Dempseys, but the overall number of supply stores in the area shriveled, until in 1958, after Doc Hoffman's retirement, there was but one left.

In 1944, Forest Oil sold all of its Allegany County operations to Quaker State. It started a trend. Albert Shaner had been approached by Messer Oil about his property on Shaner Hill in the 1920s, and he had decided to sell rather than lease it for a royalty. He died in 1945, and in 1946, his estate sold another 1,000 acres to new operators. The Phillips Estate sold a large block on Phillips Hill. Dennis McCarthy and the McEwan Brothers got out of the business of operating leases. More often than not, the new owners were investors who could only see dollar signs when they thought they had the chance to be in the oil business. The days when these leases would throw off enough cash to build another Hilltop were long gone. The sellers wanted to get out while the numbers still made sense to prospective buyers.

The population of the town of Bolivar, including those who lived in the village, peaked in 1930, when the census bureau counted 4,538 people here. 566 of them left town during the Depression. The return of the soldiers after the war, the starting of new families, and an apparently stable economy led to a count of 4,170 souls in Bolivar in 1950, a gain of nearly 200 from before the war. But, the petroleum industry was still declining, and there was little or nothing that could be done to reverse that trend. Most people knew that fact, but efforts were still made to reverse course.

Some tried to do so by experimenting with more ways to recover the oil remaining under ground. The Bradley Producing Corporation was one of the leaders with these experiments. On their Knight Farm property, on the Messer Hill Road near Hilltop, they tried using a method to start a fire in the Richburg sand, the proponents theorizing that the increasing temperature would allow the oil to flow more easily to the producing wells, and the gasses produced by the fire would help drive the petroleum through the formation to the producing wells and up to the surface. Bolivar petroleum engineer Tom Hungerford oversaw the experiment, and watched the lowering of an electrically heated metal stem into the selected well, which would be heated beyond the flash point of the gas and oil. Tom gave the order to turn the device on, and soon thereafter heard noises and felt rumblings that told him to get away from the rig fast. Thirty years later, he told me that as he ran from the platform he thought he was the fastest man alive, until he was passed like he was standing still by a college student named George Holbrook, Jr., from Wellsville, a member of the extended Bradley family who owned the company. After that incident, the experiment was abandoned.

In a separate exercise on Bradley's Sawyer lease, now the site of the Baldwin sawmill near Vosburg, the company injected carbon dioxide into the Richburg sand. That process worked. Oil production from nearby wells increased. However, there was no readily available source of cheap carbon dioxide, (the company got the CO_2 used for the experiment in the form of dry ice), and the added production did not come close to paying for the expense of using the method, so the experiment was considered a commercial failure, and it too was shut down.

Others in the Bolivar community tried to tackle the problem of the decline of the oil business by making an effort to attract small manufacturing businesses to the community, who would hire and keep a workforce here, and who could solidify the tax base. On the plus side was the school system, which had a wide reputation as one of the best in western New York. Also, the village was considered one of the wealthiest in the country, based on the number of millionaires per capita who lived here. But there were already downsides. One of the most prominent of those was the weak financial condition of the Pittsburg, Shawmut & Northern Railroad.

The Shawmut, as it was commonly known, had been on shaky financial ground the entire time it existed. It had been formed in 1899 through the merger of half a dozen small, narrow gauge lines in central Pennsylvania and western New York, roughly connecting Brockway, Pennsylvania with Wayland, New York. Due in part to the failure in 1905 of the company which underwrote its bonds, the Shawmut went into receivership. It never got out, but it did manage to stay in operation for another forty-two years, a record amount of time for an insolvent to stay in business.

Having the Shawmut running through Bolivar allowed for the delivery of much of the pipe and heavy equipment which had been installed around the oil field as it was developed. In its early years, the Shawmut had offered regular passenger service to Olean and Friendship, where long-distance travelers could connect with trains going to Pittsburg or Buffalo and beyond, but the growing popularity of the automobile had brought that business to an end in the 1930s. Even as its other traffic declined, the railroad's continuing presence was essential to the operation of the Bolivar Refinery, which used it to distribute its finished products.

In the early 1930s, as the local refineries in Wellsville, Farmer's Valley and Bradford cut back on the amount of crude oil they bought, they became choosy about which petroleum they would buy. The Allegany Field is not filled with just one type of crude, but rather with at least three. The Richburg sand around Bolivar is filled with a emerald-colored, paraffin-based petroleum. The lower Waugh and Porter's crude is of an amber hue. But that which is produced from the pool around Nile, New York is black. When the purchasing cutbacks were first made in early 1931, the area refineries announced they would no longer buy the black crude oil because it complicated their refining process.

The extended Shaner family owned many leases in the Nile pool. Under the initiative of Albert L. Shaner, plans were quickly made to build a new refinery just outside Bolivar village which could process 500 barrels a day of this black petroleum. The Shaners took a substantial ownership interest in this enterprise, but stock in the company was sold to many others throughout the community. When first announced, in the summer of 1931, the Bolivar Breeze treated the news like a front-page message from heaven, in no small part because the construction alone would create seventy-five to one hundred sorely needed jobs.

It took a few months to conclude the sale of the company's stock. It used some of those funds to buy the pump station and storage tanks of the Bradford Transit Company, which allowed it to transport the crude oil from Nile to the refinery by pipeline. Construction was sufficiently complete that the refinery started operations on January 6, 1934, able to handle 750 barrels a day, and employing twenty. The opening was marked by a parade made up of Legionnaires, the school band, school children and all others who wanted to get in line, all arranged by Neil Sullivan, who had become the refinery's executive secretary.

Over the first few years of operation, the company reinvested in its plant, broadening its product offerings, branding its motor oils and gasoline as "Bolivar" gas or oil. Three years after opening, in March 1937, the refinery proudly announced that it had purchased, thus far, 933,000 barrels of oil for which it had paid more than $2,300,000. A.L. Shaner was hailed as Bolivar's foremost citizen for bringing the refinery into being at a time when it, and the jobs it provided, were most needed.

But in 1946, the Shawmut Railroad traveled onto the terminal skids. The company existed mainly to transport coal from mines it also owned. An inspection turned up deplorable conditions at the mines and in the company towns where the miners lived. The railroad had operated under a receivership since 1905. As a result of the complaints, it was turned over to a trustee in bankruptcy, who made the decision to liquidate. The winning bidder wanted the mines and the scrap iron. It did not want to operate the railroad. So, the Pittsburg, Shawmut and Northern Railroad was sold with the proviso that the railroad would continue operating south from Bolivar only until March 31, 1947. After that, the refinery would lack a bulk carrier for its products. Had Albert Shaner still been alive, perhaps an effort would have been made to acquire the trackage from Bolivar to Olean; but he had passed away eighteen months before, and no one else stepped forward to lead the charge. Instead, plans were made to go out of business. Quaker State bought the refinery, and immediately closed it. Quaker State kept the gathering system, connected it to their own, and that source of local employment disappeared.

The refinery complex basically stood empty until 1956. Walter Pohlig, a German immigrant who had arrived in the United States in 1923, operated a small cutlery in Allegany. In the mid-1950s his business was growing and he needed more and better space. He and his wife, Helen, had made their home in Richburg, and their son, Brad, had been a star athlete for Bolivar Central, who graduated that year and headed to Harvard, so far as I know, the only "Harvard Man" Bolivar has ever produced.

A group of Bolivar businessmen and boosters agreed to co-sign with Walter on bank notes to finance the move and to do the necessary remodeling and equipping of the refinery's office building. Pohlig's Expert Cutlery came to Bolivar, bringing in twenty jobs with the hope of soon expanding to forty. This was one of the biggest success stories the Bolivar Chamber Of Commerce would be able to talk about. As an aside, it was suggested at some point that Walter might like to become a social member of Bolivar's American Legion post. He agreed. As part of the process, he had to answer a series of questions, one of which was, had be ever born arms against the United States? His answer? "Did I! DatDat-DatDatDat!" (Walter had been in the German Army in World War I). They took him anyway. Expert Cutlery was reorganized as Heritage Cutlery in the 1990s, and in 2007 Heritage was sold to Klein Cutlery, who remain on Refinery Road today.

The decline of oil and gas production led to trying and exasperating times for Bolivar taxpayers. The school system, such a source of community pride, had been built on oil money. As said earlier, in the 1930s, seventy-five percent of the assessed value of the real property in the town was that which had been placed on the oil and gas produced here. As production declined, the share of the tax burden to support the school system gradually, but steadily, shifted from the oil producing properties to those who owned homes, land, and other real estate.

Prof. Davis left Bolivar in 1951 to take over the Olean School System. In 1929, when the new school was built, and in 1945, when Prof. Whitford retired, the school board had gone to great lengths to find someone to head the school who would make it the special place they envisioned. But when Davis left, that didn't happen. Instead, vice-principal Anthony Perrone moved up, first as "acting principal," then as principal.

Perrone had come to Bolivar as vice-principal in 1945, and had been granted tenure for that position in 1950. A.L. Shaner had headed the school board during almost all of the Whitford years, and when he stepped aside attorney Chester Bliss became president of the board. The success of the Latimer athletic program kept the community focused on the school, which was bursting at the seams as the "baby boom" generation started to work its way into the system, necessitating in some grades the creation the three sections to accommodate the ninety plus students enrolled in them.

Whoever had been the head of the school during the 1950s would have been in a difficult position. An expanding student population, coupled with increasing state-mandated spending, and a shrinking tax base was a perfect storm for an administrator. And so it proved for Tony Perrone. The details are now lost to us, but these conflicting pressures frustrated the principal and the board of education. (The creation of the parochial school seemed to be a factor for some). In the spring of 1955, the board needed to decide whether or not to grant Perrone tenure as the principal. They informed him that they would not renew his contract, and set off a firestorm. The high school students walked out, en masse. The faculty voiced its support, and Perrone fought back. He tried to reclaim his previous position as vice principal, based on the grant of tenure given in 1950. He sued the board, saying they were discriminating against him for being an Italian and a Catholic. But, recognizing the weakness of his position and growing unpopularity, he found a teaching position in Wappinger's Falls and went east.

The board replaced him with Delbert Goranson, who left a principal's position in Bradford, New York to take over in Bolivar. Del had grown up in Jamestown, was thirty-four, and had been a Marine Corps officer during the war. Goranson soon discovered that he faced the same situation as had his predecessor, of a large enrollment and declining tax base, and after four years in Bolivar found himself at increasing odds with both the school board and the local community. This was despite the continuing success of the athletic program. The Bulldogs went undefeated in 1955, won the Alle-Catt League football title in 1957, and Bob Cawley's basketball team won the Section V title in 1958. The baseball team went to the Sectional championship game, but lost to Naples.

In May 1959, Goranson put on a presentation for the Men's Club, on one of their "ladies nights" at the Country Club, saying that he felt the need for better public relations between the school and the public. He passed out rough drafts of the upcoming budget and went through it line by line, explaining that most of the increases were the result of state mandates. Asked if keeping in step with state guidelines for teacher's salaries was adequate, he said no. He had a number of openings on the faculty, and had to compete on the open market to attract competent teachers. He then went into a discussion addressing complaints that the school was "over administrated," and then had to explain that there was a misconception that the school had been designed to accommodate 1,000 students, so there should be lots of room for 800. Recommended maximum class sizes had been lowered. Potential classroom space had been used for band rooms, machine, print and wood shops, art and homemaking. So, there was crowding, not lots of room. He closed by saying that if the locals wanted an A-1 community, they needed an A-1 school."

Behind his back, he was plagued by rumors that he drank too much and simply wasn't up to the job of keeping costs down while keeping the quality of the school high. He left the principal's post soon after, also told that his contract would not be renewed, but, unlike his predecessor, not complaining about the decision in public. He took his family and moved to St. Catherine's, Ontario.

There was one clear beneficiary of this turmoil. Many male members of the Bolivar faculty thought one of Goranson's problems had been that he had been seen drinking too often within the school district. Their solution? The faculty "club house" became Frank's Casa Nova Grill in Richburg- handy, but outside the district. Frank's, as it was best known, remained a popular stop as long as Frank and Katie Mucha were able to keep it going, into the 1990s, thanks in great part to the lunches Katie cooked on Saturdays. Frank would gladly sell you a beer, accompanied by a small, six ounce glass, his thinking being that the beer would stay colder longer in the bottle. He might fix you a whisky and water, or a bourbon and ginger, but he disliked fixing any drink more complicated, which was just fine with his regular customers. Katie's cheeseburgers, Texas hots, sauerkraut , goulash and potato salad were so good that when deer season arrived, there was standing room only in the Casa Nova during lunch hours. Frank wrote out the menus, which varied from week to week and season to season, on the inside of empty cigarette cartons, which he would pass around, usually no more than two to a table. Once a leading Olean restauranteur came for lunch during hunting season and ordered a Texas hot. He ate it,

Frank & Katie Mucha

and as Frank came by the table he said he would like to have another. Frank's replied that if he had wanted two, he should have ordered two. He would have to go to the back of the line!

The 1950s saw much in the way of transition. In 1953, Glenn McCoy, who had bought the Breeze just eight years earlier, was offered the opportunity to take over the management of two newspapers located in Owego. He sold the Breeze to Jack and Harriet Moore of Belmont. Jack Moore, once a B-24 Liberator bomber pilot with the 8th Air Force in England, was at the time the president of Belmont's school board, and their ties to the county seat ran deep. They did not move to Bolivar.

The village had great difficulty keeping the police patrolman's position filled. Archie Hatch, who lived in Olean got the nod as police chief in 1953, on the condition he move to town. He didn't, and was fired. The village board gave the job to Fenton Yehl, who had the highest score of those taking the civil service test for the position. He resigned seventy-two hours later. Hatch was rehired on the same condition as before, but rather than move, he resigned in November 1954. Don Moore eventually stepped into the post.

The major event of 1955 was the Matson Block fire, which destroyed a wood-frame building located between the State Bank and the Dwyer Buick Agency, the future Bowl-O-Var Lanes. The second floor of the building had been used by A.J. Matson for his law practice. Up there too was Bob Bentley's dentist office, and the offices of the Sawyer Producing Company. The bottom floor had housed the Matylas billiard parlor and Hollis's Youth Shop, which sold children's clothes. A.J. took over the ground floor of the old Methodist Church building on Boss Street. Dr. Bentley moved his practice to Wellsville. Matylas went out of business. Hollis's made plans to relocate a little way down Main Street, but it didn't take them long to decide to move out of Bolivar too.

The Bolivar Hotel underwent a renovation when it was acquired by Walt and Viola Reisen in 1956. They converted the dining room into the "Alpine Room," and coaxed local artist Dick Monroe to paint large murals on the walls which evoked alpine scenes, and started serving first class meals. Walt Reisen was a fifty-year-old Swiss immigrant who had a background in baking. Not long after coming to Bolivar, he and his wife started a second restaurant in the Miami, Florida area, and within two years had left Bolivar for Florida permanently. Reisen sold the hotel to a Buffalo policeman named Robert Grunion and his wife. In the fall of 1963, they sold it to Ken and Mary Stedman, about whom more later.

The Bolivar Little League was born in 1956, thanks mainly to the efforts of three men: school custodian Versil Goff, perpetual youth sports promoter J.F. "Old Dutch" Dunning, and Dr. Ernest Allison, a Bolivar chiropractor. Doc Allison was the head of fundraising, and by April he had come up with $1,400, (about $16,000 today). This was thought enough to kick start a Little League in Bolivar, but not enough to outfit a set of "minor league" teams. Work began to build the field at the end of Leather Street. The coming of Little League started the era of parental involvement in youth sports, which has evolved and spread to midget league football, youth soccer, softball, wrestling, and you name it. Over time, this organizing brought an end to the decades-long era of children simply gathering on the diamond or in a field to choose sides and play a pickup game of their choosing. I recall in the late 1950s being part of a football team when I was in the fifth and sixth grade, before a midget league was even thought of. We boys who lived in town, organized ourselves, and practiced often after school in Ferris's side yard on Olean Street, and would set up a game, sometimes a home and home series, with our friends and classmates from Little Genesee. The only adult involvement was driving us to Paffie's house in Little Genesee for the "away game." We had a ball. And none of us ever had to listen to parents yelling at us from the sidelines…. (That last line was written by a former youth soccer coach).

Bolivar's first Little League Park, before 1960

The Trial of the Century

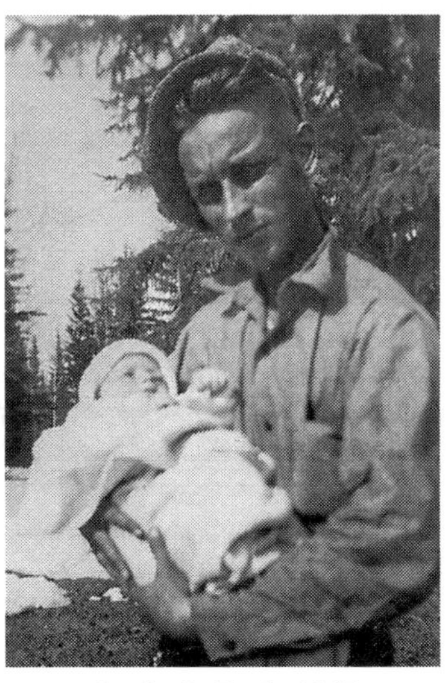

Rocky DeRock, 1947

One of the other players on the Bolivar youth football team was my classmate, Dennis DeRock. Dennis is the oldest child of Larry and Virginia Paffie DeRock, who made their home on South Street. Larry, better known as Rocky, had spent three years with the Marines during the war, more than half of it as a Marine Air Corps crew chief, keeping Corsairs flying as the Corps pushed its way through Peleliu, Okinawa, and the New Hebrides islands. When he took off his uniform, he found work in Bolivar at the Magneto, married Virginia, and took his place as an active member of the community. He became a foreman and vice-president of the Fire Department, joined the American Legion, and managed a Little League team. Then he was asked if he would run for the position of village police justice, said yes, and won. In only a few months he was put to the test.

On July 9, 1958 State Police arrested Bolivar's chiropractor, Dr. Ernest E. Allison, and his two female assistants, for practicing medicine without a license. Doc was famous for having a huge selection of "electrical machines" which could give a person mild jolts and magic diagnoses. Those were seized as evidence. Rumor around town had it that the Doc had advised a diabetic patient of his to stop taking her insulin. She did, and nearly died. That did not go over well in the medical community.

One of Doc's assistants pled guilty to the misdemeanor charge, but Doc stood his ground, entered a not guilty plea, and asked for a jury trial. Because it was a misdemeanor, the court to hear the case would be in Bolivar, and there hadn't been a jury trial in Bolivar since the 1920s. Justice Rocky had no training in law, and very little experience on the bench, having been in office less than a year. He poured through books and manuals trying to get ready for the trial. He was not alone.

Doc Allison hired future District Attorney Ed Merger; Ed in turn brought in the most highly regarded trial attorney in the area, Bob Fleischer from Wellsville. New York State appointed a special prosecutor from the attorney general's office in Buffalo, Michael P. Geraci, replacing District Attorney Norm Fitzer, himself having a great reputation for handling trials. A series of delays put the trial off until October. On the first scheduled date, October 8, Special Prosecutor Geraci dropped the charges against Doc's assistants, but jury selection proceeded. David Curtin, Merle Hollister, Robert Nicholson, William O'Conner, Larry Rossman and foreman Gordon Hahn were selected for the six-man jury, and Rocky set the trial date for the following week.

The prosecutor gave both of Doc's assistants, Amelia Sallazzo and Ruth Faulkner, immunity from prosecutions, using their testimony to document how the office worked. Then he called two other witnesses, both of whom had been patients. In every instance, there were motions and frequent objections that Justice DeRock had to rule on. Their testimony and cross examination filled two evenings, and Fleischer's cross examination of the diabetic patient was so rigorous she fainted on the stand. The whole drama played out to a packed house, every inch of space in the Library's Sorosis room packed with participants and spectators. The press reports lauded Rocky's impartiality. When asked by friends later how he had made his decisions, he admitted that basically he tried to keep things even. If you won one objection, you would probably lose the next one.

On the third night, Doc Allison was called in his own defense, and so many people showed up to watch the conclusion of the trial that the crowd ran out into the hall and up the interior steps to the library itself. When pressured, Doc admitted to using an instrument to take patient's blood pressures, but said he only did so to make certain he did not need to refer them to someone else. That was about as far as the prosecution got. Ed Mergler summed up the defendant's side of the case, saying the thirteen hour trial was a "tempest in a teapot." The jury agreed, taking little time to return a verdict of not guilty. The defendant wept. The audience cheered. As special prosecutor Geraci worked his way out of the building, he was overheard to mutter, "Bah. Frontier justice!"

Rocky DeRock was picked a couple of weeks later as the Bolivar Breeze's Citizen of the Week. Doc Allison put his electrical gizmos back to work, carried on business as usual, and kept on helping with the Little League. Justice DeRock went back to coaching his boys' team, fought to keep the movie theater open, and stayed in office for another four years. He ran for reelection and won in March 1962, but resigned that November because he had taken a new job, which, he said, would require lots of travel. In the summer of 1963, he joined the exodus and took his family, including my buddy Dennis, to North Carolina.

1958 was a gubernatorial election year, and Governor Averell Harriman came through town glad handing and looking for votes. His opponent, Nelson Rockefeller, never quite made it to Bolivar, but he did meet with the Allegany County Republican Committee at the LongVue Restaurant on top of Norton Summit when locking up the nomination. While there, he struck up a conversation with my father, and asked Dad what he did. When father replied that he was in the oil business, Nelson smiled as if pleasantly surprised and said, "You know, my grandfather was in the oil business!" Dad knew.

It was in June of 1958 that Doyle Green took over operation of the convenience store in Kossuth from Benny Turner, and in September when WKBW television started broadcasting, with Irv Weinstein asking parents every Saturday night at 10:00 if they knew where their children were. That year also witnessed the passing of three of Bolivar's most important citizens.

The Hogans

William J. Hogan, known his entire adult life as W.J., had arrived in Bolivar with his Irish immigrant parents in 1883, when he was seven years old. After attending Blackman's school, his first job was with the Tidewater Pipeline Company. W.A. Nichols, father of Bill Nichols, Bolivar's insurance man in the 20th century, taught W.J. telegraphy. He was transferred to Olean, and was later sent to Bensons' Mines in the Adirondacks as a telegraph operator. Not liking the climate, he returned to Bolivar and found work at the State Bank as a jack-of-all-trades, starting on Feb. 1, 1893. He was just nineteen. At the time, the bank had only two employees: president James M. Curtis, and cashier George A. Root. W.J. learned the ropes of the banking business quickly and in 1900 was promoted from clerk to assistant cashier. On June 12 of that year, he married Genevieve J. Moran, daughter of the man who drilled the Richburg discovery well. He became active in local athletic circles, usually as an official or timer.

By 1910, he had fathered his two children, Mary age eight, and William F., age 4, and had settled into his home on Wellsville Street. He had been promoted to cashier at the bank. In 1919, he was elected president of the State Bank of Bolivar, and kept that job until he retired in 1958, when he was given the honorific title of chairman of the board. He was then obviously in declining health, and resigned other volunteer positions that summer. He died on November 17, 1958, aged 82.

William F. "Bill" Hogan, W.J.'s son, had a position as a board member of the State Bank for a time, but he showed no real interest in following his father's career. Bill Hogan had married one of the daughters of Raymond B. Moore, and his heart was in the oil business. He worked for Moore as the company's credit manager, even after his first wife died. He remarried Mary Sherwood and raised a family of five.

Bill Hogan

He spent his long life operating the Daggett oil lease, and serving as the secretary-treasurer of the New York State Oil Producers Association. It was Bill who organized the annual, wildly popular, Oil Producer's Clambake, which was first held at the Wellsville Country Club, but which out grew it and moved to the Bolivar County Club. In the 1940s and 1950s, when there were still hundreds of people producing oil, it was difficult get tickets to the event. In its early years, the New York State Oil Producers Association worked hard as a lobbying group, being formed to get legislation passed to legalize water-flooding. But by the mid-1950s, as both the number of lease operators and leases declined, it was suggested that the name of the organization be changed to, "the New York State Clambake Association," since organizing the clambake was what took up most volunteer time. (That idea did not sit well with Bill). Bill's grandmother, Mary Moran, lived for a century. Bill had her genes, and his life ended just five months short of reaching 100 too, passing from the scene in the summer of 2005.

Bill and Mary Hogan named their first son Paul. Known as “the Bear” in high school and after, Paul became a local celebrity, He took up weight lifting as a teenager, and the power he developed got him the position of center and nose tackle on the undefeated football team of 1961. The following spring, a physical fitness promoter came to Bolivar to do a program in the school auditorium, and placed on the stage a 200-pound barbell, which he would lift using a technique called the clean and jerk to get it over his head. Before he attempted the lift, he asked if anyone would like to try to pick it up, and the entire assemblage of students began chanting “Bear! Bear! Bear!” Paul somewhat sheepishly walked up on to the stage, in part because he had never lifted more than 180 pounds above his head before. Paul did not “clean and jerk,” where the lifter quickly drops under the bar, straightens his arms, and stands. Paul did the “military press,” where the lifter gets the barbell up to his chest, then simply pushes the barbell into the air using only the power in his arms. While the performer explained the clean and jerk technique to the audience, he had his back to Paul, and the Bear was pushing the weight up into the air. The audience went wild as the 200 pounds of steel went aloft.

Paul stuck with the sport. In the oil field, he was the only person any of the old hands had ever seen who could single-handedly pick up and the move the end of a solid steel drilling stem. He took a job with Air Preheater which required that he travel, and he carried a set of York barbells everywhere he went. In Bolivar, he set up a studio called “Tool dressers” on First Street, and welcomed any young person who wanted to workout to use his equipment and space, listen to his stories, and tell their own. Steve Cooper and Jim Gardner became two of his most devoted acolytes. Paul did not compete very often, but he once won the title of “Weight Lifting Champion of France, North of the Seine.” When on a job in Brazil, he met his future wife, married, had a son of his own, the “Little Bear,” but then was killed, in 1987, in an industrial accident while in Minnesota. He had an infectious wheezing laugh, which frequently ended with a snort. It is now silent, and missed.

Paul “The Bear” Hogan

Bliss Family

Chester Bliss, 1949

The second prominent Bolivar citizen to die in 1958 was attorney Chet Bliss. Chester M. Bliss was one of the five sons of Walter T. Bliss, who had set up his law practice in Bolivar not long after the boom took place. Chet, as he was commonly known, was born on April 4, 1898. He graduated from Bolivar High School with the class of 1915, and followed his father's example by studying law at the University of Buffalo Law School, graduating in 1919.

Walter T. Bliss was a devoted member of the Prohibition Party. All of his sons joined the Democratic Party, including Chet, whose first foray into politics happened in 1922 when he was nominated for village treasurer, losing to Doc Hoffman as everyone would. In 1932, one of those rare years when a Democratic presidential candidate carried Bolivar, Chet ran for Allegany County district attorney, but carrying Bolivar by 400 votes was not enough to win the office.

Chet married Pearl Hooker in 1926 and had a son, Thomas. As the years passed he gained respect throughout the community. When A.L. Shaner stopped serving as president of the school board, Chester Bliss took his place. When W.J. Hogan stepped aside as president of the State Bank, Chester Bliss took his place. Chet stepped down as president of the school board in 1952 so he could accept the position of being attorney for the district instead. He also became the attorney for the village. He was a devoted Mason and Shriner, an active member of the Bolivar Men's Club, and of the Bolivar Country Club. His wife, Pearl, died in 1944, and in 1946 he married Madoline Childs Walchli. Madoline became active in Masonic affairs, and in 1952 accepted the office of Grand Conductress of the Order of the Amaranth for New York State, essentially being the head of the New York branch of advanced members of Eastern Star.

On July 25, 1958, Chet, Ed Gibbon, Irv Swarthout and a relative of Irv's, Warner Templin, decided to take in the harness races in Hamburg, New York. Just as they went through Delevan on the trip home, about 11:30 that night, they came on the scene of an accident, where an automobile had collided with a milk truck. They stopped to help. Irv ran off to a neighboring house to call an ambulance, while the rest looked to see if they could help the occupants of the crashed vehicles. As they did so, a station wagon approached from the south. All three stepped out to warn the oncoming driver. The station wagon hit the crashed car, and careened off. Gibbon and Templin jumped out of the way. Chet could not. He was hit and dragged a long way, breaking his neck, fracturing his skull. He was gone well before his body was found nearly half an hour later.

Chet was the second of the Bliss brothers to die. His oldest brother, Laurence, was six year's Chet's senior. He too had become an attorney, and had worked out of the family law office in Bolivar. In the early 1930s, he had been the Democratic Party's Allegany County chairman, but he died of kidney failure at the age of forty, in 1933.

The second of the Bliss brothers was Hubert, born July 1, 1894. After graduating from Alfred, Hubert decided on journalism as a career. After serving in the medical corps during World War One, he got his first job as a reporter in New Bedford, Massachusetts. Next, he landed a position as an assistant editor for the *Syracuse Post Standard*, then became the city editor of the *Hornell Tribune*. In keeping with the family's politics and his own ambition, he purchased the *Allegany County Democrat* in 1940, and published it for the rest of his life. In a special election held early in 1948, he ran for a seat in the New York Senate. Not making it, that fall he ran against Dan Reed for Congress, polling the largest percentage of the vote of any Democrat who had tried to unseat Reed. He died in Alfred in 1963.

The fourth Bliss boy, Burton T., went into the newspaper business, and took over the editing and publishing of the *Hastings News*, in Hastings-on-Hudson, New York in 1933. He ran that paper until 1960, when he retired to West Palm Beach, Florida, where he lived out his life, passing over on June 6, 1988, the last of his generation.

The fifth Bliss brother was George Walter Bliss, born in 1907, who was known throughout his life as Pete. He followed the examples set by his brothers Chet and Lawrence. He was deeply instilled with the patriotic spirit which so typified the time he grew up in. In 1923, he was chosen to recite the Gettysburg Address as part of the Memorial Day services, which was a traditional part of the ceremony. Pete was the miler on the track team, and vice-president of Bolivar's Class of 1924.

George "Pete" Bliss 1928

From Bolivar, he went on to Alfred University, and from there to Columbia Law School in New York City. He passed the bar, but decided to clerk in a Buffalo firm before returning to Bolivar to put out his shingle alongside that of his father and brothers. One of his first volunteer positions when he returned to town was as part of the Boy Scout Committee. In 1935, he was seriously injured in an automobile accident near Gorham, New York on the way home from a Colgate-Syracuse football game, fracturing his skull and being hospitalized for three weeks,. He had two passengers with him. Wilkins Newell suffered the most, with two broken legs, while Malcolm MacDivitt incurred only a few bruises.

In 1938, he became president of Bolivar's alumni association, and also a candidate for the New York Assembly, losing to the incumbent, Bill MacKenzie. In 1941, he was asked to head up the local branch of the Red Cross, which he did until he volunteered for the Army in February 1942.

After the war, he accepted the position as head of the Bolivar Industrial Development Corporation, led the local March of Dimes anti-polio campaign, and in 1953 became county chairman of the Democratic Party. The Industrial Development Corporation looked like it was getting off to a strong and quick start in 1948. Paperwork was signed with the Jeffers Electronic Company to lease the refinery property to make radio, television and radar parts. It was hoped that the company, which was based in DuBois, might bring seventy-five jobs to town. In April 1948, it looked like the company would be moving in equipment and starting operations, but negotiations dragged on regarding the building the company required, and that fall the project fell through, Jeffers deciding to build the new plant in Driftwood, PA.

After his brother Chet died, Pete stepped in and became president of the school board. Among other members of the bar, he was recognized as one of the most experienced lawyers in the area in the field of oil and gas property law and the transfers and sales of leases. In those days, New York designated an attorney in each county to supervise the opening of safety deposit boxes when a person died, and Pete served in that position for many years. Bolivar lost a devoted community servant when George Bliss died on July 14, 1976.

You could hardly ignore Winfield Guinnip's car when he came through your neighborhood. My grandfather, John C. Bradley, who took this picture, was not a fisherman. But plastic night crawlers were a new item in the 1950s, and he would buy dozens from Win Guinnip, and Grandpa would usually have half a dozen in his coat pocket. For what? He and my grandmother often ate out, and Grandpa did not eat salads. He did like to joke around with waitresses, and would take one of the night crawlers, tuck it into the lettuce, and ask the waitress to take it back. Most hurried...

Curt Jordan

W.J. Hogan died in 1958, but had not been part of the efforts to salvage the Bolivar economy as the much younger Chet Bliss had been. Younger still was Curtis M. Jordan, who had been born in Bolivar on April 3, 1911. Curt progressed from Bolivar High to Rochester Business Institute, and from there to Georgetown University. He was a devoted Bolivar boy, and after completing his education he returned to the area to make his living and raise his family. He was an accountant, and from the time he began working up until the mid-1950s, he maintained a public accounting practice, gaining the respect of many of the area's business owners for whom he kept the books and prepared tax returns and governmental filings.

As time passed, he started becoming a businessman on his own. He either owned or was a partner in a number of ventures, which included the Greene Supply Company, based in Richburg, the Larkin Packer Company, headquartered in Butler, Pennsylvania, Bolivar Gas of Canada, and the Bolivar Pallet Company, a new business he created to manufacture wood shipping pallets, as one of what he hoped would be many small manufacturing ventures that would help put a new economic base under the Bolivar area. When Doc Hoffman retired as village treasurer in 1956, Curt agreed to accept the appointment, and also filled the positions of village tax collector and clerk of the water department. Busier than he wanted to be with these appointed positions, his activity with the various entities trying to bring businesses into Bolivar, and his own business interests, he closed his public accounting practice in 1957. But on August 26, 1958, he was stricken with a fatal heart attack, and was removed from the scene . No one was able to fill his shoes.

Downtown

Bolivar's main intersection as it looked shortly after the war's end.

I was born in 1947. I never recall thinking that Bolivar's Main Street was anything out of the ordinary. The predominance of wood frame buildings set it apart from Cuba and Wellsville, both of which had far more structures built of brick than we did here. But every storefront in Bolivar was occupied, mostly with retail stores, and if not then with offices for those who offered things less tangible. I don't recall just how old I was when I was taken up to the main intersection to learn how to read the stop light and when and how to cross the street, but I do remember it was my grandmother who took that job, and it was no later than in the summer of 1952, to prepare me to walk to school by myself, which I began to do that September.

Soon enough I became George the Explorer, quickly bored with the monotonous trek up and back down Wellsville Street from our house on First Street to BCS. There was the alley between Louis Wilson's house and the Post Office, and a narrow passageway from it, between Sam Hardman's and Max Richardson's garages, which took me to a point on First Street directly opposite my parent's house. I discovered Cuba Street, which had been forgotten, but which would take you along the north side of the hotel and through various back yards to Kincaid Street. Friendship Street was always a good alternative, with the rumble of cars moving along its brick surface, just as they did on Boss Street past my grandparent's house.

What was best was that once I was trusted to cross on the green light and watch for traffic, I was given free rein to explore the village all I wanted, on foot, or on my bike, from Salt Rising Road to Prospect. "Be home for lunch," or "be home by five to clean up for dinner," were the only rules or limits on my freedom. No helicopter parent hovered over my head or tracked my whereabouts. In winter I might end up on Casey's farm with my sled, or in warmer weather at the end of Plum Street playing cowboys and Indians with the Hogan boys, or drilling a well with my buddy Doug Reeland beside his house on Belmont Street. (Doug's father Bronco set up a pipe tripod with a pulley at the top, and also made up a four foot piece of steel to use as a drilling bit, and another piece of tubing with a flap valve at the bottom to use as a bailer. At six feet down, the well started flowing. We had struck water, and lots of it- the water main leading up Belmont Street). On other days I could be found playing football either in Ferris's side yard on Olean Street or up at the school, or heading up to Prospect Street to see if Bobby Sallazzo was home, or to check on happenings at the pool.

As small as the town was, it took no time at all for all the shopkeepers to get to know me, and for me to know them, other than the barkeeps, who were off limits to a kid my age. My father was a very close friend of Al Glintz. I remember the transition when Al got into the argument with Atlantic, bought the Cowles house, and moved to the corner of Olive and Main, soon after coming up with the idea of opening a convenience store rather than a service station. I don't know if Al had the first convenience store in the town. Benny Turner's store in Kossuth, which I frequented on occasion after I got my driver's license, and after Turner had sold it to Doyle Green, may have been the first, or it might have been the little store operated in the early 1950s by the Froelichs out toward Little Genesee. I know both Al and Doyle used fresh cut Shinglehouse cheese as a draw to get people to buy their gas and shop for snacks, smokes, suds, shells and sundries. I miss the Shinglehouse cheese. I miss the sticks of pepperoni in the box next to Glintz's cash register, and I miss Al telling about his latest coup, or showing me the most recent watch he had taken in trade for a tank of gas.

Early on, directly across Olive Street from Glintz's store was Harvey Chambers' Pontiac dealership, and I always admired the blue, neon Pontiac sign mounted on the building. But my family were Ford drivers, so I never had occasion to go in there until Ferrises bought that building and moved their showroom into it. Of course, the Ferris and Forbes Ford-Mercury dealership sat across the creek from Harvey's Pontiac. My grandfather was a close friend of Glenn Ferris, and they both were horsemen. When I was young, Glenn Ferris lived in Richburg, and he kept horses there. My grandfather's religious experience was to go for a nice long ride on Sunday mornings, and often he and Glenn would cross paths on Richburg Hill, and would ride together to some scenic overlook, sometimes just over to the top of Shaner Hill, to look out over Bolivar and on down to Little Genesee, other times to Phillips Hill and views to the east.

Glenn Ferris was born near Hornell on October 6, 1900. When he started his working life, he soon found himself in Olean working with a older man named Forbes, selling used cars. He came to Bolivar in 1935 doing the same thing, managing the Ferris & Forbes used car agency. But not long after his arrival, the Bolivar Garage, which had the Ford franchise in Bolivar, suffered financial difficulties that caused it to go under in early 1936. That April, Glenn Ferris bought a new wrecker, and took over the Ford dealership in Bolivar, which three generations of the Ferris family would operate for the next fifty years.

Glenn built his business around his own reputation for fair dealing and an eagerness to please his customers, and around a service department which included half a dozen of the best mechanics in the area, all overseen by service manager, Tommy Tompkins. Tommy was a racing enthusiast who took his pick-up truck to Watkins Glen with great regularity to camp out and see the big races there. The first time I saw myself on national television was when I was sitting up on a platform Tommy had set up on the roof of his truck, watching one of the early United States Grand Prix races one October about 1960. Tommy always parked at the same spot at the end of the back straight, to hear the cars downshift as they entered the Big Bend. It was a great spot. Tommy built up a team of mechanics to keep Glenn's customers coming back. Dick Davison was one, who took over as service manager when Tommy retired. Joe Collins rebuilt the engine in my Thunderbird. PeeWee Greisch was another regular who did good work for decades.

I was often in the company of my grandfather, and there were many evenings when he would stop and go into the showroom just to chat with Glenn, and who-

The staff of Ferris & Forbes, early 1950s. L-R, in back in the truck: Ed Kemp, Arnold Pettit, Dick Davison, Dick Burdick. Front row: Bob Benson, Ed "PeeWee" Greisch, ???, Shirley Ferris, ???, Joe Collins, ???, Tommy Tompkins, Glenn Ferris, Dick Allen. The woman in the cab is unidentified.

ever else had stopped by to do the same, Sherm Lyons being one of the regulars I recall, who would mosey over from his house across the street. Sherm was about my grandfather's age, born in Kentucky in 1894, and a little-known fact was that his middle name was Boliver, yes, spelled with an e rather than an a. He had survived a career as a shooter, but I don't recall any great stories about exciting moments and close calls, just quiet conversation about recent events, with the occasional joke tossed in to keep the mood light.

Each year, Ford supplied their dealers with a boxful of model automobiles, to put into a display case so customers could get a good idea of what the various color options actually looked like, and at the end of the model year those would be given away. I still have one. Glenn gradually expanded the dealership's footprint. Beginning in a two-story brick building just south of South Street, his first expansion was to take over a long, single story building that stood on the north side of Root Hollow Creek. During World War II, at least part of it became the Liberty Roller Rink, when gas rationing limited the ability to get to the Coliseum. But by the time I came along, it had become the showroom in front, and car storage in the rear.

When the Pontiac dealership on the south side of the creek closed, Ferrises bought that building, and moved the showroom over there. Glenn added the lot across the street at the corner of Leather Street as a used car lot, and then picked up the former service station on the other side of Leather. Bolivar had been home to at least half a dozen new car dealerships over the years, but it was Ferris & Forbes that thrived, and which was the last man standing. Inflation, a spell of astronomical interest rates, and the steadily shrinking local economy finally forced the closing of its doors in the early 1990s.

Next door as you walked north along Main Street was a house, a fine, fair-sized clapboard home with extensive porches. It had been built in the nineteenth century by E.R. Kilbury, but had been, since 1916, the home of Dr. Lawrence Hackett.

Doc Hackett had been born in Ceres in 1890, son of a doctor who had his practice there. He graduated from Olean High School, then went to the University of Buffalo Medical School, from which he graduated in 1914. He initially took over his father's practice, but in less than two years moved his office to Bolivar. He served with the Army Medical Corps from January 1918 until July 1919- and that was the only time he was away from Bolivar and his practice. For the next forty-five years, he never even took a vacation. His wife explained, "There is always someone sick, and he would never leave town for any length of time as long as this was so."

Dr. Lawrence Hackett

During World War II, he was an examiner for the Draft Board. He served for many years as the doctor for the Richburg School system, and as a health officer for the towns of Wirt, Genesee and Bolivar. I remember clearly getting in line in 1954 to get my polio vaccination. There were two lines, one handled by Doc Hackett, and the other by Doc Morrison, whose line I happened to be in.

Doc left home every day at 8:00 a.m. to make his house calls., and kept office hours in the afternoons and some evenings. Early in his career, he went out one night on a call in his buggy along a road that "was then almost wilderness." Returning home, the buggy got stuck in a quagmire, and it cost $15 to have it pulled out. On top of that, he was never paid his $5 fee for the call. At what point he replaced the horse and buggy with his black Buick we don't know. It is the Buick I remember pulling up to our house in the early 1950s.

As mentioned earlier, for much of his career, he never slept on Saturday nights, instead spending those hours in a back room of the Washington Restaurant waiting for the inevitable calls to treat accident victims, calls which the operators knew where to direct, and which would not disturb his family sleeping at home. By 1960, Doc had slowed down and given up that routine. He spent those Saturday nights watching Gunsmoke, and being entertained by his three grandchildren.

Doc Hackett kept his office in the second floor of the State Bank. Standards of cleanliness and sanitation were different then than they are now. Doc's office had a sink with running water where he could scrub up. Patients were often asked to produce a urine sample during an examination, and, if the patient was a man, that sink where Doc washed his hands doubled as the urinal where you produced the sample. He was kind and competent, once put a staple in to close a wound on my hand, and he made almost daily visits to check on my grandmother during her last illness in 1963. He died on October 7, 1965.

After passing Hackett's house, you crossed South Street and came to the Kendall Service Station. Kendall Refining had purchased that corner lot in the spring of 1934, as part of its plan to develop a chain of stations between Olean and Corning. The Marchisi house stood on the property, but it was torn down to make way for a modern service station, which went up in its place. From the 1930s until about 1960, there were always three or four service stations in the village. The main east-west thoroughfare across the Southern Tier was New York Route 17, which connected Jamestown with New York City. Plenty of traffic came through. Many drivers needed gasoline, others looked for lunch or a coffee break, and kept those gas stations profitable. Al Glintz's location at the south end of Main caught the locals who knew the shortcut over Olive Street. The Kendall station caught everyone's eye with its bright red and white decor. The Main Service Station at the corner of Wellsville and Main, was the first available location for drivers coming in from Richburg or along Wellsville Street.

In early 1956, Mobil acquired the vacant lot on the west side of Main between Fagouri's and Colgrove & Wood's hardware, and put up another new station, about the first new construction in Bolivar's business district since the Kendall came in. Originally leased by Bob Hawkes, in just a few years it became Kenny's Friendly Mobil, operated by Ken Dunbar, then by his son, Richard.

Across the street from the Kendall Station stood four two-story, wooden buildings. The one on the left was used in the 1950s as the office and warehouse of Sherm Lyons, who had an oil well shooting operation. (His magazine was elsewhere). Next to the right was a related business, the tin shop where Jim Swarthout fabricated the metal cylinders used in shooting wells. Beside that had been Voorhees Hardware, which had faded out of existence during the Depression. In the 1950s, Hazel Glase kept a fish and pet food store there. The northernmost of these four was the Main Street Restaurant. My grandfather and I would often head there for breakfast on Saturday mornings for fried eggs and toast, and to listen to Edie Greene hold her own with the workmen who had come in for coffee.

To the north of this group stood another wood frame structure that was larger and taller than the others. Ira Cooper was born in Wheeler, Illinois in 1853, but the currents of his life brought him east rather than west, and in 1870 he was helping out on the family farm near Eldred, Pennsylvania. In 1879, he thought he saw an opportunity, and built a store building here in Bolivar, where he and his father David worked in partnership, settling on groceries as their business. Ira and Olive Cooper had a boy in 1882 they named Wallace, and Wally took David's place behind the counter when he came of age. Wally and his wife, Margaret, in turn raised their son Jack, who began working with his father in the store shortly after he graduated from Bolivar Central in 1939. Jack made the hard decision to shut down the store at the end of 1964, closing the door on what was then the oldest continuing business enterprise in the village, having been there for eighty-six years, predating the boom.

My grandmother and mother did their grocery shopping at Appleby's Red & White, but my grandfather spread his business around. Grandpa had a pony farm up in Pleasant Valley on the north slope of Richburg Hill. He had there two refrigerators. One he kept stocked with pop for the kids, and the other with beer for himself, the hired hands and guests, and he bought the beer and the assorted flavors of NeHi pop by the case from Coopers. Wally and Margaret were near neighbors of his, keeping house on the other side of Boss Street. All five of those storefronts were turned to ashes on February 4, 1974 during the Cooper Block fire. It is now the site of the Shop 'n Save grocery and its parking lot.

Wally Cooper and Sliv Root anxiously await their customers in Cooper's store, 1926

Beside the Kendall station stood the City Club Grille, into which I never ventured until I was out of high school. At that time, in the mid-1960s, it was run by Gordon Clark, himself an interesting character to look over and chat with from the other side of the bar. The City Club began operating under that name in 1950, then owned by Harvey Chambers and O.P. Taylor. Earl Freeman ran the kitchen, and he offered Friday night fish fries, "the best spaghetti and meatballs you ever tasted," and fun for everyone on Saturday nights. By that they meant music and dancing, and for a time at least, they booked the Tommy Fitch Orchestra to play Saturday nights and on Sunday evenings, 6-10.

I don't remember Clarks offering either music or meals, but they may well have. It seems to me that one of the more entertaining regular customers of the City Club of my time was Johnny Greene, the youngest son of the waitress Edie who worked across the street. He was hilarious when drinking, but what was more impressive was how funny he was in the years after he stopped. Three of the four Clark children were roughly my age. The twins, Janice and Janet, better known as Pickles and Tony, brought their humor to the Class of '67. Their older brother John, class of '64, set himself apart by wearing the only letterman's sweater I ever saw with five stripes: he made the varsity in football, basketball, wrestling, track and baseball. Mine has only two.

On the north side of the City Club stood the Lyric Theater. Bolivar had a movie theater in that building as far back as 1909. It started out as the Dreamland Theater, owned by A.L. Merritt. In the summer of 1910, Merritt did a major upgrade, installed his own twelve horsepower engine and a dynamo, which put out enough electric current to power the "motion picture machine," electric lights, and ceiling fans. The next year, Merritt sold it to F.H. Brewer of Jamestown.

The grand reopening of the Lyric, September 10, 1940

Ralph Ressler managed the theater in 1930, when the time had come to switch from silent to sound films. In June, the switch was made, and to emphasize the coming attractions, he changed the name from Dreamland to Lyric, and built a large electric sign touting the films being played, which changed three times a week. The first "talkie" shown was *The Night Ride*, a crime drama about a gangster who kidnaps two reporters, starring Joseph Schildkraut as a reporter, and Edward G. Robinson, naturally, as the gangster.

The theater was gutted by a fire in June 1940. The owner, Sam Gandel, took the insurance money and poured it back into the building, putting on a forty-five foot addition, hiring an architect to redesign the interior, and adding the triangular marquee which lit up that end of Main Street for the next thirty years. There was a grand re-opening on September 10, with Ginger Rogers and Ronald Coleman playing in *Lucky Partners*, a "screwball comedy" about two strangers who share a winning lottery ticket.

George "Gabby" Hayes

One of the highlights of happenings at the Lyric took place on June 10, 1938. George "Gabby" Hayes was Allegany County's gift to Hollywood. Actually a handsome, urbane and cultured man, Gabby Hayes had become the most beloved of the many cowboy sidekicks who appeared in the thousands of westerns churned out by the studios since the beginnings of the movie business. He first gained fame riding alongside Hopalong Cassidy, and was called Windy, which is how he was still known in 1938. He soon jumped ship to take the side of Roy Rogers, but had to change his moniker, being *Gabby* for the rest of his career. Hayes's father had run a hotel in Stannards outside of Wellsville, which is where George grew up. He got into performing early, and recalled appearing in a minstrel show on the stage of the Bolivar Opera House about 1898. He had a brother who lived in Portville, so when he came back to the area, he quite regularly passed through Bolivar.

On Friday evening, June 10, Sam Gandel got Hayes to make a personal appearance to add luster to a triple feature: *Rascals*, starring Jane Withers, *Alcatraz Island* with Ann Sheridan, and a "thrilling chapter" of the serial *The Lone Ranger*. Hayes did not play in any of them. Although Hayes would not appear on stage until 9 p.m., the first show started at 6:00.

The first movie I ever saw was at the Lyric about 1950. My grandmother took me to *The Wizard of Oz*. We left when the witch started skywriting. The first television in town was set up in the men's faculty lounge of the school, with the antenna attached to the chimney, and when the Friday night prize fights were broadcast, it was standing room only to see them. As the 1950s progressed, thanks to the growing popularity of television, the size of the audiences at the Lyric steadily shrank, and in 1956 Sam Gandel saw the writing on the wall. He leased the theater to Bronc Reeland and Don Moore, who took over at the start of 1957.

Reeland and Moore ran the place for two years and nine months, then in September 1959 turned it over to Larry DeRock and his brother-in-law, Fran Paffie. They gave it the old college try. About the first movie they booked was a top-notch, first run feature, *The Diary of Anne Frank.* In October they showed Alfred Hitchcock's *North by Northwest.* Soon they started having "kiddie matinees" on Saturday afternoons. Some of my favorite memories are of those afternoons, with the theater packed, every seat taken. Often there would be a delay in getting started, and the whole place would rock to the chorus of hundreds of young voices calling out, "*We want the show! We want the show!,*" which would continue until the problem was solved and the screen came to life. I was very tall for my age. The cutoff for the price of a child's ticket was twelve. But Lois Crandall, who usually sold the tickets, knew I was bigger than my classmates and never questioned me. But she lost track of time and let me have the kids deal until I was fourteen. Admission? Twenty-five cents, Jujy Fruits for a dime.

Rocky DeRock was always concerned about the children in town, and looked for ways to provide things for them to do. Two examples were Little League and the theater. But the theater was a family affair, and my friend, Dennis DeRock, was required to help clean up the place and to sweep out all of the spilled popcorn on Saturday mornings. Many was the Saturday when I would show up there too, to help with the cleanup so Dennis would be free to do other things.

Next to the theater was a simple, single-story building that had been the home of Bolivar Motors in the 1930s. When I knew it, it was first a Market Basket grocery store, then Short's Building Supply store. After I became a lawyer, a dentist from Olean hired me to represent him when he purchased the building and Short's business, in the late 1970s. I recall just as all the paperwork had been signed and money exchanged, the doctor leaned back and exclaimed that he just couldn't understand where the people of Bolivar had been buying all of their building supplies. I thought that during the thirty years I had then lived in Bolivar, I could recall a total of four homes being built: my parents on First Street; Tom and Mary Hungerford's on Prospect, and the Kuhn and O'Connor residences at the top of Plum. But, he was my client, so I kept the thought to myself.

At the corner of Main and Olean stood the Fire Hall. The ground floor was full of equipment, from the old, original American LaFrance, to the new ambulance. Upstairs, which had been a bowling alley before the war, was largely vacant. It held the village archives, stored here and there in boxes, but was little used otherwise. The Bolivar Fire Department, together with the Firemen's Auxiliary, was the largest service and social group in town. They regularly welcomed county and regional conventions in the summer months, and worked hard to raise funds to help defray the cost of equipment additions and upgrades.

Their most ambitious project was undertaken beginning in the early 1950s when they started raising the funds and contributing the labor to build a well proportioned clubhouse on Salt Rising Road. The work started in 1953. Progress was steady but slow. The clubhouse opened in 1960, and into the 1990s the Bolivar Firemen's Clubhouse served as a popular venue for alumni gatherings and other community get-togethers, when not rented out for wedding receptions and similar private events. *(Continued on page 220).*

Volunteer Firefighters

by Tom Manning

In the township of Bolivar for its first fifty-seven years, efforts to extinguish destructive fires were hit-and-miss scrambles by the victims plus any available neighbors able to pitch in. Picture the "bucket brigades" seen in the movies, with strong arms frantically filling pails at water well, horses being rushed from burning barns and women smothering flames with wet blankets. Of course, even in the quiet Bolivar village, homes and businesses were mostly scattered about with little "grouped" fire risk. That all changed in 1881-82, when the oil boom multiplied both the village population and the number of wooden structures along its old and new streets.

With all of the oil and gas permeating the ground and the air, amd with natural gas being plumbed into virtually every building, where it was set aflame to provide heat and light, everyone was acutely aware of the risk of fire. The first action taken was to hire an engineer named Thomas Farrell to design and install a water system feeding hydrants around the village. He oversaw the construction of three 1,200 gallon wooden tanks on the hill above the village, which were connected to a system of three-inch water mains that led to hydrants on most of the street corners in the village. Next, concerned men organized themselves and trained as "volunteer firefighters." On August 8, 1882, the first of two hose companies was formed in the village. It adopted the title of "J. B. Bradley Hose Company No.1," honoring Justin B. Bradley, the part owner of the Empire Gas & Fuel Company, who donated the hose cart and hose.

The Bradley men got uniforms in addition to equipment: white shirts with blue trim, black britches with white belts, and white caps. At first no "fire hall" existed, so their meetings and training drills were held at several available places in the village, usually twice a week. A month after the Bradley Hose Company was organized, a steam whistle was set up to serve as an alarm. But steam power requires a ready supply of steam – problematic at times. So in March of 1883 a large steel triangle placed in an elevated village space replaced it; when struck with a heavy rod its clanging alerted the available firemen to an emergency.

In 1884 a second firefighting unit, the Citizens Hose Company, came into being. Citizens Hose soon occupied "an attractive hose house" located on the south side of Friendship Street, just off of Main Street. (That building became the home of the American Legion Post when the new village hall was built in 1923, and served in that role for five decades.) Meanwhile, the Bradley Hose Company established a permanent home on the north side of Liberty Street, erecting a two-story structure set back from the street, with equipment bays downstairs and meeting space above. Both of those 1880s buildings were still standing in 2025. In an ironic 1924 twist of fate, the Legion Post – formerly the Citizens Hose home – suffered a partial fire that "started in one of the card rooms." The new

Bolivar Fire Department responded from its new fire hall one block away, and saved the structure.

Fire departments share attributes with military units. Its members must practice and employ teamwork to carry out their missions. They have a sense of camaraderie, of "having one another's back" in dangerous situations. From all that, there springs social fellowship, friendly competitions in professional skills, and unit participation in public events like parades. The early hose companies developed such qualities. "Running teams" were selected for hose cart competitions like Bradley Hose's of August, 1891, against the Alma Hose Company. It was the first of many contests with the region's other companies.

John Herrick of the *Bolivar Breeze* wrote that in the 1880s "some of the most colorful civic spectacles were the parades of local and visiting hose companies with their gaily decorated hose carts, blaring bands, silken company banners and roistering songs which enlivened the streets periodically." He also recounted a memorable Citizen Hose Company summer trip "by special train" to Butler, Pa., where they marched with fourteen other companies and won first prize for the largest unit (44 men) and "the finest hose cart."

To supplement the village water system and introduce "village water" to homes and businesses relying on their own wells, the Bolivar Water Company, Inc., formed in 1898, built a second system., but only after the village voters had refused to authorize the village itself to float a bond issue to build a municipal system. Springs on the Peet farm, 2.5 miles northeast of – and upslope from – the village, supplied the utility company's water by installing, according to John Herrick, "345 tons of cast-iron pipe, seven tons of castings and seven tons of lead." This system, which stored water in a steel tank on the village's northern hillside, was acquired by the Village of Bolivar in 1935.

In spite of having up-to-date means for suppressing fires, the village suffered some serious conflagrations on the hose companies' watch. Here are the big ones:

About midnight on February 15, 1895, in a below-zero blizzard wind, a Main Street duplex residence called the Manchester House, constructed of pine, "burned to the ground like a straw stack" in spite of the firemen's heroic efforts in miserable conditions. The occupants escaped uninjured, but "it threatened to wipe the entire business district off the map," declared the Breeze. The adjoining Mead's Planing Mill was leveled as well, and across the street the Williams residence caught fire and was badly damaged. "Bolivar's firemen never did better work" as for two hours they trained three hose streams on the threats, saving the Smith Brothers grist mill and thereby the rest of the business district. By 3:00 AM the threat was ended and the fire fighters were thawing out in the Clark House with hot coffee. (The disaster site was likely in the area south of Olean Street).

On March 21, 1901 the Great Opera House Fire "wiped out three buildings in 50 minutes" and "five persons narrowly escaped cremation," quoting the Breeze. At 5:15 AM the steam whistle alarm and the "fire bell"roused the hose companies' men to attack flames spreading through three wooden Main Street buildings.

The Opera House occupied the north corner lot at Olean Street, another hugged the brick Masonic Temple/bank building, and the third sat between those two. All were two-story structures, and all were reduced to ground level by 6 AM. The fire's heat was so intense that paint blistered on buildings across the street and the hydrant connection at Main and Olean had to be abandoned. Alerted by phone, Richburg's Ackerman Hose Company arrived "after a hard run" to assist, but the Bolivar volunteers had by then prevented further damage by saving the Masonic Temple's roof and dousing ember-ignited flames on the Clark House's roof across Olean Street. The disaster destroyed seven first-floor businesses, plus second-floor apartments in the center and left ones. The 1881 Opera House dominating the corner was the largest, with its entertainment space covering the entire upper floor.

On April 6, 1906, the Crandall Block burned. It stood beside the State Bank. The smoke from the fire drove the operators of the telephone company away from their switchboards, located in an office above the bank, destroyed Harlan Scott's meat market, severely damaged J.M. Van Gorden's cigar factory and pool room, and dispossessed him and Archie Moore from their second floor apartments. It was thought the blaze probably started when a cigar butt was thoughtlessly thrown into a trash bin in another vacant room upstairs.

Having hosted and warmed the firemen after the 1895 Manchester House blaze, opposite it on Main Street, and being saved by them from the 1901 Opera House fire's flying embers, the fates caught up with the Clark House on November 25, 1915. Allegany County's oldest hotel fell victim to flames as midnight approached. (Its original portion, dating from 1831, was pine-built as a general store.) The origin was likely a guest room's lace curtains contacting a gas heating stove. "Both Bradley Hose and Citizens Hose companies were there a few minutes after their alarms sounded and quickly had seven hose streams on the building," the Breeze reported. The newspaper added that the local firemen, led by chief LeRoy Root, deserved much praise for confining the blaze to the Clark House. The wall of M. E. Williams' restaurant (on the south corner of Olean at Main) was very close, but an hour's steady hose stream and that building's metal shingles saved it. Behind the old hotel, off Olean Street, was the Maxson & Graves garage. Cars and supplies were rushed out as it appeared threatened, but the firefighters kept it hosed down until the threat was ended. The Clark House, however, was badly gutted, and was left to the demolition crew as a complete loss for its owner, the Dotterweich Brewing Company of Olean.

One of the things my grandmother, Edith Bradley, was most embarrassed about had to do with that fire. She taught school in Bolivar, and rented a room in a house on South Main. My grandfather came courting that evening, and they missed all the commotion, completely unaware that the Clark House had burned while she and my grandfather were otherwise occupied.

Bolivar Fire Department

By the late 1880s, whenever one or both of Bolivar's hose companies responded to fight a fire, newspaper reports often credited "the Bolivar fire department." The term was especially common in Western New York papers other than the *Breeze*. But the actual "Bolivar Fire Department" wasn't created until four decades after the hose companies were organized. In February 1921 plans for a new Village Hall building were announced – a large, two-story, brick edifice located on the southeast corner of Olean and Main. The original concept pictured a new home for the Bradley and Citizens hose companies plus other features that would create a community center. Sharing the first floor with the firemen's equipment would be a reception room, a kitchen and a dining hall able to host eighty people. On the second floor would be two "hose parlors" for the Bradley and Citizens membership meetings; a small auditorium with a stage and dressing rooms; and boys' and girls' reading rooms. Each floor would have a pair of restrooms. Finally, the basement level would hold the furnace system and – best of all – a bowling alley! Upon review, the village board altered the original plan by deleting the reading rooms and adding a meeting room and a clerk's office for the village government.

But the intended late 1921 completion for the new building was derailed. by the death of its architect-designer, which led to a reconsideration of its functions. Construction finally began in early 1922, and the project was completed in July. The first floor included firefighting equipment space with a concrete floor, a the firemen's "hose parlor," and a reception room, checkroom, dining room and restrooms. (The *Breeze* noted that the hose companies hoped to soon have a fire engine behind the garage doors "as they are badly in need of new equipment"). The high-ceiling upstairs became an auditorium with a stage at the east end, flanked by restrooms. Its new maple floor was intended for dances and basketball games to be hosted by the high school and town teams. In an apparent concession to practicalities and finances, the village government was *not* situated in the new Village Hall and the bowling alley idea was forgotten. The village was satisfied with their office location in half of the Bolivar Free Library's ground floor, one that lasted for decades to come. The name of "Village Hall" did not stick to the new building for long. Its primary function as the fire department's home soon changed its identity to "the Fire Hall" – its title for the rest of its life.

At a joint meeting of the Bradley and Citizens hose companies in November, 1922, the firemen voted to accept their new spaces in the Village Hall and occupy them "as soon as possible." (They also agreed to host voting for town and village elections). The moves from Liberty and Friendship streets were not completed for ten months. As reported in September of 1923 by the *Breeze*, "the Citizens Hose Company's furniture, etc.,was moved to the new quarters, where their members have the west room and the J. B. Bradley Hose Company has the east room." Finally, in April of 1924 the local weekly could declare on its front page, "Bolivar Fire Department has been organized," and beneath that headline the story began: "The J. B. Bradley Hose Company No.1 and the Citizens Hose Company No.2, both organized here in the early 1880s, although not yet disbanded, have been merged into one organization known as the Bolivar Fire Department." The official act was accomplished at a meeting of both companies' members (32 attending) on March 27th. And they elected the department's first slate of officers: president, W. L. Dunning; vice president, P. J. McMillan; secretary, A. E. Mix; treasurer, C. M. Dunning; chief, H. P. Hockenberry; 1st assistant chief, Herbert McIntyre; 2nd assistant chief, Frank Thurber; foreman, K. C. Cowles; 1st assistant foreman, Joseph Dempsey; and 2nd assistant foreman, Willis Neely.

Meanwhile, as the evolution from hose companies to fire department inched along, so had efforts to solve the problem of outmoded equipment. In June, 1923, a *Breeze* article reported a "Reo" fire truck demonstration in Bolivar that concluded with these biting lines: "Why not hold a special election to appropriate [village] money for the firemen to buy a new fire truck? They have been badly in need of one for the past 20 years and their present equipment is a joke. Richburg, Allegany, Scio and other villages all have fire trucks. Bolivar, conceded to be one of the wealthiest towns of its size in this state, must be a tightwad with its firemen if it cannot afford to buy them modern firefighting equipment." Before the month ended, fifty residents had presented a petition to the village board for such an election, and the board authorized a July 10 vote to borrow $5,000 toward a fire truck. (The firemen themselves had conducted fundraising campaigns and events which by mid-'23 had generated $1,700 toward a "standard fire truck" purchase.) Voters approved the plan and in September the Village of Bolivar ordered a $6,000 "Type 36" American - LaFrance fire truck, on a Brockway chassis, with a pump rated at 300 gallons per minute, 1,000 feet of hose, a 40 gallon chemical tank for oil fires (with special hose), plus ladders and accessories. Such a unit was sometimes called a "chemical truck" for its added ability to smother burning petroleum with a foaming chemical mixture.

On February 2, 1924, the new pride of Bolivar's firemen emerged from a Shawmut railroad box car to take its place in the "hose room" of the Village Hall. Building on four decades of traditional pride and *espirit de corps*, Bolivar's firemen now had modern, motorized equipment to accompany them in a local parade. Typical of early fire trucks, it lacked one very beneficial part – a windshield. After nearly two years of its drivers needing goggles, one was added in December of 1925.

Just one month before that delivery, in the first hours of 1924, a fire had frustrated the firemen still limited to their hose carts. The new year had begun with weird weather – a windstorm with thunder and lightning – and folks surmised that a lightning strike had ignited the second floor of A. L. Shaner's barn on Shaner hill, at the village's eastern edge. The fire had spread quickly before Frank Best, passing by on his way home, spotted the flames. He entered the barn, trying to save one of the four "team horses" inside, but had to retreat without success. The responders rushed to the site only to learn their hose could not reach the nearest hydrant. The horses perished along with harnesses and rigging, a sleigh, a buggy, a buckboard wagon, one and a half tons of hay, tools and lesser items. Besides reaching the fire faster, could the new truck have saved the night?

What about the creek running at the base of the hill as a water source? Probably the A-LF Brockway's powerful pump could have tapped into that supply – with results that can only be speculated upon.

The new fire truck got its first call-out in late March of 1924, when "it made a record run to the Crandall farm" on Foreman Hollow only to find the family's home engulfed in flames and nearly destroyed. The firemen were able to save only a nearby outbuilding. Six years later, on the eve of the annual Southwestern Association of Volunteer Firemen being hosted by the Bolivar and Richburg departments, the B.F.D.'s second fire truck arrived. It was a major step up for the department's firefighting capacities. Delivered in late July of 1930 and costing $13,000, the American - LaFrance "Master Series Metropolitan" toured the village on that Saturday and attracted lots of onlookers. Among its features: a powerful six cylinder engine, pumping capacity of 1,000 gallons a minute, special 4-wheel brakes, hollow-spoked cast steel wheels and a double ignition system. Of course, it also carried a chemical tank and hose system for shooting Foamite at oil fires. And the state-of-the-art Metropolitan was a "range extender" for the ability of Bolivar's firemen to efficiently reach and battle fires. An April 1931 Breeze issue gave an example – a personal "Thank You" from Mrs. John Williams "for saving my home on Streeter Brook [near Little Genesee] when it caught fire a few days ago."

"The Metropolitan" has been treasured by Bolivar firemen and kept in their "stable" for decades after it was retired from service. As a noisy crowd pleaser it participated in numerous local parades of the 20th Century. As of the township's bicentennial year it was stored in a village building, hoping for a transmission rebuild.

"Southwestern" Convention of 1930

Through most of their history, volunteer firefighting units have been affiliated with county and regional associations of fire departments that have held annual conventions. Local fire departments, in conjunction with their local governments and communities, have tended to host conventions on a rotating basis. But some locales have long seemed more inclined than others to play host, and Bolivar has been one of them. The 22nd annual convention of New York's Southwestern Association of Volunteer Firemen was one of the best and biggest, so big that Bolivar and Richburg combined forces and resources to host it. In advance of the event, from August 6-8, 1930, the *Breeze* described the plans in a long front page article, saying that the two villages "will be in gala dress for the occasion to warmly welcome several thousand guests. Various committees had been working hard to make it Western New York's most successful ever.

August 6 would include the opening exercises, a business session at the Lyric Theater, afternoon entertainment for the firemen, and an evening banquet at Richburg's high school. On August 7 all would convene at the Lyric for more entertainment, then an afternoon fish fry at Riverhurst Park in Weston's Mills.

That evening would feature a "grotesque parade" providing firemen's comedy, and an inspection of the host fire departments.

Friday, August 8 would include a morning welcome to all visiting firemen, the afternoon Grand Parade, a post-parade "massed bands" concert, and competitions in hose cart races, manual pump contests and first aid demonstrations. On both Thursday and Friday nights there was a dance in the Village Hall's upstairs with a different orchestra each night.

Further, "a special train of the Pennsylvania Railroad for attendees living along its route will originate in Dunkirk, leaving at 6:30 Friday morning, arriving in Bolivar at 10 via Olean and the Shawmut Railroad's line from Portville, and leaving for Dunkirk at 8 PM. Friday's Grand Parade should include about 70 fire companies and 27 bands and drum corps, in twelve divisions. The line of march is to run north along Bolivar's Main Street, go up the road into Richburg, turn at Jennings' Service Station and march back to Bolivar, disbanding at the carnival grounds."

"Best ever convention" indeed. In its next issue the *Breeze* declared the convention a great success, noting that Friday's parade stretched nearly two miles long, had 2,000 men in line and was viewed by an "estimated" 10,000 spectators. (Local "boosterism" by the editor may have inflated crowd size, but given the scale of the other numbers it had to be huge.) And all of this happened in the first year of the Great Depression. It was never equaled again in Bolivar and/or Richburg, but the spirit of it reappeared during other Bolivar firemen's conventions in the ensuing decades.

Ladies of the Firemen's Auxiliary

Throughout the hose companies' era and the 1920s and early 1930s, behind every good volunteer fireman there likely had been a good woman. The wives of many fire company members along with other civic-minded Bolivar ladies had been "backing up" the firemen since the 1880s, providing food and beverages – especially hot coffee – after a serious battle against flames, cooking dinners for membership social gatherings and helping carry out fundraising efforts. Until 1934 their group was simply "the firemen's auxiliary," but on July 26 of that year they became a formally recognized entity named the Bolivar Firemen's Auxiliary. They adopted their first set of bylaws in October.

By the end of summer in 1935, the B.F.A. had outfitted themselves in white uniforms which they wore for the Auxiliary's first parade appearance on September 6. Leading them was their first president, Winifred Saunders McCrea. Her husband was fireman Lloyd McCrea, well-known and well-liked in Bolivar for many decades to come. Sadly, Winifred passed away in 1936 at age 26, leaving behind three boys aged 5, 3 and an "infant" per the *Breeze* – a hint that childbirth complications took Winifred's life. Losing her prompted her fellow Auxiliary members to honor her and her leadership skills by replacing the "Bolivar" in

their group's title with the name "McCrea." Her name stayed there for thirty years until, in 1967, the label of "Bolivar Firemen's Auxiliary" was restored.

Over ninety years, from their formal organization to Bolivar township's bicentennial year, the women of the Firemen's Auxiliary have provided the same services and support to the emergency responders of the Bolivar Fire Department (of both genders) as did their "organizational ancestors" of the 1880s. And they have marched in several styles and colors of crisp uniforms in parades where they have earned numerous awards and trophies. Going forward, Bolivar residents can count on a continuation.

Firefighting Evolves

As the decades of the 20th Century rolled along, the Bolivar Fire Department and Firemen's Auxiliary progressed in their capacities for protecting and serving the greater Bolivar area. Firefighting vehicles and other items of equipment, along with protective gear, were retired and replaced by increasingly advanced versions as required to safeguard lives and property, and as finances allowed. Notable developments in the social activities of the members and the department's interactions with the community came along as well. The following paragraphs based on newspaper accounts provide some examples of changes into the 1960s, as well as the B.F.D.'s professional consistency.

June 1938: At the Allegany County Firemen's Association convention in Bolivar, the host department's new "drum corps" made its first parade appearance (likely including some bugles and tunes). Parade units went into line from South, Liberty and Olean streets marching north, then up Wellsville Street and Shaner Avenue, down Plum Street to Main, up North Main to the Shawmut Railroad crossing (just past Salt Rising Road) and U-turning there to march to "the Fire Hall" on the corner of Olean Street. The B.F.D. Drum Corps likely lasted until late 1941when Pearl Harbor was attacked, putting many members into military uniforms in 1942.

December 1942: An afternoon fire broke out in the warehouse structure of the Main Service Station. The building sat behind the classic 1925 brick station (at the corner of Wellsville Street) where customers' cars were fueled underneath a portico projecting toward Main Street. The warehouse contained an inventory of tires, tubes, motor oils, greases and antifreeze. Also stored inside, awaiting repairs, was a B.C.S. school bus that was destroyed along with most of the contents. The station manager and an employee suffered burns. Obviously, battling a fire where petroleum products were stored was a dicey undertaking but, "by hard and efficient work, our firemen confined the blaze to the story and a half stucco building," assisted by companies from Richburg, Wellsville and Portville.

January 1943: Typical of messages relating to fire calls in the Breeze's "Personals" columns through the years was this one: "Irwin Place extends his grateful appreciation for the prompt and efficient service of the Bolivar Fire Department in extinguishing the fire on his farm in Genesee on Saturday."

The 1940s-50s-60s: Bolivar firemen trained in first aid, "EMS" as we know it now, acquired a succession of ambulances to expedite medical care for victims of fires, accidents and personal health emergencies. Their first "emergency car" was donated by the Loop family, Bolivar's home furnishings retailers and funeral home operators. The early 1940s gift was quite likely a former hearse, retrofitted to give first-responder aid to the still living but hurting. That vehicle's successors were more encouraging to stretcher riders – new factory-built ambulances: a 1952 Pontiac, then a 1960 Cadillac, then a 1971 Cadillac. Following the last "Caddy" have come the modern types built on a truck chassis.

1952: The fire department acquired its "base radio station," becoming the second in Allegany County to have the advantages of such a communication system. By 1970 it had been replaced by an extended network, with base stations in the fire hall and the Chief's home, radios in his auto and the 1st Assistant Chief's, and radios in all the emergency vehicles. Also put into use was a monitor system for alerting volunteer firemen.

1953: On the department's hillside acreage acquired along Salt Rising Road at the north edge of the village, Bolivar's firemen began construction of their new clubhouse facility. This spacious, two story block building, with its second-floor deck overlooking Bolivar and its valleys, was developed on a pay-as-you-go basis. The final touches were installed in 1960. As a gathering place, it was a vast improvement over the spaces of the 1923 Fire Hall. "The Firemen's Clubhouse" was more than a social recreation place for members; it was an asset they made available to the community for department-sponsored dances and private events. Countless good times were had and good memories were made "up on the hill" by several generations of area residents. And its activities created a revenue stream helping the B.F.D. fund the serious work of fire protection. One excellent example: the three-story metal "drill tower" they erected at the base of their hill, used by many area fire departments for training firemen in rescue and firefighting techniques.

February 1955: Risk and old age caught up with another wood-upon-wood Main Street retail site of the late 1800s. At 1 AM on a winter night, a fire of undetermined origin broke out in the Matson building next to the bank on the corner at Boss Street. It began with an explosion, "and within a short time the interior of two businesses was an inferno." One half was the Hollis Youth Shop, a children's clothing store; the other was the Matylas Billiard Parlor. Both were consumed by "one of the worst fires in Bolivar's history." The State Bank's brick wall was five feet south of the burning building, Don Dwyer's stucco Buick Motor Sales was fifteen feet north, and the first Boss Street building, wood-framed behind the bank, was equally exposed. Of course Bolivar's firemen were first on the scene, and as four were working a hose in front of the Hollis section an apparent "gas pocket" inside exploded, knocking them down but without injury. (Broken glass was later found atop the gas station across the street.) The B.F.D. was soon joined by the Richburg and Allentown departments in the freezing darkness with icy footing. Together they had as many as twelve hose streams simultaneously aimed at the fire or cooling the neighboring buildings. At 4 AM, the village public works superintendent declared "about an hour's water supply is left at this rate." But the tide turned – not until a wall had collapsed against Dwyer's garage – and at 4:30 AM Chief Ed "PeeWee" Greisch could finally declare the fire "under control." And this disaster is the reason why, ever since 1955, the Matson building's "footprint" has been a parking lot.

1960: Nineteen Bolivar girls, regulars as babysitters in the area, attended a B.F.D. instructional session on fire safety and how to properly report an emergency. "You could have heard a pin drop, they listened so carefully," said their instructor, Chief Floyd "Bronc" Reeland. Not long after, the firemen conducted another round of another public service: their semi-annual inspection of business locations to identify possible fire hazards for correction.

As the Bolivar Fire Department moved forward in the ensuing decades, the details of the incidents, events and tasks performed by the firemen and ladies' auxiliary members have been, of course, varied from those recapped above. But their spirit of service to their community has continued unchanged.

"If that block ever went up, it would be the horror of Bolivar forever."

For as long as Irene Greisch and her husband – former B.F.D. Chief Ed Greisch – could remember, they hoped to never answer a fire call for the 400 block of South Main Street. She spoke the words above as she watched the "Cooper Block" burn from across the street. Irene was working at the City Club Grill when, at about 2:30 in the afternoon of March 31, 1974, she and her customers noticed smoke blowing from a window of an upstairs apartment there. Once again, "Old buildings, probably 75 or more years old. They went up like a powder keg."

The Cooper Block was essentially four buildings in one – wood framed, wood finished, with four storefronts and second floor apartments. Only one of the stores held an active business, that of Glase's Hardware including Mrs. Glase's tropical fish hobby shop. The Glases lived upstairs and the other three apartments were occupied. It was bad timing for a volunteer fire department as many members were at work or changing shifts at out-of-town plants. Assistant Fire Chief Dick Smith was quickly there with three others but he later said, "It was a hell of a feeling with only four men and people are screaming about getting the kids out and you're trying to get ladders up. But the Richburg department arrived minutes later." In fact, Richburg's was one of the six fire companies that had trained for trouble at the Cooper Block, and all six were on site within an hour of the first alarm.

The immediate concerns were Karen Monger, age 17, and her toddler half-brother Duane Torrey. She had broken out a window and was ready to drop Duane into some strong arms twenty feet below. That was accomplished before a ladder went up and Karen climbed down to safety. Meanwhile, Duane's mother Shirley had appeared and hustled him away. For the next two hours everyone was uncertain as to the possibility of other persons being upstairs.

Thanks to the Mutual Aid system among fire departments, their prior planning against such a fire meant they were deployed as planned and had the blaze "contained" by 5 PM, meaning they had prevented it from torching the nearby Page residence on the corner at Liberty Street. But with forty mile an hour wind gusts in temperatures at or below freezing, the burning structure had itself been a giant torch, totally consumed by the flames in spite of the efforts to quell them. The wind-driven rain and sleet pelting the firefighters were no help in the circumstances.

Fortunately, all the upstairs residents got away safely or were not at home, but all lost whatever they had there. That included Mr. & Mrs. Robert Reisman with their five children and Francis Little and her two kids. Luckily – and skillfully as well – no firemen sustained significant injury. But as Bolivar's Chief Jon Lindquist observed that evening, "All I know is we've got an awful mess." The burn site with its blackened, tangled wreckage sat for months on end, a smelling eyesore that vexed village officials as to how, by whom and at whose expense it would get cleaned up. Finally, an arrangement came together by which Andover developer Herald Ford acquired the site for a paltry sum, helped the village government with hauling off the debris, and built a new Market Basket grocery and parking lot, to the betterment of Bolivar.

A New Home, a New Century, Carrying Forward the Old Ideals of Service

By the Nineteen Eighties, the sixty-year-old Fire Hall at Olean Street was aged, tired and cramped – not well suited to the modern firefighting ways that the Bolivar Fire Department had kept up with. But one block away, an ideal new location had come on the market. On the south corner of South Street, a modern brick row of auto service bays plus the older building it was attached to were available. They had been part of the Ferris & Forbes Ford-Mercury dealership that had "closed up shop" in that decade. So in 1988 the fire department acquired those facilities and carried out its second relocation in 100 years.

With modest modifications for a fire company's needs, the B.F.D. occupied its new home and has thrived there since. No modification was needed to the roomy paved parking area in front of the garage bays which face South Street. In 2024, it was a perfect spot to line up the department's vehicles for a group portrait.

The department's new facilities also had sufficient space for social activities and "comradeship building" that had always gone hand-in-hand with the serious work of providing public safety. The new situation, and changing times with changing priorities, called for a discussion and a decision about the future of the B.F.D.'s clubhouse on Salt Rising Road. Keep it and bear the expenses and responsibilities of owning it, or cash it out to be free of them and strengthen the organization's finances? The membership made the second choice, and early in the new century sold the property. However, the great memories made there were kept by all who had them in the Bolivar community.

The work of the Bolivar Fire Department and the benefits it bestows on its service area continue to this day, as does the hope that its members, present and future, will loyally carry on as long as there's a Bolivar to protect. The people of Bolivar, past and present, heartily salute them.

The Bolivar Fire Department: Ready for the 21st Century

A Walk Downtown, continued

Across Olean Street from the fire hall is the library, little changed since it was built 115 years ago. The Legionnaires put up the flag pole, and a war memorial monument, but otherwise the exterior is virtually unchanged. Across Main Street was Colgrove & Wood's hardware store. It was there that I bought the first tool I ever picked up for myself, a double-bladed ax, when I was about fourteen. The store had followed the decline of the oil business, for many years being an oil well supply store, transitioning to a general hardware store as the demand for oil well supplies declined, and finally giving up on that too. As a harbinger of the end of oil, it was acquired for use as an oil museum in 1965. Of note is the fact that the village at that time amended its ordinances to allow the drilling of an oil well on the Colgrove & Wood lot, as an added attraction to the museum, with the possibility that its production might help support the museum's operation. It has yet to be drilled.

Next to the museum was the new Mobil station, discussed earlier. Next to the Library were two brick buildings which had been built after the Opera House fire. The one closest to the library had been since its construction the home of Loop's furniture business, first run by F.A. Loop, then by his son, Harley. As was common in those times, the furniture dealer doubled as an undertaker. Harley kept his inventory of caskets with the furniture, and used his home on Friendship Street as his funeral parlor.

Separated by a small alley, next to the north was the second brick building, 386 Main Street. I knew it as Marie's Restaurant, but it was more formally know as Maxson's Lunch Room. Marie and Sherm Maxson went into the restaurant business in 1941. Sherman was born in Bolivar in 1899. He graduated from Bolivar High and headed to St. Bonaventure where he was in the ROTC unit there when the Great War came to America.

When the war ended, he thought he had had enough schooling, and took a job with Stimson and Bell, where he stayed for ten years. During the Depression, he switched jobs often, working for the Bolivar Refinery, Moore Producing, Bradley Producing and the Sinclair Refinery, before deciding to go it on his own with a restaurant. To begin, he and Marie bought out the C.F. Repp news and variety stand, but when World War II ended, they bought 386 Main. They remodeled, installed a large soda fountain, put out tables and chairs, set up the kitchen, and opened the door.

Sherm manned the soda fountain, while Marie tended to the cooking. They sold Coca Cola products. They had all the official equipment, right down to the original five or ten cent Coke glasses, which Sherm filled with freshly mixed Coca Cola syrup and soda water, or with any other flavor you asked for. My favorite there was a cherry phosphate. Marie was a great cook. She made her own version of Texas Hots. To me, her hot sauce tasted somewhat like Catalina or French salad dressing, and the chopped onions which went on top were courser than you got in Wellsville- but the wieners were bigger and I liked Marie's Texas Hots better than the originals.

Maxson's quickly caught on with the high school students, who filled the place after school, "chatting rapidly" once they had pumped themselves full of ice cream and cokes. Sherm could make a good sundae. Sometimes I would order a hot fudge, but more often a Puddle or a Mexican. They were all good.

In the first few months of 1959, Sherm and Marie decided to take a break. The went off on a three month road trip, their first vacation in ten years, heading first to Kansas to visit Sherm's best boyhood friend, my grandfather's brother, Ed Bradley, in Wichita, Kansas, then on to Oklahoma, Arizona and California to visit their scattered relatives. Then it was back home, catering to the town folk, Sherm behind the counter, Marie often doing double duty as cook and waitress, but always with a smile, happy you had decided to stop at her place. Sherm passed away at the age of sixty-seven in 1966. Marie kept operating on her own for years afterward, but eventually retired. She outlived Sherman by thirty years, not leaving the scene until October 24, 1996. The Loop building became Slavins' Hardware and was gutted by a fire about 1980. Maxson's building slowly but steadily started leaning to the south, was eventually found to be structurally unsound, and was torn down. Today, that part of Main Street is just another parking lot.

Our family did its banking at the State Bank, which, in 1962, merged with the Citizen's Bank of Wellsville, so I had little occasion to go into the First National that filled the ground floor of the Masonic Temple building. But whenever you walked by, you would see a small, black, letter-board sign in the right side of the window on which was posted the current price for a barrel of oil.

On the west side of Main, opposite the bank, was Fagouri's clothing store. When I was old enough to have a summer job, I bought all of my Dickie's summer work clothes from George and Vickie, and I was a regular customer in their shoe department growing up. I always enjoyed going there. Vickie had a unique voice I miss hearing, and both she and George were eager to help me find whatever I was looking for, and to chat about what was going on in my life, thereby making Bolivar's Main Street a place I liked to be.

George was an immigrant, born in Nazareth in what was then called Palestine. Vickie was the daughter of Syrian immigrants, born four years after George. They kept a pretty white house with blue shutters on the west side of South Main, and raised three children, the oldest Edward, who pursued a medical career in the military, and daughters Jackie and Marcia. George and Vickie decided to retire in 1975. Not finding any ready takers to buy the business, they instead sold the building to the American Legion, which proceeded to remodel the store into their bar and social gathering place, and moved on to Main Street from the old Citizens Hose building on Friendship street, which they had occupied since the 1920s. I remember opening night. The place was packed and rocking, but a design flaw became immediately apparent: when the door to the ladies room was thrown open, everyone on the dance floor had a good view right to the back of it. (The bathrooms were soon moved to the rear of the building, solving that problem).

The Legion had been one of the principal social gathering places in town since its founding, and had become a sort of home away from home for many of the unique characters that set Bolivar apart. One of those characters was Joe Meek. Born near Manchester, England, in 1889, he enlisted in the Royal Navy at the age of sixteen. He was assigned to a new cruiser, the HMS Duke of Edinburgh, and while there learned to play the alto horn and became a member of the ship's band. That set off his life-long interest in music. Supposedly he survived a four-round exhibition boxing match with British welterweight Bombardier Billy Wells, who went on the be the British heavyweight champion form 1911 to 1919. In 1909, his ship crossed to New York City to take in the Hudson-Fulton Centennial celebration. Joe jumped ship and stayed in the USA. He found work on farms in the Nunda area until 1916 or so, then headed for Bolivar, hoping to find work here.

When World War One came, he was drafted. He was initially assigned to a machine gun battalion, but when it was discovered he could play instruments, he became part of the Headquarters Company of the 302nd Engineers, and made it through the war unscathed as a musician. Joe was very entertaining and well-liked by a generation, being featured in an article in the Bolivar Breeze in the late 1950s. Music and entertaining always seemed to be his passion. In the 1930s, as a member of the Allegany Mountaineers, he played the harmonica, "second fiddle," and whistled, "his notes trilling clear and sharp above any roar of traffic or machinery," which begs the question, just where was he playing that he had to compete with the sounds of traffic and machinery?

The Mountaineers appeared on stage at the Lyric in 1933, and Joe, as the character "High Pressure Pete" brought down the house with his vocal rendition of "Where, oh where, has my little dog gone" For an encore, Joe sang two more verses of the same song to wild applause.

Not long after he returned from France, Joe had married Alice Walkley, a Geneseo graduate who taught at the Rochester Normal School. And although they brought into the world four children, Joe was not a good provider nor family man. He found work as the janitor for both banks in town, but many was the night he spent entertaining his friends at the Legion or in the local bars, which did nothing to help his family's finances.

First living in South Bolivar, Joe found a house to buy on Second Street, but the second mortgage on it was foreclosed in 1936, and Joe scrambled to sell most of his other possessions and appliances to raise money. His wife took the kids and left for a teaching job in Addison. That fall, Joe was one of the first veterans in the area to receive a generous war bonus. He took the money, quit his jobs at the banks, and used the bonus to take his children to England to meet his family. They were gone six months.

When he returned, in July 1937, he built himself a three-room cabin across the road from the cemetery, was hired as the town dog catcher, and continued making music. When the eight-member Allegany Mountaineers broke up, he formed the Original Kentucky Nighthawks. After World War II, the group shrank down to three and became the Dirty Shame Camp Band, and Joe, joined by Walter Hinman and Shorty Nolan, entertained at parties, mostly at camps kept by his friends, like Al Glintz or Bob MacDonell, but also in the minstrel shows put on by the Bolivar Men's Club.

As he approached seventy, Joe's health began to fail, and he spent his last years at the Bath Soldier's Home. He died there on May 10, 1971, and rests in the National Cemetery not far from another Bolivar character, Happy Jack Stoops.

Bolivar had other musicians, some home grown. Perhaps we had more than our share because of the oil field. Especially when the secondary recovery spread over the field, there were many farmers and landowners who received royalties from the oil and gas production who no longer needed to farm to pay their bills. And the presence of rod lines running everywhere across fields made it difficult to harvest hay, to grow other crops, or graze animals. Thus, many

Shorty Nolan, Joe Meek, and Walter Hinman, the Dirty Shame Camp Band, entertain during a Bolivar Men's Club show in the BCS auditorium, probably in 1951

people had spare time, spare money, and looked for ways to entertain themselves and their friends.

There were five Williams brothers: Midge, Major, Minor, Fred, and Burleigh, who formed a band, and who on occasion, when it was time to take a break, might call out, "Let's join hands and urinate in the hall!" Fred Williams owned a big old hound dog. He would often take the dog for an evening walk along Main Street, and Fred would start singing. The hound would join in and sing duets. (Joe Meek did not have a dog, but was often seen with Jiggs, the "well-known Main Street rooster").

Burly Lewis had no known musical talent. He had been born in Potter County in 1887, and came to Bolivar in the 1920s, finding work as a pumper on a lease up Foreman Hollow, and bringing with him a wife and two sons. His children grew up and his wife died, so Burly sent away for a "mail order bride." Her name was Sylvia Ames, but she soon became well known around Bolivar as Roxy Lewis. She found a paying job on a poultry farm. Mac MacDivitt for years tried to get Roxy to apply to be a contestant on the television show, "What's My Line," confident the panel would never figure out that Roxy' occupation was, in her own words, "a chicken de-asser."

Roxy was better known and appreciated around Bolivar for her music. She played the accordion for a dollar an hour, most often in the old Legion on Friendship Street, and would stay after hours, the patrons passing the hat to keep her going, which she did while chain smoking, and always happy to play and sing her theme song, *Listen to the Mockingbird.* She went so far as the write an operetta, but there is no record of it being performed. She lasted until 1984, when she took her spot in Maple Lawn.

Joe Meek, third from the left, and Neil Sullivan, in the white hat, are the only men identified in this photo in front of the old Legion in the 1920s

Fagouris remodeled the storefront of their building when they took it over, replacing the 19th century wood facade with brick. It had been for most of its life the Hoyt & Cowles mercantile. Next to it is another long-term survivor, a building that had been for many years the Seibert Drug Store, and also the nineteenth century office of the Doctors Cutler. Mike Italiano, born in Calabria, Italy in 1895, landed in Montreal, Canada in 1914, and soon after headed to Olean where he had an uncle. In 1920 he worked as an auto mechanic, but in 1930 operated a restaurant in Richburg. In October 1935, Mike's liquor license application was approved, and he opened the Chef Grill in the old drug store in Bolivar. He became active in the local Democratic party, was a founding member of the Bolivar Industrial Development Corporation, and ran his bar and restaurant business for the rest of his life, which ended on August 14, 1968.

I don't think I ever set foot in the Chef while Mike was alive, and only recall doing so twice after it was taken over by Ruebens Iatorno. That was about 1980. On the second occasion, I had to use the rest room, and as I stood at the urinal, I read the following written on the wall just above it. It said, "Was George Bradley really in here?" "Yes, and he had two beers!" I didn't write either the question or response, and I have no idea who did. But it was accurate.

Next to the Chef stood a store I went to often, usually running an errand for either my grandmother or my mother. Many a morning, I sat by when my grandmother would pick up the phone, ask the operator for number 1-8, and listen to her read off her carefully prepared grocery list, which would be gathered together and delivered to the house not long after from the Red and White store. That number was easy for me to remember. Our home phone was 218, and my grandparent's was 189.

The Red and White Grocery store had its roots in a meat market operated by Claude "Earl" Potter, beginning in 1918. The Potters had two sons, both of whom began careers of their own elsewhere, and three daughters. Two of them married and moved away, but their oldest daughter, Helen, married her high school sweetheart, Sealand Appleby, and stayed put. Sealand got a job as a lease foreman for Messer Oil, and in the 1930s moved Helen over to Courtney Hollow to be near the lease. Then Helen's father died of a heart attack, on October 17, 1942, and help was desperately needed in the store. So it was that Sealand Appleby became a grocer, and he and Helen worked side by side in the Red and White for the rest of their working lives. You could enter the store from either side, with aisles running down both sides, the center of the store filled with produce bins and floor displays. But, you didn't hunt to find what you needed. You just told Helen or Sealand what it was you were there for, and they would either point it out or fetch it, and gather the items into a paper bag to be carried home. In 1952, they obtained a liquor license and added beer to their list of offerings. The meat and beverage coolers were out back.

Helen and Sealand never advertised much at all, but they didn't need to. They were always upbeat, helpful, welcoming. Although ten years older, they were friends of my parents, members of the Country Club, enjoyed good times, and were good to their customers. It was a sad day for us when, in the mid-1970s, Helen and Sealand decided to retire, packed up their things, and moved to Kissimmee, Florida. They got to enjoy it for nearly twenty years. Helen passed first, in 1994, and Sealand less than a year later, on May 13, 1995.

Sealand & Helen Appleby, about 1935

Across the street sat a small little building to the north of the Masonic Temple, in which Forest Shaner's mother, Doris, had a doll shop. Later on, Forrest took over the space and used it for his clock and watch repair business. He was a certified watchmaker, and did excellent work, but he closed the shop and worked out of his home in Little Genesee until he retired. Next door, on the corner of Friendship Street stood a cast stone building put up in 1906, which I knew as the Quality Market. I was an infrequent customer, since the Red and White was so close, but there were times when I would check there to see what they had. Franny Green's was a familiar face there. Both are now gone, replaced by the village park.

Next to the Red and White was the Bolivar Diner, which I ate at only on a few occasions. Known as Walker's up into World War II, it served as the clubhouse for the Country Club during the war, when gasoline rationing was in effect. On it's north side was Parker's Alley, which ran down to First Street next to old Tom Hungerford's house, and to its north was Parker's Drug Store, which was in operation in that location from 1910 until 1955. I remember it as Bryant's, which first advertised in the Bolivar Breeze in 1957, and who operated until 1966.

Across from Bryant's was Neill's Department Store, owned and operated by Richard and Marion Neill. I usually went in there in search of penny candy, of which they had cases full, but I never felt like I was trusted by the Neills, who kept a very close eye on me and my young fingers, just as they did all young fingers who came in. Both Dick and Marion were hard working and contributing members of the community, Dick as a village trustee and secretary of the Masons, and Marion with the Methodist Church. When they retired, the store became O'Lear's, and it has since seen a series of occupants, and has now been remodeled to save on heating costs to be nearly unrecognizable as the dark green, big-windowed department store it was in the 1960s.

The prime part of Bolivar's downtown business district stood between the Mobil station and the Odd Fellow's Hall at the corner of Boss Street, and with the exception of the Legion Hall and the Chef Grill, it is all gone. Most of the boom-era buildings were taken down to make way for the senior apartments which now fill the block. Next to Bryants stood a building with a brick front, owned by Edgar Dillie, where he kept a man's clothing store. Next to that was a building with two store fronts. The southern-most was Eberl's Insurance most of the time I lived in town.

The north half of the building was the Sugar Bowl Restaurant, just as often referred to as "The Greeks." Nick Cretekos was born in Sykeau, Greece in 1890, and came to the United States in 1902, following his older brother George. The third and oldest brother, Gus, arrived in 1904. The three brothers found their way to Wellsville, where Gus established a candy shop, in which all three worked. Although not yet a citizen, Nick was prime military age when the First World War came, and he spent two years wearing the uniform of Company G, 325th Infantry. He was in Europe from April 1918 until May 1919, and was discharged as a sergeant.

Nick Cretekos. 1918

In April 1924, he bought the former C.F. Repp store building from Gus Dunn, and opened up a confectionary store and ice cream parlor he christened The Sugar Bowl. Before the war, Nick often operated his candy making separate from the restaurant, bringing in chefs to do the cooking, Nick Murtos and Louis Brown being two examples. In the 1950s, Nick's son Jack became active in the business, and it was he, in 1959, who brought the first pizza oven to Bolivar. The Sugar Bowl had a well-worn floor of small tiles, mostly white, booths along the south wall, and a long counter in front of the soda fountain on the north side, where Nick would fix me fresh creme soda. My favorite Sugar Bowl meal was a hamburger steak, which was pounded thin and cooked well-done, over which I would pour French's Worcestershire Sauce and Heinz ketchup. I have tried for years to cook that meal for myself, but I have never gotten the recipe right. Jack Cretekos saw the writing on the wall as Bolivar's economy shrank during the 1950s, and he relocated, opening a restaurant in Rochester, where he prospered. Nick retired and went to Rochester too, where he passed away in 1981.

Next to the Sugar Bowl was my favorite store in Bolivar: Hall's Department Store. Charlie Hall was born in Olean on St. Patrick's Day, 1903. He married Marie Langworthy on October 12, 1925, and moved her to Connellsville, Pennsylvania where he managed a department store. Managing a store was not owning a store, so as he learned the business, Charlie kept his ear to the ground seeking a good location for a store of his own. When the McDonell and Brennan store location in the heart of Bolivar's downtown became available in 1936, Charlie was ready to move. Hall's Department Store came into being in 1937.

It seemed to have room for everything, candy counters in the middle, men's and boys' clothing on one side, women's and girls' on the other, but it was to the back room I made a beeline, to the toy department, where on the rear-most shelves Charlie had stacked the latest editions of Revell's plastic model kits. What I looked for were the model airplanes, and as the 1960s arrived, model rockets, which could be had for a very reasonable price of $.98 each. For others, there were model cars and ships, which I would buy once in a while. Cars were much harder to paint to get them to come out right, (the Milliman brothers were master model car builders), and ship models were much more expensive, meaning I might have to save my allowance for weeks, to get the Thermopylae or the Cutty Sark, or the battleship Missouri.

I remember when Charlie's son-in-law, Phil Morrison, worked there. I remember Margie Kalkhof, and Mrs. Hall. Charlie was always Charlie, but Mrs. Hall was to me Mrs. Hall. Both Charlie and the store became the victims of changing times. In late 1961, Thrifty Westie's store opened in Weston's Mills. It was the first large floor space discount store in the area, now the home of Ashley Furniture. Charlie confided to a friend that the first month Westie's was open, his sales were off by sixty percent. Charlie was not alone in feeling that pain. Many small town business districts would share in it, as shoppers headed to Westie's or K-Mart or Walmart to find the latest deals. But the stress of seeing his business decimated by this changing business strategy proved too much for Charlie. On March 13, 1962, he died of a heart attack. Mrs. Hall tried to carry on, as did others for a while, (Margie Kalkopf and Presher's both tried), but when the proposal was made to rejuvenate Main Street by building the senior apartments on that site, it met with little opposition. Times had indeed changed.

On the north side of Hall's in the next building was Dickerson's Barber Shop, complete with the revolving red, white and blue barber pole, a Regulator wall clock, and classic barber chairs. How Leland Dickerson got the nickname "Squeak" is something I never knew, but that was how he was known as long as I patronized the shop. Squeak was born in Alma on Dec. 4, 1913. His parents moved to Mead Hollow before 1930, where his father worked as a pumper. Squeak got his first job in the oil field, working as a roustabout for the Bradley Producing Corporation, but decided there were better ways to make a living. He went off to barber school, and in the 1940s opened his shop on Main Street next to Hall's.

In the early 1950s, there were four barbers in town, and they were all busy. Squeak had a second chair in the shop, and usually a second barber to make use of it, the last of whom that I remember being Les McKay. Across the street, Dick Guise had a shop. Dick was born in 1895, and kept his shop in a building owned by his wife, the Munich block, in which she also had her millinery store. Both had retired by the end of the 1960s.

The fourth barber had a shop inside the Bolivar Hotel. If Squeak was too busy, I would head to the hotel shop. My earliest memory is of a kindly older barber with a grey mustache. But by the late 1950s that shop had been taken

Hall's Department Store not long after it opened

over by a Bolivar boy, Louis Schiralli. Louis, a section V wrestling champion, had done a stint in the Air Force after getting out of BCS in 1952, then had gone to barber college. He could make good use of his clippers and scissors, whether you wanted a DA or a flat top, but more importantly he was fun and funny, which made waiting your turn to get in the chair worth the time. He accumulated a good clientele, and when the space opened up, he bought the building next to Munich's, and had his own place.

Changing times and styles put a big crimp in the barbering business beginning in the mid-1960s, when brush cuts and short hair around the ears gave way to shoulder-length hair and sideburns, which required trimming much less frequently. Squeak carried on until 1980 before he retired. He sold the shop to a

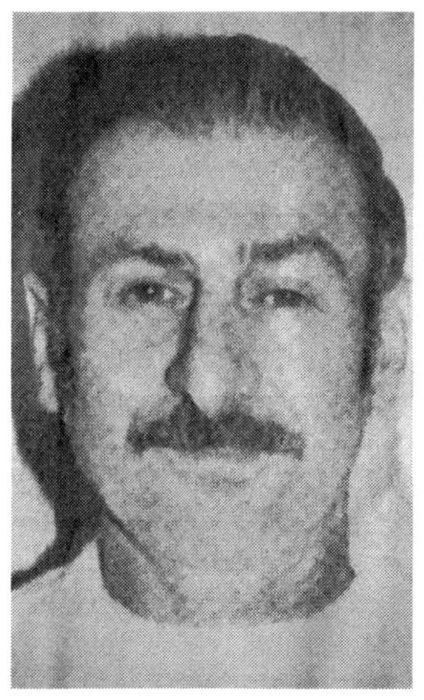

Louis Schiralli

young fellow who could not keep Squeak's customers, and the classic barber chairs ended up in the rec room of a Wellsville building contractor. Louis held on a while longer, until a serious automobile accident forced his early retirement. While active, Louis won office as a Democrat on the town council. He spent his retirement on his farm on Bartlett Road, just south of town, which lasted until he left us on Aug. 3, 2017.

As you kept going toward Boss Street, you came to Nicholson's Flower Shop. I loved the smell when you walked in. The space was divided into two rooms, front and back. The front room housed the cooler the roses and other flowers were kept in, and the counter to meet customers, while the back room was the work space where bouquets and wreaths were assembled and packaged for delivery. Bob Nicholson had grown up in Hornell, but he and his family moved from Wellsville to Bolivar in 1936, when it was bustling with secondary recovery oil money. His daughters, Anne Saunders and Barb Thomas, completed their educations at BCS, and he did his part serving as a village trustee. He and his wife, Betty, worked in the shop, providing flowers for weddings, funerals, anniversaries and birthdays, and decorative green roping and wreaths for Christmas. They also sold paint and wallpaper. That building is now gone too, to make room for the apartments.

The Odd Fellows Hall still stands. Irv Swarthout was born in Genesee township on May 28, 1890, and the Swarthouts had an oil property there which Irv pumped. When the Great War came, he was already married with two kids at home, and was still working as a pumper, living on Dean's Flats. But before 1920, he decided to do something else. He became the proprietor of a billiard parlor, and he would keep at that business, located in the south half of the Odd Fellows building, for the next sixty plus years. (*See the photo on page 128*).

I started going to the pool hall when in grade school, not to play, but to buy comic books. Irv always had the latest issues of DC and Action comics, and I was enthralled with Superman. And he had an old fashioned, "fill it with ice" Coca Cola cooler for the pop tucked away on the south wall, which had racks that the necks of the bottles could slide along, keeping the contents cold and the necks high and dry. I don't know when I first went in to play pool, probably in junior high. It was fascinating to see the range of men in there, chalking their cues, pacing around the table to see all the angles, planning shots two or three in advance. Everyone was there, from Doc Morrison to the pumpers and roustabouts who looked for a place to relax before or after their tower, (what a work shift on a rig was called).

There was a stigma about the place that I never understood, many parents making the pool hall off limits to their sons. But other than cigar smoke, I never noticed much of anything dangerous or potentially damaging to a boy's well-being. I do think I was about the first boy to take his girlfriend in for a game. We got a couple of odd looks, but no one complained.

The wizard of Swarthout's was C. Maynard Stohr. Born in 1902, Maynard was too young for World War One, and too old for the Second World War. He and his father, Robert, ran a sawmill, and he worked for a while as a building contractor. Maynard's wife died in 1945, when the oldest of his four children was eighteen. But by the mid-1950s, they had all grown, and if Maynard wasn't at the mill, he was usually at the pool hall. He wasn't a hustler. He was simply good, and open to playing just about anyone in a game of eight ball, or nine ball, or straight pocket pool. He just liked to play.

Irv liked sports. In the 1920s, he managed the town baseball team, and during all the years I remember him being open he had a pair of cast metal baseball players posed in the window left of the door on Main Street. He liked to attend the horse racing at Batavia Downs, and was happy to place bets for you if you couldn't get there yourself. There were four tables in his hall. Three were for pocket pool, which cost you a penny a minute, or ten cents a rack, depending on the game being played.

Irv's principal assistant in my time was Jack Hay, who watched over the tables. His given name was James W. Hay, born in Beaver County Pennsylvania in 1886. He had made his living most of his life as a painter and paper hanger. When my parents first set up housekeeping on First Street, Jack rented a room in the house next door. One night, he had way too much to drink and stumbled into our house by mistake, stripped, and passed out in the pantry. Dad helped him home. In later years, his hearing gave out, and one of my wise-acre friends, instead of calling out, "Rack 'em up Jack," would say, "Jack 'em up Rack," to the amusement of our friends. Jack never seemed to mind.

The west side of Main in 1958: The new Mobil station; Fagouri's Clothing, the Chef Grill, Appleby's Red & White grocery, Walker's Diner, Parker's Drug, Dillie's Men's shop, Eberl Insurance, Sugar Bowl Restaurant, Hall's Department Store, Dickerson's Barber Shop, Nicholson's Flowers, Swarthout's Pool room, Dunn's Drug, the State Bank, Dwyer's former Buick dealership, being converted to the Bowl-O-Var Lanes, and the US Post Office

In the front of the pool hall, nearest Main Street, was the billiard table, with three balls and no pockets, where the objective was simply to shoot one ball and hit the other two. Or, if you wanted to pretend you were Willie Hoppe, you could play three rail, meaning your ball had to hit three sides of the table before contacting the second ball. That game took quite a while. Irv stayed in business until very near the end of his life, which happened on March 22, 1983. Like Squeak's barber chairs, at least a couple of the pool tables are now in Wellsville. Jack passed away in 1972.

Next to the pool hall was Dunn's Drug Store, started by W.A. "Gus" Dunn. He had graduated from Bolivar High in 1916, enrolled in the pre-med course at the University of Buffalo, but from there decided on pharmacology rather than medicine. He completed his education in 1922, then worked as a pharmacist in Bolivar, Washington, D.C., and Olean. In the summer of 1926, with the backing of a boyhood friend, he opened his first pharmacy in Bolivar.

In 1934, when Ralph Ressler's dry goods store vacated the north half of the Odd Fellows Building, Gus grabbed the opportunity to relocate from his spot across the street, and the Dunn's Drug Store sign that became so familiar to everyone went up at the corner of Main and Boss. Gus had greater ambitions, and opened a second, larger pharmacy in Hornell in 1941. I often accompanied my grandfather on business trips to Hornell, and we usually had sandwiches at the lunch counter in that store, where I acquired a taste for egg and olive sandwiches.

Gus brought in Bolivar boy Gene Salzer to work in the Bolivar pharmacy in 1941. Gene graduated from pharmacy school in 1944, and began preparing drugs for Gus in Bolivar in 1945. He bought the store in 1953. In my earliest memories of Dunn's in Bolivar, there was a small soda fountain there too, just inside the door on the south side, but when he took over Gene converted the area into the space for Kodak film and cameras. The first money I ever earned was ten dollars for helping "hay it" on my grandfather's farm. I took the cash, went up to Dunn's, and bought myself my first Kodak Brownie camera.

In warm weather, the doors to the store were often propped open. I had a pet cocker spaniel named Rusty who loved to play fetch, and she and I would often walk up to Dunn's, where on a lower shelf Gene kept a box of rubber balls. Rusty was free to roam at times, and she learned so well that on occasion she would walk up to Dunn's on her own, go down the aisle, and take a ball. Rusty was the only dog I knew who had a charge account. Melba Root, who tended the store, would simply add the ball to my parent's bill, with a notation saying who picked it up.

Across Main Street is the old Barse Block, built at the height of the boom. In the 1950s, the corner store front was Bill Nichol's insurance office, and next to it a hardware store that became a Western Auto outlet, and next to that was the Washington Restaurant, which I was never in until Randy White bought it and changed the name to The Bulldog.

On the south side of the Washington was an alley, and on the south side of that was the storefront office of Rochester Gas and Electric, which provided electricity to the area. Gus Dunn opened his first Bolivar pharmacy in that location, before going into the Odd Fellows hall. Before the internet, most people paid their utility bills in person, many times in cash, which was an important reason to have a physical office in a community.

To the east of the Barse Block on Wellsville Street was the home of Bob and Elsie Bartlett. Elsie, born in 1910, established an insurance agency there in 1942. Three years later, she bought the insurance businesses of Frank Henderson and C.J. Amsden, and in 1954 was elected president of the Allegany-Cattaraugus Association of Insurance Agents. She passed the exams to become a licensed real estate agent in 1952. She and her husband had a vacation cabin in Canada they enjoyed, and at the end of 1961 she sold her business to Bernie Hilton. Bob Died in 1965. Elsie carried on until October 10, 1982.

The State Bank is where my family did its banking, where I opened my first savings and checking accounts, and where I got my first mortgage. Louis Dunn always wanted to visit when I came in, and I knew all the staff, Bernice Hitchcock and Joanne Dunning being two who come to mind. Cece Cawley Root was a long term branch manager, LaRae Witter being the last manager before the two banks merged.. But it was the area just past the bank that saw the most dramatic changes when I was young.

Upstairs in the bank building were the offices of both Doc Hackett, and of Dr. John Leahy. Doc Leahy started life in Olean in 1904. He went through St. Bonaventure as a pre-med student, and went from there to the Jefferson Medical College in Philadelphia, where he made the honor society, and went on to do his residency at the Albany Medical Center in Albany, New York. He opened his office in Bolivar in October 1929.

He joined the Navy when the Second World War came, and reached the rank of Lt. Commander while doing duty in the Pacific, and joined the Bolivar Legion when he arrived back home. He made his home at 98 Davis Street. He had a young hired man, a valet of sorts, named Albert Bundy, who had a serious speech impediment. The story goes that one night a fellow was injured in an accident, and crossed paths with Albert, who brought him to Doc's house. Albert let himself in and called for the doctor. "Eh, Doc! I godda a guy down here needs your help." Doc replied, "What's the matter with him?" Albert said, "His leg's broke," to which Doc shouted back, "Shoot him!" Doc carried on until he died in January 1969.

Don Dwyer

The "Matson Block," which stood next door to the bank burned to the ground in February 1955. There was no desire to rebuild. A.J. Matson moved his offices over to Boss Street. Don Dwyer bought the property, cleared away the debris, and leveled the lot to be home for his used car inventory.

Dwyer owned the large building to its north, the home of Dwyer Motor Sales, a Buick dealership.

Dwyer had started selling Buicks in Bolivar in the 1930s, at 263 North Main, now the CR Printing location, but had closed down in the summer of 1942 because Buick stopped making cars for the civilian market. Dwyer promised to reopen when the war ended. He started advertising again in January 1947, moving the dealership to 303 North Main, where the Dollar General is today.

Don Dwyer was born in November 1909, and lived his entire life in Wellsville. In 1948 he married, became the father of three daughters, and but kept his house and family in Wellsville. On Friday, May 13, 1955, he closed up the showroom about nine o'clock, and headed home. The rumors surrounding that trip said he had agreed to race one of his new Buicks to Wellsville over Norton Summit. Whatever the truth to that rumor, there was no doubt that he built up a big head of steam going down the hill into Wellsville.

He lost control of the car, tore out five guard rail posts, went down an embankment, snapped a telephone pole, uprooted two trees, and knocked over another tree before coming to rest against a fourth, near the road to Petrolia. He died a few hours later. The sale of Buicks dried up. Cliff Unverdorben kept the repair shop going through 1956. The Dwyer estate set up a date for a public sale of the building and adjoining lot in 1958, but it failed to sell. 1959 would see a change in the market.

The 1950s saw a huge growth of interest in the sport of bowling. I spent many a Saturday evening watching WBEN as Chuck Healy hosted *Bowling for Dollars*. Bowling had come and gone over the decades in Bolivar. There had been a couple of lanes in the second floor of the museum building in the early 1900s, where my grandfather had his first job as a pinsetter, and other lanes had been set up on the second floor of the village fire hall in the 1930s. Leagues were formed, and those lanes were heavily used. But there had never been in town really high-class, dedicated hardwood lanes, as were found in Wellsville and Olean, and those lanes disappeared during World War II.

In early February 1959, the Breeze ran a front page article about a proposal made by Bill Greene and Joe Slavin to set up four lanes in Greene's store building in Richburg. Bill and Joe said they were thinking of selling stock to raise the money and "to get the ball rolling," so to speak. The Brunswick machinery rep failed to arrive for a meeting, but Slavin and Greene got lots of people talking. At the end of the month, word got out that Truman Kreamer, who managed the K of C lanes in Olean, had taken an option to buy the Dwyer building, planning to install eight lanes there. The option lapsed and a year slipped by.

Emmet Karl was born in 1907 in Eldred. He had worked most of his life in the Bolivar area, much of the time running a bulldozer and doing contracting work around the oil field. In May 1960, he stepped forward. At an initial public meeting at the Bolivar Hotel, Emmett proposed that a group come together to buy the Dwyer building and remodel it, which he estimated would cost a total of $40,000. In return, he would lease the building for fifteen years on terms that would pay back the acquisition cost, and he would spend $80,000 of his own to install a dozen lanes equipped with AMF pin setting machines. When no group got together to act on the building, Emmett decided to do it all on his own.

In mid-August, the Elite Dress shop started advertising "bowling blouses." The Bowl-O-Var Lanes & Lounge had their first customers on September 15, and had their Grand Opening party on September 24. It was a big hit. Just a year later, Bowl-O-Var played host to seven adult bowling leagues, and junior and senior high school leagues with four teams each. For the parents who had worried about things for their children to do lest they become pregnant or juvenile delinquents, the bright lights and clean, fresh atmosphere of the Bowl-O-Var was an answer to their prayers. It offered burgers and pizza, soft drinks and beer, hours of exercise and recreation in any kind of weather, had shoes you could rent, balls you could use, and drew scores of people to Bolivar who might have otherwise gone to Wellsville or Olean to relax on their evenings or weekends. It was the largest investment made in a downtown Bolivar business venture since the construction of the hotel in the 1920s. (In today's dollars, more than $1,500,000 went into building the lanes).

This team of junior bowlers posed in front of Bowl-O-Var's "high roller's board" in 1968: L-R, Bill Cossaboon, John Barnes in front of Jim Presher, Joe Yehl, Johnny Greene, Tim Torrey, Wayne "Bud" Allen, and Bill Pinney.

Emmet, aided by Don Moore, ran the bowling business for years, and he also oversaw the town landfill in the early 1970s. He passed away on October 10, 1979. The generation of men and women who filled the bowling teams over time aged out of the game, the businesses that sponsored them did too, and eventually Bowl-O-Var became a thing of the past. So the building at 303 North Main has evolved from auto dealer to bowling lanes into the Dollar General store of today.

On the north side of the Dollar General is the US Post Office, which has operated out of the same location since 1928. That too was a welcoming place during my youth, with friendly faces and banter whenever you went in to drop off mail, buy postage, or look in your P.O. box, if you had one. What has changed is the volume of mail handled there, and the drop boxes which were thoughtfully placed around town to save you the walk if you wanted, and where the letter carriers back in the day could stash the stacks of mail to be delivered to that neighborhood. Rarely used in the twenty-first century, those too are now gone.

The Bolivar Post Office did a bustling business until the computer age arrived. We had a string of competent postmasters and postal employees who kept the wheels greased and who made it a pleasure to come in there, whether it was to buy stamps, pick up a package, or check your box. When I was born, in 1947, Frank Hughes had been Bolivar's postmaster since 1940. He died in 1950, and was replaced by Joseph S. Dempsey, Sr., who kept the job until the end of 1955. When he resigned, Bolivar haberdasher Edgar Dillie received the appointment. When I needed to do something at the Post Office, I always looked forward to the possibility that Bob "Whipper" Appleby would be the one who came to the window. He loved to talk and to banter, no matter the business that brought you into the office. We had a series of competent, home-grown, post masters, so everyone there was happy with their work, and it showed no matter who had to deal with the public that day. Stanley Dempsey was the first I remembered. Edgar Dillie had the job for only about two years, then Harry Sackinger until he died in 1966. Tom Mooney stepped into the job. Tom had been a lieutenant in an artillery battalion in Europe, stayed in the reserves, and was called up for Korea. In that war, he had served in an intelligence unit studying aerial photographs, and came out a major.

Tom resigned as postmaster in1970, and Glen Milliman became the first postmaster appointed pursuant to a new policy of promoting career employees working in their home area. Glen, born in Fillmore in 1918, graduated from Richburg in 1938, served as a navigator in the Air Force, getting his wings in 1944, and started working as a substitute mail carrier in Bolivar in 1946. Made the assistant postmaster in 1966, and postmaster in 1970. After his retirement in 1974, he moved to Olean, where he died in 2006. Glen was the last postmaster to get the post as a political appointee. During his tenure, the system changed to a merit system.

Under the new merit system, Bill Nagle became the acting postmaster when Glen vacated the position. Bill had a close connection to the Bradley family. His grandparents lived in a house we referred to as the old homestead at a crossroads named Sawyers, along what is now called Homestead Road. That was where J.B. Bradley first lived when he came to the area in 1881. When Bill got out of the Navy, and before he found a position at the Post Office, he often drove my grandmother when she needed to get to Olean or Wellsville, since she had never learned how to drive. Back then, one of the better known character actors was a man named Andy Devine, and to me he and Bill had very similar, distinctive voices. Bill married Maureen Dougherty, the niece of former postmaster Mattie Dellone.

Bill was promoted to postmaster in 1975, but stayed in Bolivar only until 1977, when he took the postmaster's position in Wellsville. He was succeeded here by Bob Dunbar, BCS class of 1966, but Bob's tenure was even shorter, only five months. He then began a professional odyssey through eight positions, the last being postmaster of Georgetown, Delaware. Since Bob left his position in Bolivar in 1977, twenty different people have served as either the officer-in-charge (assistant postmaster), or postmaster, in charge of the Bolivar office. Of those, only Bob's brother-in-law, Mark Miller, has Bolivar roots. Mark took charge of the Bolivar office for just two months in 1982. He was then the top executive at five other post offices, and retired as the postmaster of the St. Bonaventure, New York office.

Bill Nagle, Bob Appleby, and postmaster Stanley Dempsey digging a post hole for a drop box at the corner of First and Boss Streets about 1950. In the background is the original Hungerford homestead, lived in then by World War One veteran Thomas Hungerford.

Bolivar's Hotel

In the year 1900, Bolivar still boasted two hotels. The Clark House, on Main just south of Olean Street, dated back nearly to the founding of Bolivar. But it had been remodeled and extended over the years, and continued to be a satisfactory place for travelers to spend the night, and to get a drink or a meal. It had meeting rooms for larger gatherings, too, so remained a central venue of the village social life. But, it burned to the ground in the fall of 1915.

The Newton House had been thrown up in a hurry at the start of the oil boom. With its porches and verandas, and its three stories of rooms, it presented an imposing site at the corner of Main and Wellsville Streets, but by 1918 it was showing its age and was in need of substantial repair. A.J. Matson, acting as a real estate agent, offered in up for sale in July 1919, the hotel itself for lumber, and three lots: the hotel lot, the associated barn and lot, and a garden lot. The Newton House was gone by the end of 1920. For 1921, the hotel lot served as a community park, hosting a carousel for some of the time, but in 1922, the Motor Age claimed the park, when the firm of Seversen and Shaner bought it and built a new state-of-the-art service station there, complete with three Bowser gasoline pumps under roof, so you could fill up and stay dry no matter the weather. But, the many traveling salesmen or business partners who came to town no longer had a place to stay.

This situation was a community problem, and discussions began about how best to solve it. The agreed course of action was to form a corporation, and raise the money to build a new hotel by selling stock to local residents. The prime movers behind the proposal were A.L. Shaner, Dorr Graves, Dr. H.L. Hulett, W.J. Brannen, Harry Goodrich and W.J. Hogan. Graves served as the first president of the corporation.The idea was floated in 1924, but sales of stock proceeded slowly, delaying the start of construction to July 1, 1925, 100 years ago. Then work began on a twenty-eight room hotel, with appropriate lobby and restaurant spaces, at a cost of $42,000, which would be more than $750,000 today. It opened for business on May 30, 1926. That was an opportune time to open. The improved, paved road to Wellsville running over Norton Summit was completed the same year, a modern switchboard vastly improved Bolivar's telephone service, and an electric fire siren went up on top of the village fire hall.

The new hotel was designed by A.W.E. Schoenberg of Olean, fireproof, two stories high. The first manager was J. Charles Webb from Ellicottville, who engaged his wife and children to work with him. Mary Richmond ran the dining room. The hotel changed management fairly regularly. In the late 1920s, J.W. Forney, who had previously operated the Olean House, took over for Webb, who in turn took over a hotel in Perry, NY. As the Depression set in, Forney was replaced in 1930 by Ferd West of Wellsville. In 1941, it was managed by Frank Dunlavey, but he retired back to Olean in 1945, and it was purchased by Ray Christman and his wife, Elizabeth, who lived in Wellsville.

In 1951, Almon Kittle, from Elmira, and Richard Deschler of Wellsville, went in together and took over the property, with the Kitttle family moving into the residence. They did their best to keep the hotel going until March, 1955. George and Agnes Asbel were the operators for most of 1955, but in November, turned the hotel over to Walter and Viola Riesen. The Riesens were first and foremost restauranteurs. They hired Bolivar artist Dick Monroe to paint a series of large murals, and converted the dining room from "The Apple Blossom Lounge," as it had been marketed in 1940, into the "Alpine Chalet," where diners were surrounded by scenes reminiscent of the Swiss Alps the Riesens grew up in.

The Alpine Room was a hit. The food was good, the surroundings fresh and attractive, and it quickly became one of the area's favorite dining spots, and a popular place to host parties, banquets, and wedding receptions. But the Riesens kept the hotel for only two years, selling it in December 1957 to Mr. and Mrs. Bob Grundon of Buffalo, while they pursued new business opportunities in Miami.

The Grundons kept up the restaurant, and the hotel appeared to run well while they owned it, but after just five years, they too tired of the business and looked for a buyer who would have the energy needed to make the hotel a success. The buyers they found were Ken and Mary Stedman. The Stedmans had been in the restaurant business for a while, owning and operating the Hotel Belvidere outside Belmont. Mary Stedman was an excellent cook, and their dining room had been packed, especially on Friday nights for fish fries. In Belvedere, they had booked live music for dancing on Saturday nights to fill the place through the weekend. In October, 1963, they brought both the fried fish and the music to the Bolivar Hotel, which had many more tables, and a much bigger space for music and dancing, than Stedmans had had before. And they turned the tables and filled the dance floor over and over again for decades. Mary was the head chef, and it didn't matter if it was fried haddock, a T-bone steak, or spaghetti and meatballs, the customers liked what was ordered, and kept coming back for more. Ken ran the bar, and was glad to fill and refill as needed, tuned in every Yankees broadcast, and kept on going and going until closing time.

In the 1930s and 1940s, music attracted couples who were used to doing slow dances to the sounds of the big bands, and perhaps an occasional jitterbug to tunes with a faster beat. Tom Hungerford said the proper sequence in the 1940s was two slow dances, then a fast one. But rock and roll demanded dancers with more energy, and they were usually younger and single. Ken and Mary found the right musicians, and on Saturday nights the Alpine Chalet and Kenny's barroom were packed to overflowing. Bolivar band director Ralph Butler was part of the Doug Bushnell Trio which played on many a Saturday night. Tom Manning, Scott MacDonell, Mike Appleby, John Cornelius and Doug Milliman formed a band which started out as *Michael and the Archangels*, but which played as *The Spider's Web* for most of its existence, many times at the hotel, and during the summers at the Cuba Lake Pavilion. The hotel drew customers from Salamanca to Wellsville, and built a reputation as one of the rockingest places in the Southern Tier.

Ken Stedman was fifty-one years old when he bought the Bolivar Hotel, and Mary was forty-three. In the late 1970s, Ken thought about retiring, and looked for someone to buy the hotel so he and Mary could do so. I handled the other side of the transaction for an Olean banker, and for a short while Ken and Mary got to step away, but not for long. The Stedmans took a mortgage from the buyer to help get the deal done., and the buyer stopped paying. They got the hotel back, and Kenny moved back behind the bar. Bolivar's shrunken business district and economy, and a hotel roof and heating system that was fifty years old,

Kenny Stedman poured the drinks, while Mary tended the stove at their Bolivar Hotel

kept potential buyers at bay. Mary stopped cooking, but Ken, helped by his children, stayed there behind the bar for another thirty years, until he was in his nineties and living in the twenty-first century. Mary passed away in 1988. Kenny joined Mary on the other side on July 2, 2013, three days past his one hundred first birthday. They rest in St. Anne's Cemetery in Hornell. The Bolivar Hotel building will turn 100 during the town's bicentennial, in June 2025.

The Bolivar Breeze, the community's only newspaper, started up in the summer of 1892, and from then to 1950 had known only three owners: brothers John then Frank Herrick, and Glenn McCoy. McCoy grew up in Chicago, and was by all accounts an interesting and enterprising man, and a mid-western Republican through and through. In 1952, the Republican National Convention was held in the Drake Hotel in Chicago. My father, John D. Bradley, had business to do in Illinois around the time of the convention. Having finished his work there, he headed up to Chicago just to see what was going on. Somehow in the throng. he ran into Glen McCoy. McCoy, based on his livelihood as editor and publisher of the *Bolivar Breeze*, had landed press credentials, and invited my father to follow him where ever he could get.

Those were different times. The Drake Hotel is enormous. Everyone was there. At the coat room, my father actually heard John Wayne say the words, “Well, hello little lady” to the hat check girl. There were two main contenders for the nomination, Senator Robert Taft of Ohio, and General Dwight D. Eisenhower. McCoy was impressed that when my father attended the Taft School in Connecticut after high school, he had been a classmate of Horace Taft, a son of the senator. So, they thought they had an in there. The Taft delegation took up one entire floor of the hotel. The Eisenhower party occupied another. They managed to track down Horace, but never got to interview the Senator. Unperturbed, and wanting to show what press credentials could do, McCoy said to Dad, “well, lets go meet Ike!” So, they simply walked up the flight of stairs to the next floor, and started asking where the general’s room was. They got there and knocked. An aide told them that he was sorry, but it was two o’clock in the morning, and the general had retired for the night. Dad got back to Bolivar first. McCoy, unable to land a scoop, never mentioned in the Breeze that he had been there! One of the prize possessions of my youth was the huge “I Like Ike” poster which filled the window of Nichol’s Insurance office at the corner of Wellsville and Main during the 1952 campaign season.

McCoy could see as well as anyone that with oil production steadily declining, and with it fewer people wanting print advertising, that the Bolivar Breeze was not going to provide him with a comfortable retirement. The following year, he found a position in Owego where he could run two newspapers, and he sold the *Breeze* to Jack and Harriett Moore, who lived in Belmont, and also had control of Whitesville’s newspaper. They in turn put the Breeze under the corporate umbrella of Allegany Printing, essentially in partnership with Robert Wilson, who was known around town as Luke.

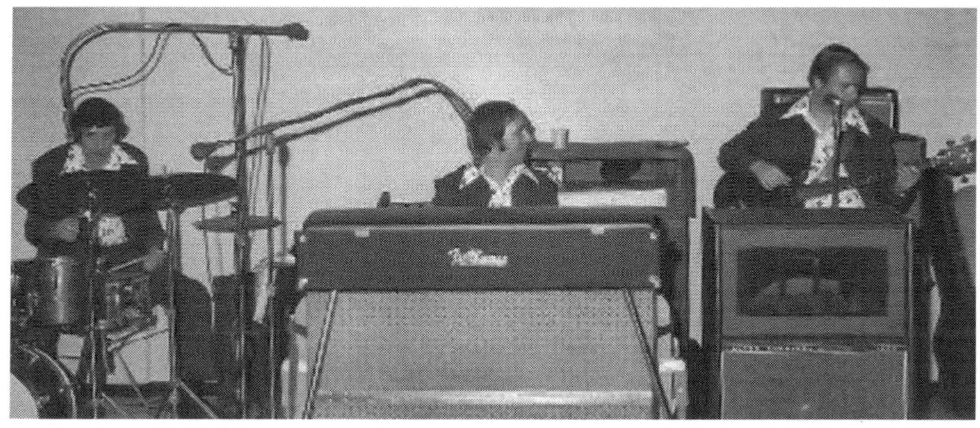

Doug Bushnell Trio, Ralph Butler on the right

Moore only lasted a little over two years. During that time, the *Breeze* was moved from its tight quarters on Friendship Street, to much larger accommodations in the former Bolivar Garage, two doors north of the post office. Moore sold out to Luke and his father, Roy Wilson, and took a job in advertising in Rochester. Luke had come to Bolivar with his family to edit the Breeze when they first took it over, and he stayed. In 1961, Luke asked insurance man Bernie Hilton to write a column, and Bernie put out many fun to read "Off the Cuff" columns, one involving the dilemma my mother and my future mother-in-law encountered when they tried to retrieve a golf ball from a cow pasture and came face to face with a bull.

But Westies was driving out small businesses and drying up their ads, putting their own advertising exclusively in the *Olean Times Herald.* The last issue of the *Breeze* was dated October 14, 1965. Perhaps appropriately, it ran on the front page its last obituary, of Bolivar's longest lived man, Merritt Starr, who died on his 102nd birthday, October 7. In his column, Bernie said this: "It is with a twinge of sadness that we pound out these last chapters of "the stuff" column. As you already know, this is the last edition of this old pioneer oil town's newspaper. Most of the oil wells have now disappeared, so maybe it is natural that the time has come to bury this tired sheet along with it." But along with the demise of the *Bolivar Breeze* went the intimate, detailed record of all the things bad and good which happen here.

The Breeze never had any direct competition as a newspaper, but it did have it for advertising. Not only from the *Wellsville Daily Reporter* and the *Olean Times Herald*, but also from Bolivar's own *Moneysaver*, then put together on North Main Street by William Jones. Bill Jones had two sons, Jim, and William W., whom we, his schoolmates, knew as Wayne. Wayne, known in Wellsville where he lived his adult life, as Wiley, put on Facebook a picture of his father's first advertising venture, which was called, *Bolivar's Pennysaver*, issued in March 1938. Here is Jim Jones' description of the founding of this publication, as he wrote it for the Bolivar Fan Page on Facebook:

"*This early venture into the advertising business by my dad William O. Jones and his sister Isabel's husband, Paul Rose, did not end in success. Bill worked a number of jobs, was a Theatre Manager for Sam Gandel in Salamanca, NY, (where I was born in 1940), and eventually ended up being a meat cutter for Market Basket and then Quality Markets in Bolivar. During that time, my mom, Marian V. Jones, and dad started a silk screen business in their home at 142 North Main Street in Bolivar, and eventually after 20 years, he left the meat cutting job and started the Moneysaver Shopping Guide which enjoyed a great success over many decades.*

After I graduated from high school in 1958, I looked for work and there was none available, so in conjunction with Mom & Dad, I started a second Moneysaver in Eldred and Portville which eventually expanded to a large area of McKean, Potter and Cattaraugus Counties. Mom and Dad continued to publish both these papers after I went off on other ventures and sampled other occupations. My brother William "Wayne" Jones bought the papers and Mom and Dad retired as my dad's health began to fail. Wayne continued the papers until last year when he sold the papers to Tioga Publishing Company. The papers provided our family with a good income for many, many years, and my brother Wayne came on the scene and used his abilities (he was the smart one of the family) to carry on a very successful business with the help of his wonderful and talented staff at the Moneysaver."

The Moneysaver contained almost nothing but paid advertisements, but Bill Jones did regularly feature old photographs of the Bolivar, New York area that readers would bring to him. Although we have few, if any, complete copies of any issues of the *Moneysaver*, many people clipped out these photos, and many of those have been scanned and added to the collection of the Bolivar New York Fan Page on Facebook. Both the *Moneysaver* and telephone books are valuable historic records which are rarely preserved.

Wayne Jones moved the operation a short distance from his parents' garage out on North Main into the Bronc Reeland house at the corner of Plum and Main. He was highly regarded not just in the business world, but more so by the people who worked for him. When he sold, he left the area to be near his grandchildren in Georgia, and the buyers closed the Bolivar office. There is still activity in the old Breeze printing plant, under the name of C R Printing, but all in all the printing business in Bolivar is a shell of its old self, as is true across the country.

Across the street from the Breeze office was another restaurant. In the 1930's, up to 1945, it was Mary Miller's. I knew it as Elliott's, although the official business name was the Bolivar Lunch Room. The Elliotts, Rueben and Doris, took over in October 1946. I went in there at least once a week from the mid-1950s on, because that was where I picked up my parent's copy of the *Sunday New York Times*. There were other occasions when I would go there to grab a sandwich or a milkshake, but never on Sundays. Doris and Reuben were in their mid-forties when they bought the restaurant, and I seem to recall it went away in the late 1960s when they reached retirement age. Reuben died in 1980, Doris in 1989. Their lunch counter was the only one in town which was semi-circular. Everyone else, Marie's, the Sugar Bowl, the Main Street, were straight.

On the north side of Elliott's was Stoll's Dry Cleaning Service. John, born in Wellsville in 1897, was a Navy veteran who came to Bolivar in 1929. He was a shirt tail relative of mine, because his half-sister married my mother's uncle. Before coming to Bolivar, John worked as a tailor in Wellsville, and could do alterations as well as clean your woolens or other delicate garments. His wife, Helen, did the bookkeeping. John became active in community affairs, served as a village trustee and deputy mayor, and also helped with the maintenance of the Christ the King Seminary in Allegany. He passed from the scene unexpectedly in 1970. Helen outlived him by four years.

The Bolivar Town Hall went up in 1926. The town of Bolivar moved into the first floor, which was the first time the town government had a place of its own to store records, have meetings, hold court, and otherwise conduct the town's business. One of the key positions in town government is the town clerk, who has many duties, one of which is the keeper of vital statistics: the births, marriages, and deaths which happen here. In 1926, that person was Maude Maxson. In 1918, the supervisor, A.J. Matson had resigned to enlist in the Army. The town clerk, Edwin M. Strayer, was asked to take the supervisor's spot, and the town board appointed Maude to fill the clerk's position.

Maude Maxson was born in her parent's home at the corner of Boss and First Streets on March 23, 1885. Her name first appeared in the Bolivar Breeze in 1900, when she passed the United States History regent's exam, along with Frank Dougherty and Lotta Hearons. Maude and Strayer had to run for their positions in 1921. Strayer kept his job, winning by a single vote. Maude kept hers too, the votes being 272 for her, and eighty-seven for her male opponent. After that mauling, Maude, a Republican whose father's name was Sherman Ulysses Maxson, was rarely opposed, and often ran on both party lines.

In 1954, she celebrated being on the job for thirty-six years. Bill, Nichols, one of the two town justices, had almost as much seniority, having then served for thirty-two years. Supervisor MacDonell had been in charge for eighteen years, and had thirteen to go. Ralph Bentley had been the other town justice for fourteen years, and the town constable, Frank Moore, was appointed again, going into his twenty-second year. The next year, the state retirement board gave Maude special dispensation to keep on working as the clerk of the village water department.

Maude never married. She lived with her father in the house where she was born until he died in 1951, and she never moved. She continued in office until December 31, 1961, when at age seventy-seven she completed forty-three years of service to the town of Bolivar, the most of anyone during the twentieth century, and probably of all time. When she died, at the age of ninety-three in 1978, she had been a contributing member of the Methodist Church for seventy-three years.

Her place was taken by Erma Jandrew. She and her husband, George, a pumper in 1950, had raised one boy, Walt, and had another, much younger, named Jack, who would graduate from Bolivar Central in 1964. When she ran for clerk in 1961, she was endorsed by both parties, as she was again in 1965, when she ran for another term. George Jandrew died, Erma remarried, resigned as the clerk in August 1969, and moved with her new husband to Port Allegany, where he was employed. Betty Butler, who had lost her job as a telephone operator when dial phones came in, received the appointment.

All the clerks we have had whom I got to know were really good people, but earlier this year, when I asked around for suggestions about who to include in this book, only one was suggested numerous times, and justifiably so: Ruby Allen. Born in Pennsylvania in 1928, she married her husband Wayne Allen in Alma in January 1948. Before he had gone into the Army, Wayne had been living with his step father in Allentown, and worked for Harold Miller in Wellsville. The Allens set up housekeeping in Bolivar, where he sold automobiles, and Ruby paid attention to the two daughters and three sons they brought into the world: Janet, Wayne jr., called Bud, Bob, Ray, and Brenda.

Wayne Allen did his best to pitch in around Bolivar. He joined the Legion, brought the family to the Methodist Church, and became active with the Cub Scouts. During the 1950s, Ruby Allen only got her name in the papers once, for winning the weekly prize given out by the Elite Dress Shop. Then the roof fell in. In 1960, Wayne's heart began to give out. He was only forty-two. The headline on page one of the Bolivar Breeze of July 6, 1961 broke the news that Jack Root, a star athlete at BCS five years before, and popular manager of the pool summer programs, had been killed in an automobile accident. The next column let the village know that Wayne Allen had died on July 2.

Ruby Allen

Ruby needed employment, and she found it in the bookkeeping department of the Bradley Producing Corporation in Wellsville. She was very competent, completely reliable, and very well liked by everyone in the office. The Bradley companies were reorganized in 1984, and its Wellsville office closed in the early 1990s. It was then she became a familiar face to the few town residents who didn't know her, when she became Bolivar's town clerk in 1991. She kept the job until 2010, not as long as Maude, but earning every bit as much admiration for the work she did.

Ruby was also for many years the treasurer of the Methodist Church Women, and was a founding member of the Bolivar Sports Boosters. She was given an award in 2010 for being the softball team's "Best Fan." Why? For years, she supplied the football teams with bananas, the softball and soccer teams with licorice, and cooked the sloppy joes for every football homecoming game. If someone needed something she was always there to provide what she could, whether it was offering time, money or food. Ruby was always willing to help raise money for various organizations or to improve the community. She made spaghetti sauce for scores of dinner fundraisers in town. She was a supporter of local businesses, even refusing to travel to Olean to get groceries. She was Grand Marshall along with Hank Lindquist for Pioneer Oil Days.

But to me, the most remarkable part was how well she carried on raising her five children as a single mother. The proof, as is said, was in the pudding. All of her children were as well known around town as she was. Janet won the office of town justice. Years later, she moved out of town. To retain her as the justice, the town managed to get the New York State legislature to change the law which required town justices to be town residents. Wayne Allen, Jr., who we all knew as Bud, was a four-letter man in high school, captain of the football team, was on the student council for four years, and president as a senior in 1968. He and his brothers stayed in the area and earned similar levels of respect as they served the community as adults. Through her children, Ruby amplified her contribution to Bolivar, New York.

When first established in Bolivar, the telephone company set up its equipment in the second floor of the State Bank, which was the only brick "fireproof" building in the village at the time. When the new brick town hall went up, the phone company decided to move its switchboards and operators over there, making the bank available, and both doctors Hackett and Leahy relocated there after World War II.

In May 1964, New York Telephone announced plans to build a new facility in Bolivar to house a dial system. The last five communities New York Telephone served which still had operators and switchboards at that time were Wellsville, Salamanca, Belfast, Cuba and Bolivar. The company was upgrading them all, and would have no switchboards in 1966. By then, all five of these towns would have much more modern dial systems, (which first came into use in 1919!), and the second story of the town building would become vacant.

My grandmother Bradley came from a tiny village overlooking Keuka Lake, and whenever I would accompany her up there to see her sister, or decorate her family's graves for Decoration Day, her first stop would be at the home of her life-long friend, Mae Hess. Why? Mae was the telephone operator, and had the switch board in her home. Mae could fill Grandma in on everything going on in town in just a few minutes. That was true in Bolivar too. The ones who knew all the town doings were the operators, who were free to cut themselves in on any conversation they chose, unless times were busy and they had to help others make connections. They could also sound the fire alarm, and set up group conference calls, once in a while by request, but other times either accidentally or facetiously. I started dating my wife, Connie, in 1965, when we were both in high school at BCS. I recall one evening when we had been talking to each other on the phone for a couple of hours. All of a sudden there was a loud click, and a booming female voice saying, "Annie- Get Off That Phone!" How long Annie had been listening in we never found out.

All that ended on April 17, 1966, when all five manual switchboards were shut down, and the dial system went live. Our home phone number changed from 218 to 928-1095. Never again would you pick up the receiver and hear the words, "Number please," or hear a third voice say, "Annie, get off that phone!"

Doctors Leahy and Hackett had their offices over the State Bank. Dentist Bob Bentley had set up next door in the Matson building, and Doc Claflin over Hall's Department Store. Our third medical doctor at that time did not have an office on Main Street. Instead, he kept his office in his home on Wellsville Street. At the time my grandfather Bradley died, in March 1965, his sister, Naomi, came and stayed a few days. At some point she asked me if "that nice young doctor, the one who had treated her mother during her last illness, (in 1930), was still practicing." I had to think for a while about who that "nice young doctor" might have been.

Phillips Lovering Morrison came into the world on April 14, 1903 in Merchantville, New Jersey. He grew up in and around Swarthmore, the youngest of the four children of Bayard Morrison, a chemist, and his wife, Carline Lovering. Phillips graduated from Swarthmore High, attended Swarthmore College, and went on to medical school, completing his residency at the Hahnemann Medical School in Spring Lake, New Jersey in 1928. He then began looking for a good place to establish his practice.

At that time, the area's population was growing fast and we were losing doctors. Dr. Orry Latham, who had come to Bolivar during the boom, had served for many years since as the town health officer for both Bolivar and Wirt, but he died in 1918. This left Bolivar with three practitioners: Charles Hoffman, Lawrence Hackett, and Horace Hulett.

Doctor Hoffman, who had his office on Boss Street, took over as the health officer for Bolivar, Wirt, and Alma, and kept those appointments until he died in 1925. Horace Hulett, born in Little Genesee in 1871, had his office in the back of his house at 144 Wellsville Street, and being a hometown boy was the health officer for the town of Genesee. When Charles Hoffman died, he took over the positions Hoffman had held, and thus became the health officer for all four towns, and for the schools there. But the Hulett's children had grown up and were then living in Wisconsin. The good doctor, approaching sixty, was looking for a way to get closer to his grandchildren.

In August 1928, into town over freshly paved highways came the recently licensed Dr. Phillips Morrison, and his father, Bayard, to check the area over. They stayed with the Keith Hardmans in Richburg, who undoubtedly acted as their guide, and introduced them to Dr. Hulett. The Morrisons also met with the various town officials, hoping to land the health officer appointments held by Dr. Hulett, if the decision was made to buy the practice. Dr. Morrison impressed everyone, with one caveat. He was a bachelor, and they would be reluctant to have a single man in the position of doctor for the school districts, (which were at the time being consolidated into the central school).

Doc was single, but engaged to the very pretty daughter of a New Jersey real estate broker. Her name was Sarabelle Brooke. The new doctor told the local officials he thought he could solve the bachelor problem, and he hurried home to ask Sarabelle if they could move their wedding day up so he could get to work. They were married in the Bala Cynwyd, Pennsylvania Episcopal Church on October 5, 1928. He bought Dr. Hulett's house and his practice, and hung out his shingle in Bolivar within a month. Dr. and Mrs. Hulett moved to Milton, Wisconsin, where their daughter had attended college.

Dr. Hulett had his office in the back of his home. Doc Morrison remodeled the west end of the house, and in the summer of 1929 he put his office in the new space. If you wanted to see him, you could ask the operator for number 6-9 and arrange for a house call, or you could just drop in during office hours, which were two to four in the afternoons, and six thirty to eight o'clock in the evenings. There was a fireplace in the waiting room area, which Doc kept burning nearly year round, bartering his services for a steady supply of firewood.

As the youngest doctor in town, he was also the one with the most up to date ideas and equipment. In 1930, he installed his own x-ray machine. Having the only one in town, any time a fractured bone was suspected, Doc Morrison usually became involved to make the determination and properly set the bones. There

Among the last telephone operators in New York State were, top: Marion Skinner, Sandra Friar, Sheila Freeman, Athlene Wight, & Amelia Sallazzo, and below, Lyla Monahan, Eleanor Wheeler, Mary Newell, Helen Fenner, Betty Butler, and Lois Filips.

were many ways bones could be broken. In the fall of 1932 a sixteen-year-old girl who had been hit by a car in Little Genesee was rushed to his office, but too late. She died of a fractured skull before she arrived. Harry Jennings's new horse kicked him in the leg, and once the x-rays were seen, Doc put him in a cast. As the community health officer, he would be looked to for decisions in times of emergency, such as the influenza epidemic, and to otherwise bring new information to the people in the area. One of the last things Health Officer Hulett did was to arrange for showings of a film about the prevention of tuberculosis at the Dreamland Theater.

Doc and Sara enjoyed life. Soon after arriving, they were playing bridge all around town. Doc was a chess player, and became part of a Bolivar chess club, which took on opponents in Olean, Cuba and Smethport. He usually won. When the country club was organized, Doc put his golf clubs to use, and often won there too. And almost as soon as they settled in, they began a family, which over the next nineteen years would grow to include three sons and six daughters.

Not all calls came during office hours. Daughter Lynne recalled answering the phone one day during lunch hour, from a woman frantically looking for a doctor. Was he in? Her husband had caught his had in a thrashing machine. Lynne said no, but told her to bring her husband in right away. The doctor would be there before they arrived. Lynne then hung up, and literally ran down Wellsville Street to Swarthout's Pool Hall, where Doc went at mid-day, and he was ready when new patients arrived.

Doc gained hospital privileges in both Olean and Wellsville, had a nice bedside manner, whether it was when he made house calls or hospital visits, and kept on working into the 1970s. One of his last acts as a health officer happened in October 1971, when he declared Richburg's water unsafe because of an unexplained high bacterial count. In 1955, both he and Dr. Hackett administered the new polio vaccine to long lines of grade school children, including myself. Doc Hackett wanted to avoid inflicting pain, but as a result very slowly pushed the needle in. Doc Morrison simply asked you a question, knowing that thinking about something other than getting the shot would smooth things along, and before you could think of an answer, he had given you the shot and was getting ready for the kid behind you.

Doc left his family from August 31, 1942 to March 28, 1943 to put on an Army captain's uniform, but otherwise he and Sara were inseparable. They enjoyed Caribbean cruises and attending the horse races around Buffalo on the weekends. The Morrison family regularly filled the back pews of the Episcopal Church on Olean Street. In his later years, as his hearing grew weaker, Doc often raised smiles on the faces of those sitting in front of him when, during the sermon, he would ask Sara in his booming voice, "What did he say?" (The Bradleys also attended the Episcopal Church. My father told the story of one day when the minister, Father Peatross from Wellsville, lost his place and train of thought while delivering a sermon, resulting in a very long pause. My grandmother asked Dad what the problem was, to which Dad said, "He wasn't listening either").

Dr. Phillips Morrison, and his fiancé, Sarabelle Brooke, 1927

Dr. Hackett died in 1965, which meant that when Dr. Leahy passed away in 1969, Doc Morrison was the only physician left practicing in Bolivar, and he was then sixty-six. When he turned seventy, he wanted to slow down and retire. The community needed another medical man. The town fathers decided to make the second story of the town building available to a doctor who would agree to come to Bolivar, and a few of the more well-to-do citizens agreed to furnish it. The search resulted in the coming to town of Dr. Hwang, an Indo-Chinese emigre. In 1974, my two-year-old younger son, James, found a fishing filet knife and sliced his thumb lengthwise down to the bone. I ran him right up to the new doctor's office. He examined James, then said very clearly, "Need stitches. I give him special shot, novocaine and tetanus. Kill two stone with one bird." The stones died. James lived, and healed up just fine.

Doc Morrison died in the Olean General Hospital on October 23, 1979. To be near some of her children, Sara took her smiles, good cheer and fifty years of memories of being the wife of a country doctor in Bolivar, New York to New Jersey, from whence she joined Doc on May 12, 1993. They rest together here in Maple Lawn.

In 1980, after the time Dr. Hwang had moved on to larger pastures, Dr. Rick was finally ready to start work. True to his word, he came back and started taking care of the people of Bolivar, and did so until he too retired. Initially, he occupied the space above the town hall, but eventually moved his offices to First Street, where he had a modern set up of a waiting room and multiple examining rooms.

There was another project going on at this time to bring a medical practitioner to Bolivar. Richard P. Cudahy had graduated from Bolivar with the class of 1967. He said "God told me I was going to be a doctor when I was five years old." The realization of that dream was delayed by the difficulty Rick found in being admitted to a medical school. With the backing of some local citizens to help him defray the cost of his education, he was accepted by the University of

Dr. Rick

Guadalajara in Mexico. He spent three years there, then two more at the University of Buffalo Medical School, followed by three additional years doing his residency there in internal medicine. Rick gained a great reputation for his wry humor, keen insights, and eminently practical advice. He was a devoted western New Yorker. He enjoyed to the hilt his winter Thursdays off on the slopes at Holiday Valley with his good buddy, Jim "Spider" Webb, the local conservation officer, and the "Road Kill Gang." Every spring he dug leeks, and planted a garden. Every fall, he hunted. He lived on a farm up Willowbrook Road, outside Little Genesee, where he had grown up. But I think he most enjoyed conversing with his patients, and of living his dream of being a country doctor in his little home town.

In 2007, changing times and the aging process forced Dr. Rick to place an announcement in the Cuba Patriot, saying he would no longer provide hospital care for his patients, but that he would continue to treat them before and after discharge. What caught my eye when he published this announcement was how he addressed it: "To My Very Special Patients." I was one of them, and that is the way he made me feel. He retired, much to the dismay of his patients, in 2012, but only got to enjoy his retirement for ten years. He died on October 14, 2022.

As part of his retirement planning, Rick sold his practice to Jones Memorial Hospital, and brought in a daughter, Dr. Elizabeth Osborn, to take his place. She too has moved on, (with her husband to Geneva), but thanks to Dr. Rick's planning, Bolivar still has active medical practitioners in the office on First Street.

Back to Main Street. One day back in the late 1970s, while I was still practicing law, Frank Stimson came into my office with a problem that had nothing to do with law, but which I found fascinating. Frank was then approaching eighty, and he still had his store building at the corner of Main and Plum from which he had conducted his heating, plumbing, and electrical business for decades. He handed me a picture he had had Dick Monroe draw of an animal he had seen many decades before on the banks of the Allegany River, done as sort of a police sketch, with Frank detailing what he had seen, and correcting what Dick drew until the drawing matched up with what he recalled. Frank swore the drawing was dead on, even though his memories of this thing were far from fresh. I was impressed by the fact that whatever Frank saw must have really given him a jolt, to be so clearly imbedded after all of these years. It was a mystery he wanted solved while he was still here and still with it.

What the picture showed was a spotted, four-legged, lizard-like creature with lots of appendages where ears normally are. He described it as a little less then two feet long, not very tall, walking on all fours. He thought it must be some sort of remnant of the dinosaurs. He had seen it only that one time, He wanted to know what it was. Because it seemed to be bothering Frank so much, I agreed to see what I could find out. I took a respectable amount of time to conclude that it must have been a mud puppy, not common, and being nocturnal, not commonly seen. Just seeing how relieved Frank was to learn that he hadn't been seeing things was all the payment I needed. Frank passed away in 1982.

Opposite Plum Street on the west side of Main was what had been the Oil Well Supply Company Store. The first mention of the Oil Well Supply Company in the Bolivar Breeze appeared in May 1894, when the village bought two dollars worth of nails from it. In 1899, the store and grounds were completely remodeled, the changes being made possible by the removal of the railroad grade which crossed the property there on the route to Wellsville. The office was described as "light and airy," and the store manager, J.C. Craig, lived upstairs. In 1900, Bolivar's was one of four Oil Well Supply stores. The others were in Bradford, Oil City, and Pittsburg. It was at that time the company began advertising the equipment it could supply to power leases, as well as equip wells. They ran the same ad every week for five years.

Oil Well Supply began offering used pipe for sale in 1909, everything from drive pipe to tubing, and had a repair shop and warehouse near the railroad depot. Craig became well known around town, owned oil properties of his own around the area, joined the Macedonia Lodge, and ran the store until he died on April 1, 1924. Ace Root, W.L. Dunning, and A.L. Shaner were among his pall bearers. His place was taken by Sam Hartman, who ran the first ad for the business in years in the September 1925 issue of the Breeze. D.O. Smith took over for Sam, and he left to work in the Bradford store in 1937, his place filled by Elmer W. Rice, who may have been the last manager of the store. He was fifty-nine when he filled out his draft registration form in 1942. The story of oil well supplies in Bolivar is probably best told by some simple statistics. Competition was most fierce in the first decade of the twentieth century. The term "oil well supply" appeared in the *Breeze* 141 times in that decade. After dipping to just thirty mentions in the 1910s, it jumped back up to sixty in the 1920s as secondary recovery kicked in. But during the 1930s it dropped to twenty-seven, in the 1940s to thirteen, and in the 1960s those words appeared only twice.

The last business building on the west side of Main before you get to Pleasant Street was, when I was young, the home of F&S Sales. F&S was a partnership between Alyn Shaner and Tony Sallazzo, where they dealt in sporting goods. It marked the start of Tony's professional career. He would go on to become the east coast or United States sales representative for various well known brands of sporting goods and hunting and fishing equipment. He loved to tell the tale of traveling to Finland to meet with Mr. Lauri Rapala, and gaining the rights to bring Rapala filet knives to the United States. The only reason I visited the store was to buy golf balls, which came in plastic tubes, rather than in sleeves. That would have been in the late 1950s, when my friends and I started to play golf. I don't think the partnership lasted long after that. Alyn Shaner went back to school to start a career in hospital administration, and Tony went all the way in to finding hunting and fishing goods manufacturers he could represent- and do a little hunting and fishing along the way.

After F&S vacated, a laundromat was installed in the building. Then, in one of the best developments for Bolivar in years, it was remodeled to become Cafe Jacob. Due to health concerns for the woman who created it, the Cafe Jacob had but a brief run, but has reopened as Debbie Sue's Restaurant and Specialty Coffee. We wish her well.

Vietnam

The Vietnam War was just starting to develop when the Stedmans came to Bolivar, and the late 1960s were a much different time than the 1940s or 1950s had been. I can recall one of my contemporaries standing on a table in the hotel shouting their complaints about the war to a room packed with people there just to relax on a Saturday night, when many other Bolivar boys of military age were in harm's way Then, like now, there were huge disparities between those who ended up in the war, and those who didn't. That wasn't so in the 1940s. Almost everyone physically able then put on a uniform. Everyone at home supported what they did, knowing the war needed to be fought and won. No one thanked anyone for their service, because virtually every family had done their part.

None of that was true in the 1960s. I graduated and arrived at Cornell University in 1965. That fall, President Johnson decided to send 500,000 soldiers to Vietnam. The military draft was still used to fill the ranks, but the Army did not want or need every man in the country. Just some. That fall, I took an examination. How well you did determined how long you would be granted a student deferment, and need to worry about fighting in southeast Asia. I was the only person on my floor in the dormitory to score high enough on that examination to be exempt all the way through graduate school. Another student exemption was offered to anyone at any college who stood in the top third of their class. Harvard announced that all of their students were in the top third.

You were subject to the draft through age twenty-six, and the older you were, the more likely it was you would be drafted. That all changed in 1968. Student deferments ended. The 365 days of the year were put in a hopper and drawn out one at a time. If the first one drawn had your birthday on it, you would be in the first group drafted. I became number 47. The Army announced how many men it was going to need, and would go through enough birthdays to get that number to fill the ranks. That year, it was up to 189. But, after that first year, the maximum age subject to being called was nineteen. If you weren't picked that year, it was over. You could go to school, or work, and get on with life. I was called, reported, failed my physical, and got on with it.

Although there is a large monument in Maple Lawn Cemetery dedicated to the service of our Civil War soldiers, there is no equivalent monument tied to the service of either those who served in World War One, World War II, or Korea. Thanks to the leadership efforts of Fred Cole, a Vietnam veteran himself, Bolivar does have a monument thanking those service members for their service in that conflict. More than 120 memorial bricks have been purchased and placed near the monument, each with the name of a local soldier, most Vietnam era, but for many others who served in other places at other times.

Of all those, one stood out to me: Greg Metz. Metzie was a classmate of mine. He went into the Navy and ended up on CVA-59, the aircraft carrier USS Forrestal. In 1967, also assigned to the Forrestal was future presidential candidate John McCain, and the ship headed to the Gulf of Tonkin off Vietnam. On

July 27, while planes were being readied for a strike, a rocket misfired, hit a second plane on the flight deck, and started a huge fire. It destroyed 21 aircraft, killed 134 sailors, and injured another 161, including McCain. Greg could not be located, and his obituary appeared in the Olean Times Herald. Two years later, I was driving out West State Street in Olean, when I heard a familiar voice call out, "Brads." I turned to look, and saw Metzie sitting on the hood of a car. I looked ahead again, did a double take, and while confirming it was Metz, ran into the car ahead of me. By the time I got things straightened out with the driver I had collided with, Metz had disappeared, again.

What happened on the Forrestal? Greg had been below decks in his bunk when the fire started. The water tight doors closed, and in order to control the fire, many compartments were ordered to be flooded, including the one in which Metzie was then trapped. As the water rose, and stayed deeper than he was tall, he tied himself to a top bunk so he could get some sleep, and waited it out. As I recall it, he was there four days, tired, hungry, thirsty, but not a ghost.

We did lose at least one man to the conflict. Jerry McKay was a victim of Agent Orange, a toxic chemical defoliant used with abandon on the forests of Vietnam. He held on until March 1976. He deserved better.

One of the scores of bricks bought as remembrances for the men who served in Vietnam

The Ambassadors: Hahn & Schaffner

When World War II came to a close, many men and women took off their uniforms and began looking for work. Some were able to come back to their old jobs. One of those was Clarence Schaffner, Jr. Because he bore his father's name, Clarence responded to the nickname Mike all his life. Mike Schaffner had been born in Franklin, Pennsylvania in 1915, and arrived in Bolivar in 1923, when his father was transferred to Bolivar to be the machinist in the newly opened Oil Well Supply store.

Mike lacked neither intelligence, nor gumption, nor charm. He did well in the Bolivar School, won some debate and public speaking contests, and graduated with the class of 1933. Noticing his diligence, charm and wit, Oil Well Supply put Mike on the payroll as one of its salesmen. He was still a salesman in 1940, but shortly after the company promoted him to be a store manager in Indiana. Then came the war. Oil Well Supply closed its Bolivar branch, and moved Mike's father, Clarence Sr., to Oil City. Mike was called for duty and went off with everyone else into the Army in the summer of 1942. He ended up in Europe with the Air Force. When the war ended, he wanted to work closer to home, and took a salesman's job with the Bradford Supply Company. In 1949, the company made him the manager of its Bolivar store.

Mike's principal salesman was a Bradford paratrooper named Gordon Hahn. Gordy Hahn was two years younger than Mike. He decided to get ahead of the draft and joined the Army in June 1941. In October, he was transferred to the 82nd Airborne Division, and became a paratrooper. He left the United States in May 1942, and campaigned with the division through North Africa and Sicily.

Clarence "Mike" Schaffner

Once Sicily fell, the 82nd moved into Italy, and there in November 1943, Gordon Hahn , "while afoot," crossed paths with a land mine. The shrapnel tore into his upper thigh and stomach. It also took him away from the fighting for the rest of the war. It wasn't until March 1944 that he was well enough to be shipped back to the United States. Once back in this country, he went straight to Ashford Hospital in White Sulphur Springs. While there, Staff Sgt. Hahn met Petty Officer 2nd Class Gail Andrews serving with the WAVES, and he married her on October 23, 1944. All of Gail's attendants were also WAVES, and they did double duty that day, serving both as the bridesmaids and as the ushers.

When the war ended, Bradford Supply sent the Hahns to Bolivar to work for Mike Schaffner, and thus were sewn the seeds of Hahn & Schaffner. Gordon was quick to fit in. In 1947, the Bolivar Legion tried to raise money to build a Legion Memorial Park, which would house a bandstand, picnic grounds, memorial plaques, and appropriate landscaping. One of the first events used to raise funds was a "Grand Ol' Opry" style show, starring Bob Paffie, Bob Appleby, Rocky DeRock, Tony Sallazzo, Harold Cossaboon, Gordy Hahn, and a line of chorus girls. By 1953, Gordon was president of the Bolivar Men's Club.

A man named Murray C. Bascom had set up an oil well supply business in 1920, and over the years created something new. The property Murray acquired was at the edge of the village, on the west side of the railroad tracks. He had a lot much larger than that of the other oil well supply businesses, giving him the room for a pipe yard. As old wells were pulled and plugged, Murray bought and reconditioned the used pipe, offering it as a cheap alternative to new pipe. Murray died at the age of fifty-six in 1937. Bradford Supply bought the business from his estate in 1945, and as a result had the largest pipe yard in the area, as well as the store building from which to sell tools and fittings. All they needed was good management. In 1946, they made Francis "Funny" Foster the local manager, but Funny was seventy-five years old. In 1949, Bradford Supply brought Mike Schaffner back to town and made him the store manager. To work alongside him, was Gordon Hahn, who had worked for the company before the war. As time marched on, the company promoted Mike to regional sales manager, and put Gordy in charge of the Bolivar store. The business provided work for seven other employees.

The parent company, Atlas-Bradford, made a corporate decision to move out of the eastern oil fields, and moved its headquarters to Houston, Texas. But they decided to give their local employees the first chance to buy the business where they worked. Mike and Gordon approached a few prospective partners, formed the corporation Hahn & Schaffner, Inc., and bought the business, keeping their "World Headquarters" in Bolivar. Mike became its president, Gordon the vice president, Tom Dunn its treasurer, and Phil LaBella the secretary. Hahn & Schaffner thus became the "last man standing," the last oil well supply company in the Allegany Field.

It was a happy place to work at. Mike and Gordon had a wide circle of friends and admirers before they went into business for themselves. They put an old church pew in the main section, not far from their office where they shared a partner's desk, and had an endless supply of coffee and a steady stream of takers. They opened early so their customers could pick up whatever they needed so as not lose much time building or repairing or doing whatever job was at hand. The pew became the nerve and news center of the area.

Mike was responsible for an article in a nationally syndicated publication which appeared in 1964. It was a three-page spread titled "A Mayor and his Village," which appeared in the spring issue of *Petroleum Today*. It included photographs taken by Werner Wolff, a renowned New York photographer. The article contained this quote of Mike's: "*Being Mayor is a great experience. Everyone should do it. I think all of us should seek public office. It's a small down payment on the debt we owe our ancestors and this system we live under.*"

Bolivar, New York has only been mentioned in the *New York Times* a handful of times. One of the most recent was in the issue of May 27, 1985, when the shale gas play was developing. The article carried the headline, "Miniature Oil Rush Lifting Economic Hopes in Southern Tier." The reporter obtained much of his information by carrying on a conversation with Mike Schaffner and Karney Cochran during a stop at the Hahn & Schaffner store early one morning. Another example of the Hahn and Schaffner store being the source of instant news happened in 1993, when my younger son James brought his fiancé home for a few days. She needed to do some school work, went up to the library, found a quiet spot behind the stacks, and lost track of time. The librarians forgot about her, left, and locked up. Wyn, the fiancé, soon discovered that she was locked in, (once locked, you needed a key to get in or out), and made a series of calls. Finally, my son tracked down Chief Whitney, who unlocked the door and let her out. The next morning, James took her down to Hahn & Schaffner to meet Gordon and Mike. Before he could say a word, James was asked, "is this the girl who was locked up in the library last night?"

I gave this chapter the title, "The Ambassadors," because that is what Mike and Gordon became. People came to know Bolivar in the greater world because of them. When they started the business, Mike was just starting to serve the first of his three terms as a Democratic mayor of Bolivar. When Leon MacDonell died in 1966, Gordon, a Republican, was picked to fill Leon's role as town supervisor until an election could be held, so for a few months Hahn & Schaffner stood at the head of the town government, the village government, and one of the community's most important businesses.

But where they spread the word about Bolivar the farthest was with their backing and promotion of the New York State Oil Producer's Clambake. The clambake was held for its first years at the Wellsville Country Club. However, the WCC's parking lot was small, limiting the number of tickets that could be sold. Gordon and Mike both were directors of the New York State Oil Producer's Association. Mike was a vice president, and Gordy took command of the clambake committee. They solved the parking problem by moving the event to the Bolivar Country Club. Ticket sales grew from 400 to 1,600, and ultimately to 2,400, in just a few years. Bill Hogan handled the ticket sales and the collection of dues, (anyone could come, but only members could buy the tickets), and Gordon assembled the support crew to get ready for the party. My father, John D. Bradley, had the job of putting the lights up in the big tent, while the Hahn and Schaffner employees put the tent up. Bob MacDonell handled parking the cars. For the first few years the event was in Bolivar, the Castle Restaurant catered the bake. The Castle was succeeded by the Johnstons and the Hilltop staff. People came from all over the country on the fourth Thursday in August to meet and greet faces not seen in a while, to eat endless supplies of clams washed down with draft beer, and to enjoy themselves in Bolivar, New York. If you weren't given a ticket, if you knew Gordon or Mike, you knew where you could get one.

At one time or another, Gordon Hahn was president of the Country Club, president of the Bolivar PTA, and was on the advisory board of the Citizen's Bank. When county government was reorganized and Ham Shaner became a county legislator, Gordon ran for and became town supervisor again, and took the lead in forming a town supervisor's association. For decades, Gordon would take his constitutional stroll around town after dark, perhaps puffing on his pipe as he did so, if he wasn't down in Olean playing racquetball. Mike's interest in politics had come to the fore in the 1940's when he started forty years of service on the county Democratic committee. He spent twenty of those years as a member of the New York State Democratic Committee, and in 1958 was the Democratic candidate for assemblyman for our

Delores Ingalls Wilcox, Gordon Hahn and Pat McQueen in the Throne Rom of the Castle Restaurant, for the company Christmas party

area. In 1968, he received an appointment as our congressional district's representative to the meeting of New York's presidential electors in Albany.

But time marches on. Some of the last oil wells drilled in the Allegany Field were drilled in the early 1980s on forty acres of land that bordered the Hahn & Schaffner property on the west. Those wells are still producing, but Hahn & Schaffner is long gone. Mike was the first to go. A smoker most of his life, emphysema caught up with him, and he died in the Jones Memorial Hospital in Wellsville on Christmas Day, 1988. Gordon carried on afterward, but joined Mike at the interstellar clambake on January 17, 2003. They both brought smiles and good cheer to everyone around them, family, friends, customers, associates, employees. They won't be replaced.

With the old wells pulled and plugged, and the supply of used pipe disappeared, where still needed spools of plastic pipe replaced the stacks of twenty-foot joints of two-inch that had been the staple of the industry since the first powerhouses were built, and which the Hahn & Schaffner pipe yard had been set up to recondition and resell. An attempt to keep the business going as a hardware store met the same fate as all the other attempts to convert had met, and all that was left of Hahn & Schaffner was the "World Headquarter's" sign at the end of Boss Street. Now, if you are one of the odd ones left who needs oil well supplies, you need to go to Bradford!

As the oil business winds down, Jim Day picks up a load of concrete to plug wells, rather than a a load of pipe to set them up, and compares notes with Gordie.

Tom Cawley, George Green, Smiley Weber, and Bud McQueen on break.

Pioneer Oil Museum

contributed by Kelly Lounsberry & Tom Manning

Mike and Gordon were fully aware of the state of the Allegany Field when they went into business. They saw the end in sight, but were great supporters of the Bolivar community. An oil industry expert had come through this area in 1937, as secondary-recovery was reaching its peak, and had issued a warning. He said that both Bradford and Bolivar had better start conserving their resources, because without oil, neither community had a reason to exist. Hahn & Schaffner did their best to stave off the devil at the door. Gordon had been a member of the joint village and town planning commission established in 1956 to address the "economic doldrums" which had descended on the area. In 1964, the Colgrove & Wood Hardware Store, in an 1851 building at the corner of Main and Liberty streets closed, an early example of the difficulty of an oil well supply business continuing as a hardware store. It left a vacant store front right across from the Library.

The question was, how to fill it? Hahn & Schaffner came up with an idea. At the 1965 Oil Producer's Clambake, they proposed an increase in association dues from $5 to $10. The additional money from the 500 or so members would provide the funds to buy the Colgrove & Wood store, which would be converted into a museum. The proposal passed. The Pioneer Oil Museum was born.

Mike Schaffner was the first person to serve as a chairman of the museum committee. But operational funding had not been thought through. They did manage to lobby the village into amending its 1882 ordinance to allow one well to be drilled on the Colgrove & Wood lot, presumably on the small, grassy space on the north side of the main building, to be both a display and a source of revenue. However, it is probably a good thing that so far such a well has not been drilled. County Historian Bill Greene loved the place, and came up with a grant to put new board and batten siding all around the structure. The museum first saw heavy traffic in 1975, when it served as the headquarters of the Sesquicentennial Celebration.

Following the 1975 celebration, the Pioneer Oil Museum on Main Street remained open until September, staffed by a handful of volunteers during limited hours. Each succeeding spring volunteers were recruited as museum "hosts" for the summer months. Tom Manning headed this task as ongoing oversight of the museum fell into his lap, a willing one driven by a lifelong interest in Bolivar's history and family roots tracing back 150 years.

Soon the museum provided, (again thanks to assistance arranged by County Historian Greene) part-time summer employment to a pair of retired oilfield roustabouts — Gordon Burdick and Max Richardson. Following Tom Manning's suggestions and directions (and their own, based on their working lives' experience), they created displays like "The Old Rig Floor," a scaled down but authentic replica of a 1900 work space for a driller and his tool dresser, displaying their tools and equipment around a new well's casing pipe with a hemp drilling cable working inside it. Gordon and Max also handled the mundane tasks of building maintenance and making small improvements. They, along with Gordon's wife Ethel, took in artifact donations and greeted visitors, showing them around the museum and explaining the functions of its contents. During the five-year run of the original Pioneer Oil Days in the late 1970s to the early 1980s, the museum was central to those community heritage celebrations.

Such was the "Memorial Day thru Labor Day" routine at the Pioneer Oil Museum into the late 1980s. Volunteers often staffed the Saturday hours after Max and the Burdicks kept the lights on during the week. Eventually, age and health issues forced the regulars to retire. From then on and through the 1990s, a few ever-helpful museum fans such as Ray Payne and Dick Fitch, with Tom Manning's continued oversight, ensured the museum carried on. Every spring Ray and Dick would recruit a summer staff of local volunteers to keep the doors open. In the spring of 2000, in anticipation of a southward relocation later that year, Tom contacted Kelly Lounsberry, Barbara Webb, Jim Day, Rose Fenaughty, Steve Yehl, Diane Mountain and Paul Plants, asking them to form a new board of directors to take over management of the museum. All seven were quick to agree to a meeting that established the museum's new leadership whose first goal was to incorporate as a charitable nonprofit entity and take it to a new level.

All that has flowed from that meeting has been superlative and incredible, especially the museum's acquisition of the former Hahn & Schaffner site and what the Pioneer Oil Museum of New York has become since its origins on the corner of Main and Liberty streets. All that is needed to confirm that statement is a visit to the west end of Boss Street. Several years later, Paul Plants, president of both the Oil Producer's Association and the museum Board of Directors, had the brainstorm to move the museum to the Hahn & Schaffner property. The building on Main was old and had numerous repair issues. It was obvious a new site was needed, one that would allow the museum to expand and thrive. Consequently, in 2009, the museum was able to purchase this 6.5-acre property.

Not having been used for decades, scrub trees and weeds covered the site. Rusting pipe racks had to be cleaned up. Seven buildings came with the property, all needing repair. Three were torn down, four were renovated. Three of these were redesigned as exhibit areas for the museum's growing collection of tools and artifacts. The Museum built a large, new engine building which now houses more than ten antique oil field engines, all in working order. After many years of effort at the Hahn & Schaffner site, enough work had been completed to allow the Museum to move from Main Street to this new location. At the new site, a large annex has been constructed on the main building. There will be many new exhibits there, while incorporating those from the Main Street site.

Paul Plants had dreamed of a way to honor those individuals who had played a vital role in the growth of the local oil and gas fields. To do this, he instituted the New York State Oil Producers' Association Wall of Fame. Each year worthy individuals are inducted if they have played a prominent role in the local energy industry. The induction ceremony takes place during Bolivar's Pioneer Oil Days in June. On this evening, the inductees are posthumously honored, and this event is followed by a wine-and-cheese tasting, often with 200 people in attendance.

In order to attract people to the museum, the museum has instituted various events and outreach techniques. An antique tractor pull is held on the museum's grounds on the first Sunday of Pioneer Oil Days week in late June. A Facebook page has been created to help share information about the museum and reasons to visit it. As of 2025, more than 1,600 followers have "followed" the Museum and are aware of its goings on.

Each year the museum publishes a newsletter to help inform the public about what has gone on over the past year, and explain how the museum is expanding. Museum personnel have developed several PowerPoint presentations, and they participate in speaking engagements for various groups in the area. In addition to being open to the general public, museum personnel often lead private groups/ families on tours. Numerous local groups have used the museum buildings as space to hold meetings.

With the advent of the STEAM (science, technology, engineering, arts, math) curriculum in schools throughout the region and the country, the museum is a logical place to visit. Working with local schools on this program could prove a boon. Over the last 25 years or so, there has been a solid school-museum connection with local students completing a number of projects related to our local oil and gas heritage.

Various activities such as festivals, farmers' markets, swap meets, etc. have been considered. Each of these events would bring more people onto the museum grounds and keep the museum in the public's eye. Maintaining a vibrant, hard-working board of directors is essential to the future. Recently, the board expanded from seven to fifteen members, and four are younger, which is a critical component. Financial support is, of course, the backbone of any cultural group. The museum has a number of resources. An annual fund-raising appeal is included in the newsletter. These donations from supporters provide the largest chunk of our budget. The Wall of Fame ceremony produces a huge amount of publicity, but has a limited financial impact. The museum is always on the lookout for grants and other revenue sources to help provide for the future.

Much of what appears above was written by Kelly Lounsberry, which explains why his name did not appear there. Kelly has been for many years the key to keeping the museum open and growing. He has raised the funds to rebuild the Hahn & Schaffner property, and expand the museum's footprint so that it has the room to fully preserve and explain the natural resources businesses which were the foundation of the Bolivar Community for fully half of its existence. He has recruited new board members. He has pursued the money needed to create all that is there now. It's not all Kelly Lounsberry, but had he not been here and did all that he has done, it is hard to imagine who would have.

Bolivar Police Department

Bolivar has had dozens of police officers and chiefs over the years, but few kept the job for long. Fenton Yehl probably holds the record for the shortest tenure, having kept the job for just seventy-two hours. Only one, Charles Hoffman, who was the first patrolman hired during the boom, quit, decided to better himself by going to medical school, and came back to Bolivar to help his friends stay healthy until he himself passed away in 1925. In 1960, the village finally hired as a patrolman someone who lived in town, who wanted to stay, and who needed the job. He was a fifty-one year old pumper whose lease had played out. His name was Oak Marsh. He was fifty-one.

Officer Marsh, who had previously driven a school bus, was immediately put in a tough spot by the village board, which insisted that he get busy writing parking tickets. The village had spent good money installing parking meters, at the urging of New York State, but they were never going to pay for themselves unless there was a penalty for taking a spot all day for a dime, or for nothing at all. He went right out and wrote a stack of them, and in the words of the Breeze, "Much furor seemed to have arisen" over the rate at which they were handed out, and many local citizens were loudly and vocally abusive to the new cop. It was the Breeze's opinion that Bolivar shouldn't have parking meters at all; but so long as it did, no one should complain that the local patrolman was doing his job.

Oak was Bolivar's patrolman when I got my driver's license, in 1964, and I was one of many teenage wise acres who showed little respect for Oak and his position. Officer Marsh would often drive around the village at night in the patrol car with his headlights turned off, hoping to sneak up on unsuspecting troublemakers. But whenever I or any of my contemporaries saw this, the game became to quickly drive around the block, turn off our lights, and follow Oak as he went from street to street.

It wasn't all fun and games. In May 1965, at 12:30 on a Sunday morning, eighteen-year-old Brooke Matylas called Officer Marsh to the scene of an altercation between two men in front of the Main Street Restaurant, where Matylas worked. Oak asked a crowd of onlookers to move on, and as they did he was attacked by Leon Sadler, from Wellsville, one of those who had attracted the crowd. State Police came in as reinforcements and carried Sadler off to Belmont.

Perhaps chastened by the reception he got when he first took the job, Oak tried hard to be lenient and understanding with village residents. There was an often repeated story about one night when a well-known resident went through the stop light headed toward Little Genesee. Oak saw him, flipped on his revolving red light, and took off in pursuit. The unlucky driver decided to try to elude the police, pulled into the Ferris and Forbes used car lot, turned off his lights and engine, and lay down in the seat. Soon enough, a flashlight shined into the window. The hapless driver exclaimed, "Oak! Thank God it's you! I thought it was the Troopers!!" He was quietly escorted home, and if he hadn't told the story on himself, no one would have known.

The Bolivar Police Department on Nov. 2, 1965. L-R: Oliver Taylor, Harold Cossaboon, Don Moore, Oak Marsh, Earl Skinner, and Al Hollister

Oak stayed on the job until he was old enough to retire, and for a year more as the village searched for a suitable replacement. The change occurred at the end of 1975. Oak did not get to enjoy a long retirement. He passed away on April 29, 1977. But the Bolivar trustees struck gold when they hired as Oak's replacement a young man fresh out of school, who had trained to be a policeman. His name was Rick Whitney. Here is Rick's story, in his own words:

"I started full time in Bolivar on January 1, 1976, as Officer in Charge. When I arrived, there were three part-time officers: Dick Smith, Bob Wilcox and Harold Cossaboon. The police car only had a CB radio with six channels 8-9-10-19-20-21. The former Police Chief, Oak Marsh, had the police phone in his home. There was a yellow light on the building at the corner of Main and Wellsville streets that Oak could turn on if he got a call. When I saw the light, I had to drive to his house and see what the call was. Later that year they added an extension to the police phone at my apartment. There was also an answering machine at the office (downstairs in the library) that was the size of a small suitcase, that I could turn on if Oak was not home, and I would stop at the office occasionally to check the messages.

In 1978 I talked the Village Board into purchasing an actual police vehicle through state bid, and I got to drive a new 1978 Plymouth Grand Fury. I also made an agreement with the State Police to have calls transferred to the barracks in Wellsville and got permission to have a radio with their frequencies installed in the car. Our car number was 1757, and I believe we were the first local police department to have the state police dispatch us. In 1980, I took the civil service test for Chief of Police and was the third officer in the county to pass it. In August of 1980 I was certified as the Chief of Police and was the youngest civil service certified Chief of Police in New York State. In November 1997 I received notification that I was selected to attend the FBI National Academy at Quantico and attended the 193rd session of the academy from April 5 through June 19, 1998.

Chief & future sheriff, Rick Whitney

Probably the most memorable incident I was involved in happened on November 8, 2007. I was on my way to Belmont to meet with the District Attorney about an upcoming trial when I heard the Wellsville police department being dispatched to an armed robbery at the Rite Aid Pharmacy. I was just East of Allentown, and they asked me to respond. I hurried to the pharmacy and exchanged gunfire with the suspect as he fled the scene in a van. I chased the suspect, along with the other agencies (Wellsville police, State Police and the Sheriff's Office). The suspect was heading back toward the village of Wellsville, when Sheriff's Deputy Kevin Ross rammed the van head-on. The van continued forward, and I rammed it again, stopping it in front of the NAPA store. A State trooper and I then took the suspect into custody. In 2008 I was awarded the Medal of Honor from the New York State Association of Chiefs of Police for that incident. In 2010, I decided to run for Allegany County Sheriff. I beat the incumbent, ending my career in Bolivar on December 31, 2010."

I, the author, became village justice at about the same time Rick began in Bolivar, so I had ample opportunity to observe him, and from the beginning I was impressed with the way he handled his position. I tried to be innovative in my sentencing, especially of young offenders, and I often gave them a stack of garbage bags and sentenced them to walking the streets picking up trash until they had filled a certain number of the bags. I had few repeat offenders.

My wife and I liked to entertain, and we had the idea of hosting a "champagne Monopoly party" one Saturday night. The party was getting into full swing about 10:00, when I got a call from Rick saying I was needed in court. Why? "I just picked up Tom Hayden." Tom Hayden- you mean Jane Fonda's Chicago Seven boyfriend? "No. This is the Tom Hayden I picked up a few months ago for no license and registration. You gave him a week to produce them, and he never came back, so you issued a warrant." "O.K. I'll be right up."

My friend Tom Ferris accompanied me on the walk to the Library. As we entered, there stood Rick beside a tall, thin young man wearing a beautiful, polished leather cowboy hat: Tom Hayden. So, Tom, what about your license and registration? He replied that he really did have them, just as he had said before, but, as usual, did not have them with him. I said, in that case, I am requiring bail of $100. Ferris nudged me and said, "Take the hat!" I said no, it was $100 or go to jail, Hayden went to jail. A few days later, I ran into Rick and he asked me how the Monopoly game had turned out. I was surprised by the question, and asked how he knew we had been playing it. He replied, "Well, you had Monopoly money sticking out of every pocket you had when you came into court Saturday night." Rick was very observant.

Who Else?

In all this discussion of times past, there are any number of people who did things that made a difference and largely volunteered their time to better Bolivar who have yet to be mentioned. Here are a few who should be remembered decades from now,

Clarence R. Shaner was born in Bolivar on Dec. 17, 1906. In high school he played the saxophone, and had a reputation as the class "jazz hound," perhaps one step up on Harry Hendrickson, "the sheik." He left school after his junior year to work in the oil field. In 1927, he married Catherine D. Kahn, and in 1929, their son, Kenneth A., arrived. In late 1933, he moved to a rented home on Phillips Hill Road, near or on the lease owned by J.P. Herrick, of which he was the foreman. In 1939, he left the job, bought a home at 92 Olean Street, and opened a business on Main Street selling and repairing electrical appliances and radios.

Clarence was his name. "Ham" was how he was known. With an antenna tower attached to his garage on Olean Street, using the callsign W8ELK, he would put on his headphones and spend his evenings as a HAM radio operator, turning his dial to connect with other radio hobbyists around the world. He built a reputation as a reliable radio and appliance repairman and dealer. At that time, the county relied on amateur radio operators to provide the quick response network, and Ham was Bolivar's member of the Radio Amateur Civil Emergency Service.

Radio was his profession and hobby. He also became seriously interested in the church next door. He led the Episcopal men's group and the church vestry, and after World War II the congregation grew from a dozen or two congregants to near capacity, with the holiday crowds filling the little church with more than 100 attendees, packing every pew and all the extra folding chairs that could fit in the rear. He organized fund-raising suppers, where the men cooked and served a buffet in the church basement. His middle initial was R. It stood for Roosevelt, for the man who had been President when he was born: Theodore. Clarence Roosevelt Shaner was destined to be a Republican. For two decades, beginning in

1959, Ham served on the Bolivar Town and the Allegany County Republican Committees. In that role, he felt it his duty to provide candidates for every town or village office, so voters could have a choice. Because there were equally fervent Democrats in town, local politics was interesting.

In 1959, he became a town assessor. In 1966, when supervisor MacDonell died, Ham replaced him and took a seat on the county Board of Supervisors. The county board was made up of the supervisors of all towns in the county. Thus the citizens of the Town of Burns, where almost no one lived, had as much say in county affairs as did those in the Town of Wellsville. Federal court decisions forced a change. Ham put forward a plan to divide the county into five districts, with three representatives for each. The plan was adopted and is still in effect today. Ham won a seat, becoming the first person from Bolivar to serve as a county legislator. He stayed until he turned seventy, in 1976, then served on an unpaid Citizen's Advisory Committee into the 1980s. Ham Shaner was typical of the quality people who were engaged in making and keeping Bolivar a good place to be and live in the 20th century. He died in Olean June 6, 2000, having lived through nearly all of it.

Ham Shaner and Ed Mergler, 1970

Edward F. Mergler was born in Buffalo in April 1915. He came to Bolivar with his wife, Laura, after World War II to join the law practice of A.J. Matson. Highly respected for his diligence as a attorney, he served as Allegany County's District Attorney for a number of terms, beginning in the 1970s. It was in the early 1970s that he recruited Leslie Hagstrom to join his practice. Leslie was the first attorney to establish a practice in Bolivar who did not come here to live. She kept her home in Angelica. Because of his position as the district attorney, Ed never took a position in local government, but he was an active participant in the Allegany County Republican Party. He remained in Bolivar after retirement, and passed away in early 1997.

James P. "Doc" Hoffman. Doc was born in Bolivar in 1893, and attended the local school until he got into high school. His was the son of Dr. Charles Hoffman, who had the hope that all of his sons would follow him into the profession. James, by his own description, "had too much deviltry" in him to stick with his studies. He dropped out of high school and went to work in a store. He did go to business school in Olean, then came back to Bolivar. His diligence and good-naturedness resulted in his election as the village treasurer in 1920, a post he would hold for thirty-six years. It also landed him an offer to open the McDonell & Brannen oil well supply store on Main Street in 1923. He ran the store

for three different owners and two different locations until it closed in 1956.

The McDonell & Brannen Main Street store location was taken over by Charlie Hall in 1939. But while Doc ran the store there, it was memorable for two things. He kept a pet snake on prominent display in one of the windows. The other related to the metal park bench which sat on the sidewalk outside another window. This is where most people experienced Doc's "deviltry." He wired a magneto up to the bench. If someone sat there too long, or if Doc just felt like playing a prank, he would give the magneto a crank, and give the sitters "just a little jolt." Doc left us on July 31, 1975.

Leon J.D. MacDonell. Election night, November 5, 1935, resulted in the election of four men to offices in Allegany County for the first time, and all four would keep their offices for extended periods. William H. MacKenzie of Bel-

mont became Allegany County's representative in the New York State Assembly, where he would stay for twenty-five years. "Genial" Vanama Jones, from Friendship, won the office of County Sheriff, where he too would remain for decades. Ward Hopkins, from Cuba, became the County Judge. All three were Republicans.

The fourth man elected that night was a Progressive Democrat, who would hold his office for thirty-one years, and who would be on the County Board of Supervisors for the rest of his life. He won the votes of 421 Bolivar residents, against just 269 for his opponent. Once in office, he gained the respect of nearly everyone, and frequently ran unopposed when it was time to run again. In addition, he was chairman of the Allegany County Public Health Committee for the rest of his life.

Leon, known to many as L.J., worked as an oil producer for his entire adult life, operating a lease near the mouth of Beers Hollow. As a member of the Allegany County Selective Service (Draft) Board in 1943, along with hundreds of other young men who were called to serve during World War II, "LJ" and the board called up his own son, Robert, who served with distinction in Europe.

He was born in Bolivar on July 27, 1891. He went off to war in 1918 as a private in the 329th Guard & Fire Co. QMC. During World War II, he worked on behalf of the New York State Oil Producers Assn. as a lobbyist in Washington, making trips and appearances there to defend the depletion allowance for small producers.

Once, before the coming of the First World War, his close friend John C. Bradley asked Leon if he would like to see New York City, riding there in the sidecar of Bradley's 1914 Henderson motorcycle. Leon agreed. Neither had been there before. They arrived in the city late at night, covered in smoke, grime and road dust, and then began looking for a hotel room. Night clerk after night clerk took one look at the filthy pair and sent them away, until one attentive clerk saw something glinting on Leon's hand. He asked, "Is that a Masonic ring?" When the answer was yes, they were welcomed like long lost brothers by this fellow member of the craft, and had comfortable quarters for their stay in the Big City.

Leon MacDonell on left & John Bradley, 1914

Leon was a charter member of the Kenyon Andrus Post 772, American Legion. He was also a founding member of the Bolivar Country Club. He was not only a proud member of Macedonia Lodge, No. 258, Free and Accepted Masons, but also of the Corning Consistory, Ismalia Temple, Buffalo, and of the Allegany County Shrine Club, as well as the New York State Oil Producers Association. "LJ" was placed on the Pioneer Oil Museum's Wall of Fame in 2013. He was still the town supervisor when he died, on September 1, 1966.

Leon and his wife Trina were the parents of Herbert MacDonell, who is covered in another section of this story. Their oldest boy was Robert, or Bob, MacDonell. After the war, Bob married Nancy Campbell. They settled on Wellsville Street, and Bob pumped the family oil property until it no longer paid to do so. He then bought and operated the Evergreen Dairy, which delivered fresh milk all around town and to the school. As part of the business, they ran a dairy bar, which was located on the north side of Wellsville Street near the school, where Lance Shaner built apartments after the dairy closed.

In 1963, the high school was reorganized to have nine periods. The ninth was for activities: band, choir, or study hall. At the time, I had not joined either band or choir, and on the first day of classes, at the end of the eighth period, I disappeared and hid in the locker room until classes ended and football practice began. No one realized I was missing. The homeroom teacher assumed I was in band or choir, and Mrs Young and John Humphrey were not in the business of looking for students who hadn't signed up, so for that period of that semester I was free. Fairly often that fall I would exit the rear of the school building, saunter over to the dairy bar, order my favorite concoction, a pineapple malted milkshake, and shoot the breeze with Bob or Nancy, or whoever was "tending bar." But when football season ended, I had to find a new routine. I instead headed to the auditorium balcony to watch band practice. It took a couple of weeks for Mr. Humphrey to look back to see who my buddy, Sousaphone player Jimmy Crowley, was communicating with using sign language; and he soon informed me that he needed a second sousaphone player. From there on out, I spent activity period at band practice.

The MacDonells sold Evergreen to Crosby Dairy in 1965. Bob served the town for decades as an assessor. The end of oil meant that many of the large parcels of land owned by oil producers were broken up and sold as hunting camp properties, so during Bob's tenure the number of properties to be assessed, and bills to be sent out, skyrocketed. Bob, with his patient, light-hearted nature was a great person to have as an assessor, who were so very often unfairly abused for making honest attempts to do a good and fair job.

Nancy MacDonell was a transplant, having spent her early years in Belmont. She quickly became a familiar face when she worked for Gene Salzer in the drug store. In her later years, she took the office of town historian, and used her talents to help genealogists and other curious people discover what they could using the town's records. She and Bob raised two boys, Scott who made a career in school administration, and Craig, who made his around Bolivar, being the last owner of the Sterling Gas Station at the corner of Main and Wellsville Streets, before it was town down and converted into a Unimart.

Nancy MacDonell
BCS 1946

Bolivar has produced two other artists of note.

Alice Cranston Fenner was born in Bolivar Nov. 13, 1894, daughter of Allen and Inez. She received an BFA from Alfred in 1918, and went on to study at the Royal Worcester Potteries in England. She married Glenn Babcock Fenner, also an Alfred grad, in 1920. Glenn made the molds for her vases and art pottery, and as a chemist created a new and improved method a producing her bas relief plaques, which they marketed using the business name Artyle Studio. With these, she built a wide reputation as a source of bas relief items for home decoration. In 1936, she produced a memorial plaque of Will Rogers, which was highly praised and sought after as "one of the best likenesses of Will Rogers ever modeled..."

They maintained her studio in Belmont, NY from about 1930 to 1940, then moved to New Preston, Connecticut and changed the business name to the Cranston-Fenner Studio. In the 1950s, it was moved to Portville, then Olean. In 1962, they settled in Wilmington, NC and opened the Alice Cranston Fenner Art Gallery, and sold mainly her country landscapes, harbor views, and scenes of dogs, horses and gardens. For a season in the 1960s, she had her own local television program on art in Wilmington. She designed clock faces for the Westclox Company, and did plates and greeting cards. She wrote and published a number of books, including *The Philosophy of Art: Petite Essays, Poetic Jingles, and Dreams Do Come True*. Glenn died in 1974. Alice passed away in 1982.

Richard "Dick" Monroe graduated from BCS in 1946, served two years in the Army in Japan, then obtained a bachelor's degree in industrial art from RIT. He made his reputation as the chief designer of murals for the Olean Tile Company. Among his most viewed works are the Mickey Mouse logo on Disney's first cruise ship, of the Twin Towers for New York City, and a portrait of Corporal Jason Dunham placed on board the Navy guided missile destroyer USS Jason Dunham. One of his post-retirement projects was to do portrait of all the Bolivar boys lost in World War II. These are on display in the Kenyon Andrus Post on Main Street in Bolivar.

Dick relaxed fishing. He was a frequent visitor to the Allegany River, Kinzua, the Genesee, and area lakes. He was a fixture among the group who made an annual Memorial Day weekend fishing trip to the Rideau Chain of Lakes in eastern Ontario. And invariably, he caught the most and had the most fun doing it. After he retired, he turned his attention to golf, playing in sneakers in fair weather so he could get around faster, and painting some of his balls black so he could keep playing when snow was on the ground. Dick, called "Lucy" by many of his friends, had an endless supply of jokes you could enjoy if you sat near him in the Bolivar Hotel, or at the Legion, or the Country Club, or at Frank's Casa Nova Grill in the evenings. We all loved Lucy. He left the scene July 30, 2020.

There is one more Bolivarian, a photographer, who should be remembered generations from now. He suffered with epilepsy his entire, but short, life, and found his calling behind the lens of a camera, recording scores of great moments along the sidelines of Bolivar's sports fields all through the 1950s and 1960s. His name was Bruno Christini. Born in Olean in August 1923, he graduated with Bolivar's class of 1942. If you run across a great photo of a sporting event or player of that era, thank Bruno. He left us in 1972.

Back to School

There are many Bolivar faculty members who have inspired their students, and of whom hundreds of students have fond memories. On February 1, 1963, our biology teacher, a fine gentleman named Marshal Hills, attended a basketball game, drove home, and died of a heart attack. His replacement was one of the best remembered teachers over the next thirty years: Ron "The Flea" Stabley. Whether it was in the classroom trying to explain the intricacies of amino acids, or outside encouraging his cross country teams, or manning the counter of the Olean Sub Shop he started with "Fast Eddie" Forrest, or just trying to create smiles while pushing his "Fun Seekers" T-shirts, everyone knew and liked Ron.

My father-in-law, Roger Francisco, came to teach high school science and math in Bolivar in September 1960, filling one of nine empty spots supervising principal George Kuhn needed to fill over that summer. Roger would also take over the science classes taught by Bob McMahon, who took Roger's spot in Belmont teaching junior high students. Roger soon moved his family to Bolivar, and became very active in the community. He headed the greens keeping committee at the country club, and planted many trees along the creek to control erosion. He became a lay reader at the Episcopal Church, and took an active part in local politics, winning the race for mayor in 1967, taking over for Mike Schaffner, who had held the office for six years. Roger stayed in Bolivar through the 1970s. In the 1980s, he decided to move to Maryland, where he continued teaching at a the school for the Seafarer's Union, where he gave instruction in everything from basic math to celestial navigation.

Another notable faculty addition in 1960 was Joe O'Toole, who had just graduated from SUNY Cortland. Coach Craumer had decided not to come back. Dutch Dunning took over as the athletic director, and Coach O'Toole came in to help with coaching and physical education. Joe would go from Bolivar to a career working as a trainer in professional sports, most of the time with the Atlanta Hawks. He was "a catalyst in the formation of the National Basketball Trainer's Association," acted as its first chairman, and was named its first "NBA Trainer of the Year." In 1997, the award was named in his honor. He worked with the Hawks for twenty-eight years, and never missed a game. He is a member of the Georgia Athletic Trainer's Hall of Fame, and received the National Athletic Trainer's Association's Distinguished Athletic Trainer Award in 1996.

Bob Cawley, who began his coaching and teaching career in Bolivar in the 1940s, had a similar retinue of admirers, while in his junior high science classes he gently tried to guide adolescents through the arrival of their hormones, and led the school basketball teams to sectional titles. I can't write a history of Bolivar without including the longest serving member of the faculty, one I first knew as Miss Theresa DeRose, but who most of her students knew as Mrs. Crowley.

Theresa DeRose was born in Olean on November 16, 1927. She attended Ithaca College and did graduate work at St. Bonaventure. Her first teaching job was with the Livonia School District, where she began in the fall of 1950. The

Theresa DeRose in 1945

following year, she resigned in order to take the position of physical education director for girls at Bolivar Central School, so as to be closer to her home. When Terry came to Bolivar, there were virtually no interscholastic girls sports. There had been a field hockey team, whose only opponent was Richburg. She taught grade school students how to square dance and polka. She organized intramural basketball teams. She set up the archery targets, badminton nets, ping pong tables and gymnastic equipment. Her most visible athletes were the school cheerleaders, which she personally chose. In those early days of her career, cheerleading was an all year commitment. There was a varsity squad and a junior varsity, but those squads led the cheers at both the fall football games and at winter's basketball games.

That held true until the 1970s, when the laws changed and women's sports started the climb to be on a par with men's sports. Then girls were recruited to play softball and basketball, soccer, and now, even wrestling. And the school still needed cheerleaders! In 1955, Miss DeRose married Jim Crowley, brother of her fellow faculty member, Robert "R.T." Crowley, who famously drummed into his upper level English students the intricate uses of sesquipedalians, and who broke up eraser fights that might have erupted out in his absence by waving a white handkerchief to signal the need for a cease fire before he reentered the classroom. In our freshman English class, I recall a very nice spring day when the windows were open, the classroom overlooking the school's front lawn. The teacher, not R.T., stepped out for a few minutes, and a chain of the more mischievous students started passing the erasers to those closest to the windows, who threw them out onto the lawn. The last erasers in the room had scarcely hit the grass when Babe Ford, one of the custodians, rounded the corner driving the tractor equipped with reel mowers to do the front lawn. All of a sudden every student in the room was craning to see the cloud of chalk dust and eraser bits flying into the air. The bell must have rung just about then, for I don't recall any repercussions inflicted for the eraser disappearance. Alan Gensamer, a year behind me, a very imaginative student, came to school one day with pet fly. He and his brother Mike had managed to catch a fly and tie a thread around its neck, so it could still fly, but on a tether. It was last seen going out a third story window. I digress….

Terry DeRose Crowley never had children of her own. She had her students. She loved those students and her job, and so she stayed on as the girls physical education teacher for fifty-three years. She retired in 2004, a few months shy of her seventy-seventh birthday. More Bolivar school students had the guidance of Terry Crowley than they did any other member of the school faculty.

The new girls sports teams were coached by men and women other than Terry Crowley. Instrumental music instructor Ralph Butler had success with the girl's basketball teams in the 1980s. But none have matched the attainments of the softball teams of the twenty-first century, nor that of girls wrestling. Bolivar's first high school state champions were the members of the 1929 440 relay team, but there have been few others between then and now. And none has the incredible back story of Bolivar's state champion wrestler, Teagan Sibble. More about all this when we get to the merged schools and the Wolverines.

After the turmoil of the 1950s, and the refusal of the school board to grant tenure to two successive principals, Bolivar Central settled into a prolonged, twenty-year period of smooth operation, when, in 1959 George Kuhn moved into the principal's office, and Gil Brinnier took the post of assistant principal and guidance counsellor. George, who had worked as a printing and industrial arts instructor, received his masters in education from St. Bonaventure in 1949, in a ceremony where Anna Duggan was awarded a Masters in Spanish, and Margaret Sherwood a bachelor's degree in biology. For the 1950-51 school year, he taught printing in Bolivar, and industrial arts in Allentown. In the summer of 1951, he took charge of Bolivar's summer recreation program, and led a class in fly fishing, using equipment donated by F&S Sales. At the end of that summer, George put his degree to work, beginning his years as Bolivar's vice principal, and in those first years also as the golf coach. It was in the fall of 1953 that students were excused early on Mondays to attend church school. Initially, only the Catholic Church offered instruction, but soon enough the Methodists and Episcopalians set up programs too.

As vice principal, George had also been in charge of the adult education programs. In 1954, the program awarded a record of more than 200 certificates in twelve areas of study, which included bookkeeping, typing, shorthand, cake decorating, hair styling, (taught by Ernestine Sadler), fly tying, and woodworking. In 1959, high school principal Kuhn inaugurated a plan to issue report cards every five weeks, or eight times per school year, to help parents stay on top of their children's progress.

Bonnie Peaslee

On the departure of Delbert Goranson, George Kuhn took the reins of Bolivar Central School on July 1, 1960. The turmoil had led to twelve vacancies in the faculty. However, all but two spots had been filled before Principal Kuhn took over. There was no overriding theme to the Kuhn years, like instrumental music had been during the Whitford era, or football and sports during the Davis years. George Kuhn's emphasis was on maintaining a smooth running apparatus, controlling costs as much as they could be in the face of so much budgetary control coming from Albany, and maintaining good academic standards so that graduates could prosper in the wider world. 1959's valedictorian Bonnie Peaslee had become the first woman from Bolivar to be admitted into the Cornell University Engineering program. (She was one of only six women in the Cornell engineering school her first year). Those academic standards reached an apogee by one measure early on in George's tenure, thanks to the efforts of the Jordan family on South Street. Robert and Marguerite Jordan had three children, Kay, class of 1960, Barry, class of 1962, and Brian, class of 1965. Marguerite was a familiar face to everyone who went through high school, because she was vice principal Brinnier's secretary, and was thus the first face you saw when you set foot in the high school office. Kay Jordan graduated in 1960 with a grade point average of 97.83, the highest ever attained in the records of the school. Try as he might, Barry, who also graduated as valedictorian of the class of 1962, fell short of besting his sister, posting the second highest average known in Bolivar, of 96.7. Competition in the class of 1965 was fierce, with nine of its students having averages of more than 90. Brian followed his siblings as valedictorian, but his actual numbers were never published. All three Jordans won Herrick academic scholarships to Alfred University.

Gil Brinnier

Throughout his stay, George Kuhn had by his side Gil Brinnier. Gil, who was raised in the Hudson valley, came to Alfred University for college, and there he met Virginia Shaner, a member of Bolivar's class of 1938. They became engaged in 1942, and married a year later. When the war ended, Gil headed to Albany Law School, but decided, as many do, that lawyering is not what he wanted to do. He and "Ginny" married, and he came to Bolivar to teach high school social studies in 1950. During the turmoil which surrounded the end of Anthony Perrone's career in Bolivar, Gil taught for a year in Wellsville. But when Del Goranson took over, George Kuhn became vice principal in charge of the high school, and the decision was made to bring in a full time guidance counsellor. Gil took the new job and came back. When Goranson left and George Kuhn became the supervising principal, Mr. Brinnier moved up into the vice principal's office, but retained the responsibilities of the guidance counsellor.

There are many faces who become familiar to the students who spend their childhoods in the school systems. The school building erected in 1929, which is the core of the current Bolivar Richburg complex, has *always* looked brand new. That is so in part because there was plenty of money to build it right in the first place, but also because of the skilled effort that has gone into maintaining the building ever since. During my time there, that was true because of the determined effort and good work of a small group of custodians. Mr. Thorwart, Lowell Button, Babe Ford, and Ray Peaslee, seen at right, had decades of experience each in not just keeping the plant running, but also keeping it looking like it had hardly been used. The standard set back then by them was the foundation for the pride still taken in the school complex in Bolivar as it exists today.

Keeping the place in good repair was only half the job. The other half was keeping the kids who filled the two cafeterias fed, and the kitchen up to.and

The Mrs. Messler, Goodliff, McKay, Taylor, Stives, Smith and Ford, ready to serve up lunch for 800 plus students in 1959.

The Bolivar Central custodial staff of 1960

above, health department standards. Of course, on of the essential elements of keeping the kids fed was fixing meals that tasted good. During most of my time as a Bolivar student, Mrs. Goodliff was the head cook, and one of my favorite meals was on Thursdays, which was usually spaghetti day. I have forgotten the menu rotation, but each day usually had one of two offerings, which included sloppy joes, hamburg gravy on mashed potatoes, tuna melts, and chili; but each came up only once a week, and on a set day. You only got spaghetti on Thursdays. But, it was really good spaghetti!

Bolivar's Military Academy Graduates

Ben Francisco, USNA '73 *Kelly Monahan, USMA* *Bob Matheny, USNA '81*

Stacy Manning USMA 1991 *Julie Stopha, USNA 1993* *Todd Ferris, USNA 1995*

Before 1969, no Bolivar graduate had attended any of the United States military academies. In 1955, Brad Pohlig had obtained an appointment which would have made him part of the very first graduating class at the US Air Force Academy, but he chose Harvard instead. That all changed when Roger B. "Ben" Francisco earned an appointment to the United States Naval Academy in 1969, and graduated from there in 1973. He made the Navy a career, spending most of his time in the cockpit piloting a P-3 four-engine sub-hunting airplane in the Pacific.

Perhaps inspired by Ben's admission and success there, Kelly Monahan, salutatorian of the class of 1971 and student council president, left Bolivar for the United States Military Academy at West Point. Robert Matheny, class of 1977, followed Ben into the Naval Academy and also became a pilot. Lt. Matheny died on June 20, 1988, when the engine of his single engine plane quit, and he chose to ride it down to keep it from crashing where it would harm others.

In 1988, Bolivar's star female athlete, and valedictorian of the class of 1987, became the first woman from Bolivar to receive an appointment, which she, Stacy Manning, accepted, graduating from West Point in 1991. She was followed two years later by Julie Stopha, salutatorian of the class of 1989, who went to Annapolis. And finally, Todd Ferris, BCS 1991, also gained an appointment to the United States Naval Academy, and went from it to the Marine Corps where he too made a career as a pilot.

One other Bolivar student of the Kuhn-Brinnier Era should be added here. Charles David Hahn, known as Dave while in school, and as Charlie afterwards, graduated at the head of the class of 1964. Charlie did not attend one of the four national military academies, but instead attended the Empire State Maritime College at Fort Schuyler, from which he graduated in 1968.

Charles D. Hahn 1964

Upon graduation, he became an officer in the U.S. Naval Reserve, but went to work for Exxon. A year later, he was assigned the position of 3rd Officer aboard the SS Manhattan. This ship, which was 1,005 feet long, and which displaced 105,000 tons, was at the time the largest US merchant vessel in existence. It had been refitted with an icebreaker bow, and was assigned to attempt the first successful transit in history of the fabled Northwest Passage, going from Chester, Pennsylvania on Delaware Bay, around the north coast of Canada to Prudhoe Bay, Alaska, and back. The ship departed in August 1969, had to alter its route because of heavy sea ice in the M'Clure Strait, but successfully returned to Chester in November. And so it was that Charlie Hahn became part of history, one of the leading officers of a crew which accomplished what scores of expeditions through history had failed to accomplish. Unfortunately, he died as the result of an accident at the Southwestern Firemen's Convention in Silver Creek in August 1977. He was only thirty-one.

The SS Manhattan, with its new ice-breaker bow

Three other Bolivar people also broke out onto the national stage during this era.

Bill Blowers

Although Gabby Hayes passed through town many times, and even appeared on our stages on two occasions, our town has never produced anyone who has made it in the movies. (Unless you want to count Mel Van Curen). But we have come close. Each year for almost all of the last century, the Academy of Motion Pictures and Sciences gives out what are called the Academy Awards, and the winners get a small statue of "Oscar." Those who have watched a few of those awards ceremonies should also be aware, because they always mention them, that the Academy also gives out a stack of special technical awards in a separate ceremony that usually occurs a few days before Oscar Sunday. Those winners do not get Oscars, but the do get Certificates of Merit from the Academy.

In March 1989, at the Sixty-First Scientific and Technical Honors of the Academy of Motion Pictures and Sciences, hosted that year by Angie Dickinson, an award was presented for the design and development of the Spectra CineSpot one-degree spotter, (used to measure the brightness of motion picture screens), to William L. Blowers and a partner. Bill Blowers was the vice president of Bolivar Central's class of 1959.

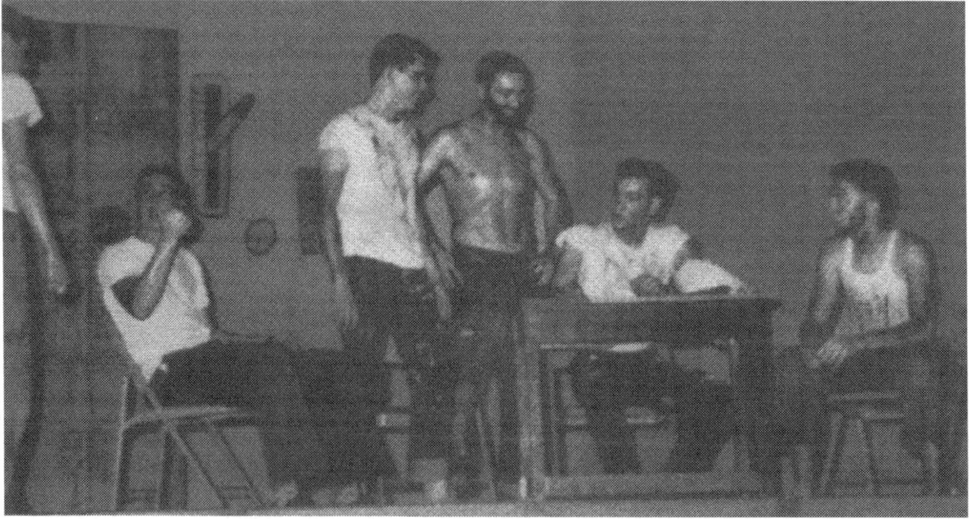

Seen here are Rad Parker, Tom Grantier, Bill Blowers, Don Smith, Dale Wood and Doug Polen in the one act play, "Submerged." It depicts a failed attempt to refloat a crippled submarine. I vividly recall the end, as the lighting turned blue and faded to black. Bill Blowers liked to act, and later that year appeared at the Alfred Ag Tech Drama Festival, in a select cast performing in the play "Winterset," written by Maxwell Anderson, in front of the late playwright's family.

Doug Reeland

Four doors down the street from my parents lived another kid four months older than me. His name was Floyd Douglas Reeland, the last of Bolivar's Floyd Reelands. Floyd Sr. lived on Wellsville Street near the school. Floyd II was called Bronco. Floyd III was Doug.

Bronco had been a running back in high school, and as many boys do, Doug looked to his father's example to get his sense of direction. There was no midget league at that time, but when we were old enough we got footballs and helmets from Santa Clause and started organizing pickup games in the fall. One of my earliest memories of Doug was an occasion when a big snowball fight was organized on upper Main Street, probably at the base of Casey's fields where we all went sledding. Doug and I were on the same side, but the other side had better range and accuracy, and our compatriots faded away, until there was just the two of us against a horde of others who had made us retreat into the L formed by the new Reeland house Bronco had built at the corner of Main and Belmont. We became great and trusted friends.

We were only classmates until the fifth grade. Doug had learning difficulties with the result that he fell back from the class of 1965 into the class of 1966, but we played for the Bulldogs three years together, double dated on occasion, and then went our separate ways for a long time. I got my law degree and started a family. Doug, who had a great athletic career in Bolivar, setting records in both the long and high jumps, had wanted since junior high to be an athletic trainer. He got his degree from Oklahoma in 1972, where he had been recruited by football coach Daryl Royal, but never made the playing squad, and on graduation went to work for the Dodgers baseball system. He became a certified trainer in 1979 and found a full time job as the head trainer for Hobart-William Smith College in Geneva. Then he married and settled down too.

The author & Doug Reeland, 2005

Doug very quickly gained wide respect for his abilities as a trainer, so much so that in 1986 he was named the official trainer for the United States National LaCrosse Team competing in the World Championships. He served for eighteen years on the Ethics Committee of the National Athletic Trainer's Association. Then, at age sixty-two he discovered he had an advanced cancer, and he died in April 2011. One person accurately described Doug as, "loud, robust, and completely honest. He was a pleasure to be around." I, the author, gave one of three eulogies at his funeral. Afterwards, four different men came up to me to tell me that they had lost their best friend. Doug Reeland was that sort of guy.

Bob Torrey

In the earlier chapter about the Bulldogs, Wayne Torrey played a prominent part. His son, Bob, born on January 30, 1957, was part of Bolivar Central's Class of 1975, and was a big part of the success of Coach Bob Dunsmore's football teams of that time. His father taught Bob how to catch a pass, and how to kick, so during his junior and senior years as a Bulldog Bob Torrey, the biggest guy on the team, kicked off. When he was freshman here, the team never won a game. But as the Dunsmore system kicked in, and as Bob grew, that changed. In the 1974 season, when Bob was a senior, the Bulldogs had another undefeated run, finishing with a 9-0 record. That garnered a Coach of the Year award for Bob Dunsmore, and allowed Bob Torrey to catch the eye of Joe Paterno. He headed off to play as a running back for Penn State.

On the team with Torrey was a running back named Matt Suhey. Suhey was a Paterno relative, and although smaller than Bob he saw lots of playing time. When the 1977 season arrived, both Bob and Matt were juniors, and I had the opportunity to take in a game at State College. I kept looking and looking for number 39, Torrey, to get into the game, which PSU was trailing. I wasn't alone. There came a point when the spectators started chanting, "Tor-rey, Tor-rey, Tor-rey." He got in, was handed the ball, and dragged a group of tacklers down the field for twenty yards, and the crowd went crazy. Penn State came back to win the game. Bob rushed for 456 yards that season, his 5.8 average yards per carry more than a yard more than Suhey's, But, Suhey was in for twice as many plays, for reasons the spectators never quite understood. Penn State had started out number 13 in the national polls. The last regular season game was played against number 10 ranked Pitt, in what Bob considered the coldest game he ever played in. Bob caught the game winning screen pass, which led to a spot in the Fiesta Bowl. There Bob rushed for 107 yards, half of them during a fifty-five yard sprint, where he was dropped on the two yard line. The Nittany Lions beat Arizona State 42-28, and ended up ranked number 5 in the polls

There were high hopes in State College for the 1978 season. Bob was in the best condition of his life. The team travelled to Columbus to play Ohio State, and won 19-0. Rocks were thrown at the team bus as they escaped back to State College. Torrey played in all eleven regular season games, but still alternated with Suhey, with Suhey getting about 2/3s of the playing time. On average, Bob still out gained Suhey by half a yard per carry, but Suhey was favored as a receiver and had the better numbers when he caught the ball. The closest game of that season was the one the week after Ohio State, when they beat SMU 26-21.

TCU fell 58-0, Syracuse 45-15, which lifted the Lions to number 2 in the polls. When they beat North Carolina State 19-10 for their tenth win of the season, they topped the college poll. They went to the Sugar Bowl to play Bear Bryant and number 2 Alabama for the national championship on January 1, 1979. Joe never put Bob in that game and Penn State lost, 10-14.

He was drafted in the sixth round by the New York Giants, listed as standing six feet four inches, weighing 231 pounds. Midway through that first season, the Giants, who had yet to use him in a game, traded Bob to the Miami Dolphins. He first saw action there on November 11 in a game against Baltimore. Bob carried the ball four times, and the Dolphins won 19-0. He next played on December 9 in Detroit, where he picked up twenty-two yards on 5 carries, and Miami won again, 28-10. The next week against the Jets, he carried the ball five times, caught two passes, and scored his first, and as it turned out, only NFL touchdown, in a losing effort against the Jets, who won 24-27. He got to play one play in the divisional playoff against Pittsburg, which Miami lost 14-34.

Bob came back for the 1980 season, but after seeing no action in Miami, was traded to the Philadelphia Eagles, and with that team he caught a ticket to the 1981 Super Bowl played in the Super Dome in New Orleans. Unfortunately, Bob did not get a Super Bowl ring. Jim Plunkett and the Oakland Raiders rolled over the Eagles 27-10. Bob had seen enough of the Big Time. He decided to hang up his cleats and to make his way back home in western New York. As many readers know, Bob has suffered numerous serious health setbacks in recent years. He deserves better. He is still Bolivar's all time best on the gridiron.

Bob Dunsmore

Contributed by Kelly Lounsberry

Bob Dunsmore took the reins of the BCS varsity football program for the 1971 season after several years as an assistant. That year was a learning process for both the players and the head coach, as the team limped to an 0-7 final record. The next two seasons finished with solid records, and the building blocks were set in place for 1974. That was the season in which the Bulldogs finished undefeated with a 9-0 record, the first undefeated season since 1961. After a long drought, the Blue and White had returned to the upper echelon of area football!

As a salute to his success with this program, Dunsmore was named "Big 30 Coach of the Year," an honor well-deserved. The Bulldogs dominated the Tri-County League with a 4-0 record, and the second annual Big 30 All-Star Game roster included Bob Torrey, Dave Button, and Brian Morrison. Final recognition went to Bob Torrey who received a full scholarship to play football at Penn State University. The next four campaigns were mostly successful with a cumulative 21-13 record. By 1979, the team was ready for another run to perfection. They steamrolled all their opponents with four shutouts along the way. In the Section V championship game, the boys lost a heartbreaker, 7-0, although they dominated every phase of the game, which featured some of the most controversial calls ever seen on the gridiron. Once again, for his tremendous accomplishments, Coach Dunsmore was named "Big 30 Coach of the Year."

The 80's continued as an era of unparalleled success. During that decade, the team won numerous league titles, and on six occasions, they earned a place in the Section V playoffs. In 1991, an undermanned Bulldog team barely snuck into the playoffs where they upset the number two seed Elba. What followed was a battle against a MUCH larger team in number one seed Dundee. Often outweighed by 80-100 pounds per man on the line of scrimmage, the Bulldogs scrapped to the very end, scoring a touchdown with a minute left, but ultimately losing 32-28. The fact that Bolivar could even compete with these two superior teams exemplifies the job that Coach Dunsmore did, taking a squad of overachievers and leading them to the doorstep of football immortality. It would be difficult to argue against the fact that this was the finest coaching job (of many superb coaching jobs) of Dunsmore's career.

By the time of his retirement at the end of the 1992 season, Bob Dunsmore had guided the program for 22 seasons, racking up seven league victories and eight trips to the playoffs. His cumulative record was 115-72-5, with only four losing seasons. His career was highlighted by two undefeated teams (during the regular season) with two selections as "Big 30 Coach of the Year." Of course, it must be remembered that very often he took the field with much smaller players than his opponents. It was also a common occurrence for the Bulldogs to be lined up against players from schools with much larger enrollments.

For his efforts, the football field at the high school was named "Dunsmore-Latimer Field" to honor the two greatest coaches in the program's history. Dunsmore would go on to be honored by selection into several organizations that acknowledged his achievements. He was inducted into the Allegany County Sports Hall of Fame in 2005 and the Clearfield County (P.A.) Scholastic Hall of Fame. In 2009, he was selected for induction into the Section V Football Hall of Fame where his induction ceremony barely contained the word "I", as that's the type of coach and man he was. He never looked for or wanted the individual accolades, he simply wanted to do what was best for his players as he always made sure to praise them. The following quote found in the coaching world describes Bob Dunsmore, "A good coach can change games; a great coach can change lives."

Coach Dunsmore on the far right, with members of the undefeated football team of 1979. They are: Mickey Bliss, Jeff Greene, Dave Stives, John Molisani, Andy Ingslls, Rick Gould, Bill Darling, Stan Dunsmore, Rich Matheny, and Joe Johnston.

Photo courtesy Olean Times Herald

My Time as Superintendent of Schools, 1980-1986

by Tom Boedicker

As I approached the school building at 100 School Street in the spring of 1980, I was impressed with the building and surrounding landscape. I came for my first interview as a candidate for the position of superintendent of schools. I had arrived early in the village and stopped in the local café in the downtown area. While having a piece of pie and coffee, I heard two customers chatting about who would be the next superintendent of school. They said it would be the current elementary supervisor, Vince DiTanna. I thought to myself, it looks like a forgone conclusion. Approaching the board room on the second floor, I was greeted by the Board President, Neil Dempsey and Vice President, "Dutch" Dunning.

As I left the interview, I felt I had done a fairly good job and drove back to Skaneateles, New York to wait to see if I would be back for a second one. A few weeks later, I was called back for a final interview which was held at the Hilltop Restaurant. I was impressed with that restaurant and had many enjoyable evenings there while living in Bolivar. The next week, I received a call from Neil Dempsey that I was the selected candidate to be the new leader of the Bolivar Central School District.

I arrived in July of 1980 and one of the first visitors to my office was a senior student who wanted to meet me. He welcomed me and then informed me that there were certain ways of doing things here in Bolivar. I said I was glad to meet him, and as superintendent of school, I will abide by the policies and procedure of the Board of Education. During the summer, the athletic director asked if I would like to announce the Bolivar Bulldogs football games. I said I would love to do that, and quickly found out the importance of Friday night football in Bolivar, I was told that Bolivar was the first high school in the area to install lights for high school football games. Along with newly elected Board member Fred Shaner and teacher Ron Stabley we called many Friday night games.

The 1979 football season, the Bulldogs went on to the district final. My first year, the team did not win a game! I am glad I was not to blame for the season. The football field was not in the best shape, so I investigated replacing the sod. Trying to keep the cost down, the Board decided to level the field with local help, buy sod from Batavia Sod farms, and install it with student and local help. We also needed a watering system to make sure the new sod took. The fire department helped by watering the field when it was first put down.

After the old sod was stripped and ground leveled, I asked football coach Bob Dunsmore to accompany me to the third floor and look at the field. It was May. Coach Dunsmore saw the field was just dirt, and said: "How am I going to play on this muddy field in a couple of months?" I told him it will be ready by then and he reacted; "IT BETTER BE!" Thanks to the community, staff and students, the field was ready, I believe Bolivar then had the best natural grass field in the area.

One other Coach Dunsmore story. Assistant coach and teacher, Jud Foy, came into my office one day and said a salesperson had sample football pants for Bolivar. It had a pinkish/red strip down the side. I told Jud to have Bob come up to my office and while he is there, put the pants on his desk. Bob arrived and I told him there is a sample of new football pants I want to order for the team. Bob went to his office, came back, and declared:" if you want me to use those pants, I quit!" Jud came in laughing, as he knew Bob would never change from Penn State colors! And he never did. Coach Dunsmore is a legend in Bolivar, and I am so glad I had the privilege of working with him.

One of the concerns I had as superintendent was the need for more gym space. With the rise of girls sports, one gym could not meet the requested use. So one day, an architect of Habiterra Associates, (who did the window installation) was in my office, the old Board room. Looking out the window, I asked him if he could build a gym where the old merry-go round and monkey bars were located. Sure, plenty of room along with some classrooms. That was the start of many future construction projects.

With the assistance of State aid, money from capital reserve fund, and community approval, we were able to build a new gym and classrooms with no additional taxes. This was the second major building project since the completion of the building in 1930, and the first since 1939.

Another concern of the Board was the accessibility of programs for handicapped students. The school had four levels , and no easy access for students and staff. The architects evaluated the building, and determined an elevator could be installed in the south end of the building, where the current elementary supervisor was located, and straight up through small offices used for speech and special education. The basement floor had a store room that was assessable.

One side note. Following the pouring of the foundation and footers for the new addition, I received a call from Buck Reeland, head custodian, one Saturday morning saying the toilets were plugged up and he could not unplug them. After investigating, we noticed that one of the pilings was poured over the main sewer line. We had to pull up the piling, repair the main sewer line and then a form a new piling!

When I arrived in 1980, the only computerized functions being used by the district were payroll and accounts payable, through ERIE I BOCES. There were no computers in the school building for staff or student use. One day, I received a flyer advertising Commodore PET Computers. Buy two, get one free. We had some money available, and the district purchased three Commodore PET Computers. They came with cassettes holding **8K** of memory! Shortly, Commodore offered floppy disks with 16K of memory, twice as much, and we thought it was great. The storage room (on the second or third floor) became the first computer lab in 1981-82.

David Stanton, high school English teacher, had an interest in computers, and became the lead teacher in this modern technology. Dedicated computer rooms and equipment were added to the new gym/classroom addition in 1987-88.

Along those lines, my secretary, Carol Greene, was using an electric IBM typewriter. I asked her if she would switch to a personal computer. She said no, she liked her electric. IBM came out with a electric typewriter that included a floppy disk that saved correspondence. Carol agreed to this upgrade. After a year, Carol liked the floppy, and requested a personal computer. Change came slowly.

In the central office, there was safe for storage of documents and small amounts of cash. One day I noticed a red box containing a baseball. It had several autographs on it, all former New York Yankees, Babe Ruth was among them. I showed it one day to a Yankee fan and he told me this ball was signed over a period of years, as many of the players did not play at the same time. I never found out the origin of the autographed baseball.

I arrived in July, 1980, following the retirement of George Kuhn as supervising principal, and of Gil Brinner, guidance counselor and secondary principal. The administrative staff then consisted of a supervising principal, secondary principal/guidance counselor, an elementary supervisor, Vince DiTanna, and the district treasurer, Lucille Barnes.

With the retirement of Mr. Brinnier, I told the Board I would like to evaluate the current administrative structure during my first year. During that first year, I recommended we hire a full-time guidance counselor to take Mr. Brinner's place, and I would take over the duties of secondary principal. The elementary supervisor's job would remain the same.

Following the 1980-81 school year, I recommended a reorganization: one building principal, one guidance counselor, a superintendent of schools, and a part time business manager, contracted through BOCES. With additional BOCES aid, the cost to the Bolivar district of a part-time business manager would be minimal, and would be shared with Wellsville School District. The treasurer position would remain the same. This freed up the superintendent to spend more time on long range planning, facilities and space needs, as well as new curriculum mandates coming from the State Education Department.

Wellsville decided it needed the business manager full time and hired the part time person. This left Bolivar without a business manager. After discussion with the Board, it was decided a full-time position was needed here too. Following a search on the Civil Service List of eligible candidates, we appointed Neil Dempsey as business manager, where he remained until his retirement.

Around this time, the State Education Department mandated health instruction during the middle school years. Around 1984-85 the Board hired a part-time health teacher with part time curriculum duties. This was Robert Mountain, the future superintendent.

Another room change took place around 1984-85 when the men's and women's faculty rooms were combined. Because space was becoming hard to make, the guidance office was moved to the third floor, north end of the building, previously the men's faculty room. The men's faculty room was then merged with the ladies faculty room on the second floor. (There was some weeping from the men faculty members).

The merger of the Richburg and Bolivar School Districts had been talked about for many years. In my discussions with the Richburg superintendent, the

Richburg Board was not interested. At that time, the State was not mandating merger; however the State Education Department was offering additional state aid to schools who would consider merging. I recall it was 10% additional foundation aid first year and dropping 1% each year for ten years. Additional aid for any building projects was also given. These were great incentives to merge. Since there was no interest from Richburg at the time, Bolivar commenced to look at their needs, and the first major capital improvement project was started: an additional new gym and classrooms. Several years later under Superintendent Bob Mountain, Bolivar and Richburg merged to form the current Bolivar- Richburg Central School.

The concept of running a Pre-Kindergarten program became popular during my time, and we researched developing one. The old True Value Hardware store was available and renovated to become the first Pre-School Program. I believe Jim Margeson was the first director. The new facility was built after I left.

Tom Boedicker on the left, with the student council: In front: C Lindamer, T Mitchell, R Monahan, P Stopha. In back, S Reesher, D Ferguson, T Dempsey, and K Majot

My Time in Bolivar

by Bob Mountain

Our test scores, (grades 3,6, and 8) were not good when compared to other schools in Allegany and Cattaraugus counties. We took various steps to improve the situation, and in 1988 we were one of twenty-two schools across New York State showing vast improvement of these test scores. About 1987 or 1988, the Appalachian Regional Commission released information about a grant for schools in Appalachia. *[Editor's note: Sen. Robert Kennedy, while representing New York State in the mid-1960s, had the government's definition of Appalachia expanded to include Allegany County and much of the Southern Tier].* My focus as superintendent was on at risk students who were very challenged by the New York State regents program, who often fell behind, and often dropped out of school. With the help of my wife, Diane, who wrote a grant proposal for Bolivar Central School emphasizing our desire to help these at risk students, we presented this idea: we would purchase run down, but restorable homes, and develop a plan to use these targeted students to renovate the homes, which would be resold to fund another purchase and renovation project. In Bolivar at that time, there were many properties that needed improving.

The renovations done while I was with the Bolivar school system were fully tied into education lessons. An example: science might center around electrical and HVAC. Classroom education was in the morning, and renovation in the afternoon. Thanks to Dave Evans and Mary Lou Nichols, the program became very successful and well organized. Our representatives in Albany, Senator Jess Present and Assemblywoman Pat McGee, among others, loved the program and had us giving presentations often around the state. They were also great at supporting us with a number of items which I was able to get yearly until I retired.

The leaders of the education department fell in love with the program and the more support we got the more we asked for, and were given. We even received an international award for it. The village was also responsive, since the program kept these homes on the tax rolls. I was even asked to apply for a BOCES district superintendency, but I declined. My heart was with working my all for the less fortunate, underserved of our district. They in turn returned the favor of supporting our programs by passing each budget as proposed.

The creative genius Bob Mountain brought to his position leading the school system was truly remarkable.

The last house we were able to do with this program was the former Erie Wilson house on Wellsville Street, which had been used during the mid-twentieth century by Doctor Allison as both his home and office. The program turned it back into a showplace. My goal was to turn it into a bed and breakfast location which would be run by our program, led and guided by the school business and home economics departments. This never came to pass because I moved on before we could get it going. This property subsequently sold for $230,000, a record price in Bolivar at the time. The proceeds were used to acquire the old Manley property on the corner of Friendship and Kincaid streets.

The early 1990s was business as usual, always with the challenge of passing school budgets. In 1993, we embarked on the merging of Bolivar and Richburg Central schools. It began with a comprehensive study measuring all aspects to determine if a merger was feasible and made sense. There were many incentives to merge, not least of which were the financial incentives offered by New York State, one of the most significant being the promise of increased state funding for fifteen, perhaps more, years following the merger.

After many pre-merger meetings, some heated, the vote was taken. Bolivar, at least three times in the past, had given voter approval to the proposal, but Richburg had never come close. This time they did, and the wheels were set in motion for a merged school district to begin operating for the 1994-1995 academic year. It was a large undertaking which created many headaches. However, the bottom line was that it would create opportunities to add and strengthen the programs offered within the system, and to upgrade the facilities, where both of the main school buildings were approaching seventy years of age.

With the merger, the state offered to reimburse us for ninety-five percent of any building upgrades approved by the education department. To begin, we focused on the changes required to convert the Richburg building into a dedicated elementary school, and the Bolivar facility into the secondary school. I saw the merger, and the available funding, as an opportunity to create a team of educators and community members to create a comprehensive plan. From 1997 through 2000, we put before the voters a series of projects which were brave and required finesse on our part to gain voter approval. At the time, we had a pre-kindergarten program set in an older store building on Main Street, which the owner wanted to sell to us. My thought was that the rented structure was too small, and was in the midst of a run down block, which included the seventy-five-year-old village fire hall, and the even older and unused former Lyric movie theater. I led the drive to acquire the entire block. It was a difficult sell, but the resulting facility, across Olean Street from the village library which it was designed to resemble, was well worth the time, trouble, and expense. However, as large and difficult as that project was, it was not the biggest project we had in mind.

We next presented a proposal for a total upgrade of the Bolivar building and grounds, including installing artificial turf on the outdoor athletic fields. I knew it would be a hard sell because after much study we decided to go with artificial turf for the baseball field. In that regard, one of the biggest challenges was convincing the public that we, the students and the community, deserved the best. Im recall during one presentation an upstanding citizen stating that the project was a Cadillac; why not go for a Ford instead? I remember my response, which I think helped to sway the packed crowd. I said, “What kind of superintendent would I be if I didn’t want the Mercedes, the best for our students, which you should also. We deserve it for our students.” The project was approved, and we were ecstatic. All our work was not for naught. We were the first school in the area to install an artificial playing field. Now you see them everywhere.

It is worth noting that all of the projects, $40,000,000 in total, were done at no direct cost to local taxpayers In many cases, we were able to make money, because once a project was approved we could borrow the money to begin. Interest rates were such that we could borrow at a lower rate than we received for the unspent funds in the bank, and keep the difference. When all this work was completed, in 2003, I decided to retire. It was a real pleasure to serve the Bolivar community. I haven't spent my entire life in Bolivar, first arriving in 1973, but after fifty years I think of myself as a native. So do the rest of us, Bob.

84 Wellsville Street. This was the home of Erie Wilson, and thanks to him it was the first home in Bolivar to be electrified. (Erie generated his own). Later it was the home of Dr. Ernest Allison, who had his office in the rooms on the lower right. It was also the last house in Bolivar renovated under the internationally recognized program created by Bob Mountain during his tenure as the superintendent of Bolivar's school.

My Years Teaching in Bolivar

by Norene Crowley Ferris

I was asked to try and recount some memories of my years in the BCS-BRCS music department. I was one of the privileged people who not only graduated from Bolivar Central School in 1965, but returned to teach at my Alma Mater from 1970-2000. While a student at BCS, I felt every teacher there was looking out for our best interests, preparing us for life beyond graduation. Of course my father and high school English teacher, RT Crowley, was my main mentor, but Evangeline Young, choral director, encouraged and nurtured my love of singing, and led me down the path I would pursue and teach—vocal music.

In 1970, after graduating from Fredonia State, I applied in Bolivar for an elementary music position, which was vacated, but Mrs. Young had other ideas. She told George Kuhn, supervising principal, that she would move down and teach elementary classes for her last year so I could be hired as the 6-12 vocal music teacher, and follow in her footsteps. What a treasure she was! And so it began. Ralph Butler was hired as the new band director the year before I graduated high school, and we would work together in a flourishing music department until his retirement in 1997. Bolivar had always had a reputation for strong band and choral music, and Ralph and I worked hard to continue that tradition. Pam Graffius was hired a few years after I was, and she stayed on for our thirty year journey together as well. In my opinion, the three of us couldn't have had better partners! Pam and I both retired in 2000.

Ralph developed one of the largest and finest award winning marching bands in the area. In the summer of 1967, the BCS band, now led by Ralph Butler, returned to the NY State band Exposition in Syracuse, the first time since the 1940s. By 1974, 125 students were participating in the band and color guard, which won six first place awards that summer. The Bolivar Bulldog Marching Band, along with the color guard, traveled many summers competing in area parades, bringing home dozens of trophies and prizes. The color guard, later led by Dick Greene, also BCS '65, marched with the band, but also competed separately, continuing to bring in more awards. I remember the Tuesday night practices on the village streets, with residents coming out of their houses to watch the students march by—often clapping as they passed. Small town pride! The 135 member band won an invitation to participate in Gimbel's 1978 Thanksgiving Day parade in Philadelphia. The whole town watched the blue and white marching Bulldogs on television that morning to cheer. Ralph's high school band and stage band were also exceptional. The Friday night home football pep band helped the crowd cheer on the Bulldog football team! The Bolivar Hotel saw Ralph in a different light on Saturday nights for many years, as the bass player in the Doug Bushnell Trio. What fun we had dancing to their music.

I was blessed to take over a large and skilled high school chorus from Evangeline Young, and continued her tradition of an extra curricular Senior Girls' Ensemble—-a select 16 member treble choir—and also formed a Jr. Girls' Ensemble of seventh & eighth grade girls. Both these groups went to state competition every year, and the Senior Ensemble maintained over 20 years of level 6A+ ratings, the highest possible.

Our senior choir also received consistently high ratings at spring competitions. In 1986 the eighty-five voice chorus traveled to Albany for "Music in Our Schools Month". We were invited to perform on the mall outside the capitol, and Senator Jess Present greeted us. Every year in December, a BCS (and later BRCS) tradition for the senior choir was to perform the "Hallelujah Chorus" at the close of the Christmas concert (when we could still call it that), and many alumni would join us on the risers. It was always a highlight of the evening. From elementary through high school we were blessed to have many students interested in singing and entertaining. It always amazed me that for such a small school, we had so many outstanding voices, both male and female. In my thirty years teaching, I was privileged to help mentor many fine voices, having dozens of students audition and be selected for New York State Conference Choirs, with several going on to the All-Eastern Choirs as well. Pam Graffius, elementary vocal teacher, also doubled as our accompanist, and we couldn't have performed many of the selections without her amazing hands!!

Our music department also worked together to bring new opportunities to our students. In 1977 I begged the senior drama advisor to let me direct a musical for their senior play. She agreed, and "*You're A Good Man, Charlie Brown*" was the first musical to be done since the days long gone of the Junior High operetta. What a time we had, and with the talented cast of David Herne, Jim Hahn, Mike Petzen, Emilio Rende, Beth Bucher and Tami Kuhn, who wouldn't have fun?

The curtain goes up on Bolivar's first high school musical, presented by the senior class of 1977

This was so successful that we decided to do a musical every other year, alternating with another new endeavor—-the Bolivar "Best of the BCS" Variety Shows. These featured not only students, but faculty, alumni and community residents. Oh, the stories I could tell about behind the scenes, as well as some of the infamous faculty numbers. The emcees included favorites—RT Crowley,

Ron Stabley, Steve Yehl, Tom Boedicker, Jim Margeson, Jim Danaher, and not to ignore the ladies, Betsy Greene and Pam Graffius. They never failed to entertain! Some of my fondest memories are working with students who had never been on stage and watch them blossom into their character. A highlight was always having faculty accept their call to participate. Two musicals, "Bye Bye Birdie", and "The Sound of Music", featured my daughter Katie as the lead. She was serenaded in "Bye Bye Birdie" by quite the array of men faculty, playing the bar patrons and bartender! In earlier musicals, my sons Matt and Todd ran the spotlight and microphones. I'm not sure they thought it was as great as I did! So many faculty members stand out as fantastic role models for the students——helping behind the scenes, playing a role (Deb Melaro, Mary Bernstein, Ron Stabley, Steve Yehl, Jim Margeson, Jim Danaher, RT Crowley, Tom Boedicker, Vince DiTanna, Betsy Greene, Sue Cameron, Pam Graffius come to mind), creating, sewing and organizing all the costumes (Sharon Dimmig)—and the students loved having them involved. The art department—Dave Bosworth, and later Jodie Nothem, designed and helped students create our sets. The whole school supported the music department. Several Mother's Day Dessert Theaters provided ways to feature our talented students, choral and instrumental, with Thelma Zeh's Home Economics classes providing desserts. The Bolivar (and after the merger), the Bolivar-Richburg community always supported the fine arts, as well as athletics, and I am forever grateful for that! I was honored and invited back in 2003. The auditorium was being named the "Norene Crowley Ferris" auditorium, and I didn't even have to die first!! It was my second home The memories I have of time spent there are treasured. The band and choir are continuing, and so will their successes. I was glad to be a part of it for as long as I was.

Ron Stabley came to Bolivar, as seen here, fresh out of college in January 1963, and he never left, spending his entire teaching career here in Bolivar. Although he struggled during his first years to stay ahead of his chemistry students, his persistent happiness and warmth made him popular with every class he worked with.

"The Flea" coached, he advised, he taught his science courses. He cooked his pirogies and made his submarine sandwiches, and he kept his classroom light-hearted. But he never generated more or heartier laughter than he did during the variety shows of the 1980s, when Ron alone would perform the duet "To The Many Girls I've Loved Before," made up so that half his body was a male, and the other half a female, so when he faced left he was one character, and when he faced right he was the other. Everyone's sides ached for hours afterwards. He was one of those you miss the most.

Our Music Madam

The Crowley family has been in Bolivar since the 1880s. Michael J. Crowley, the son of Irish immigrants, was born in Harbor Creek, Erie County, Pennsylvania, in 1855. In 1885, he married his wife Johanna, and came to Bolivar to pursue the oil business. Their son, Thomas R. Crowley, was born in 1887. Michael worked hard and became well established. In 1910, he won a seat on the school board, and later on served as a town assessor. Thomas married Norene Davis in 1924, and moved her into a nice, new home he had built on Pleasant Street. That Tom and Norene had three sons, Robert "R.T.", the well-known long-term Bolivar English teacher, Jim, the husband of Terry DeRose Crowley, another fixture at the school, and the youngest, Tom jr., who made his way in life away from Bolivar. Norene Crowley II was the first of the nine children born to R.T. and Mary Congdon Crowley. Her "Irish twin" brother, Jim, (born less than a year after her), was the most devoted friend I ever had.

I, the author, had only three members of my graduating class who were younger than I was: Tom Ferris, Bob Richardson, and Norene Crowley, who was the youngest member of the Class of 1965. (I am one month and four days older). Our parents were very close friends, so to say I have known her my entire life is about right.

Norene has always been on top of things, organizing, suggesting, tackling the things that needed to be done. Her position as the oldest of nine probably helped her develop that attitude and those skills, but you never doubted that if Norene set out to do something, it would get done, and it would be done well and right. We appeared together in our Junior class play. During the main evening performance, I completely missed a line which was a cue for others. She covered up the mishap so well I was unaware it had happened until after the show ended and I was told about it.

In the summer of 1966, friends talked her into entering the Miss Dunkirk-Fredonia Beauty Pageant, a preliminary qualifier for the Miss New York State and Miss America Pageants, which sixty years ago was a very big deal. She won at the first level, (she won the swimsuit competition, but not the talent, still winning overall), so moved on to the Miss New York State event, which in those days was held in Olean. We all found tickets to go see her perform, and cheered and glowed in her limelight as we watched a Bolivar girl take center stage. When the field was narrowed to the final two, Norene was still there; but she lost to a baton-twirler, and came in first-runner up. Still, we were all impressed.

More impressive was her thirty years as the choral music teacher in the Bolivar and Bolivar-Richburg systems. As she described, the quality of the concerts her choral groups were able to give was first rate. But the extra effort she put in, of turning school plays into musicals, of the amateur nights and variety shows was just astonishing. It was Norene's persistence and ability to attract and recruit performers that set her apart, so that all of these things happened, and came off as memorable events. She was able to get a large proportion of the student body involved in her programs, and also the faculty, parents, and the wider community. It was no wonder that when she decided to slow down, twenty-five years ago, that her auditorium became *her* auditorium. That was only fair, so the memory of all that she helped create there will be perpetuated.

Norene Ferris, and son Matt
1971

Of course there is no better evidence of the quality of a teacher than the success of her students. Much earlier in this book, readers learned of A.J. Glennie, who had depart from his school two students who made it on to the national stage, Patsy Dougherty and Frank Gannett. In Norene's case, she didn't need to look any farther than her own children, one the head of a major local employer, another an Annapolis graduate and career military pilot, and the third a teacher and mother much like herself.

Norene stopped teaching and moved to State College, Pennsylvania, where he husband, Tom Ferris, was working. While there, she kept herself busy working with the PSU teaching program, evaluating student music teachers. When Tom retired in 2009, they returned to Bolivar. Although Tom passed away in 2013, she has stayed, and continues to be a community organizer and activist, helping most recently with organizing the bi-centennial celebration for the summer of 2025. As the community always has been, it is very lucky to have such a actively committed and talented person in its midst to help make good things happen.

Harvey Girls

It should be no surprise that two of the more successful twenty-first century graduates of the Bolivar-Richburg system were products of the school's music program: Joelle Harvey, BRCS 2003, and her younger sister, Melissa. Melissa, After receiving her bachelors and masters degrees in voice from the University of Cincinnati's College-Conservatory of Music, has performed a number of times with the Cincinnati-based Catacoustic Consort, and with the Cincinnati Opera. She is skilled in the performance of earlier music, performing Bach Cantatas and works by Handel, Haydn, and Mozart, and has performed premieres of twenty-first century works, including the role of Flora in the New York City Opera's The Turn of the Screw, and as Hebe in La Ville Morte with the Greek National Opera in Athens, Greece.

Joelle Harvey, also a graduate of the University of Cincinnati's College-Conservatory of Music, has appeared with many of the world's great symphonies, including the New York Philharmonic, Chicago Symphony, San Francisco, Los Angeles, Boston's Handel & Haydn Society, the London Symphony, Amsterdam's Concertgebouw, the Royal Opera House, at Carnegie Hall, and at the Festival d'Aix-en-Provence.

Her 2025 season includes appearances in Des Moines, Cleveland, The Lincoln Center in New York, and the Metropolitan Opera reprising her role as Pamina in The Magic Flute. At least ten of her performances are available on YouTube, and at least four appear in the iTunes catalogue.

Joelle Harvey
courtesy JoelleHarvey.com

Melissa Harvey
courtesy Jessica Osber Photography

Wolverines

Athletic Director Dustin Allen

I moved away from Bolivar in 1993, before the schools merged, when there were still Bearcats and Bulldogs, before there were any Wolverines. In 2075, when some of you gather to celebrate Bolivar's 250th, hopefully a caring historian will have good access to the records and materials to write a good account of the first eighty plus years of the merged schools, and of the Wolverines. I lack both the experience and access to the materials needed to do this.

However, having moved away, and now looking at Bolivar from the outside in, I am struck by the similarities I see between the present time, and the Bolivar of the 1890s. As described in earlier chapters, the 1890s were a very difficult time to be in business in Bolivar, business of any kind, because of the shrinking oil production and the shriveling economic base. And yet, that era produced two people of national stature, and a generation of others who weathered the storm and prospered later.

I see that going on now. I took a virtual drive down Main Street the other day, and doing so made me think of my good friend Doug Reeland and the story he told me about the time when the installation of artificial turf was being debated, and he as an athletic trainer was asked by the school board to come down and talk about the pros and cons. Doug was eminently practical, and he asked a question: when he came down from Geneva to meet, where could he have dinner? At the time, there were no restaurants open in the village, and he was told, "Wellsville." He then asked a second question: "if you folks can't support a restaurant, how are you going to raise the money to replace all that carpet?" I recount this only to demonstrate how bad things have been for people wanting to support themselves in Bolivar, a problem that has yet to be solved.

What is remarkable to me is the quality of the graduates of the school system, as the Harvey girls are shining examples. Further proof of this statement is the persistent success of the school athletic program since the Bulldogs and Bearcats became the Wolverines. As a product of the Bolivar system when FOOTBALL was far and away the prominent sport, when, in 1963 104 high school boys came out to play, it is hard to fathom a time like the present where BRCS can no longer field a full team. Knowing that now there are fewer than 700 students in the system, it is more easily understood. But, there is plenty of talent doing many, many great things. Athletic director Dustin Allen, who himself has demonstrated great coaching ability, has developed a coaching staff who have helped the Wolverines become some of the best teams and individual performers, not in Allegany County, but in New York State. I asked him for a summary of the successes in the athletic department since the merger. Here it is.

In 1997, the Wolverines won the Sectional Cross Country championship. In 1998, the girl's softball team first demonstrated its success, winning the Section V tournament. They won the sectionals again in 1999, 2000, 2004, 2005, and in 2006 brought home the New York State Championship. They continued winning, taking the Section V tournament in 2008, 2010, 2014, 2015, 2021, 2022, and 2023.

The baseball team has won the Section V title in 2000, 2002, 2008, 2010, 2013, 2014, 2016, 2018, 2019, 2021, 2022, and 2024, and qualified for the State Championship tournament four of those times.

The football team reached its apogee in 2007, winning the Section V championship and reaching the final four in the New York State championship tournament. The girls basketball team won Section V in 2015, as did the basketball cheerleaders.

In track and field, the boys won the Section V title in 2022. Since the merger, the Wolverines have seen forty of its boys and girls win individual Section V titles, and two of those qualified for the State Championships. The depth and variety of these successes are such a marvel to record. I can't help but think that part of the foundation for the present level of success is the long winning and "being the best" tradition which has endured for so long in the Bolivar community, in sports, music, and academics. I had the privilege, many decades ago, of working in the oil field summers digging ditch, running electric line, and repairing pressure leaks with Dustin's father, Bud Allen. Dustin I am sure has made his family proud; but to have remained in the valley of the Little Genesee and accomplish so much is the sort of act that has kept Bolivar, New York a great place to be from. It is.

And then there are the wrestlers. In 1950, the point of community pride was the football team. Seventy-five years later, it is the wrestlers who put the icing on a this very multi-layered cake. Under the coaching most recently of Andrew and Todd Taylor, the Wolverine Wrestling team has won four Section V championships in this century, in 2002, 2018, 2019, and 2020. The team has included in its ranks twenty-nine individual Section V weight class champions, and thirteen who qualified for the State Championship tournament.

In 2022, junior Trent Sibble was the runner-up in the New York State 220 pound class Championship Tournament. In 2023, Trent moved up to the 285 pound class, and won the New York State Championship. in the 285 pound class. He won 198 career high school wrestling matches in his high school career, and was chosen for three NHSCA All-American teams. He was also a four-time Section V all star in football, and was the Section V defensive player of the year, All the while, he as a high honor roll student. At this writing, he is a student at Binghamton University, and is destined to do much more.

New York State Wresting Champion
Trent Sibble

This is Trent Sibble's "little sister," Teegan. She may be less than half Trent's weight, and stands only five feet two, but inspired by his example, she too has reached the top of her sport, as a New York State wrestling champion. This year, 2025, she gave up only two points to other wrestlers the entire season, and those in the semi-final match of the State Championship tournament. She won the final contest and the championship with a chin whip takedown, in one minute and eleven seconds.

Teegan learned to be tough early, from the beginning of life. She arrived with serious birth defects. She has cystic fibrosis. She hasn't become who she is by herself. Obviously, the Sibble family has provided both Trent and Teegan with a tremendous foundation, helping them develop the drive to overcome adversity, no matter the magnitude of the challenge. But the Bolivar school and community certainly have helped too, providing a broader base of support in which the Sibbles, and so many others, can grow, learn to persevere, to overcome, and to prosper. For an old timer, looking in from out, that is a wonderful thing to witness.

In the long line of principals and superintendents who have headed up the Bolivar school system since the formation of the first Union school in the 1880s, Jeff Margeson is only the second who was also a student in the system. And he was that at the most pivotal time for Bolivar schools since the formation of the central school district in the 1920s. What he has to say here should give everyone great reason to think Bolivar's present and future are in good hands.

From Superintendent Jeff Margeson

My grandparents, Robert and Mary Cawley moved to Bolivar by way of Eldred, Pennsylvania in the middle of the 20th century. They raised six children in a little house on Plum Street and both worked as teachers at the Bolivar Central School. I was raised one block to the west, on Kincaid Street. My parents, Jim and Nancy Margeson both worked for the school, with my father playing a part in the first Pre-Kindergarten building on Main Street. I was a Bulldog for the first ten years of my educational journey, and during my Freshman year I served on the Merger Committee by way of the Bolivar Student Council. The merger with Richburg took place at the beginning of the 1994-95 school year, as I was entering the 10th grade. In 1997, I graduated as a Bolivar-Richburg Wolverine.

Dave Bosworth was my high school art teacher, and one of the driving forces for my decision to attend Art school at the Columbus College of Art and Design in Columbus, Ohio. After graduating, although I did not have any classes in formal education, in 2002, Bob Mountain called me to see if I would be interested in the High School Art position at Bolivar-Richburg. I agreed to take the job, and took classes at night while I taught and coached during the school year. During the summers, I painted houses on the "Teacher Paint Crew" that my Grandpa Cawley, Dave Evans, and Coach Lindamer started decades earlier.

I continued on this path for the next 18 years, teaching and coaching basketball and baseball for BRCS. I served as a Union Representative for the Faculty Association while increasing my involvement in the community. During those years, I saw many administrators come and go. I saw Federal and State mandates implemented, revamped, and thrown away completely. Unbeknownst to me at the time, all of these events and observations were helping to plant the seeds of future growth down deep in my soul. I found myself reading books about leadership, culture-building, and effective communication. I was questioning more than complying, and I was struggling internally with what I could do to help. I got that chance in March of 2020.

COVID-19 changed everything for everyone. It made us rethink our processes and protocols, our priorities regarding teaching and learning, and it put an overwhelming stress on the mental health of our society. I felt that leadership was needed now more than ever. So, at 40-years-old, I decided to go back to school for my Administrative degree.

Two years later, in 2022, I passed my final test for certification from the Warner School of Education at the University of Rochester. I also accepted the job as Secondary Principal at Bolivar-Richburg. I had no formal training or experience in Administration, so every day was like drinking from a firehose. In the two years that I served as Middle/High School Principal, I was happy that we were the first school district in Allegany and Cattaraugus County to ban cell phones district-wide. We also installed vape detectors in each of our bathrooms, which dropped Disciplinary Referrals by up to 60%. Through relationship building and listening to our teachers, I felt like we addressed many of the core problems that kept kids from learning.

In July of 2024, I was honored to be offered the job as Superintendent of Schools. Once again, the learning curve was reset and I found myself in charge of not just one building, but the entire district. I am currently finishing up Year 1 and I can confidently say that the reason I still love getting up and going to work is because of this great community that is so supportive of the work we continue to do for the betterment of our kids.

My goal for Bolivar-Richburg is to be the best steward as possible. I see myself as the current caretaker, guiding our community and our students through the next wave of educational obstacles such as declining enrollment, alternatives to state assessments, and the socio-economic problems associated with our rural way of life.

Currently, I am raising my three kids in the same house I grew up in on Kincaid Street. My wife is an 8th grade Special Education teacher at Bolivar-Richburg, and our plan is to continue our lives helping and serving the community as the years pass. I have seen first hand the positive power that comes from good people planting deep roots in our community. Service to our community is something that was ingrained in me from an early age. It is my hope, as a third-generation educator in this community, to guide the ship to the best of my ability, build lasting bonds between the school and the community, and do what is best for our students.

Hopefully, one of them might just decide to settle down, raise a family here, and carry the torch for the next generation!

Second Growth

Should you visit the museum and travel Boss Street to enter or leave the former Hahn & Schaffner property, you will pass the old Bradley home at the corner of Boss and First. My great grandfather, George Hiram Bradley lived on that corner from 1884 until 1938, when he died there. He liked the corner lot so much that when his family outgrew the house he first built, (five children and the in-laws), in 1907 he built the home which stands on the corner now. My grandparents moved in after doing some remodeling in 1939, when my father and his brother were in high school. I spent the first forty-five years of my life there. I grew up in it with my grandparents. I moved my family into the house when I finished my formal education. It is still the house I think of as home.

I have included little in this book about the Bradleys. Especially from the 1920s into the 1950s, the family owned companies, Empire Gas & Fuel and the Bradley Producing Corporation, with 450 employees were the largest employers in the area. Until the 1930s, my great-grandfather also owned the Bolivar Water Company. It was thought best to stay out of politics and community affairs, and leave that to others. So, my great-grandfather, the first George Bradley, only held office once. He served one term as the town highway superintendent. My grandfather, John C., was a famously kind individual, who shied away from the limelight. In 1940, a census taker asked him what church he belonged to. He replied that evidently he belonged to the church that needed a new roof. He gave to all who asked. He helped a number of World War II veterans pay for their educations. He was once asked if he would say the greetings at a Boy Scout banquet. At the dinner, he was introduced, rose, said the word "Greetings," and sat down, to the amusement of most of the others present. My father, John D. Bradley, ran for a seat on the school board in the 1960s, won, and did not run again. With the exception of a window in the Methodist Church, gifts were always made anonymously.

When I first came back to town in 1973, I was asked to run for town justice for the Democrats. I did no campaigning and lost. A couple of years later, I was asked if I would serve as the assistant village justice, and was appointed. The village justice immediately quit, and I inherited the position. I ran when the term expired and won, but resigned in 1980 because I had taken a new job that required a great deal of travel.

In 1970, I was back in Bolivar for the summer, and so were a number of my contemporaries. We started playing croquet in the evenings, and I started keeping score. At the end of the summer, I declared my close friend and classmate, Professor Michael Edward Starr, the New York State Champion. The next summer, my wife and I decided he should have the chance to defend his title. For sixteen years afterwards, on the Saturday after the New York State Oil Producer's Clambake, we hosted the New York State Croquet Championship Tournament. It grew from a couple of dozen people playing on one court, to 200 people playing on thirteen courts, most of them set up in the large field behind what is now Morris's house on First Street. The championship game was always held under the lights in the side lawn beside the house on Boss Street. But by the mid-1980s, my wife Connie and I burned out, and had to let the series end.

In 1990, my oldest son was seriously injured in an automobile accident. We soldiered on in Bolivar for two years, but concluded that if he was going to recover, we needed to get him to new surroundings. In the summer of 1993, we moved to Carlisle, Pennsylvania. About the hardest thing I have ever done was to close the front door on the home at 71 Boss and walk out to the moving van.

Before I close, I have to admit that there are people who should be included who have not been. Jim "Buzz" Dunn, with his crazy nicknames for people, and his razor sharp mind was a great engineer, and an enterprising mayor. Charlie Church was not just a carpenter, but an artisan with wood, an art he passed down to his sons. Dave Sisson has shown in recent decades that a real entrepreneur can prosper anywhere. I know there are more, but it is time to close.

The history of Bolivar up to the 1960s is mostly a story of oil and the businesses which came to be as a result. The story since 1980 is the story of the school system, because by and large most of the businesses have disappeared. In his piece above, Jeff Margeson expressed his concern about the declining school enrollment. At last count 699 students are in the system, down from a combined student population for Bolivar-Richburg in the 1940s of more than 1,200. Only a restored economic base can keep families in the area, and children in the system, and give the story the basis it needs to continue.

The discovery of oil here is thought of as the primary stage of recovery. Water flooding was called secondary recovery. Despite all the effort to recover all the oil they could, it is generally understood that about half of all the oil that was in place in the Allegany oil field is still there. Experiments were done both in the 1950s and in the 1970s with "tertiary recovery" methods, to see if more oil could be produced here. All resulted in additional production, but at the time, none were economic.

We are living in a time when climate change is finally being recognized as a reality, and it is. It is also known that adding carbon dioxide to the atmosphere is a major cause. One proposed solution is "carbon capture," separating the carbon dioxide out of the air, and pumping it underground. One of the experimental tertiary techniques tried to extract more oil was the injection of carbon dioxide into the oil sands. It wasn't economical then because the CO2 was too expensive. But now, when we want to get the carbon dioxide out of the air, couldn't plants be set up to do that, and put the gas into the oil sands to recover much more oil? Yes, if New York State would agree, that might work.

Would it make much of a difference to the local economy? Probably not much. Mineral owners would benefit, but few live locally. It would not result in the hundreds of jobs which were created by water-flooding, and thus would not draw many people to the area. The jobs created would be well paying, but many could be done anywhere, no need to be on location. In my estimation, despite the large remaining reserves of oil, it will never again be a significant contributor to the local economy. So, what might be?

The forest was the first natural resource exploited in Bolivar. The coming of oil had the added effect of speeding the end of farming in the area, and when the fields were no longer tended nor grazed, the forest grew back. That regrowth climaxed in the 1980s, when logging again became a major enterprise in the area. But, the valuable species were largely harvested then, and it takes eighty years for another crop to mature.

I now live in New Hampshire, in an area in many ways similar to Allegany County; except it is in New Hampshire. In New York, the state is the most important governmental unit. In New Hampshire, it is the town that counts. There has never been a culture where I live now of exploiting the natural resources it has. Perhaps one-third of the town is in formal forest preserves, or in land trusts which seek to do the same thing: keep things as they are, so they can be enjoyed now and in the future.

It was Bill Jones with the Moneysaver who invented the term, "The Land of the Deer and Derrick." What may strike many as odd is that derricks had been much more common than deer up until World War II, not long before Bill came up with the phrase. By the end of the nineteenth century, deer were considered extinct in Allegany County. In June 1930, the sighting of a deer on a lease made the front page of the *Breeze*. In 1931, a flock of five deer in Beers Hollow made similar headlines. But, as the forest recovered, the deer herd grew to such an extent that hunting was allowed again for the first time in 1939.

Perhaps the greatest charm the Bolivar area has to offer is its scenic beauty, the forested hills at the heart of what can been seen that is attractive. The forest, which is in the heart of the area in North American to grow the best hardwoods, will continue to regrow, fill the fields and openings created in years past, and mature. Where I live now, there are miles and miles of trails, for hiking, for skiing, for enjoying what nature has provided. Where I once lived, in Bolivar, New York, that is also true. Thanks to water flooding, there are trails leading everywhere, although many need reopening, and are not currently marked or open for public use. The forest is regrowing on virtually every hillside, but none of it, as yet, has been set aside to be preserved. When the entire history of an area has been based on the commercial exploitation of its natural resources, it may not be possible to change the community mindset to one of protection and preservation, to create in its stead a town which celebrates and preserves the beauty it contains, and which perhaps builds a tourist and service economy that prospers within it. But that would be one route ahead, a route that would give new school graduates a economically sensible reason to return and raise another generation.

I mentioned this before. In 1937, an expert came to the area to consult on the water flooding phenomenon. His advice to both Bradford, Pennsylvania and to Bolivar, New York was to carefully conserve what they had, for without oil, neither community had a reason to exist. The oil is gone. Bolivar still exists, but that advice is more pertinent now than it was then: preserve what we have. Make it last. If you do, so will the community.

Bibliography

Anselmo, Ray *Patsy Dougherty*, Soc. for American Baseball Research, found at https://sabr.org/bioproj/person/Patsy-Dougherty, originally found in David Jones, ed., *Deadball Stars of the American League, Washington DC, Potomac Books Inc., 2006.*

The Bolivar Breeze. Virtually all of *The Bolivar Breeze's* 3,757 issues over 73 years, from 1891 to 1965 can be read (and searched) at NYS Historic Newspapers – https://nyshistoricnewspapers.org. The details of daily life in Bolivar contained there were essential to the writing of this book.

Other local papers, such as the *Cuba Patriot*, *Friendship Register*, *Belmont Dispatch*, and the *Wellsville Daily Reporter*, can also be viewed and searched online at https://www.nyshistoricnewspapers.org. Unfortunately, at the present time, the *Olean Times Herald* is not.

Herrick, John P. *Bolivar, New York, Pioneer Oil Town.* The Ward Ritchie Press, Los Angeles, 1952

Herrick, John P. *Empire Oil. The story of oil in New York State.* Dodd, Mead & Co., New York, 1949

MacDonell, Herbert L., and Alfred Allan Lewis, *The Evidence Never Lies*, Henry Holt & Co., 1984

Minard, John Stearns. *Allegany and its People, a Centennial Memorial History of Allegany County, New York, illustrated.* W.A. Fergusson & Co., 1896

Old Oil Field Waterflood Operations and Enhanced Oil Recovery Potential, Draft GEIS Vol. 2, found at https://extapps.dec.ny.gov/docs/materials_minerals_pdf/dgeisv2ch12.pdf

Paquette, William A. *Abel Root, Sr. of Bolivar, New York and his Descendants,* New Dominion Press, 2020

Index

About the Author

George Christman Bradley was born to parents who lived at 91 First Street in Bolivar, New York, in a house built in 1884, which was torn down in 1960. He spent most of his childhood next door at his grandparents, seen here with his grandmother, Edith Bradley, about 1950, or with his grandfather at the Pony Farm up in Pleasant Valley. He was part of Bolivar Central's Class of 1965. From there, he went to Cornell University as a history major, and to Albany Law School, finishing there in 1973. He practiced law in Olean and Bolivar until 1980, when he went to work for the Bradley Producing Corporation. As a result of the liquidation of that company in 1984, he ended up in the timber business, and conducted business as the Homestead Timber Company around Bolivar until 1990.

He married Connie Francisco in 1968. They have three children and five grandchildren. In 1993, he moved his family to Carlisle, Pennsylvania. In 2008, they moved to the Fort Lauderdale, Florida area, and summered at Cuba Lake. In 2024 they consolidated living quarters and moved once again to southern New Hampshire.

George has always been an historian at heart. He was the principal author of the book produced for the Bolivar Sesquicentennial in 1975. Since then he has written or co-written six other books: The first two were *The Bradley Companies, 1860-1980*; and *The Spire On the Square, the 250th Anniversary History of St. John's Episcopal Church, Carlisle, Pennsylvania.* With Richard Dahlen he wrote, *From Conciliation to Conquest: The Sack of Athens and the Court Martial of Colonel John B. Turchin.* He has also written *Surviving Stonewall: Part One of the History of the 46th Pennsylvania Volunteers*; and *They Knew No Glory; Part Two of the History of the 46th Pennsylvania Volunteers.* Two companies of that regiment were raised in Potter, County, Pennsylvania, and a few of its men are buried in Maple Lawn Cemetery, Bolivar.

Over the years, he has enjoyed sailboat racing, officiating at important sailing events, including the Youth World Championships, coaching soccer, and teaching sailing. Now he writes and edits photographs.

Anyone wishing to offer comments about the contents of this book, or who would like to share their own memories of this little town we called home, is welcome to send them to SurvivingStonewall@gmail.

Made in the USA
Columbia, SC
14 June 2025

e2b89f0c-6351-45d7-9679-c7be7ecdad17R01